The GLASS GAFFERS of NEW JERSEY

CAPEWELL CRUET remarkable for architectural precision and imaginative concept of patterning amber and clear flint glass. Amber container, on a clear, hand-cut base, has six applied clear strips ending in petal shapes. Hand-cut neck and faceted stopper. Blown at Capewells of Camden (1841–1859). H. 6 7/8 inches. *Photo by E. Ralph Capewell.*

COBALT BOWL, base shaped in a wooden mold, has some lead content, scattered bubbles. C. 1840s. H. 3 3/4 inches. PRECISION WORKMANSHIP in rather coarse metal marks this cobalt pitcher of outstanding detail: ear handle with balanced curve ends in gauffered ridges; globular base is formed in a mold, with unusual drawn foot; mouth of pitcher has edge folded inward. C. 1840s. H. 9½ inches.

PLATE I

DURAND CAMEO VASE, acid etched, is iridescent opaque white etched to clear green flint in a design hitherto not published, which appears to be a quetzal bird. Signed in silver script: V Durand, with the number 1970/10. H. 10 inches. *Collection of the Chrysler Art Museum, Provincetown, Mass.*

RARE CORNFLOWER BLUE VASE with opaque white swirls has clear, baluster, applied pedestal with 1842 U.S. dime in hollow knop of stem. H. 10 inches. Miniature cobalt blown pitcher has applied handle. H. 1 3/4 inches.

GOLD RUBY AND FLINT PITCHER of exceptionally harmonious design and cutting was blown by Ralph Barber and cut by Charles Reeves about 1900, at Whitall Tatum of Millville. *C. S. Reeves collection. Courtesy, Wheaton Glass Museum.*

The GLASS GAFFERS of NEW JERSEY

and their creations from 1739 to the present

by Adeline Pepper

CHARLES SCRIBNER'S SONS • NEW YORK

A-9.71 (MH)

Printed in the United States of America
SBN 684-10459-8

Library of Congress Catalog Card Number 70-123831

Fig. 1 WITCH BALL COVERS date this unusual pair of jars as early holders for pharmaceuticals or candles. Shaped entirely by a dip mold and tooling, with the foot hollow instead of being applied. Golden amber such as Whitney works favored. H. 12½ inches.

WILD ROSE PINK pitcher with ice-clear handle was blown in Atlantic City by John Ruhlander. Similar exquisite glass was made for a few weeks in the summer of 1901 by Ralph Barber, Marcus Kuntz and Emil Staner at a furnace started by Arthur Saunders H. 6 inches. *Edward Griner collection. Ex-collection, Charles Pepper.*

RUBY CUP AND SAUCER with white peacock feather pattern matches parfait glass blown at Durand, probably by Emil J. Larson. 1925–30. *H.M. Smith collection.*

AMPHORA TRANSLATED FROM THE GREEK ceramics has winged handles that soar, instead of collapsing as soft glass is wont to do. Slender tooled stem rests on circular applied foot. Deep aquamarine looped in white. H. 11 inches. *Crawford Wettlaufer collection.*

PLATE 3

BIRD SALTS, hand tooled, not pressed, are very rare. Blue-green glass matches a simple early Jersey bowl. *H.W. Smith collection.*

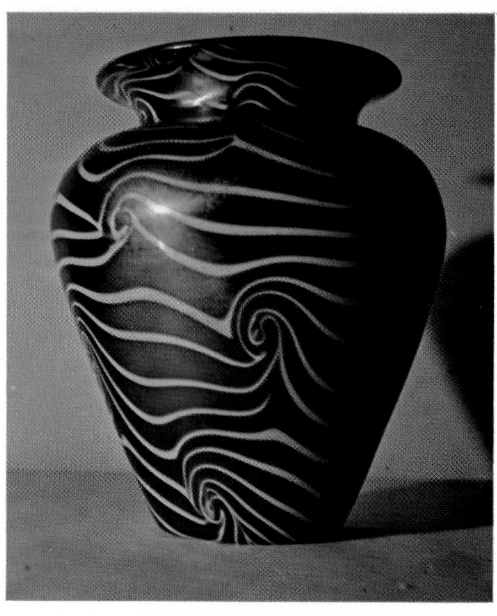

KING TUT DESIGN in deep peacock luster swirled with white. Blown at Durand by Emil J. Larson and decorated by Harry Britton. H. 7½ inches.

PERFECTION, JERSEY-STYLE, swirled pitcher in gold-ruby, clear and opaque white. Broad loopings harmonize with the generous curves of the body which has a sheared mouth and clear, applied circular foot. Graceful handle with lavishly crimped base appears to be sculptured in ice. C. 1840s. H. 9½ inches.

COLUMBIA GLASS WORKS PITCHER, light aqua with threaded neck and strap handle curled at base which has a hole probably caused by "stone" or heat crack. History of remaining in a single family who lived to present times at Delaware, two miles from Columbia. C. 1820s; 9 inches high. *Hope Historical Society.*

Fig. 2 EARLY JERSEY sugar bowl has charm, lent by the slightly primitive shape. Cover, with wafer finial and folded edge, is set in flanged rim. Tooled, applied pedestal is attached to thick circular foot; rough pontil. Clear, with some lead content; several "stones." H. 8¾ inches.

In Appreciation. . . .

Much of "The New Jersey Glass Gaffers" has been founded on "living" history: first-hand reports.

So common—and ephemeral—were New Jersey glassworks where only handblown articles were made that little was recorded of anything except statistics like tons of sands used. Yet museum and private collections of truly great New Jersey glass attest to the artistry of glassblowers who eked out a living blowing medicine and beverage bottles but whose true talents surfaced in spare-time creations.

The low regard in the 19th century for New Jersey's glass industry is graphic in a report by State officials for the 1876 United States Centennial at Philadelphia. Although various industries of New Jersey are duly and even fulsomely praised there is scant mention of glassmaking, except for notes about glass-sand pits; and this at a time when Whitall Tatum & Company, the Whitney Glass Works and large Bridgeton factories were shipping to world-wide markets.

Although Edwin Atlee Barber in 1900 was a collector of New Jersey blown glass, it had few collectors until the 1920s and 1930s and then suprisingly, not at depression prices.

First major recorder of New Jersey glass was the late Charles S. Boyer, a president of the Camden County Historical Society, from whom Stephen Van Rensselaer and most subsequent writers obtained their basic information.

With limited accurate information in print, it became imperative to trace families of New Jersey's glassblowers and documents relating to them. Far from being a chore this has been an exciting detective search, especially one of discovering that many gaffers are long-lived and eager to talk about their glassmaking. With notes dating back to 1960 my records show I have interviewed over 300 persons, to all of whom I am most grateful. I hope that their interest and that of other readers will spark a move to delve into attics and cellars and files for added facts about New Jersey glass.

I want to thank particularly the following persons who have given me very special help in preparing this book. I shall long remember their enthusiastic and generous encouragement. My warmest thanks to: Mrs. Lilla Abrams of the Wistar Institute, Mrs. Martin Bach, Jr., Mr. J. Lawrence Bacon, Mrs. Alwina D. Bailey, director of the Millville Public Library, the late Mr. Harry Barber, Dr. and Mrs. Harry Barber, Mr. and Mrs. James C. Barbetti, the late Mr. Melvin P. Billups, Dr. and Mrs. George A. Bourgeois, Mr. James B. Byrnes, director of the Isaac Delgado Museum of Art, Mr. E. Ralph Capewell, Mr. and Mrs. Charles F. Carr, Mr. H. Millard Chew, Mrs. Evelyn Campbell Cloak, assistant director, the John Nelson Bergstrom Art Center and Museum, Mrs. William Coffin, Mr. and Mrs. L. Otis Coleman, Mr. Stephen H. Costa, the James H. Dailey family, Mrs. J. R. de Arellano, Mr. Lewis De Eugenio, Mr. and Mrs. John H. Fisher, Mrs. Harry P. Folger II, Mr. Harry P. Folger III, Mr. Jesse Ford, Mr.

and Mrs. Philip Glick, Mr. Edward Griner, Mr. Calvin S. Hathaway, curator of decorative arts for the Philadelphia Museum of Art, Mr. A. Woodruff Harris, Miss Eugenia Calvert Holland, assistant curator, Maryland Historical Society, Miss Magdalena Houlroyd, curator of the Frank Stewart collection, Glassboro State College, Mr. Frederick Jackson, Mrs. Michael J. Kane, Mr. Howard R. Kemble; Mr. Robert Kerr, Mr. Gordon Buffington, Mrs. Marianne K. Ditzler, Mr. Michael Polonus and Mr. George Scattergood of the Kerr Glass Manufacturing Company; Mr. Dwight P. Lanmon, assistant curator of the Henry Francis du Pont Winterthur Museum, Mr. and Mrs. Louis Lapetina, the late Mr. Emil J. Larson and Mrs. Larson, Mr. and Mrs. C. F. Link, Mr. and Mrs. Henry Lupton, Mr. and Mrs. George G. McConnell, Miss Mary O. Merrill, chief curator of glass, the Chrysler Art Museum, Mr. and Mrs. Everett F. Mickle, Mr. Alonzo Norcross, Mr. Peter Parker, chief of manuscript division of the Historical Society of Pennsylvania, Mr. and Mrs. G. Vernon Pepper, Mr. Paul Perrot, director of the Corning Museum of Glass, Mrs. William Plummer, Jr., Mr. and Mrs. Ernest C. Stanmire, Mr. and Mrs. A. L. Smith, Dr. Harold Morrison Smith, Mrs. Henry C. Stockman, Mr. Herbert A. Vanaman, Sgt. E.J. Watson, Jr., Mr. Martin Weber of the Wheaton Glass Company and the staff of the Wheaton Museum, Mr. Crawford Wettlaufer, Mr. and Mrs. John Winslow and Mr. Howard Wiseman, curator of the New Jersey Historical Society.

ADELINE PEPPER

Batsto, New Jersey
April 30, 1970

Fig. 3 PRESERVE JAR from Alloway area. Bubbled green glass. *Yoerger collection.*

Contents

Illustrations in Color

Black and White Illustrations

Fig. 4 The seal of the State of New Jersey, 1776

Fig. 5 THE GADROON SWAG is superimposed on the body of this footed dark-amber pitcher executed with great flair. The broad lip of the pitcher balances the curve of the superb pitcher. H. 9¾ inches. *Fish sale of 1940. Photo by Taylor and Dull.*

Some Guidelines for Reading This Book

THIS IS A BOOK not only for collectors and would-be collectors but also for the non-addicted who would like to read about New Jersey's early settlers and their customs, the lives of great American glassblowers and New Jersey's historical role in shaping the American glass industry.

Because so many books have told the tale of ancient glass-making that history will be sketched only briefly here. It is also assumed that educated readers have a general background in United States history, so that will not be expanded upon. Local history, however, may be highly significant and will be so treated.

Place names described are in New Jersey, except for such obvious ones as New York and Philadelphia. When there might be doubt, as for Newport, N.J., the New Jersey locale is stated.

As collectors usually want to zoom in on their specialties, there may be repetition from chapter to chapter. This is intended to be helpful.

So multifarious were New Jersey's glassworks that it is a problem to decide how to arrange them for best understanding and memorability. One writer chose to group the glasshouses in three layers—early, middle and late—often regardless that the history of some covered all three periods. Some other authors listed the factories strictly chronologically according to major management. Both methods break up the continuum of events. Believing that the rise and fall of owners, the intermarriages of glassmaking families and their struggles against historical and natural calamities will interest readers and will help in associating needful facts I have chosen to report the stories as they occurred, that is, around a certain town such as Millville which has a history of over a century and a quarter of handblown glass, or around a family like the Stangers who shaped the mold for the South Jersey style of glass and spread the tradition as far afield as New England, New York state, Pittsburgh, Ohio and Kentucky.

The casual reader or even a collector may ask, why bother about so many dates or names of numerous glassblowers or a one-pot furnace. Such basic information is essential in sweeping away rumors and misconceptions about New Jersey glass and gaffers. For example, some of the most desirable American paperweights, the Vineland roses, were made by Emil Larson at a one-pot backyard furnace. If one "authority" had known the year of Ralph Barber's birth he wouldn't have had him making perfect Millville roses at the age of 12. As for the names of long-gone glassblowers, these may help in determining the provenance of handblown glass, an essential part of documenting a collection.

In preparing this book the author has of course searched all standard—and substandard !—histories relating to New Jersey glass, but a new approach has been that of interviewing hundreds of persons within and outside the state to uncover unknown documents, glassworks ledgers and store books, courthouse records. A pioneer researcher in the history of New Jersey glasshouses was Charles S. Boyer who, though he published with Stephen Van Rensselaer, was the investigator *in situ.* Subsequently, most authors mentioning Jersey glass simply referred the reader to these two men, with little attempt at new research. In the meantime many valuable records were lost. It is hoped that this book will stimulate readers to search for documents that may still be packed away in attics, storerooms and office files.

Although this book is designed primarily to show the artistic creations of workaday Jersey blowers in their spare hours, many of the attractive, hand-made, commercial bottles which first appeared in The Glass State are also described. Scores of distinctive and highly collectible fruit jars, including the first Masons, also originated here, and many of these are discussed in relation to the glasshouses where they were blown.

New Jersey had so many fine glass-cutting shops that space does not permit mention of all, but those noted for excellence in such centers as Jersey City, Hammonton, Egg Harbor, Flemington and Bridgeton are described.

Note: All glass from the author's collection unless otherwise described.
All photos by the author unless otherwise credited. Flask numbers such as GII-49 McK. refer to chart identification numbers of bottles and flasks in McKearins' book *American Glass.*

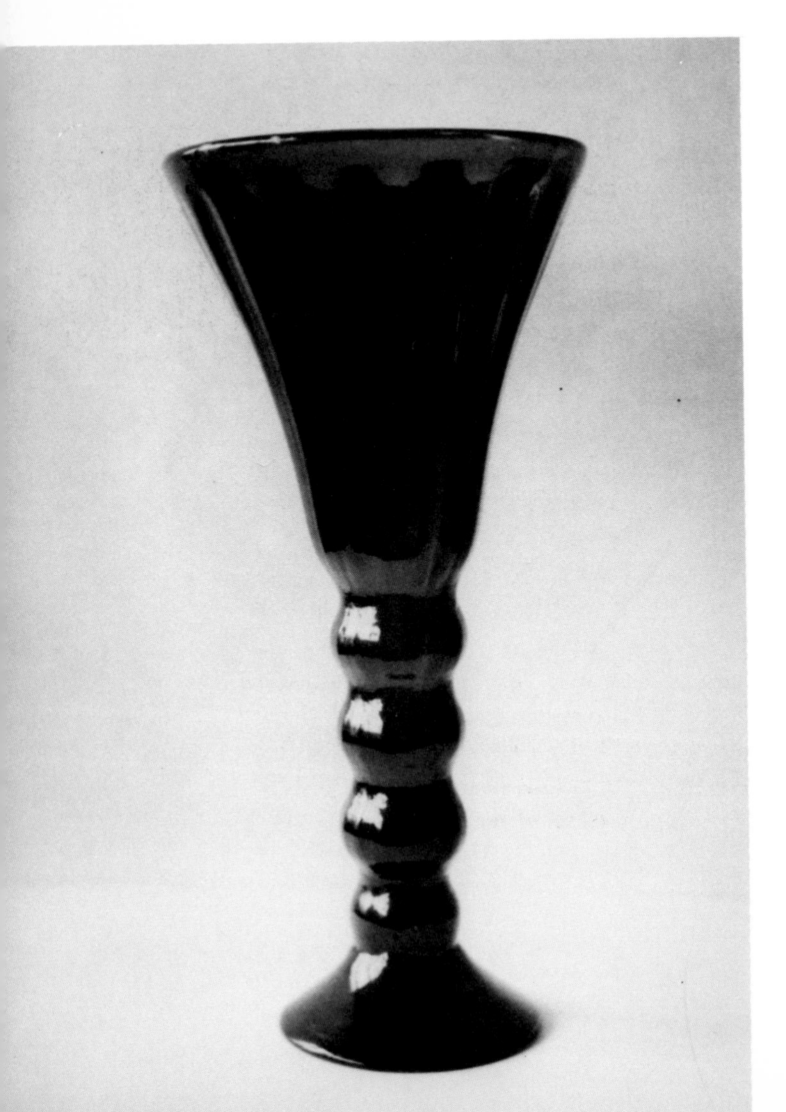

Fig. 6 ELLENVILLE, N.Y. made glass in the Jersey style, like this trumpet-shaped vase with candlestick stem. Molasses-colored glass indicated period before Jersey sand was used here.

The New Jersey Glass Gaffers and Their Creations 1739 to Present

AND WHAT might a glass gaffer be?

In the ancient, traditional and honorable art of glass-making, a gaffer is a master of the craft. It's as simple as that. But the road of attainment to the summit has ever been arduous.

"Gaffer" is an old word but by no means obsolete. It is still indispensable to the language in southern New Jersey or West Virginia or Indiana or wherever else glassmakers gather to fashion glass by hand or to talk about the old days before The Machine.

A gaffer is a blower, par excellence, but more than that he is "master of the chair." In his world the "chair," usually a beat-up bench with flat arms on which his blowpipe can be manipulated to give final shape to the blown glass, carries as much status as a university "chair" in other circles.

To assist him the gaffer has a servitor, who is also a blower. Another assistant is the "gatherer" who thrusts the 5-foot iron blowpipe into the blazing furnace and collects a "gather" or ball of molten "metal" or glass for blowing. Hovering near to be of service at the precise moment of need may be a "mold-boy" to hold a mold that gives shape to the glass and "carry-in" boys who rush the articles which the gaffer has finished to the annealing oven or "lehr."

If this sounds like 15th century Venice or France, the system is still the traditional way of creating glass by hand. A gaffer's dependence on gatherers, servitors, foot-makers, mold-boys and other helpers is not a caste system handed down through the centuries but a vital inter-relationship demanded for fast co-ordinated action before the molten glass "freezes." A marvelous example of how a gaffer like John Ruhlander and his favorite assistant A. Woodruff Harris worked phenomenally as a team is the 16-part bottle illustrated on page 263. A false move anywhere in the procedure would have meant disaster instead of a work of art.

It has been a great pleasure to meet and talk with many Jersey glass gaffers such as Emil J. Larson, Otis Coleman, August Hofbauer, Allie Clevenger, and to learn from the families of other master blowers no longer living something about their work and their times. Believing that collectors would like to know more about these people I have set down as much as I could learn about the lives of gaffers as well as their creations.

The New Jersey Style of Glass Making

First of all, nearly all New Jersey glass with appeal to collectors has for over two centuries been entirely hand made! Those who admire New Jersey glass and gaffers who have shaped and decorated it are inclined to be shocked by pressed glass, for which as Frederick Carder, co-founder of the Steuben Glass Works, once said, "All you do is press a lever." The pride and creativity of the blower go into every piece of hand made glass, each as individual as are finger prints.

Some collectors of old glass, when they see a primitive style of blown ware, are wont to exclaim, "Oh, that must be early South Jersey." This mistaken impression may have arisen because New Jersey had a glassworks as early as 1739 and in a primitive region, to be sure. But Caspar Wistar's Glass Works at Alloway in "the Jersies" became the first successful one in the western hemisphere, a place not achieved by careless workmanship. Wistar went to great expense to import four of the most experienced glassmakers he could find in the German Palatine and set up a profit-sharing arrangement with them, not one of master and redemptioner. The tradition of expert glassmaking has been scrupulously carried on over the decades, even by descendants of original glassmaking families, and the charming style has spread to Pennsylvania, New England, New York, Ohio, Kentucky.

This book will try to tell not only what the early South Jersey style and its gaffers were like but how new designs and colors have evolved in the 19th and 20th centuries.

Household Objects

What kinds of articles were made from glass in New Jersey from the mid-1700s to 1830? As in many primitive American settlements from Maryland to Massachusetts, the objects were basically the same when local glass became available to a village. These were large, spreading milk bowls in which cream could rise to the top and be skimmed off for churning into butter; similar bowls with folded edges, but smaller, for serving foods; porridge bowls; mugs; pitchers; flagons for wine; covered bowls for that precious commodity, sugar; bowls for jams and preserves, with high domed covers to include a spoon; salts; small bowls or deep plates for pastries or other desserts such as wild strawberries or blueberries; candlesticks and whale-oil lamps; farmers' jugs for field use; preserve jars; pocket bottles and flasks; tumblers; demijohns for water and liquors.

For more sophisticated circles, say, for glassworks owners and their visitors, there was need for water and wine goblets, even cordial glasses, decanters, hurricane shades for candlesticks, finger bowls, vases and mantel ornaments. And of course washbowl and pitcher sets.

All of these articles blown by New Jersey's craftsmen have been found in the state.

Most have been sold out of New Jersey. Many are in museums far away, where sometimes they may be labeled Coventry, Conn., or Redford, N.Y., or Kensington, Pa.

Color and Clarity in New Jersey Glass

An English authority on glass, E. M. Elville, stated in 1967 that the purest deposits of glass sand in America were to be found in Pennsylvania and New Jersey. This fact explains why South Jersey sand is ideal for making either clear sparkling glass or objects with fresh bright colors.

In the depression year of 1932 when thousands of Americans didn't know where their next meal was coming from, an "Unsurpassed Wistarberg Deep Claret Footed Pitcher" sold at auction for $900. The magic words which brought this price, fantastic for its time, when other good Jersey glass sold for $40, were "Wistarberg" and "Deep Claret." Through what is now recognized as the faulty research by Hunter and Kerfoot at the site of Caspar Wistar's 18th century furnace, almost any glass that looked South Jersey in style was mistakenly termed "Wistarberg" in the 1930s and '40s. The point of this look at high prices of the past is that an 18th century American furnace would not be likely to have produced reddish or claret-colored glass. This was all the less probable inasmuch as there was no documentation of Wistarberg for the above-mentioned pitcher.

As any American glassworks before the Revolution was a *sub rosa* or bootleg operation because England taxed such manufacturing in order to keep the Colonial market dependent on the mother country, 18th century glassmakers here would not have wanted to disclose their hands by ordering exotic or expensive chemicals for making colored ware. Moreover, popular need for household glass was so great that color was not required to increase demand.

The most common color, therefore, of New Jersey glass in the 18th century, and even the first half of the 19th century, was a rich aquamarine obtained from the unusually pure South Jersey sand. Wistar's skilled German craftsmen had found a glassmakers' paradise, with sand so low in impurities that for all practical purposes it did not need washing.

When made into flat sheets for windows this aqua glass looked almost clear but when blown into shapes such as pitchers the true aquamarine was intensified. The color is often called "Jersey green," a misnomer as this gives the impression of "apple green," a shade not typically New Jersey. The aqua of early New Jersey has no hint of yellow but some reproductions of the 1960s are made from heavy yellow-green metal. At Lancaster and Lockport in New York state, Jersey style articles were made in aqua verging on cornflower blue and turquoise. Both are quite easily differentiated from Jersey aqua.

A prevalent but erroneous impression exists that early Jersey glass was never colorless. Wistarberg bookkeeping records show that even this first successful glassmaking venture in the western hemisphere produced "white" glass, the craft name for colorless metal. "White" glass was easy to obtain by adding manganese which, because it cleaned or cleared the metal, was known as glassmakers' soap.

Too much manganese turned the batch to amethyst or purple, colors that occasionally appear in early Jersey glass because the chemical was inexpensive and handy. A purple which appears to be black until held to the light is likely to be English glass from the Bristol region.

Various shades of green were obtained easily by adding oxide of iron. As little as one part of iron oxide in 5,000 parts of sand is sufficient, says Elville, to impart a sea-green tint to glass. In northwest Jersey naturally occurring iron produced a "sour" sand giving an apple or grass green color. A blue-green could be obtained from copper.

Iron or manganese in large amounts were used in 18th century glasshouses to make the lightproof olive-amber demijohns for wine and case gin bottles. The lovely golden ambers made for the Whitneys at Glassboro in the 1840s and '50s were of course made with far more sophisticated formulas. Yet there are occasional sunlit ambers in 18th century barrel-shaped mugs with thumb-rest handles.

Opaque white or milk glass when "combed" in loops in combination with clear or colored glass has come to seem an American symbol of South Jersey glass. Made by the addition of oxide of tin, the method is as old as the history of glassmaking: spiraled Egyptian pitchers survive from the fifth century B.C. The technic is also called Nailsea and is wrongly assumed to have been first brought to New Jersey by blowers from the Stourbridge region of England. The white loops and swirls were common in German glass, however, at the time when scores of Palatine blowers arrived in America in the early 18th century. Articles such as Clementon's looped canes, scent bottles for which milk glass was used, and the early lamp from Port Elizabeth (Fig. 34) are some of the evidence that looped milk glass was made in New Jersey well before the 1840s and '50s when English workmen began to appear from Nailsea, and then only in limited numbers. As a general rule, the very thin, precise and evenly matched lines of white are likely to be English glass, the German influence showing a more casual design.

An auction catalog of the 1930s contains an introduction saying that the South Jersey colors are aquamarine, green and amber, with occasionally cobalt. Glassmakers and collectors living in New Jersey know that blue has been used lavishly even in early times. Both Coffin & Hay and Stratton & Buck made sapphire flasks, and as early as the 1830s the Jackson Glass Works was famed for its beautiful blue ware. At the site of Waterford Glass Works fragments of pitchers that are definitely early South Jersey are in sapphire as well as aqua. During the last half of the 19th century a common color was cobalt because many glassworks used this deep, nearly opaque blue for bottles. Whitall Tatum introduced one of the most luminous blues, lighter than cobalt, ever made in American glass. In one South Jersey household I have seen a tincture bottle and a finger bowl which appear to have been made from the same batch of this glowing blue. Late in the 19th century Whitall Tatum also introduced a new green, a blue-green emerald, nearly opaque.

In the late 1860s Whitall Tatum began using a fine quality of lime glass that was a close approximation of brilliant lead glass. Blowers enjoyed working this more malleable metal and began stocking kits of colored glass for spare-time blowing. Among the attractive results were vases swirled in red, white and blue and pitchers swirled in green, white and mauve.

As glass factories of the last half of the 19th century started producing millions of bottles, the Jersey ambers changed to a more orange tone. Light blues and yellow greens were often used for beverage bottles.

Red has always been an uncommon color in Jersey glass. Gold ruby, the most desirable of reds, has been very costly because it was usually made by the addition of gold; one formula was an ounce of gold for 60 pounds of batch. The legendary tale is that the owner of the glassworks would toss a gold coin into the melting pot. To many persons the name gold ruby connotes an orange red. True gold ruby, however, is the color of the precious stone for which it is named.

About 1905 Ralph Barber, John Ruhlander and John Fath made some large pitchers with gold ruby glass (see page 264). Some of Emil Larson's creations of the 1930s, especially the rose paperweights, indicate that he also used gold ruby at his small furnace at home. One of the rarest and most exquisite of Jersey colors is pale pink such as Ralph Barber used for some of his rose paperweights. Ruhlander is known to have made a cup and a pitcher in this color which is very like New England Peachblow.

Forms and Decoration of Early South Jersey Glass

Considering that the South Jersey style of glass was being made in the state as late as the 1850s and in other sections such as New England, New York state and Pennsylvania, it is surprising that the characteristics can be described according to a few rules. Yet each object, far from being stereotyped, has an individual look because it is freeblown.

Large bowls usually have straight, slanting sides, with or without foldover rims, and are rarely footed. Some of the smaller serving bowls often have a crimped circular base.

Barrel-shaped pitchers, often with a thumb-rest handle, are likely to be the earliest ones in Jersey and are considered to be an 18th century form. They are usually small and have a tiny pouring lip.

The Jersey style pitchers most often seen, and now usually only in collections or at auction, are narrow waisted with a globular body above an applied circular foot which may be either plain or crimped with a marking tool. Rims of some pitchers have a foldover edge. Others are tooled on the outside in one or two concentric rings that give the appearance of a ripple.

Most handles were ear-shaped or semi-ear-shaped, and were applied by starting at the top and swinging the ribbon of glass down to end in a curl. As they are usually flat they were called strap handles, or double strap handles, the latter with a cleft down the length. Handles made from Victorian down to modern times tend to be widest at the base, are not curled and are likely to be cylindrical; some have a claw form at the base.

Threading was a decoration used for the necks of pitchers and vases. Allover threading like that used for the sugar bowl in Fig. 85 is rare.

Leaf-shaped prunts applied to the body of an article are a form of decoration derived from early German *waldglas* or "forest glass."

Quilling, narrow ribbons of glass applied in undulating waves, was one of the earliest forms of decoration for sugarbowls, vases, gimmal bottles and banks. As the glassmakers became more and more busy producing utility ware they apparently had little time for making these spun-sugar decorations (Fig. 24) derived from the Venetians. The finials hand-tooled in the shape of a swan or a chicken were another casualty of the speed-up and were replaced with round or wafer-shaped knobs.

One of the handsomest and rarest forms of superimposed decoration was gadrooning, to form a cup at the base of a vase or pitcher (see Fig. 5). A separate gather of glass, called a pearl, was attached to the end of the parison and formed into an even band and then the whole was expanded in a fluted dip mold. Occasionally, the pearl instead of being blown in a mold was tooled in a swirl, giving the effect of drapery. A swagged design was created by adding one of these cup forms and then pulling into points (Fig. 29).

Instantly recognized by collectors as a South Jersey style is the lilypad decoration, believed to be uniquely American. Applied to pitchers, bowls and vases, this leaflike design was also made with a second dip of glass or pearl which was pulled into shape according to the fancy of the maker, more often in wavelike crests than a lilypad form.

Although glass with swirled ribbing is rarely attributed to South Jersey, now that it has been established that Pitkin ribbed flasks were blown at Clementon, the possibility exists that swirled pitchers made in New Jersey have been ascribed to glassworks in other states.

A characteristic badge of South Jersey glass is the pillared foot for pitchers, lamps, bowls and vases. The blue and white vase (Plate 1) has an 1832 dime inside the hollow knopped stem. The amber and white pitcher with gadrooning (Fig. 114) is set on a carefully tooled stem. In the latter half of the 19th century, when Whitall Tatum began selling to druggists elaborate show globes on glass pedestals, the turning and tooling of balusters and multiple knops revealed great skill.

BEN FRANKLIN said it best: New Jersey is a barrel open at both ends. One end is Philadelphia and the other is Manhattan.

Although Franklin's once sound aphorism can no longer be applied in modern times, now that New Jersey is self-sufficient, nevertheless, to understand the story of Jersey glass one must believe in Franklin's homespun theory. The fact is that Jersey glass products, from Caspar Wistar's Alloway furnace of 1739 down to the close of Whitall Tatum in 1938, had their greatest market *via* Philadelphia. Although this glass sold world-wide, especially in Latin America and Europe, it usually cleared first through the port of Philadelphia.

Checking only 19th century Philadelphia and New York directories one would think that the best glass from some of the largest firms was made in these two cities. Here are some random listings from records of 1830 to 1930:

Whitall Tatum & Company, New York and Philadelphia
George Dummer & Co. 110 Broadway, New York
Estellville Glass Works, New York and Philadelphia
Thomas W. Dyott, Kensington, Phila.
Yarnell & Trimble, Phila. and New York
Whitney Glass Works, Philadelphia

Every one of the above glassworks had its factories in New Jersey and could not have operated so successfully without the talents of scores of first-rate blowers in the state and the fine, white Jersey sand so readily available. New York and Philadelphia were merely sales offices or warehouses. Yet the erroneous attributions continue; a 1969 book on glass, which gives evidence of time-consuming research, nevertheless cites the locale of numerous major Jersey glass works as Philadelphia and New York.

Some Myths and Truths About New Jersey Glass

Myth 1: "Jersey glass doesn't ring."

Truth 1: As early as 1826 George Dummer & Company of Jersey City won a silver medal for cut glass from the Franklin Institute of Philadelphia and over the years won more awards for quality of metal and cutting. About 1865 Whitall Tatum of Millville began using, up until 1936, huge quantities of fine clear glass that "rings," for such utilitarian needs as apothecaries' ware. All Durand art glass is fine flint ware.

Myth 2: "Wistarberg glass was either dark brown misshapen bottles or colorful pitchers swirled with white waves."

Truth 2: At great cost the Wistars imported the best blowers they could find in Europe and made them *partners;* these were not clods who couldn't even blow simple wine bottles. As for rich blue or claret-colored pitchers swirled with white, which have sold at high prices at auctions as Wistarberg, these and other such swirled pieces are known to be 19th century Jersey and not from the mid-18th century when Wistar gaffers made glass.

Myth 3: "Any Millville rose paperweight is valuable."

Truth 3: Almost no Millville rose is valuable except the best made by Ralph Barber and John Ruhlander. Also valuable are *Vineland* roses made in a similar style by Emil J. Larson.

Myth 4: "All Barber rose paperweights had the same number of petals."

Truth 4: Ralph Barber, say members of his family and friends, was continually experimenting with the rose weight that he alone perfected and, modeling it after roses in the family garden, made many changes in the rose crimps.

Myth 5: "Early Jersey glass was crude and heavy."

Truth 5: Fortunate collectors of early Jersey (c. 1810) pitchers enjoy the light, thin-walled and sparkling qualities that modern imitations have not matched. One reason is that most of the earliest gaffers in Jersey were Palatines who used the "German system" which meant fire-polishing, and sparkle. Then these gaffers had, besides their own expertise, what is still acknowledged to be some of the most extraordinary silica-sand in the world, fantastically free from impurities. Sandwich glass improved greatly when the factory began importing Jersey sand. For crude, molasses-brown ware one should look, if one wants to, toward Ellenville, N.Y., before the glassworks there began importing sand from Jersey's Maurice River.

Myth 6: "All Durand glass was blown by Victor Durand whose name is signed on many pieces."

Truth 6: Most Durand art glass was not blown by Durand but by Emil J. Larson, and the decorative effects were created by Harry Britton, *neither* of whom *rarely* gets credit for his exquisite work. Yet Victor Durand had been a glassblower and his taste pervaded "the fancy shop."

Myth 7: "All Durand glass is astronomically valuable."

Truth 7: When Victor Durand was killed in an automobile accident and his death ended his firm, the warehouse was filled with glass, some abominable rejects, some great glass. Astute collectors bought the carefully made pieces at a special sale for about $5 each and are now reaping manifold profits. The rejects are worthless, except to unwary collectors. Victor Durand signatures mean nothing nowadays because of the numerous fakes.

Myth 8: "All Clevenger glass was crude and ugly."

Truth 8: For some time a famous museum displayed a 1930s Clevenger 3-mold carafe as early pattern-molded ware (c. 1815-1830), so excellent was the work. Operating from the 1930s to the 1960s when there were intermittent shortages of experienced glassmen and good cullet, some cumbersome glass was blown at intervals, best forgotten. Halcyon days were those when Otis Coleman and Allie Clevenger, lifelong friends, worked together. The Booz bottle in Fig. 30 is one of their co-operative blowings, a gift to the author from Otis Coleman.

Myth 9: "Jersey produced few historical flasks—most were made by Dyottville."

Truth 9: By "Dr." Dyott's own advertisements it is proved that many of his historical flasks were blown at the Olive Glass Works in Glassboro and the Gloucester Glass Works in Clementon.

Myth 10: "New Jersey never produced anything like the swirled Pitkin flasks, highly collectible today."

Truth 10: Many fragments of Pitkin flasks have been excavated at Clementon by Morcom, as reported in the *Journal of Glass Studies,* 1968, but no such fragments have been recorded at the Pitkin Works.

The Palatine People

IT MUST HAVE seemed like the end of the world. Or an omen of God's judgment. Perhaps He had turned His back on human wickedness.

People were fearful of what they beheld . . . terrified of still worse to come. Life had become a cold hell, such as not even Hieronymous Bosch, expert in painting hideous damnations, had depicted.

This was the winter of 1708 in the Palatine* of central Europe . . . a winter colder, grimmer than any in the memory of the oldest living inhabitant.

Even before this dire year, the peasants, the shopkeepers, the artisans, even the landed gentry were crushed, weary and impoverished, for they had all undergone the hardships and ravaging taxes of the Thirty Years War, then only recently ended.

In that winter of dreadful memory the populace in every one of the Palatine states suffered. As early as the first of November it was so cold that firewood did not burn, even in the open air. As the new year of 1709 opened, the cold was so intense that casks of wine and liquor froze solid. On January 8 the Rhone, one of the fast-flowing rivers of Europe, was covered with ice from bank to bank. Absolutely unheard of before, the sea froze all along the Baltic coast, the ice thick enough to bear wagons. On human flesh the cold clamped down like the bite of a wolf trap.

A man looking up at the threatening sky could see birds on the wing fall dead. And many a German died a numbing peaceful death by freezing.

When spring came at last it was welcomed with unutterable joy and thanksgiving. But the gladness quickly changed to gall when it was discovered that the vast acres of vineyards never did turn green. The vines which had required so many years to become fruitful and on which so many of the people subsisted—as vine-tenders, pressers, vintners—had been killed by the deep freeze. Even all free-standing trees were killed. Germany of that year was a blighted land, one seeming to be singled out by a curse. All those who had been involved in the religious wars took thought.

Word of the desperate straits of Germans reached all the way to London where the inhabitants spoke pityingly of "the poor Palatines." Quick to see a chance to lend a helping hand and at the same time to turn the situation to England's advantage, Queen Anne and some of her court offered haven to the Palatines. This was no hasty judgment. For some time, England had been searching for stable settlers who would hold the mother country's stake in America. Britain herself in the early 1700s was running short of wood for fuel, for lumber, and needed standing woodlands for naval stores to keep her armadas afloat. The

*The Palatine then consisted of the Lower or Rhenish Palatinate on both banks of the middle Rhine, chiefly between Mainz and Heidelberg; and the Upper Palatinate which included Neuberg and Sulzbach, lands contiguous to Bavaria.

new continent had an excess of trees. Ergo, America's limitless square miles of forest was the place to send colonizers to harvest lumber, tar and other maritime necessities. What better settlers than the Palatines? No hot-eyed zealots these, nor chronic beggars nor criminals, but good steady workers, many with exceptional trades . . . such as glassmaking.

London hung out the welcome sign, and starving Palatines swarmed in. Some were so weak and sick that they died soon after arrival. Between May and November of 1709 shipload after shipload of Germans arrived in London. Some estimates are that as many as 32,000 refugees reached that port.

Those leaving the German states usually went first to Rotterdam and Amsterdam, often via the Rhine, in hopes of locating a vessel leaving for London. The strong and the hopeful tried to get passage direct to the American colonies, on ships embarking from Rotterdam or London.

The wave of Palatines became so overwhelming that London set up refugee camps, perhaps the first in history, and allotted relief payments of sixpence per person a day. At that time it was said of the Palatines "they appear to be an innocent, laborious, peaceable, healthy and ingenious people, and may be rather reckoned a blessing than a burden to any nation where they shall be settled."

That benevolent attitude did not last long. When these "laborious" and "ingenious" people began competing with native Englishmen for jobs, even for food, London mobs attacked those whom they had formerly spoken so benignly of as "the poor Palatines."

Even before the appalling year of 1708, William Penn, that pioneer of real estate promoters, had by shrewd advertising made Pennsylvania the best known American province. He had even paid several visits to the Rhineland to recruit settlers and later, when thousands of Germans came pouring into England he helped draft the 1709 Statute of the Palatines, a naturalization bill to protect these Protestant refugees.

I. Daniel Rupp who in 1898 reported his studies of "Thirty Thousand Names of Pennsylvania Immigrants, 1727–1776," showed that the overwhelming number were Palatine Germans, not Dutch or Belgian even though they sailed from Amsterdam and Rotterdam. Rupp stated that in England alone some 10,000 of the Palatines died for lack of food and medical care. In despair, many of the Germans obtained passage to New York, along the Hudson river, but were made most unwelcome in this region, as Peter Kalm, the Swedish naturalist, noted in his writings in 1748. "What man will be such a fool to become a base tenant to Mr. Dellius, Col. Schuyler, Mr. Livingston . . . when, for crossing Hudson's river, that man can for a song purchase a good freehold in the Jersies," wrote Governor Bellomont.

Most of the Germans then entering Jersey came via the Port of Philadelphia, where many elected to stay, as William Penn was offering good Pennsylvania farm land at the rate of two pounds for 100 acres, and a low yearly rental.

This section of the Colonies was inundated with refugees throughout most of the 18th century. Praising the industry of these Germans, Colonial Governor Thomas in 1738 said, "This Province has for some years been the asylum of the distressed Protestants of the Palatinate, and other parts of Germany." Jonathan Dickinson in 1719 had remarked, "We are daily expecting ships from London which bring over Palatines, in number about six or seven thousand."

Of 14 vessels which in 1738 transported a total of 1,739 Palatine immigrants, clearly listed as such in immigration records, to Philadelphia, only two of the ships sailed out of London and all the others embarked from Rotterdam or Amsterdam.

From this typical fact, nearly all collectors and most writers who informed them assumed that the many glassblowers who arrived in Pennsylvania or New Jersey via such ships were Hollanders. This is like saying that anyone who travels to or from Italy today on an Italian aircraft is Italian.

Although the true facts could have been ascertained by 1900 when Rupp's figures were already in print, the error of Dutch and Belgian influence on New Jersey glass not only persists but pervades. A typical comment is this from Northend, "A characteristic of Wistar glass that strikes the eye almost at once is the shape. The first glass workers in Wistarberg, being from Rotterdam, naturally brought with them Dutch traditions. As a result Wistarberg bowls and pitchers are inclined to be broad of base and spreading of top, outlines that in any substance less ethereal looking than glass might give the effect of solidity or even stolidity."

The very first four expert glassmakers whom Caspar Wistar brought to Alloway, N.J., at great expense and who enabled him to conduct what is now known as the first successful glassworks in the western hemisphere were definitely Palatine Germans. Yet because Johannes Wentzel, Caspar Halter, Johan Martin Halter and Simeon Kreismayer sailed from Rotterdam, on Dec. 7, 1738, writers such as Mrs. Knittle refer to them as "the four Belgians."

In research for this book I have located the lineal descendants of Johannes Wilhelm Wentzel, as he signed his name, and they confirm the Palatine origin of the family. By coincidence, these present-day descendants live only a few miles from the New Jersey hamlet of Palatine. The family owns a Bible signed Mar. 19, 1803 by one of Johannes Wentzel's children who also inscribed this prophetic verse:

This Book my name shall ever have,
When I am dead and in my Grave
When greedy worms my body eat
Here you may read my name complete.

Fig. 7 EARLY JERSEY LILYPAD aqua creamer and bowl (4-inch dia.), both with folded rim. Ear handle is applied to the pitcher, as is the crimped foot. H. 4 inches.

Fig. 8 FOOTED CUP in soft cobalt is early Jersey, probably 18th century, and believed to be one of a kind. *Maclay sale of 1935 and Howe sale of 1940. Courtesy of Parke-Bernet Galleries, Inc. All photos on these pages by Taylor and Dull.*

Fig. 9 EXCEEDINGLY RARE and imaginatively designed teapot of brilliant green glass, body tooled in swirl. Flattened dome, set-in cover has finial of two applied rings with five waffle ornaments. *Ex-collection of Minnie Meacham. Maclay sale of 1935 and Fish sale of 1940.*

Fig. 10 OF RARE BEAUTY, a sugar bowl in clear translucent blue, its set-in cover threaded, the body decorated with applied leaf prunts. H. 7⅝ inches. *Ex-Jacob Paxson Temple Collection. Fish sale of 1940.*

Fig. 11 DRAPERY in glass is superimposed and tooled, not molded, for cover and body of an 18th century sugar bowl in brilliant aquamarine. High domed cover with knob finial is set in galleried rim. H. 9¾ inches. *Fish sale of 1940.*

Fig. 12 FINE SWAN FINIAL tops this superbly executed sugar bowl in pale aquamarine. C. 1880. H. 8 inches. *Fish sale of 1940.*

Fig. 13 ONE-PIECE SAPPHIRE VASE attributed to Whitney. RIGHT: rare 18th century mug, also in one piece, has hollow applied handle. Sapphire. *Fish sale of 1940.*

Fig. 14 NOTABLY 18th CENTURY in its U-shaped body and its crimped twin handles, this sugar bowl offers an interesting contrast to Fig. 15. The domed, flanged lid, topped by a swan, repeats the curve of the base. Vertical ribbing. Aquamarine. H. 8⅞ inches. *Ex-collection George Hammersley. Courtesy, The Henry Francis du Pont Winterthur Museum.*

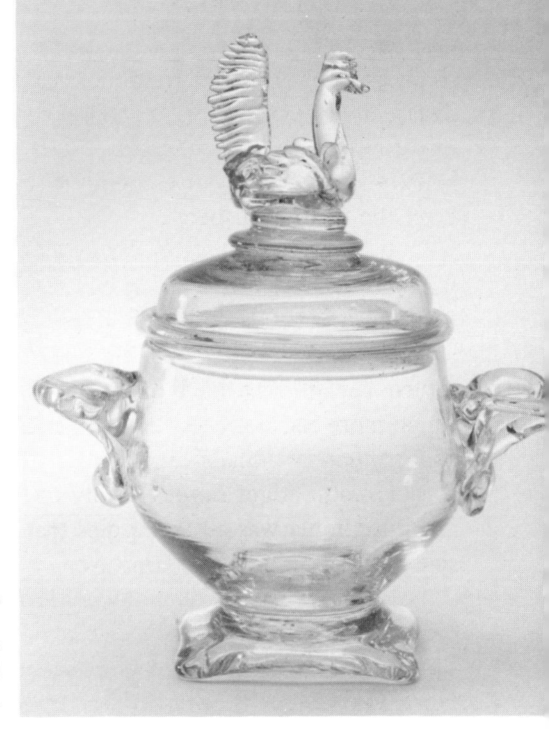

Fig. 15 INTERTWINED DOUBLE BOWKNOT HANDLES reveal incredible skill of an unknown gaffer, probably at the turn of the 18th century. The swan finial resting on a flattened dome cover is equally remarkable. Proportions of the whole are exceptionally fine. Clear, slightly bluish cast. H. 6¾ inches. *Courtesy, The Henry Francis du Pont Winterthur Museum.*

Fig. 16 REGAL SWAN tops a domed-cover sugar bowl of splendid proportions and workmanship in the late 18th century Jersey tradition. Bowl is notable for its vertical ribbing combined with diagonal swirls, as well as for flaring handles and square foot. Clear, with slight bluish cast. H. 7 inches. *Ex-collection Mrs. J. Amory Haskell. Courtesy, The Henry Francis du Pont Winterthur Museum.*

Wistarberg: First Successful Glassworks in America, 1739

Out of the Palatine gloom, Caspar Wistar on Sept. 16, 1717, came sauntering from shipboard onto the cobblestoned streets of Philadelphia, a double-barreled gun in hand, a pistareen (a Spanish coin worth about 9¢) in pocket. All this, according to Wistar family history as written by descendant Gen. Isaac Jones Wistar in his *Autobiography* published in 1914. As the story of General Wistar's life is now known to have many errors of fact, even the truth is suspect.

It is reasonable to wonder why Caspar Wistar, a Palatine, was so optimistic as to have traversed the Atlantic without funds, when most other Palatines would not have dared. One reason is that because his father held the hereditary post of *fürstenjäger* or chief huntsman to Prince Carl Theodore of Bavaria, if Caspar failed in the New World he could always return, though why his family didn't provide better for him en route is still unexplained. Much more fascinating is that Caspar evidently never looked back, only to bring his sister and brother to Philadelphia.

Horatio Alger heroes hardly had the success that Caspar Wistar did. His first meal in Philadelphia was all the apples that he could eat and carry away. After that there is a short lapse of a few years and from then on nothing but success for the rest of his life.

Caspar Wistar probably would have been successful in almost any line of endeavor. He did not hesitate to take a menial job such as hauling ashes for a soap and candlemaker. But within three years he had made money by buying cheap Pennsylvania land in Northampton county, subdividing it and selling to German newcomers. With these earnings he became a partner in the Colebrookdale iron furnace in Berks county. This obviously was a profitable venture for soon after the move he was able to set up a Philadelphia factory to make brass buttons. Advertising these as "warranted for seven years," he quickly enjoyed a steady income from this source, which continued even after his death in 1752.

Only nine years after arriving in America as a poor young man Wistar was able to invest in a second iron enterprise, Pool Forge in Berks county, and to marry into the Philadelphia Establishment, the Society of Friends. On Mar. 25, 1726, he married Catherine Jansen, daughter of Dirick Jansen of Germantown (the name later changed to Johnson). Held at the Abington Friends Meeting House, the wedding was a large one. It seems reasonable to suppose that the bride brought a generous dowry.

The Wistars' first son, Richard, was born the following year on June 7. It would be Richard who would take charge of the Wistar Glass Works after his father's death.

In 1727 Caspar* sent to Hilsbach, Germany, for his brother John and arranged for

*Born Feb. 3, 1696 with the name Würster, Caspar, when he took the oath of allegiance to the English king at the port of Philadelphia in 1721, signed his name Wister but a clerk recorded it as Wistar, a spelling that Caspar and his descendants thenceforward accepted. His brother John, however, used the spelling of Wister, as did his offspring. Thus, though there seem to be two distinct families, all stem from Hans Caspar Würster, or Wüster.

Fig. 17 HOUSE IN ALLOWAY, built in 1736 by William Oakford, contained glass attributed to Wistarberg. *Courtesy of Rutgers University Library.*

him to become a Philadelphia wine-seller, a business that quickly prospered. Was it the need for cheap and plentiful wine bottles and demijohns that stirred Caspar Wistar's interest in glassmaking?

Eleven years later Wistar made his first recorded purchase of land at what would become the glassmaking village of Alloway, 100 acres from Clement Hall. He then bought 1,000 acres of adjacent forested land and on April 27, 1739, he bought from Amos Hilton the glass factory property on Alloway creek about seven miles from Salem. In all, he bought about 2,000 acres.

This land buying was no mere speculation. Wistar in 1738 had already been prospecting in the Palatine for glassmakers. Although he knew little about the industry, he had been well advised about the basics and hence had selected acreage with abundance of pure sand, plentiful wood for fuel, even clay deposits for making furnace pots, and a stream with access to the Delaware river. Although his father, Hans Caspar Würster, had died in Hilsbach in 1726, Caspar no doubt had sound advice, perhaps from his brother George, in the selection of the four men who would be responsible for the unique record of Wistarberg: first successful glassworks in the New World.

It has too often been assumed that Wistarberg glass must have been crude because it was made in an undeveloped primitive region. The evidence is unequivocal that Wistar spared no expense in choosing an ideal site and in picking his first four glassmakers. They must have been men who had operated factories, for besides being glassblowers they knew how to build furnaces and how to make a profit. If they had not been at the top of their craft they could not have driven so hard a bargain. Wistar had to take them in as partners.

The four Palatines were Caspar Halter, Johan Martin Halter, Johannes Wilhelm Wentzel, and Simeon Kreismayer. Wistar paid their passage, amounting to 58 pounds, 8 shillings, to Capt. James Marshall. Agreeing to furnish all materials and tools, Wistar also signed a contract, ratified by the glassmakers in Rotterdam on Dec. 7, 1738, to grant them one third of profits, in addition to food and servants. The men agreed to teach the secrets of glassmaking to Wistar and his son Richard, but there is no evidence that the Wistars did any serious glassblowing, instead acquiring background against pitfalls.

The furnace was built during the summer of 1739 and ready for an autumn blast. By July 1740 the English Crown's collector of customs at Salem, William Frasor, had already passed along word to his superior Charles Carkesse at the London customs house, who in turn spread the news to the Lords Commissioners for Trade and Plantations that a glass-works had recently been erected within eight miles of Salem "by one Caspar Wistar, a Palatine, and is brought to perfection so as to make Glass." This was the first of several attempts by the snooping mother-country to find out just how much the Wistars were cutting into British exports of glass.

It must come as news to most collectors of Jersey glass that the Wistar Glass Works was recorded in its books as the United Glass Company, a sort of conglomerate for separate operations, such as the accounts of the "Pottash Company" and Furnaces 1, 2, 3 and 4. Wentzel was in charge of Furnaces 3 and 4, and presumably the Halters and Kreismayer also had special responsibilities. These men were even charged with seeing that sales were made in Philadelphia, where David Matzinger was an agent. Fortunately for the peace of mind of the glassmakers, the works had an overseer, Benjamin Thompson, a "down Jerseyman" who must have been efficient as he was with the firm for most of its life, during which sand was transmuted to pounds sterling for the Wistars.

A United Glass Company ledger of special interest is Book G, described today as a Geheimbuch or "Home book" of private records. John Stockard, the company's account-ant, wrote in the book in 1743 that it was being started because "the human memory is so frail and weak that it cannot be depended upon. . . ."

Because of Wistar advertisements for window panes and bottles (see below), it is often glibly stated that only coarse glass was made at Alloway. The Geheimbuch settles that moot point once and for all, as the records show that three kinds of *metal* (as distinct from color) were available: green-glass (used for windowlights and hollow ware), bottle glass (lightproof olive-amber for all types of spirits), and white glass. This last is highly significant for it is glassmakers' parlance for clear colorless glass and does not mean glass that is opaque white. Once the company had a clear glass, there was little problem in making flint glass for customers demanding a bit of luxury.

Having become a wealthy man through clever investments and shrewd planning, Caspar Wistar had also a reputation as a leading citizen of Philadelphia when, at the age of 56 he was stricken with dropsy and died on Feb. 13, 1752. His wife and son Richard were among the executors and major beneficiaries of his will. The glass works was pushed to even greater goals, with Richard in charge.

That Caspar Wistar had tried to make the British think his glassworks was a country

The glassmaking Wistars named their village Wistarburg or Wistarburgh but today the usual spelling is Wistar-berg.

project of not much account is clear from this letter which Jersey's Provincial Governor Belcher sent from Elizabeth on Aug. 24, 1752, to Col. John Alford of Boston:

> I have begun to make inquiry about the Glass Works in this province which are 130 miles from this town & as I know no proper person near them capable of getting the Information you desire I have hardly a lean hope of rendering you any Servis in the matter in which the Undertakers are very close and Secret. I was well acquainted with one Caspar, a German who lived at Philadelphia and was the first and principal Undertaker of the Glass Works in this Province and with whom I discoursed particularly about them . . . and he complained that the Clay of the Furnace pottery was but poor and often gave WAY to their great damage and complained also that they could not make their Glass so Clear and Strong for want of HELP their Works being near 200 miles from any quantity of it . . . This Caspar is lately dead and from a very poor man raised and left a Fortune of £20,000 or £30,000.

Obviously the Wistars could and did get plenty of help from skilled immigrants who swarmed into the port of Philadelphia, but Governor Belcher saw fit to accept this downgrading of Wistarberg.

Lord Grenville, however, preparing to enforce the hated stamp tax of the Townshend Acts, inquired of Benjamin Franklin as to manufactories in the Colonies in 1768. Wistarberg could not escape notice and so Jersey's strongly Tory Governor William Franklin answered for his father that the Salem County Glass House made "a very coarse Green Glass for windows used only in some of the houses of the poorer Sort of People. The Profits made by this Work have not hitherto been sufficient it seems to induce any Persons to set up more of the like kind in this Colony . . . It seems probable that notwithstanding the Duty, Fine Glass can still be imported into America cheaper than it can be made here."

Tory Richard Wistar surely must have appreciated this red herring to divert the tax collectors from the trail to Wistarberg. As far as we know the Wistars did not advertise "Fine Glass" but if they did manufacture luxury goods it would not have been politic to announce the fact.

In 1752, the year in which his father died, Richard Wistar published advertisements such as the following which appeared in the *Pennsylvania Gazette* of Nov. 23:

> Richard Wistar hereby gives notice that he is removed from his Father's House in Market Street Philadelphia to a house higher up in the same Street next door to the Spinning Wheel almost opposite the Prison. Where may be had Glass 9 x 11, 8 x 10, 7 x 9 and all other sizes of Window Glass and Bottles, wholesale and retail. He likewise carries on the trade of Making Brass Buttons where merchants shop keepers and others may be supplied as usual.

Seventeen years later an advertisement more explicit about the kind of glass Richard Wistar was selling appeared in the *Pennsylvania Gazette* of Sept. 28, 1769:

> Made at subscriber's Glass Works between 300 and 400 boxes of Window glass consisting of common sizes 10 x 12, 9 x 11, 8 x 10, 7 x 9, 6 x 8. Lamp glasses or any uncommon sizes under

> 16 x 18 are cut on short notice. Most sort of bottles, gallon, ½ gallon, and quart, full measure ½ gallon cafe bottles, snuff and mustard bottles also electrofying globes and tubes &c. All glass American Manufacture and America ought also encourage her own manufacture.
>
> N.B. He also continues to make the Philadelphia brass buttons noted for their strength and such as were made by his deceased father and warranted for seven years.

The "electrofying globes and tubes" were what was called "philosophical" glassware, much in demand then for electrical experiments, a fad set off by Benjamin Franklin and his kite.

In 1768 a large family of Palatine glassmakers, the Stengers, arrived in Alloway from Dornhagen, Germany, where they had owned a glassworks, from which they were not permitted to withdraw capital. The parents, Jacob and Catherine Stanger, as the name soon became known, brought with them seven sons, the eldest, Solomon, 25 and a proficient blower as were several others. In time all of the Stanger boys grew up to be glassmakers, founding numerous factories in New Jersey, and the 8-year-old daughter Sophia later married a glassmaker. The influence of the Stanger style and skill on American blown glass up to the time of the Civil War is vast, but incalculable. On arrival in Alloway they soon became members of the Emanuel Lutheran church built at Freasburg in 1748 (later Friesburg) of which so many early glassmaking families were members, among them the Freas, Zieglers (Sickler), Fralingers, Souders, Dilshavers.

One of the Stangers, though, seems to have had no use for the Wistar works and thereby got his name in the *Pennsylvania Chronicle and Universal and Advertiser* for April 18, 1770. In that issue Richard Wistar offered a $20 reward for "two German Servant Lads run away," one of them described as "Jacob Stenger, aged 18 years 5 feet 8 inches well set, good countenanced, light complexioned, dark hair." Whether or not Jacob returned we do not know. We do know that a second-generation Jacob was active at the Union Glass Works of Port Elizabeth but he was not necessarily the son of the original Jacob.

An indentured servant, Jacob Stenger was but one of many Europeans who bound themselves for several years to work for the Wistars because the latter had paid their passage money. This cheap labor was one of the reasons for the prosperity of the Wistar works. Some were bound for as long as 12 years, among them a John Lambert, in consideration of 9 pounds, 9 shillings passage money. Abraham Zimmerman was bound for eight years, Melchior Zimmerman for nine years. It is not surprising that Jacob Stanger could not face that kind of servitude.

"Find me a whole bottle, and I'll pay you $300."

So said a 1969 collector to the owners of the present day Wistarberg farm, residents here for 43 years. In that length of time they have been plowing the land and have found only two of the wine bottle "cheaters" or pontil mark fragments like those shown opposite. The residents of this famed site, now protected against outsiders' digging by U.S. Soil Bank regulations are not aware of the fine points of collecting blown glass but they do know that most of the fragments they have turned up are light green or dark amber. They have found no fragments whatsoever of opaque white and aqua so often labeled Wistarberg.

Fig. 18 DEMIJOHN "CHEATERS" FROM WISTARBERG. These unusually large "kick-ups" from the base of large wine bottles are the only ones found in 43 years by the present owners of a farm on the Wistarberg site.

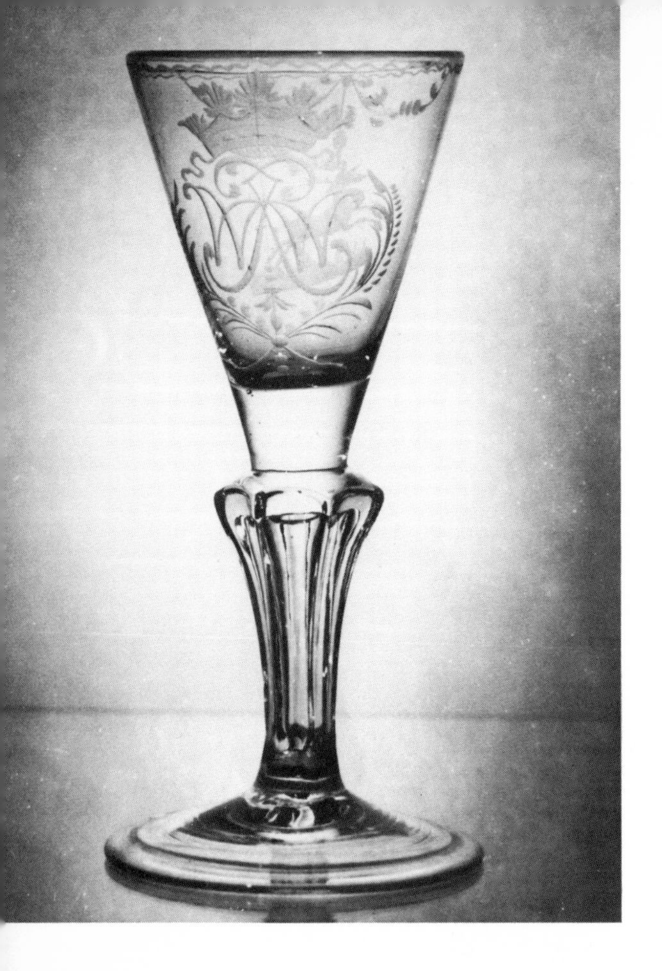

Fig. 19 WISTAR-OWNED, this is one of a dozen handsome wine glasses inherited by Caspar Wistar's descendants. Of clear glass, only two of the goblets remain, this one owned by the Wistar Institute of Philadelphia and one owned by Thomas Wistar. Most of the Wistarberg blowers, supervisors and owners were Germans. H. 5 inches. *Photo by Adolph Marfaing, courtesy of the Wistar Institute of Anatomy and Biology.*

The evidence of what is Wistarberg glass was destroyed long ago. The damage done by unscientific digging at historic sites is demonstrated by the unsystematic, uncatalogued, imprecise excavations performed at Wistarberg in 1913 by author-collector Frederick W. Hunter and his brother-in-law J. B. Kerfoot, formerly a dealer who lived at The House with the Brick Wall in Freehold.

Between the time Wistarberg was founded and Hunter and Kerfoot arrived 175 years had passed and New Jersey had seen scores of glassworks spring up, several close to Alloway, and whose products were sold, used, and broken in the area. Unfortunately, as the McKearins wrote:

> ". . . Hunter did not differentiate between fragment evidence, local tradition, and personal opinion in presenting his material . . . Apparently not even one complete vessel could be reconstructed from the fragments . . . Nevertheless an entire temple of American glass tradition was erected upon the fragile foundation of fragments, mortared with opinion and located at Wistarberg."

As a result of the careless conclusions of Hunter and Kerfoot hundreds of pieces of glass were sold as Wistarberg and at auction some highly colored articles sold in the 1930s and 1940s for $500 and more, glass that would not bring a fourth of that today. Today the waters are still so muddied that most collectors would not trust anything dredged from Alloway creek, much less word-of-mouth documentation.

The lovely goblet illustrated opposite is one of a dozen made for Caspar Wistar and bears the monogram of Richard Wistar. The reverse side has a copper-wheel engraving of a stag. A matching goblet shows the initials of Caspar Wistar and an engraving of a hunting dog. The goblet pictured is owned by the Wistar Institute of Anatomy and Biology of Philadelphia and the other by a member of the Wistar family.

Each owner is convinced that the goblets were made at Wistarberg, as General Wistar declared. Curators at the Corning Museum of Glass, however, believe that the goblets are too sophisticated to have been fashioned at Wistarberg and were made in Europe. It should be noted, however, that clear glass was made at Alloway. Then, too, the goblets have the hexagonal Silesian stem, a German style of the 18th century, one with which some of Wistars' glassmakers would have been familiar. Might one speculate that one or all of the Wistars' four partners, expert craftsmen as they were, made these goblets as a gift for their benefactor?

If one cannot depend on documentation such as the above, how then can anyone say what is Wistarberg? A lop-sided wine bottle, below, gives every evidence of having been made at Alloway. On its seal it bears the name of the owner, WM. SAVERY 1752. Savery was the noted Philadelphia cabinetmaker and the bottle has been handed down in direct

Fig. 20 WM. SAVERY 1752 reads the glass seal on this wine or spirits bottle, handed down in the family of this famous Philadelphia cabinet-maker who died in 1787. Dark olive green, bubbled. Sheared lip, collared neck. Believed to be Wistarberg. *Philadelphia Museum of Art. Photo by A. J. Wyatt, Staff Photographer.*

line in his family until presented to the Philadelphia Museum of Fine Arts, in this century. The bottle may well have been filled with wine by Caspar Wistar's brother John, a wine-seller.

The Philadelphia Museum of Fine Arts has one of the most outstanding permanent exhibits of South Jersey style glass in its George Horace Lorimer collection. Some of these beautiful objects have 18th century influences. The viewer will have to judge for himself if some of this is in the Wistarberg tradition.

The Salem County Historical Society has a small collection of South Jersey glass once called Wistarberg but present-day officers say they can document it only by family tradition. One unusual object is a nearly clear glass horn, with rigaree threading. These were said to have been made at Wistarberg for sleighing parties, which used to wind up the evening at Wistars' store.

A light green plate about 6½ inches in diameter which Mrs. William Hancock, Sr., of Salem presented to the museum seems to have a solid history of Wistarberg. Mrs. Hancock in 1970 told me that the plate came from her grandmother, Mrs. Mary House Ewen who was a descendant of a Wistarberg glassworker named Houseman. Mary House or Houseman was born at Alloway in 1828 in a dwelling known to have been built in 1736 by one of three Oakford brothers. Among other glass in the home Mary Houseman especially remembered the plate from her childhood as it was the family butter plate.

The light green, with a yellow cast, of this plate is in decided contrast to Port Elizabeth's early ware of sea-blue. The light green slag at Wistarberg is so different from that at other early South Jersey sites as to suggest that the Wistarberg batches intentionally had additions of iron oxides.

Over the years many tiny scent and "smelling" bottles (Fig. 21) in the shape of sea-horses have been found in the Alloway area and sold by Philadelphia dealers. It seems likely that these were made at Wistarberg, but of course it does not follow that all such pocket scent bottles are Wistarberg.

One of the mystifying aspects of Wistarberg is when it closed. From a highly successful venture that brought great wealth to Caspar and his son Richard, Wistar's glassworks suddenly ceased to exist some time during the Revolution and never re-opened, although Jersey, Delaware and Pennsylvania were in dire need of glass after the war.

Although Wistar's "Glass Manufactory" was being advertised for sale as late as 1780 it has been assumed that the works was then still operating; more likely this was a standing advertisement from an earlier date. Almost certainly Wistarberg had gone out of blast early in the Revolution, possibly just before 1776.

A fact not remarked on in print until now is that Solomon Stanger, the eldest and *pater familias* of Wistar's glassblowing clan of seven brothers and their in-laws, was listed as a blower at Stiegel's Manheim works in 1774! It is known, moreover, that his wife Guin Blumer, back in Salem county, was pregnant. Would Solomon Stanger have left family and his long-standing position as gaffer by choice? What he could not foretell in that year was that he would become the founder of the second glassworks in New Jersey, at Glassboro.

Besides the fact that many workers were volunteering or being conscripted for the American army, the major reason that Wistarberg must have shut down early in the

Fig. 21 GIMMAL AND SEAHORSE bottles show use of rigaree decoration. "Seahorse" scent bottles were formerly found in numerous homes in the Wistarberg area and are regarded as one of its most popular articles. Clear glass. H. gimmal 9 inches; scent bottle 3 inches.

Revolution is that the Quakers of Philadelphia and Salem county were already conducting a hot war of their own with those they dubbed "the rebel canaille."

It is amply proved that the Wistars, the Drinkers, the Walns and their wide circle of the Society of Friends in Philadelphia were intensely loyal to the British. On Dec. 8, 1777 Sally Wister wrote:

> Rejoice with us, my dear. The British have return'd to the city. Charming news this. May we ever be thankful to the Almighty Dispenser of events for his care and protection of us while surrounded with dangers.

On Sept. 2 of that same year Elizabeth Drinker wrote in her journal that the rebels "took my Henry [her husband] to the Mason's Lodge, in an illegal, unprecedented manner; where are several other Friends, with some of other persuasions, made prisoners." Henry Drinker, incidentally, had closed down the iron works in Atsion to prevent its use in making munitions for the patriot Americans.

"Richard Wister and Levi Hollingsworth put in Prison," wrote Elizabeth Drinker on May 26, 1779, "—have not heard on what pretext. A great concourse of people assembled at ye State House, by appointment, at 5 o'clock, this afternoon. Men with clubs have been to several stores, obliging ye people to lower their prices."

In his *Autobiography,* Gen. Isaac Jones Wistar (1827-1925) tells that the Philadelphia residence of his ancestor Richard was attacked by a mob and when Wistar came out

Fig. 22 FOOT OF PITCHER, WISTARBERG SITE, an unfinished reject indicates it was made there. Cloudy light green. Emerald green slag with fragment of pot attached, also from Wistarberg.

brandishing a cane he was knocked down and beaten but rescued by a rear guard of Gen. Clinton's royal troops and taken to Rahway where he died. Like many another family record, part truth, part hearsay. Indubitably, Richard Wistar's property and orchards in Philadelphia were damaged by patriots enraged over his active support of the British troops. The inescapable facts are, though, that Richard Wistar died in 1781, at Rahway, to be sure, but not in 1778 when Gen. Clinton was forced to evacuate Philadelphia.

An interesting footnote to the story of the Wistar works is that Richard married his second wife in the midst of the strife, on Aug. 4, 1776, a month after the Liberty Bell at Bridgeton pealed for the Declaration of Independence. Richard's new wife was a widow, Mary Gilbert, daughter of John and Elizabeth Bacon of Cumberland county, and the wedding took place in the Quaker stronghold of the Salem Friends Meeting House, still standing.

The following notice, then, tells not when Wistarberg ended but what it looked like in its last days.

A year before his death Richard Wistar ran this advertisement of sale of the Wistar Glass Works, which almost certainly was no longer in operation at this time, October 11, 1780, when the announcement appeared in the *Pennsylvania Journal.* Note that in this year Wistarberg had only two furnaces where once there had been four.

> The GLASS MANUFACTORY in Salem County West Jersey is for sale with 1500 Acres of Land adjoining. It contains two Furnaces with all the necessary Ovens for cooling the glass, drying Wood, etc. Contiguous to the Manufactory are two flattening Ovens in Separate Houses, a Storehouse, a Pot-house, a House fitted with Tables for the cutting of Glass, a Stamping Mill, a rolling Mill for the preparing of Clay for the making of Pots; and at a suitable distance are ten Dwelling houses for the Work men, as likewise a large Mansion House containing Six rooms on a Floor, with Bake-house and wash-house; Also a convenient Store-house where a well assorted retail Shop has been kept above 30 years, is as good a stand for the sale of goods as any in the Country, being situated one mile and a half from a navigable creek where shallops load for Philadelphia, eight miles from the county seat of Salem and half a mile from a good mill. There are about 250 acres of cleared Land within fence 100 whereof is mowable meadow, which produces hay and pasturage sufficient for the large stock of Cattle and Horses employed by the Manufactory.
> There is Stabling sufficient for 60 head of Cattle with a large Barn, Granery and Waggon House. The unimproved Land is well wooded and 200 acres more of Meadow may be made. The situation and convenience for the procuring of Materials is equal if not superior to any place in Jersey. For terms of sale apply to the Subscriber in Philadelphia.
>
> Richard Wistar

Rebellion was rife not only in the Colonies but also in the Wistar family. Richard's son, Richard II, had the family knack of making money and had become independently wealthy. As the war intensified he sided with the American patriots. For this he was later disowned by the Society of Friends. When the War of Independence was won Richard joined the Free Masons, of whom George Washington was the titular head.

And what of the four first glassmakers responsible for the initial success of Wistarberg? Their ends are obscure, to say the least.

Caspar Halter drops out of the picture so soon in Wistar account books that one suspects he must have died or changed to another occupation or returned to the Palatinate.

Simeon Kreismayer died in 1748 and his widow Susannah received a settlement of 406 pounds from the company. Johan Martin Halter died in 1769.

As noted in the preceding chapter, I have found direct descendants of Johannes Wentzel, who, although they know nothing about the glass their ancestor made, have located a Wentzel cemetery at Cohansey, near Shiloh. Here are four brown sandstone markers incised with initials only. One of the these gravestones is inscribed "J. W.," and the present generation of the family believe this to be the last resting place of the original Johannes Wentzel.

A FAMED glassworks that died suddenly like Wistarberg and was not reborn seems to be unnatural. At any rate, a rumor has arisen to cover the situation. The rumor is that in the 1830s the Stangers came back to Alloway, as owners and blowers at defunct Wistarberg.

The rumor has doubtless arisen from a very real document in the Salem County Historical Society, which shows that Lewis Stanger of Glassboro was administrator for the estate of his son George who died without will on June 16, 1836, in Upper Alloway township where Wistarberg was located. In that year the father and his son are verified as owning the Temperanceville furnace at Glassboro, as Lewis Stanger & Son.

That they might have owned another factory at Alloway seems logical. From checking records in the Salem County court house, however, I find in the Alloway inventory of the firm of Lewis Stanger & Son that a stock of dry goods, earthen and queens ware, amounting to $1,095.24½, had been shipped from Alloway to Glassboro, evidently for sale in the company store there. But nowhere is there an account of a stock of glass on hand or shipped to Glassboro. If George Stanger's property was close to Alloway creek, as court records indicate, he doubtless was importing from Philadelphia household goods for sale and not blowing glass at Alloway.

The inventory of George Stanger's personal effects amounted to only $569.17, including "1 tight Bodey coat." The only mention of glass in his household goods is "1 Glass Lamp" and a "Lot of fancy Glass," the latter valued at $2.50. Every admirer of early Jersey glass will have his own special dream of what that fancy Stanger glass might have been like.

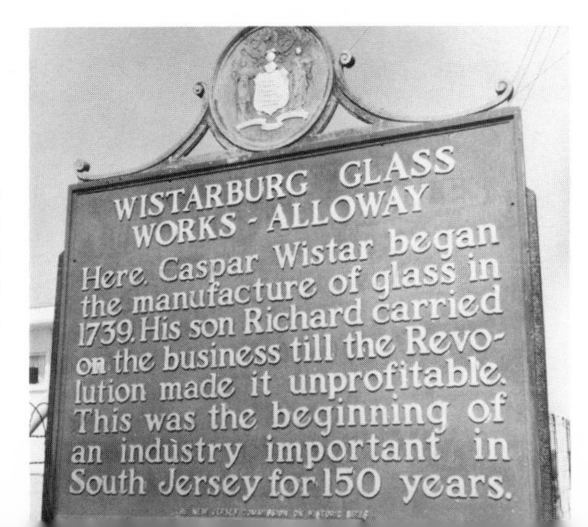

WISTARBURG GLASS
WORKS - ALLOWAY
Here Caspar Wistar began
the manufacture of glass in
1739. His son Richard carried
on the business till the Revolution made it unprofitable.
This was the beginning of
an industry important in
South Jersey for 150 years.

Fig. 23 HISTORIC MARKER at a farm near Alloway, Salem county, is the site of the first New Jersey glasshouse and the first successful one in America.

Glass House, N. J.

In 1800 there was a stagecoach leaving Camden about once a week for Cape May, traversing dense pine woods, where you'd best have a gun, and rolling through sand, mud and unbridged streams, until it reached the last stop, known as Pitch o' the Cape.

En route there was a log cabin settlement known as Glass House, N.J., a place then run by the glassblowing family of Stangers who had come from Dornhagen, Germany, in 1768 to work at Wistarberg in Salem county.

By the time Wistarberg had already closed, about 1775, and the works was offered for sale on Oct. 11, 1780, the Stangers were well established with their glass furnace—the second in New Jersey—at Glass House, N.J. This fact is revealed in the diary of Dr. Nicholas Collin, pastor of the Friesburg Church in 1780. His journal, translated from the Swedish by Amandus Johnson, makes it plain that the family glasshouse was a going concern at the close of 1780:

> A party of German Lutherans who arrived from Saxony some years ago consisting of six brothers, three of whom had wives and children, their mother, a sister and some others had erected a glassworks in the woods 2½ miles east of the Raccoon Church and as there was no German Pastor at the place they asked me to come over and preach to them as often as possible. Thereupon, I visited them on Sunday each month from June to October. German divine service was first held and then English for all kinds of people who appeared. Several children were baptized. These kind Germans paid me honorably as much as they could afford, about two Swedish Ricksthaler for every trip, which amounted to more than I received from the entire Swedish congregation during the same period. I was indeed lucky to get that amount, for the currency had now depreciated to such an extent that the man who rented the main part of the Church property in Swedesboro could legally pay off two years rent with a sum which would scarcely pay for about a hundred weight of wheat flour.

In those words Dr. Collin not only told volumes about the good character of the Stangers but also foretold, in writing about the devastating effect of the depreciation of Continental currency, the coming change in Stanger fortunes. Of 1781 the clergyman writes, "I visited the glass-works once during the winter." From Pastor Collin's journal of 1782 come intimations of changes at Glass House, N.J.:

> In the month of May I preached at the above mentioned glassworks and Baptized several children. I was not able to visit the good people there as often as I really desired nor had I since the first year accepted any payments from them, for they were not especially wealthy people and I was now in less need.

A fragile sailing vessel commanded by Capt. S. Hawkes in 1768 embarked from Rotterdam for England, thence from Cowes to America. Tossed by high seas on this voyage were a whole family of glassworkers: a father and a mother, Jacob and Catherine

Fig. 24 POCKET FLASK, olive amber ¼ pint, has quilling on four sides. H. 5 inches.

Meyer Binder Stenger (later changed to Stanger), a little daughter Sophia, 8, and seven sons. Solomon, 25, was the eldest; then there were Daniel, Christian, Adam, Jacob, Philip 12, and Franz 10.*

The family had had their own glassworks in Dornhagen but because of unsettled conditions in the German states of the 1760s the government refused to allow them to sell. Thus they came to Philadelphia virtually without capital, which by industry, however, they had built up while employed at the Wistar Glass Works in Alloway. When the strife leading to the Revolution closed that glasshouse, Solomon who became head of the family in 1774 was blowing glass at Stiegel's Manheim factory, shortly before the "Baron" was about to go into bankruptcy.

The Stangers had no choice but to start up their own furnace as there was not one similar to Wistarberg within hundreds of miles that would support a whole family and their relatives by marriage.

*The Stanger history is a genealogist's nightmare because, as Bole and Walton have pointed out, of the large families in which male offspring predominated, many of whom were named after uncles instead of parents. Philip married Mary Swope who bore him seven sons. Solomon who married Guin or Gwyn Blumer had four sons. Most of the men of the first and second generations founded or sustained major glassworks throughout South Jersey.

They chose a site inland, as much of the coastal and river banks had already been denuded of essential wood, which was to become the town of Glassboro. That city dates its founding from Sept. 23, 1779 when Solomon Stanger paid Jacob Gosling 700 pounds for 200 acres of ground in gold and silver specie, a huge sum for that site so distant from market in a time of few, and often impassible, roads. Soon after the Stangers established the furnace and attained success in selling their glass, the government devalued the currency, setting $40 of continental money as equal to one dollar of gold.

The Stangers had paid for their land in gold and silver, but were being paid in nearly worthless paper money. In order to keep going they went heavily into debt, mortgaging their land, tools and glassworks. Soon they found they were compelled to sell these hard-won possessions, which they did gradually over a period of 1783 to 1786. By that time Glass House, N.J., was in the hands of Col. Thomas Heston and Col. Thomas Carpenter, two "fighting Quakers" who had given gallant service for the American cause in the Revolution.

The Stangers were indispensable, however, for the operation of the glassworks and hence were the actual managers. Some of them left before long to start furnaces at Malaga and to operate others at Port Elizabeth, Marshallville, and New Brooklyn. Time would enhance Pastor Collin's opinion of them as good citizens and they would leave a heritage of beautiful glass.

Like their predecessors the Wistars, Colonels Heston and Thomas Carpenter believed in advertising their glassware, but not content merely with the Philadelphia market, they went after New York trade, as can be seen from the following notice in the *New York Mercantile Advertiser* of Dec. 6, 1799. The advertisement gives us a rare insight into the kind of glass the Stangers and their relatives were blowing at that early date.

> New Jersey Glafs Manufactory
>
> The proprietors of the New Jersey Glafs Manufactory have on hand for sale on reasonable terms the following articles of Glafsware, viz—
>
> Retorts and receivers, tincture bottles,
> Snuff and mustard bottles,
> Pocket, quart and two quart farmers' bottles,
> Claret and lavender bottles,
> Vials assorted, from half ounce to 8 ounces
>
> Orders received for any of the above kinds of glass by Levi Garrett, no. 120 south Front Street, Philadelphia, and the proprietors, Woodbury, Gloucester County, N. Jersey.
>
> Heston and Carpenter

It is worth noting that nowhere is the place of manufacture mentioned, a fact that still today leads researchers on Jersey glass astray.

Like most owners of early glassworks, or their clerks, Colonel Heston kept journals or ledgers of articles blown and gaffers making them. A notebook, written at the start of the autumn "firing" in 1802, tells us that Stangers were still the mainstay of the works at Glass House, N.J. We learn that on Sept. 28 Jacob Stanger blew 264 mustard bottles. Other blowers who were engaged then in making cordial bottles, pocket flasks, and ½ gallon bottles were Chris Stanger, Daniel Stanger, another Jacob Stanger, William Shough, Jacob

Focer, Leonard Neapling and N. Swaner. Another glassman Jacob Swope was absent for a couple of weeks because of sickness, and one of the Jacob Stangers had a lame finger that hindered blowing. Adding to the problems, the clay melting pots collapsed, with loss of the batch. The autumn "melt" was not off to an auspicious start.

Far worse was in store. Three weeks after starting the notebook, its unknown author ended it on October 13, "being the day," as he wrote, "that Col. Heston's left this troublesome World for a better one no doubt."

Col. Heston was stricken at the age of 46 and his widow was left with eight minor children, all girls except for a 5-year-old son. Widow Heston continued to hold her share of the glassworks, along with Col. Thomas Carpenter, but in 1808 she sold her interest to Peter Wickoff. She ran the village tavern, however, for seven years after her husband's death. Nor was this to be the end of Hestons in glassmaking. In years to come, their grandsons, Thomas H. and Samuel A. Whitney, would make Glassboro more famous for glass than it had ever been.

Enough exquisite and fragile 18th century glass has been found in New Jersey to warrant the conclusion that such unique examples were blown here, some by the Stangers as they worked at both of the only two 18th century glasshouses in the colony. Yet the one most solid association with the Stangers is the decanter shown below, a simple threaded bottle which was probably produced in quantity. It was presented to Glassboro State College in 1923 by Thomas W. Synnott, a great grandson of Col. Heston, who had been directly associated with the Whitney works. Information given was that the bottle was "made at the Heston Glass Works in 1784," which would have been the time of transition when the Stangers still owned some of the property and were the chief blowers. Edward H. Walton, Jr., recalls seeing this bottle, 50 years ago, on a mantel in the home of Isaac

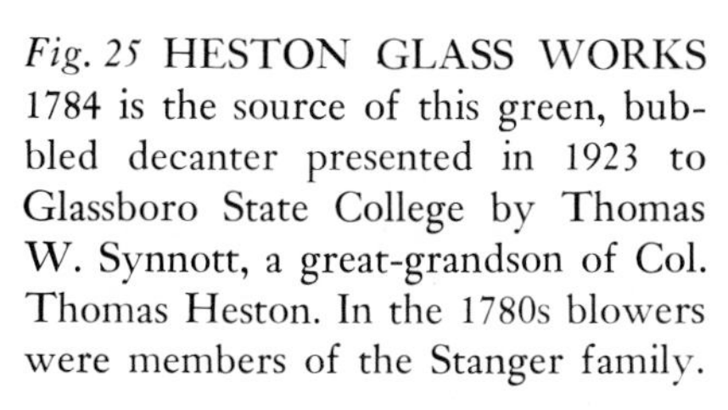

Fig. 25 HESTON GLASS WORKS 1784 is the source of this green, bubbled decanter presented in 1923 to Glassboro State College by Thomas W. Synnott, a great-grandson of Col. Thomas Heston. In the 1780s blowers were members of the Stanger family.

Moffett, another great grandson of Col. Heston. The base of the decanter has had so much wear that it must have been a tavern bottle. It is worth noting that Solomon Stanger in 1781 was licensed to operate Glassboro's first tavern, which was later run by the widow of Col. Heston. Through all the intervening years the inn has remained in operation, today as the Franklin House, at Main and West streets.

THE OLIVE GLASS WORKS

Edward Carpenter on May 18, 1808 acquired his father's share of the original Glassboro works and the firm became known as Edward Carpenter Company, Olive Works, a highly significant name because T. W. Dyott of Philadelphia announced in 1819 that he was purchasing the entire output of the Olive Works for his ever-increasing business of selling flasks, drug bottles and medicines.

The sudden death of Edward Carpenter in 1813 resulted in a decline of the Olive Works until Wickoff in 1816 sold his interest to David Wolf of Woolwich township. Wolf obtained entire control on June 25, 1817, when he bought the Carpenter estate share for $4,559.43, and began renovating the furnace and building a new pot house. By the time he was ready for the autumn blast Wolf announced on Sept. 17, 1817 in Philadelphia's *Democratic Press:*

> OLIVE GLASS WORKS—The proprietors of this GLASS WORKS beg leave to acquaint publishers and the public that as a new blast is commenced they will feel obliged by having early orders for bottles, vials, or any hollow-ware of any form in the making of which their attention will be given to please their friends, both in quality and figure, and every exertion made as to punctuality in time for execution. All orders for this factory are received at the drug store of T. W. Dyott, North-east Corner of Second and Race Street.

This news preceded by three years "Dr." Dyott's own advertisements in the Philadelphia *American Centinel and Mercantile Advertiser* stating that he was buying the output—and listing kinds of bottles available—from the Olive Works and from the Gloucester Works at Clementon (see chapters on Dr. Dyott and Clementon Glass Works).

The improvements in the furnace attracted a member of the Stanger group, Daniel Focer, son of Valentine Focer and Sophia Stanger, who bought a quarter interest, as did Isaac Thorne. By 1821 Thorne was sole owner, but not for long, as in 1824 he was bought out by Jeremiah J. Foster. Shortly thereafter he merged the plant with the Harmony Glass Works and thus ended the first phase of the Stangers in the town of Glassboro which they had founded in 1779.

THE HARMONY GLASS WORKS

The Harmony Glass Works was born in 1813 when after Edward Carpenter died and his firm was dissolved some of the glassblowers led by Stangers and John Rink built a new furnace only 400 yards south of the original one and took the firm name of Rink, Stanger & Company and appointed Daniel Focer, mentioned above, as manager. Rink in Philadelphia had charge of sales and supplies. He died in 1823 and on July 23 his interest was offered at public sale in the Woodbury *Village Herald*, a notice describing the settlement as a complete establishment with "a large Glass House, Pot House, Mill House, Packing House, Store House, several dwellings," on five acres. The proposition appealed to Daniel K. Miller, then owner of the Franklin Glass Works at Malaga, which had been founded by Christian L. Stanger in 1810.

Lewis Stanger had been the leader of the Stangers in their venture, the Harmony works, and when he withdrew in 1834 a third interest in the works was bought by Thomas H. Whitney. This was the foot in the door of the Whitney family who would eventually transform a small glassworks into a major corporation supplying handblown containers to the nation. The next step occurred in 1837 when Whitney bought out all other interests and joined with his sons Thomas H. and Samuel A. to form Whitney & Brothers. Later with his death the firm became known as Whitney Brothers until 1882, then as the Whitney Glass Works. From 1836 to 1878 glassmaking production expanded eight-fold.

STANGERS' TEMPERANCEVILLE (LEWISVILLE)

Looking back a bit we recall that when the original Stanger works in Glassboro was dissolved in 1813 after the owner Edward Carpenter died, Lewis Stanger and John Rink set up the Harmony Works about 400 yards south of the first one. This story repeated itself in 1834 when Lewis Stanger having withdrawn from Harmony, as the Whitneys made inroads, set up still another glasshouse, this one about 500 yards south of Harmony.

The firm name was Lewis Stanger & Son, the latter for George C. Stanger. Jacob, brother of Lewis, was also an organizer, and the locality was at first called Lewisville. The name that stuck, however, was the Temperanceville Glass Works, for the Stangers would employ only teetotalers. It is unlikely that any liquor flasks came from Temperanceville.

This new generation of Stangers blew window-glass and some hollow ware until 1841, when they found they could no longer carry on. To make the pill more bitter, Lewis Stanger found once again that he and his family were being sold out to Thomas Whitney. The latter proceeded to place Temperanceville in the hands of his brother Eben and his brother-in-law Woodward Warrick. The new owners quickly stopped making window-glass, concentrated on bottles, and marketed their entire production through Whitney Brothers of Harmony.

WOODWARD WARRICK AND THOMAS W. STANGER

Prospering with the help of Whitney Brothers, the plant at Lewisville in Glassboro continued as Whitney and Warrick until 1849 when the latter sold out to Eben Whitney.

After a decade, he sold out to Thomas W. Stanger, a son of Frederick and a nephew of Lewis Stanger. Thomas W. then brought Warrick back into the firm and the two reconverted the factory to window-glass, very successfully, for it ran under this management until 1883 when Stanger died. Warrick then being 76, he bequeathed the works to his three sons, J. Price, T.D. and H.S., but the new generation soon abandoned the project.

It is worth noting that Thomas W. Stanger was a third generation of that family and

Fig. 26 BRASS COINS good for 1 cent at the Warrick & Stanger Window Glass Works, Glassboro, N. J., "at our store."

not the same Thomas Stanger who operated the Isabella Works at New Brooklyn after his cousin Frederick died. The Thomas Stanger in partnership with Warrick had a reputation as a precocious child who learned to swim and to read by the time he was four years old and at age 15 was a journeyman glassblower. At age 21 he was a principal in the Glassboro school but resigned after a year, saying that "teaching is a lazy man's job." After working in Baltimore and Louisville, he settled in Pittsburgh where he became owner of a glass bottle factory, at age 25. He took time to earn a college degree, became a member of the board of education and of the city council, and was otherwise known as a civic leader. The last 25 years of his life he spent in Glassboro and proved that a home-town boy could make good—at home, too.

WHITNEY BROTHERS GLASSWORKS

Who were the Whitneys who had such devastating effect on Stanger management of glasshouses in the town they had founded? The first of these Whitneys was Ebenezer, a sea captain from Castine, Maine, whose cargo of wine bound for Philadelphia was wrecked off Cape May in 1806. As the captain himself was injured his rescuers placed him in a stagecoach bound for Philadelphia but he became so ill that he was forced to stop off at Heston's Tavern in Glassboro. There he recuperated nicely under the care of Widow Heston's daughter, Bathsheba. Within a year she had become his wife.

Ebenezer never did engage in glassmaking. He tried tavern-keeping in several towns and lastly running a general store in Glassboro. It was here that the first Whitney died in 1823 at the young age of 43, leaving a miniscule inheritance for Bathsheba and their three young sons and two daughters.

The eldest son Thomas Heston Whitney when only a boy went to work for a dollar a week at the Harmony Glass Works but at 18 chose to become a clerk there. Possibly with the help of his mother who was selling inheritances of Col. Heston's land, Thomas when only 22 bought a third interest in the Harmony works and by 1838 owned it.

His youngest brother Samuel went to work here as an apprentice and being an apt pupil he learned not only glassblowing but all sides of managing a glassworks. With a drive for accomplishment and foresighted planning the two brothers quickly prospered and forced out all unwanted competition. As previously noted, the middle brother Eben became a co-partner with Woodward Warrick, a brother-in-law, in the Temperanceville glassworks.

Where many glassworks were forced to close because of lack of fuel, the Whitneys bought hundreds of acres of timberland long before the need arose. In 1853 they began using anthracite coal experimentally. The factory buildings were constantly being modernized and expanded.

With success assured, Thomas began to delve into state politics as a member of the Whig party, and the management of Whitney Brothers became more and more the responsibility of Samuel.

In 1849 the two brothers and their mother moved into a mansion that was the talk of Glassboro. Its setting was an enchanting deer park named Holly Bush. Four years later at the age of 40 Thomas married his second cousin Josephine Allen Whitney, a New

Orleans girl who became known in Glassboro for wearing the identical fashions of Queen Victoria. The couple's six sons and a daughter, together with the bachelor brother Samuel, enjoyed life at Holly Bush as leading citizens not only of Glassboro but of the state.

The Civil War which shattered so many glasshouses had no markedly adverse affect on Whitney Brothers. That was a time when some of their most attractive bottles were issued. Considering that the Indian Queen and the Booz bottle, among others, are so desirable to modern collectors, they must have been irresistible to contemporary buyers. As many records were destroyed in a disastrous Whitney works fire on Oct. 25, 1895, no information is available as to the designers of Whitney bottles.

In the late 1870s when Glassboro's largest industry had really hit its stride the two men most responsible for this success—Thomas and Samuel Whitney—retired, but the new management was well indoctrinated, as John Perkins Whitney, son of Thomas, and Thomas Whitney Synnott, his namesake and nephew, took charge.

At this period the Whitney Glass Works was one of the major ones in the state, though not nearly so large as Whitall Tatum at Millville. The Whitney plant already dominated the town, with four 2-story factory buildings each 100 by 80 feet, and there were the usual appendages of sawmill, box factory, packing house, warehouses, wheelwright and blacksmith shops, as well as a large company store. About 100 houses, company-owned, were rented to workmen. The original Stanger tavern, now much altered and enlarged, had become the Bismarck House. The whole compound, which looked pleasantly rural because of many trees, occupied 12 acres bounded by streets known today as State, High and Main and College Avenue.

Glass blown each month amounted to 525 tons, a job handled by some 400 employees. A monthly supply of 100 tons of soda ash, 300 tons of sand, and 2,000 bushels of oyster-shell lime were required to produce this glass.

In the '70s the Whitneys were continuing to make containers such as those named in their price lists of the 1860s: bottles for mustard, catsup, horse radish, pepper sauce, olives, capers, lemon syrup, cod liver oil and castor oil. They also made ink bottles and ink stands, preserve jars, ½-gallon hexagon pickle bottles, snuff jars, patent medicine bottles and containers for porter, ale and mineral water. Although the Whitneys were active in the temperance movement they advertised "Wine and Liquor Bottles of Every Description." Their store coins, made of brass, carried a bas-relief of a wicker-covered demijohn; some of those blown held as much as 14 gallons.

Although there was considerable overlapping of the lines between the Whitneys and the Whitall Tatum Company, the former never went in for the elaborate "apothecary shop furniture" and show globes blown at Millville but concentrated more on food containers and brand name bottles. The Whitneys' largest single order was one in 1885 for 7½ million bottles for "Warner's Safe Cure," made by the H. H. Warner Company of Rochester, N.Y.

With orders of this size coming in the firm installed a new tank furnace, largest of its kind in the state. Known as "Jumbo" and weighing 40 tons it produced metal at a rate equal to four pot furnaces. About this time too the plant went into a day and night shift. All this expansion produced a labor and a housing shortage. The relatively high rate of pay, $70 to $110 a month as compared with the average of $44 in other fields of manufacturing, soon helped to alleviate the shortage of workers.

Fig. 27 WHITNEY BOTTLES. "The Indian Queen," made to hold Brown's Celebrated Indian Herb Bitters. Patented 1868. H. 12 inches. Dr. Fisch's Bitters was the original medicinal for the fish bottle, of which this is a variant without lettering. Amber. H. 10 inches.

The Whitneys developed renown for appealing figural and historical bottles which have long been favorites of advanced collectors.

"The Indian Queen," a well executed sculpture of an Indian maid, is one of the more romantic of these bottles. Usually found in amber, this figural is more prosaically known as BROWN'S/CELEBRATED/INDIAN HERB BITTERS, for the words embossed on a shield below the Indian's left hand. The back is embossed PATENTED/Feb 11./1868. Variations of the date are "Patented 1867" and "Patented 1868." Other colors reported are aqua, clear and green. The bottle has been widely copied and modified to avoid patent infringements (above).

Another popular figural is "Doctor Fisch's Bitters," a fish standing on a flat tail. In an arc beneath one eye is impressed DOCTOR FISCH'S BITTERS and on the reverse: W. H. WARE/PATENTED 1866. The 11½-inch bottle is usually found in amber but a variant with the name THE FISH BITTERS is reported also in clear and green. Still another variant is devoid of lettering, a type that was used by Eli Lilly & Company for bottling cod liver oil (opposite).

The realistic "ear of corn", a 12½-inch round bottle usually made in amber, sometimes aqua, was moldblown for NATIONAL BITTERS, the name impressed in an oblong panel on the face. Above is a plain oval for a paper label, in this case that of Walton & Zug of Philadelphia. The bottle, with a ringed collar and a circular foot, has the base embossed in a circle: PATENT 1867.all slender log cabin embossed on roof panels: S T / DRAKES, 1860/PLANTATION, X/BITTERS, shows a different date on the reverse panels: PATENTED /1862. Found in shades of amber and green, with minor variations in design, it by no means compares in value with Whitney's far rarer "Booz" bottle, a so-called log cabin. Some other unusual Whitney bottles are the tall, three-sided one for Morning Star bitters, another amber one for bitters with the word TIPPECANOE spelled out in a vertical column, and a gray clam-shaped flask with metal cap.

The "pineapple" bitters bottle in dark amber, also made by Whitney, is a pineapple-shaped decanter with deeply impressed diamond points resembling the fruit's scales. A

Fig. 28 WHITNEY'S tall log cabin, 10 inches high, is embossed on the roof: S T DRAKES/1860 PLANTATION BITTERS. Commonly deep orange-amber; rare in amethyst and dark green. *Charles F. Carr collection.*

diamond-shaped medallion on one side is embossed W & CO / N.Y. Plate 252 of McKearins' *American Glass* shows how a skillful gaffer created a jug and a covered sugar bowl from a pineapple mold. The Minotola Glass Works made ½-pint pineapple bottles in the 1890s but no illustrations have been found.

A well-shaped chestnut bottle with graceful handle crimped at the base was made by Whitney for whiskies. The dark amber bottle has a sheared lip with applied ring (below). A very rare version of this is impressed OLD / DR/ TOWNSENDS /CELEBRATED / STOMACH /BITTERS, but it is not certain if this was made at Glassboro.

The Flora Temple race horse jug is identical in neck ring, handle and color with the Whitney chestnut whiskies but the shape is flatter, the shoulders higher. Ascribed also to Whitney, the jug has a bas-relief in a square panel of the famed trotting horse and above it her name Flora Temple; below, "Harness Trot 219½." The reverse is plain.

The "hunter-fisherman" calabash is one of two of these gourd-shaped liquor bottles known to have been made for the Whitneys, although there may be others. Probably preceding the Jenny Lind, this is the earliest of the calabashes and was made also at other glassworks in New Jersey. As both hunter and fisherman are wearing high hats for an active sport, this would date these bottles at the earliest as 1840; and would certainly rule out Wistarberg, a source suggested to me by a glassblowing family! The McKearins do not mention any hunter-fisherman bottles but Van Rensselaer describes two nearly identical ones from Whitney. A Salem variant of the Whitneys is shown in Fig. 69, differing chiefly in showing the hunter with two dogs and shooting at two birds instead of one. Medium green and aqua are the usual colors, with a rare amber.

The other type of calabash made by the Whitneys is the Jenny Lind. According to the McKearins, the only two Whitney versions of this liquor bottle both have the name of "the Swedish nightingale" misspelled as Jeny. Why this should be is strange, for the Whitneys of 1850, when this bottle was probably made, were above average in sophistication. The Whitney Jeny Linds have an overall deep ribbing (unlike the Huffsey Jenny

Fig. 29 DARK AMBER. LEFT: Whitney whiskey jug, handle with fine S-curve. Sheared lip with ring. C.1840. H. 8 inches. CENTER: sugar bowl with flanged, inset cover has a drawn finial with pontil scar. Bubbled glass, possibly 18th century. H. 4 inches. Precisely made narrow-waisted pitcher has carefully drawn swag at the base and an unusual 6-pointed star foot, applied. Blown by Emil J. Larson in the 1930s. H. 8 inches, one of a pair.

Fig. 30 BOOZ BOTTLE and iron mold such as was used at Whitney Glass Works, Glassboro, in blowing these famous bottles impressed with the name E.G. BOOZ'S/OLD CABIN/ WHISKEY. Opposite side of the roof impressed with the date 1840, but it is now known that the bottles were made in the 1860s for Edmund G. Booz of Philadelphia. *Philadelphia Museum of Art. Photo by A. J. Wyatt, Staff Photographer.*

Linds which are not corrugated) except where the singer's portrait is encircled with a thick laurel wreath, surmounted by JENY . LIND. The unribbed portion of the reverse side shows a 2-story building above which is a 6-pointed star and the words GLASS FACTORY in an arc. The second version is similar but omits the star and the words. The glass factory depicted is the only one on any Jenny Lind calabash that indicates shingles on the roof.

Listing Jeny Linds as comparatively scarce, the McKearins report them in aqua, cornflower blue and brilliant green. The one Jenny Lind listed by Van Rensselaer as Whitney apparently is a Huffsey as the sides are not ribbed.

Astonishingly like a Whitney Lind in design is one with Jenny spelled correctly, and a tree in leaf filling the space of the glass factory. The provenance is unknown and the McKearins report it extremely rare.

Most prized of all Whitney mold-blown glass is the Booz bottle in the shape of a South Jersey cabin. To understand the decades of discussion about the bottle's confusing date one must know the embossing. One side of the roof is dated 1840 which led early collectors to believe that the bottle was blown that year, as a souvenir of the "log-cabin campaign" for Presidential candidate William Henry Harrison. The other side of the roof and one of the narrow walls are impressed E. G. BOOZ'S/ OLD CABIN / WHISKEY. The Booz address, shown on the opposite wall,is 120 WALNUT ST. /PHILADELPHIA. Some sharp detective work by I. Hazleton Mirkil, reported in the magazine *Antiques* of November 1926, revealed that liquor dealer E. G. Booz was listed in Philadelphia directories at this address only between the years 1860 and 1870; hence the bottles must have been blown in that decade, not in 1840.

The Whitney Booz bottle was made in two styles: one, with a straight roof line; the other with beveled roof-corners. The latter were made when it was found that the sharp corners had a tendency to break, a discovery made also by the Clevengers in blowing reproductions. Although the bottle is often called a log cabin, the 2-story house shows no logs; in style it is very like glassmakers' houses still to be seen in such Jersey villages as Batsto. The usual color for the Booz bottle was amber, deep and golden, and deep green; pale green is one of the rarities.

In 1927 the Clevengers and Ernest C. Stanmire of Clayton introduced an excellent reproduction of the Booz bottle, in orange-amber, sapphire and grass green. For differentiation see chapter on the Clevengers.

It is frequently assumed that the word "booze" originated from the E.G. Booz bottle but Webster's dictionaries show it to be an ancient word derived from "bouse" (same pronunciation) which was a Middle English term for liquor.

An identical bottle, except for the name and absence of a date, is presumed to have been made also at the Whitney Works. The roof and one end wall are impressed JACOB'S / CABIN TONIC / BITTERS. The opposite ends are embossed LABORATORY / PHILADELPHIA. Roof corners are beveled and the bottle, very rare, has been found only in clear glass.

In 1887 the official name of Whitney Brothers became the Whitney Glass Works, a fact that helps in identification. Many bottles, particularly amber whiskies, have this name embossed in capitals in a circle around the bottom. An earlier and rarer dark amber whiskey, made in quarts and pints, has an inside-thread neck with a matching glass stopper. Too costly to make, this bottle was soon discontinued.

A bottle that baffles many a collector because of a large and graceful but cryptic monogram of the letters G, K and W, is now known to have been made for Whitney Brothers. Key to the initials has been discovered to be Gettysburg Katalysine Water (catalyzing water?) which was dispensed from these bottles. An advertising booklet, owned by Charles Carr, which proclaims "Wonderful Cures" from this beverage, reveals that Whitney Brothers were not only glassmakers but were general agents for the tonic,

Choice rarities among Mason fruit jars, owned by Lewis de Eugenio of Glassboro, are a pair of tall 3-gallon ones in clear glass embossed MANUFACTURED AT/ THE/ WHITNEY GLASS WORKS/ GLASSBORO, N.J. The surprise, however, is that the jar is also embossed not only with the word MASON'S (which many factories simply "pinched") but also with the intertwined monogram of the Consolidated Fruit Jar Company of New Brunswick where John Landis Mason settled in 1873. Oldtime glassmen are on record as saying that Consolidated Fruit Jar Company made caps and liners but had the patented Mason jars blown elsewhere. Thus Whitney, privileged to use the monogram, must have been one such firm. In 1876 Mason assigned his remaining unexpired patents to Consolidated. The inventor of this great boon to mankind, a really effective preserve jar, died on Feb. 26, 1902 at 70, a charity patient in the House of Relief in Manhattan.

The years 1900 to 1930 were "boom and bust" not only for the Whitney Glass Works but for glassmaking in the town, and even for the town.

As the 20th century opened the demand for glass containers was so great that Whitney Brothers could not find enough good workers to keep up the pace. Workmen were imported from New York, from the South and finally from Greece but proved unsatisfactory. Recognizing their good bargaining position, local glassmen went on strike, to demand what the Glass Bottle Blowers Association had long been fighting for: 1) cash wages instead of wage deductions for forced purchases at the Whitney department store and 2) the right to rent elsewhere than in Whitney-owned tenant houses. Eventually Whitney employees won their demands, partly because business was booming and the Whitneys could not afford an idle plant.

Behind the scenes one man, Michael J. Owens, was working, whose inventions would displace both the Whitneys and their employees. On April 28, 1904, the Owens automatic bottle blowing machine, which had taken six years to make at a cost of $300,000, went into experimental production. It ran only one day, but perfection was quick in coming. The Whitneys bought one Owens machine in 1910 and by 1912 had installed five of them.

The reaction was instantaneous: glassmakers were permanently thrown out of work. In 1911 and 1912, 140 glassmen and their families moved out of Glassboro. One of the last of the Whitneys, George Perkins, died in 1915, and new names were added to the roster.

In 1918 a million dollar automatic factory opened and the Whitney name disappeared from letterheads, to be replaced by the Owens Bottle Works.

The new management prospered for a decade even if much of Glassboro's population did not. Then as financial storm clouds threatened the nation in 1929 the Owens Bottle Company announced a merger with Illinois Glass Corporation.

The real shock, however, struck when the new organization, Owens-Illinois Glass

ESTABLISHED IN 1775.

WHITNEY GLASS WORKS.

GLASSBORO', N. J.

Office 227 S. Front Street, Philadelphia.

Whitney Brothers,

MANUFACTURERS OF

FRUIT JARS,

Carboys, Demijohns, Wine Bottles,

And DRUGGISTS' GLASSWARE of every description.

Fig. 31 Advertisement from *The Crockery Journal*, July 8, 1875.

Corporation, closed down completely its new modern plant right after the merger. Thus ended 130 years of glassmaking at Glass House, N.J.

A cheerful postscript is that Owens-Illinois is now actively back in business in Glassboro with a large container closure division. The Whitneys' former mansion Holly Bush is now part of the campus at Glassboro State College as the home of its president. And Glassboro attained its greatest fame when Holly Bush was the scene of the 1967 "summit" meeting between Russia's Premier Aleksei N. Kosygin and President Lyndon B. Johnson. The tall white pines at the east end of University Boulevard are a reminder of the early days of Glass House, N.J.

SOLOMON H. STANGER, GLASSMAKER 1842-52

A calfskin-bound ledger for 1848 to 1852 for a Glassboro factory owned by Solomon H. Stanger may well be the last such record of Stangers as proprietors of furnaces. Owned in 1935 by S. Edna Fletcher of Newburgh, N.Y., the ledger was accompanied by five very simply made aquamarine glass pieces, including a mug and a lipless pitcher. An accompanying paper label read "Blowen by Solomon H. Stanger in Glassboro 49 years old 1876." This last date, as Ormsbee noted, probably refers to a local exhibit at the time of the 1876 United States Centennial.

Of 19 journeymen employed three were Stangers: Simon W., Richard H., and Joseph O. The most steadily employed blower was George C. Hewitt who over the course of 40 months recorded blew 22,680 bottles, for which he received $3,148.99. This was at a time when house rent was $6.25 for three months and firewood was $2.75 a cord. One of the blowers was J. L. Duffield, who may possibly have been the Joel Duffield who fashioned the lovely blue pitcher on Plate 7.

Some 30 patent medicine containers are listed as blown here, not only such standbys as Turlington's Balsam and Opodeldoc but also Blake's Bitters, and Clarke's Sarsaparilla Bitters, the source of the latter not hitherto recorded.

For the blast of 1848-49 there were 133 different types and sizes of bottles, from vials to demijohns, from jelly to pickle jars, from oval inks to "plain old." By far the most interesting are the cologne bottles because they are verified by name as tree, fountain, dahlia, lion, diamond-shaped, and grape, the latter the most expensive to blow, at 96¢ a dozen.

A second account book runs from 1852 to 1870 with no mention of glassmaking. Solomon Stanger may have found storekeeping more rewarding.

Fig. 32 HOLLY BUSH, former Whitney mansion, now the residence of the president of Glassboro State College and scene of the 1967 international summit conference between President Lyndon B. Johnson and Russia's Premier Alexei N. Kosygin.

Eagle and Union Works at Port Elizabeth

A 17TH CENTURY settlement, Port Elizabeth, today a sleepy village on the sandy banks of Manumuskin creek, a branch of the Maurice river which in turns flows into the mouth of the Delaware, is the site of two early glassworks which must have exerted as much influence in shaping American glass as did Wistarberg and the early Stanger works at Glassboro.

The Eagle Glass Works, built at Port Elizabeth at least as early as 1799, was the third glasshouse established in New Jersey and was founded and financed initially by James and Thomas Lee and other Philadelphians. The actual running of the works was handled by members of the Stanger clan. Another noted family of German glassmakers, the Getsingers, leased the works from 1816 for a period of about 30 years.

The Union Glass Works, though built about eight years after the Eagle, was founded and owned by such skilled gaffers as Frederick and Jacob Stanger, who were cousins, and later included as a shareholder Randall Marshall for whom Marshallville Glass Works was named.

EAGLE GLASS WORKS

Port Elizabeth is named for Elisabeth Bodley, a widow who inherited much land in the area and then in 1795 began plotting and selling it. In 1789 Congress had made the settlement a port of delivery for the collection of customs duties, a fact that contributed to the commerce and importance of the village.

As early as 1796 Thomas Lee of Philadelphia bought from Mrs. Bodley the first of much more land which he and his half-brother James Lee, a Philadelphia merchant, purchased here. By 1799, they had, with the help of most of the men of the Stanger family, set up a glassworks. There is no evidence that the Stangers ever owned this house, but the furnace drawings dated 1800 and 1806 in the notebook of Christian Stanger, Jr. (see page 46) suggest that they refer to structures built by Christian, Sr. for Port Elizabeth.

On Dec. 4, 1806, Christian Stanger bought of James Lee certain lots "situate near the Meurice River Glafs Works," but there seem to be no purchases of actual glasshouse property from Lee. James Lee by 1806 was already in process of leaving Port Elizabeth to organize a new furnace at Millville, its first. Described by historian Elmer as "an active enterprising man, too spasmodic in his efforts to succeed well," James Lee soon left the glass business and went west about 1817.

Port Elizabeth became such a busy place that in 1807 a hotel had to be built, the Rising Sun, of which Christian Stanger was innkeeper for a time. Brisk trade had been established with Caribbean ports, and there is no doubt that the War of 1812 cut into such commerce. Historian Francis Bazley Lee tells of one incident:

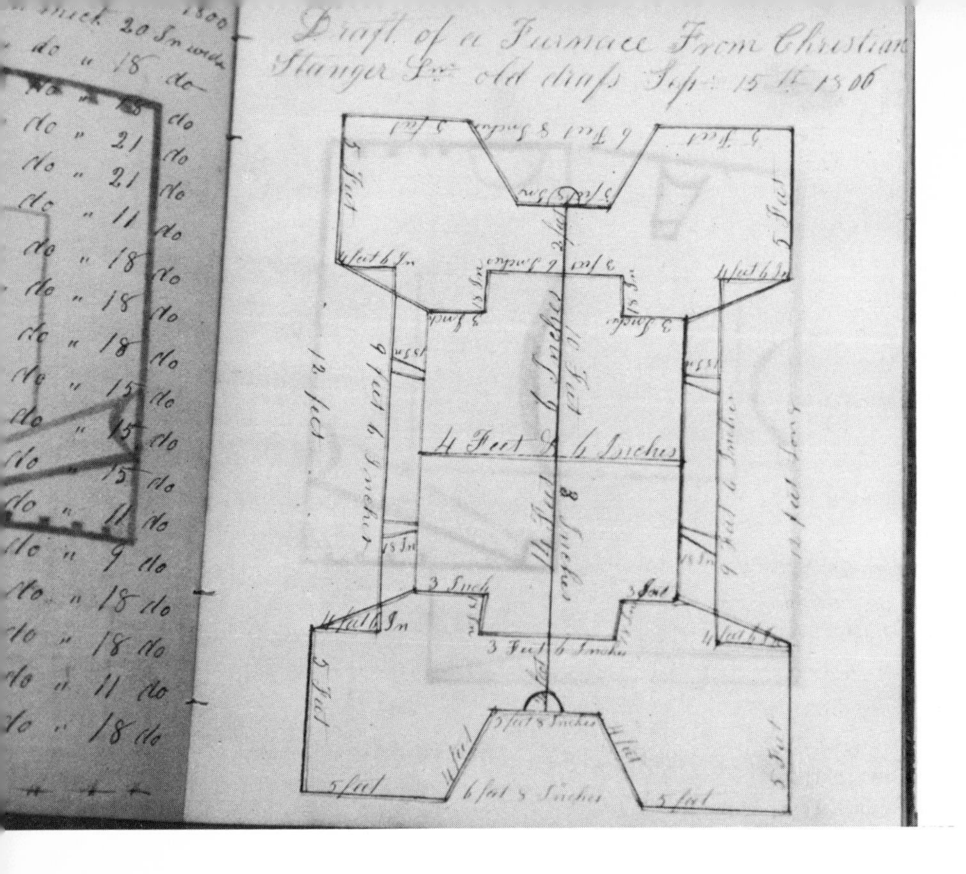

Fig. 33 DRAFT OF A FURNACE FROM CHRISTIAN STANGER, SR. 1806. Rare drawing made by his son Christian L. Stanger could be design for furnace at Glassboro or Port Elizabeth. *Courtesy of A. L. Smith.*

> Along Delaware Bay much of the minor naval activities centered in the village of Port Elizabeth, where a trade with the West Indies, the manufacture of glass, development of the woodland in charcoal and tar making, and the prominence of nearby iron forges gave the town an importance throughout the State. Here were stored military supplies in a large store owned by Joshua Brick and Thomas Lee. Upon one eventful night during the war the cry was raised that a marauding party of British were cattle hunting upon the marshes of the Maurice River. The local militia, hastily assembling to repulse an attack, and failing to gain an entrance to the building, so wrenched the key to the front door as to bend the key-post out of shape. The key is still in use [1900]. Thus without doing great damage, or securing an entrance upon any highway or minor waterway leading to Philadelphia, the inhabitants of the coast of New Jersey were kept in a constant state of alarm.

This first Port Elizabeth furnace was set up, we are told, to make window-glass but who can doubt, considering the needs of the local hotel, the neighboring industries and the potential trade in the West Indies, that much other glass was made here, especially bottles and tableware. The Stangers were particularly noted for their expert bottle making. Although much unorganized digging has been done at this site apparently no fragments of historical flasks have been found.

In 1810 the Lees disposed of a three-fourths interest to James Josiah, Samuel Parish and Joseph L. Lewis & Company. By 1817 the firm was called Josiah, Harrison & Company, with Joshua Brick and Jacob Wyckoff as silent partners, and the glasshouse appears to have been called the Eagle Glass Works for the first time. William Shough, William Riggins and Ollie Parks were blowers that year.

Samuel P. Weatherill of Philadelphia bought the entire works in 1818 and immediately leased it to a group of German Catholic glassmakers: Joseph, Johann and Christopher Getsinger, John Welser and Francis Langraff. The latter two soon retired and Christopher Getsinger died. His two brothers bought the works in 1831 and continued to manage it until 1846. All of the workmen apparently were German and carried on their work in that language exclusively. Besides having a reputation for excellent glassmaking, they were noted for choral singing.

George B. Cooper and Charles Townsend were the next owners of Eagle. After several years, with the retirement of Cooper, Townsend had a succession of partners, among them John Andrews and Francis Allen. On April 30, 1862, the works were sold at sheriff's auction and soon after this Samuel Townsend became the owner. He appears to have leased the furnace to Mitchell & Irwin for a time. At another period John Focer was manager for Townsend. In May of 1881 the factory was owned by the Whitney Brothers of Glassboro but by 1885 the plant was abandoned.

Present-day residents of Port Elizabeth know that tableware was made at Eagle Works from a canary-colored glass, and a considerable amount of such slag has been found at the site. One theory is that this color of glass was produced when the pots were being cleaned from amber to clear. An opposite theory is that some commercial tableware was made here, as red slag has also been found. In any event, various colors were used for bottle-making. One of the strangest of articles said to have been made here, during the late years, were some glass coffins for infants.

UNION GLASS WORKS

This second Port Elizabeth bottle works, on the west bank of Manumuskin creek, had a short and troubled life, but from its demise came the partnership of Frederick Stanger and Randall Marshall in the window-glass works at Marshallville.

Jacob and Frederick Stanger and William Shough built and owned the Union Glass Works some time previous to 1811 but not earlier than 1806, for in that year only one glass works was referred to in deeds describing property locations. On June 6, 1811, the three partners sold for $1,000 a one-fourth interest in the Union Works to Randall Marshall who was not a glassmaker but was owner of a tannery in Port Elizabeth. That autumn the 8-pot furnace went into blast, with the original three partners as managers and blowers and also Solomon, Philip and Francis Stanger, and Daniel Focer and Daniel Shough as blowers. Medicine vials were the main items blown.

In December of 1811 the building burned to the ground. It was not rebuilt until 1812 and did not go into blast until March of that year. As it was customary for South Jersey furnaces to close during the hottest months, that year must have been one of small profit for the partners. By September, the Union Works was again in blast with the same blowers and apparently without disasters for a couple of seasons.

Then in June of 1814 the blowers and apprentices learned that the company was being dissolved. This was confirmed by a Cumberland County Court order of Nov. 5, 1814, requiring that the property be divided into four equal parts. The workmen left for other jobs but Jacob Stanger and William Shough stayed on to build a tiny 4-pot furnace. They and Shough's son Daniel were the only blowers at that time, with Sam Huffsey as their helper.

It appears that there must have been strong differences about the proper way to run a glasshouse, for by 1816 the Union Glass Works had become two separately owned 6-pot furnaces under one roof. One was owned by Randall Marshall who had as his blowers his son Thomas, John Turner, John Collect, Jeremiah Carter, John Carter and Sam Huffsey.

The other furnace was owned by Jacob Stanger and William Shough who had taken Marshall's father-in-law Abraham Reeves as a partner. Their blowers were Samuel Focer, Adolph Button, Daniel and Samuel Lutz and Stephen Reeves.

After the court order of 1814 Marshall had moved one furnace to the vicinity of Tuckahoe where he and his son-in-law Frederick Stanger built the Marshallville Glassworks. By 1818 the Union Glass Works had ceased operations.

A Port Elizabeth mystery, seemingly ineluctible today, is what Frederick M. Amelung was doing in that village in 1811. The first guess, which may be the correct one, is that this son of John Frederick Amelung who founded the costly, short-lived New Bremen Glass Manufactory four miles from Fredericktown, Md., in 1785, was blowing glass, along with fellow Germans, the Stangers.

That Frederick M. Amelung was living in Port Elizabeth in 1811 is virtually unknown to collectors. Yet the fact is indisputable as the date of his death, Sept. 13, 1811, is recorded in the Cumberland County Court archives. He died without a will and the names of his Port Elizabeth creditors are listed in a court order to sell a half-acre of property in the village so as to settle his debts.

What is most interesting in this pathetic record is that Amelung had bought the property on Oct. 20, 1809, which indicates that he was not merely passing through Port Elizabeth but was living there. As no dwelling or other building on the half-acre of land is mentioned, it seems possible that Amelung and his wife Sophia leased or owned a house before buying this property in 1809, which was about the time when Stangers were forming the Union Glass Works.

Prior to the failure of the New Bremen glassworks about 1795, Frederick Amelung had been assisting his father, famed even then for the distinguished engraved clear glass his factory produced. Because certain handsome presentation pieces such as pokals and goblets were engraved with the name of the recipient and that of the New Bremen Glass Manufactory, as well as the date of engraving or occasion for the gift, fully documented Amelung is among the most collectible, and expensive, of early American glass. Even without a date, the smoky glass, when combined with the stylized motifs, such as leafy sprays interspersed with primitive daisies, serve as clues to identity.

After John Frederick Amelung's glassworks had failed, Frederick in 1797 married the daughter of Alexander Furnival, a well-to-do resident of Baltimore, and by 1799 had persuaded his father-in-law to join him in building a glasshouse, Frederick Amelung & Company, at the foot of Federal Hill. But as early as Aug. 11, 1802, the partnership was dissolved. By Dec. 2 Amelung had sold the works to Philip Friese. In November of 1804

Fig. 34 AND SO TO BED. This quaint lamp, only 5½ inches high, was found in the Port Elizabeth area. Asymmetrical, with tipsy stem, it was surely not made by a journeyman but nevertheless by a blower with a sense of style. Color of the bowl can best be described as moonstone streaked with chocolate. Clear handle and applied foot. *Ex-collection of Albert Silvers. Collection of Jesse Ford.*

the property was sold at a sheriff's sale. Not long thereafter, Amelung went to work for Col. James O'Hara, co-owner of the Pittsburgh Glass Works, but the pact was short-lived. Probably already in poor health he then made the long trek to join his friends the Stangers at Port Elizabeth.

From then on the Amelung fortunes spiraled downward. Only 11 days after Frederick's death, his widow Sophia had to travel to Bridgeton to testify that assets to pay his few debts amounted to $399.60, and where she consented to the sale of the half-acre to meet the total debt of $1,748.71. Major creditors were Albert Seehalp, for the sum of $800, and Josiah Parish Lee, $600. Others who were owed smaller amounts were Benjamin Fisler, probably the attending physician, Mark Stratton, Isaac Townsend, Brick and Lee, and William Barrett.

The property was not sold until Nov. 10, 1813, and the buyer was James Lee, founder of the first glasshouse in Port Elizabeth, the Eagle works. The deed was signed in the presence of Roger Males and Randall Marshall; the latter just two years earlier had become a shareholder in the Stanger-founded Union Glass Works of Port Elizabeth. The Amelung-

Lee deed was received for recording on Jan. 16, 1815, as noted by Randall Marshall who was then one of the judges of the court of common pleas for Cumberland county.

Amelung is said to have been buried in the Baptist cemetery but, as with many another glassmaker, no marker can be found today.

Adding to the Port Elizabeth mystery, the glass flask below shows the typical Amelung daisy-and-leaf spray and is engraved with the name of F. Stenger and the date of 1792. This would have been the name of Francis Stanger, next to the youngest of the original seven brothers, who was quite likely living in Glassboro at that date and blowing for the Heston-Carpenter works, to whom the Stanger brothers had lost the glasshouse they founded. Or can we speculate that Francis had traveled to New Bremen to blow? The reverse side of the Stenger flask, it should be noted, is engraved with a plow, which has been a symbol in the seal of New Jersey, both as a colony and as a state.

In any event, what is not speculation is that Francis Stanger was blowing glass at the Union Works in Port Elizabeth in 1811, the year that Frederick Amelung died there.

Fig. 35 F. STENGER 1792 is inscribed on a clear flask of smoky cast with Amelung-style engravings of floral sprays. The reverse is engraved with a Masonic trowel and square, a bottle and a plow, the latter a symbol on the original arms of New Jersey. Thought to be a presentation from the Amelungs of New Bremen, Md., to Francis Stanger, then of Glassboro. Neck ground for stopper. H. 6¾ inches. *Ex-McKearin collection. Courtesy, Corning Museum of Glass.*

Marshalls and Stangers at Marshallville

WALKING DOWN the tree-lined lane that once was the main street of Marshallville in 1815, with only a little imagination, or possibly the help of "the star wagon" or "the time machine," one can be transported back to the early 19th century when this hamlet had a window-glass works running full blast.

The founders of this village, near Tuckahoe, and the glass furnace were Randall Marshall and Frederick Stanger, of the family of pioneering glassworkers, who married Marshall's 17-year-old daughter Ann in 1812. Both Marshall and Stanger had held shares in the Union Glass Works of Port Elizabeth which Stangers founded some time between 1806 and 1810.

Still today along the quiet road paralleling the placid Tuckahoe river, whence glass was carried in sailing ships to Philadelphia, is a frame house built in 1828 for Thomas Chew Marshall, son of Randall. The brown jug shown in Fig. 36 was found in the old house by lineal descendants of the Marshalls.

A bit east, on the river side of the road, is a 3-story rosy brick house which Randall built for his wife, who died in 1847. The two separate front doors are not a modern renovation. The right door led to the office of the works manager. The left door was the entrance to living rooms. A few steps to the right of the dwelling is the thick-walled springhouse. Inside on the floor is a foot-wide channel for water from an ever-flowing spring, cold enough to preserve milk even during a humid South Jersey summer. Here, a collector likes to imagine, were set out those broad pans of aquamarine glass where milk was poured for cream to rise.

Outside are boxwood and ivy so ancient that it seems this site must have been occupied in the 18th century. Adjoining the back of the brick house is an unpainted, cedarboard, double house, once the home of at least two glassworking families, and part of a row that formerly faced the river.

Behind the brick residence and near the river in 1970 was the old cedar-covered Marshallville store where employees bought most of their supplies, purchases balanced against earnings in "store books." This bit of history, moved several hundred yards from its original site, and crumbling to ruin, with the old post office boxes and handblown window panes has since been destroyed.

At river's edge not far from the store site is a narrow-gauge marine railway, probably used for moving glass and supplies to and from vessels. Furnace slag in this area is mostly pale aqua and some amber, the latter possibly indicating that hollow ware was blown here as well as window-glass.

Traveling east down the Marshallville road, one comes to a second brick house, this one built about 1835 for Dr. Randolph Marshall, son of Randall, the similarity of whose

Fig. 36 LITTLE BROWN MARSHALLVILLE JUG. Found by descendants of Randall Marshall in the 1829 house of Thomas Chew Marshall, manager of the glassworks founded by Randall Marshall and Frederick Stanger near Tuckahoe. Reddish amber.

Fig. 37 MARSHALLVILLE'S FIRST HOUSE, built 1829, and two of Randall Marshall's descendants, one of whom still owns the property, now much modernized.

names has led many genealogists and writers astray. Still living today in Corbin City just across the Tuckahoe, not far from Mosquito Landing, is a vivacious nonagenarian who recalls the good ministrations of Dr. Randolph and his brother Dr. Joseph, also a physician, grandsons of Randall.

Marshallville was founded on Mar. 21, 1811, when Marshall and Stanger, with intent to build a glassmaking community, bought land for a sawmill adjacent to Mill Creek (flowing into the Tuckahoe) and Wheaton Branch Pond. The first fruit of the plans was the fine old mill illustrated on opposite page.

Next, the two men on Mar. 1, 1814, bought 169½ additional acres, again from Joseph

Falkenburg, for the considerable sum of $5,000. This was land upon which the glassworks and the village were subsequently built. For the reason that in 1811 Marshalls and Stangers were jointly operating the Union glassworks of Port Elizabeth, it seems certain that the Marshallville glasshouse was not completed until 1814, after the main purchase of land. By Cumberland County Court order, the Union works had been divided into four shares, and Marshall had moved one of its furnaces to the Tuckahoe river site. In the intervening years to 1814, the Marshallville partners were no doubt occupied in building the sawmill, a wharf and roads.

Marshall never lived in the town named for him, it is said, but continued to travel the short distance between it and Port Elizabeth by horse and buggy. Stanger, acting as manager, did live in Marshallville as we learn from the sad fact that his wife died in childbirth at the age of 20 and their daughter Ann was born in Marshallville.

The few surviving ledgers and storebooks cast some illuminating rays on Marshallville. There are references, for example, to Factories Nos. 1, 2, 3, and 4, which would indicate that the works had grown to four furnaces. The company store also did a large volume of business, despite the fact that the store of Estellville Glass Works was nearby and, because of Daniel Estell's shipping fleet, could import choice goods from New York.

Some time before 1827 Frederick Stanger acquired another Marshall for a father-in-law and still another for a wife. Elizabeth, his second wife, was the daughter of John Marshall, brother of Randall.

Fig. 38 MARSHALLVILLE'S FIRST MILL, c. 1814, probably the first structure at Marshallville Glass works. A serene scene photographed in 1910 by a direct descendant of Randall Marshall.

A deed of Aug. 6, 1827, shows that Stanger and his wife sold to Randall for $8,000 their share of about 450 acres constituting what had become the village of Marshallville and which the two partners had originally bought in 1814.

The purpose of this sale was to finance a new glassworks that Stanger was building at Brooklyn, N.J., where his partner would be his new father-in-law. As told in the following chapter, Stanger did not live to see the new works completed. He died prematurely from what may have been pneumonia, brought on by exposure during a snowstorm.

Soon after the Stangers left Marshallville, Randall took another partner, Samuel Stille, and the firm became known as Marshall, Stille & Company. Thomas Chew Marshall is known to have been a manager of the works, a post he may have taken when Stanger left. Experienced as he was, Thomas doubtless continued the works when his father died in 1841.

No solid information has been obtained as to when the glassworks closed but prevailing opinion is that this occurred just prior to the Civil War. The following three records of sales mention the glassworks property but give no clue as to when blowing ceased.

On June 23, 1849, Joshua Brick, master in chancery of the Cumberland County Court, ordered sale of the property. Thomas and John S. Van Gilder who bought the Marshallville works in 1849, after Mrs. Randall Marshall died, sold it in 1865 to Samuel Stille. Although the lengthy description in the deed of Feb. 2 does not state whether the glassworks was functioning, reference is made to "the westernmost end of the Wharf, known as the Glass House Wharf." A year later Stille writing on Feb. 22 from Batsto to A. Browning of Camden, said that he had advertised to sell at public auction in Camden "The Tuckahoe Glass Factory Property" and wished Browning to look after details. Stille commented that the bond of Dr. R. Marshall and T. C. Marshall had already been arranged for. The subsequent owner of the property was Timothy Henderson.

Marshallville Store Book V, covering 1825 and 1826, in which are listed running accounts and heavy purchases by Frederick Stanger and Thomas Marshall, reveals that Philip Stanger was one of the glassmakers active in the village. He was undoubtedly a second generation Stanger but his relationship to Frederick is not clear. That he was a family man seems evident, however, from his many purchases of food and household articles. On Mar. 23, 1826, he was charged $4.60 for diapers. Four days later he bought a quart of rum at $4.69. At another time, in 1825, he had bought corn, molasses, cordwood, buckwheat, butter, flour, soap, boots, gingham and coffee. His debits then were $140.92 against $116.19 that he had received in pay. Another page, in 1826, shows that he was buying chocolate, sugar, beef, lard, a quart of brandy, mackerel, flour, molasses, candles and tea. For the home-remedy painkiller, laudanum, he paid $8.92 a vial.

David Scull, of one of Jersey's early families, and John Madden were glassblowers whose purchases and wages were often recorded in 1825 and 1826. Lee & Willetts are listed also, but this would not have been the original James Lee who with Willetts founded the Port Elizabeth glassworks. John Rosenbaum who was an owner of the Malaga glasshouse and later of the Estellville works is recorded as a purchaser in 1826.

A ledger of 1835 to 1837 lists the new firm name of Marshall & Stille in 1835. One ledger with accounts ranging from 1841 to 1868 lists 29 glassblowers or cutters, about 10

Fig. 39 THOMAS CHEW MARSHALL, an early manager of the Marshallville Glass Works, founded by Randall Marshall and Frederick Stanger.

Fig. 40 COMPANY STORE AND POST OFFICE of Marshallville is still on the glass works site.

Fig. 41 MARSHALLVILLE LEDGER of 1826 shows accounts of Frederick and Philip Stanger.

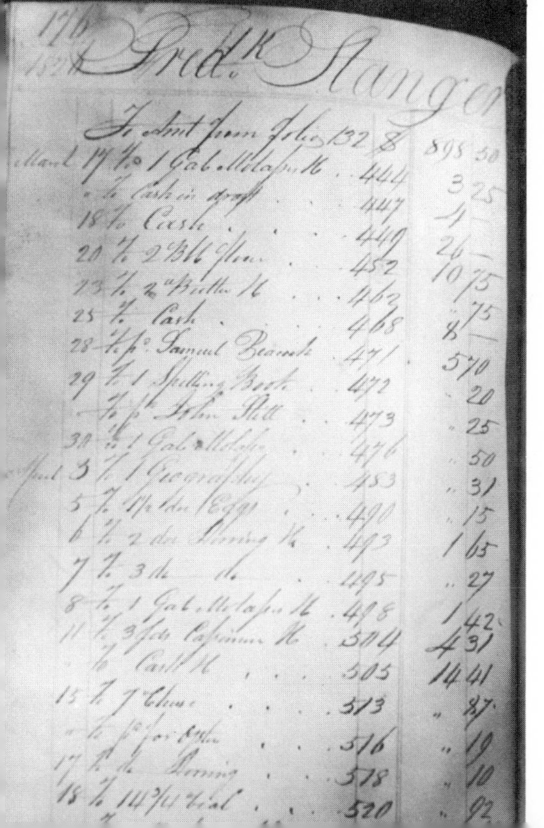

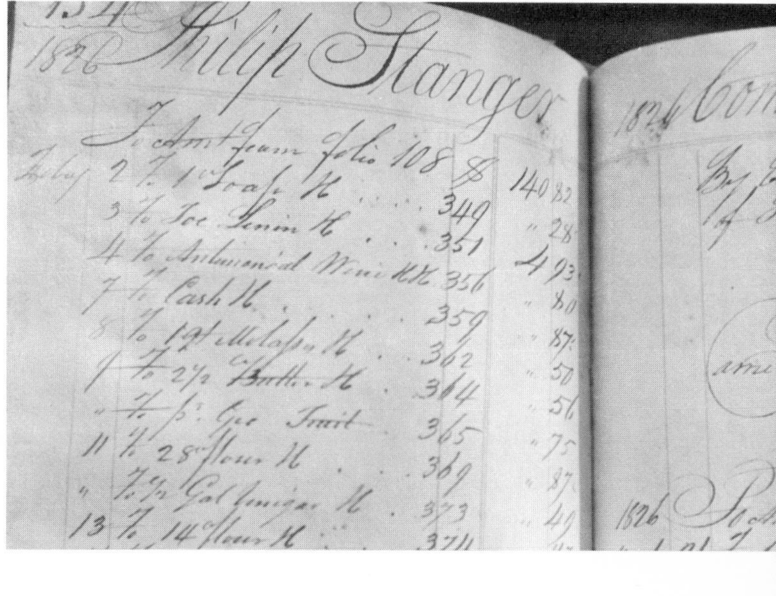

Fig. 42 FREDERICK STANGER'S office and home when he was co-owner of Marshallville Glass Works (1814-1827) is now a private residence in this riverside village.

of them from Estellville and one or two from Port Elizabeth, Gibson's Creek, Millville and Bridgeton. It seems possible that the out-of-town workers may have been men employed for one season. Local blowers listed, each for a single year, between 1846 and 1859 are Reeves Louder, Francis Sweeney, Lewis Hirsch, Japhet Hann, Joseph Stadler, Ephraim and Richard Scull, Isaac Steelman, Lewis Neipling and Martin Madden. Oliver W. Towne was listed as a glass cutter and Bennet Muley as a shearer. John Getsinger is listed as a glass manufacturer in 1855. In that year he and John Rosenbaum jointly owned the Estellville glassworks.

Except for the amber field-jug mentioned earlier which quite likely was blown at Marshallville, no other hollow ware articles have been identified. A glassworks of this early date and so far removed from cities most certainly made many household utensils for use in the community.

Note.—It is sometimes said that Cumberland Works was an alternate name for the Marshallville glasshouse. It is known that the Cumberland iron works was in the region, but Jesse Ford, formerly a Millville glassworker, states that an elderly member of the local Steelman family informed him that a Cumberland Glass Works did once exist at head of navigation on the Tuckahoe but that it had a brief life because of poor draft of the furnace.

Stangers and Marshalls at Isabella Works

AFTER A PARTNERSHIP that had lasted from 1811 when he and his father-in-law, Randall Marshall, were buying a mill site off Tuckahoe creek preparatory to building a glassworks that would become Marshallville, Frederick Stanger and his wife Elizabeth in 1827 were making plans to depart. From Cumberland county indentures I find that the Stangers had just sold to Marshall their share of 450 acres of valuable built-up land that constituted Marshallville and its glassworks. The price paid was $8,000 which Stanger was about to invest in a glasshouse which would be built at Seven Causeways in partnership with Stanger's *other* father-in-law who then lived there.

If this sounds confusing, it has been so, even to descendants of the Marshalls. After much genealogical research it is learned that Frederick Stanger married Randall Marshall's daughter Ann who died after childbirth, on Feb. 15, 1815, and that some time later he married Elizabeth, daughter of Randall's elder brother John, a large landowner near Williamstown. Seven Causeways was also known as Brooklyn and later as Old Brooklyn when a new furnace was erected about a mile away at New Brooklyn, better known as the Isabella Glass Works.

As a second generation member and son of the original Philip in the talented pioneer glassmaking family of Stangers, Frederick had charge of building the furnace at Brooklyn, since his father-in-law was not a glass man. The project was well along and the furnace nearly ready to go into blast in 1831 when Stanger, returning from Camden with a load of lime, was caught in a snowstorm and then developed a respiratory disorder. On May 14, 1831 he was dead, at the age of 45. He lies buried in the old Episcopal graveyard at Glassboro, the town his ancestors founded in 1779.

John Marshall went ahead with the Brooklyn works, which had its first "fire" in 1832. He was assisted by Frederick's cousin Thomas Stanger who in 1835 married Frederick's widow.

Marshall's wife Abbie died on Mar. 27, 1838, at Brooklyn Glass Works, the Woodbury *Constitution* reported. Although the furnace was operating full blast for the next couple of years, Marshall withdrew in 1839 as he was then 71 years old.

The firm soon became known as Stanger & Dotterer, a partnership that was still in effect in 1846, according to Marshallville store books I have seen.

About a mile from the original furnace Stanger in 1848 built a new one of seven pots,

Fig. 43 STANGER HOUSE AT ISABELLA glass works, which was demolished for a highway in the 1960s.

the Isabella Glass Works named for his only daughter, a glasshouse also called New Brooklyn. At one time 100 persons were said to have been employed here.

In 1856 the Woodbury *Constitution* announced that the glassworks and gristmill of Thomas Stanger at *Old* Brooklyn were destroyed by an incendiary fire. The following year this property was bought at sheriff's auction by C. B. Tice who operated it until 1868.

As the *Constitution* report specifies the burning of *Old* Brooklyn, it is probable that Thomas Stanger continued to operate Isabella furnace for some time; he did not die until 1892, aged 91. It is well to note, in view of the confused Stanger genealogy, that a Thomas W. Stanger of Glassboro lived much of his life in Pittsburgh, then returned to be part of Warrick & Stanger glassworks in Glassboro.

Few collectors realize that New Brooklyn made flasks embossed on a scroll, ISABELLA GLASS WORKS, with an anchor centered on the obverse, moldblown at this furnace. The reverse side of the flask shows a glass factory. The Isabella flasks were first reported by Barber in 1900 who at that time had not determined the locale. Usually aquamarine and in quarts, pints and ½-pints, these flasks cannot compare in subject and interest with those from Coffin & Hay or Stratton & Buck but are worth having because of being marked and for their association.

Several pieces of freeblown glass, typically South Jersey, have been attributed, apparently quite soundly, to New Brooklyn. As Isabella Stanger did not die until the age of 97, in the year 1936, and even in her nineties was alert with visitors, she may have helped in accurate identification. The McKearins, for example, in Plate 14 of *American Glass* show a quaint footed lamp with handle, bought from a Miss Stanger of Brooklyn and said to have been blown by Julius Stanger at Isabella. A handled mug in aqua with loopings, Plate 21, is also attributed to this furnace.

Some pleasing objects in New York auctions have also been ascribed to Isabella, among them No. 463, a wide amber bowl from the William W. Wood sale of 1942. In the 1932 sale of the Herbert Delavan Mason collection No. 262 was a light green lilypad vase with double handles, described as "One of the finest pieces of Isabella glass in existence."

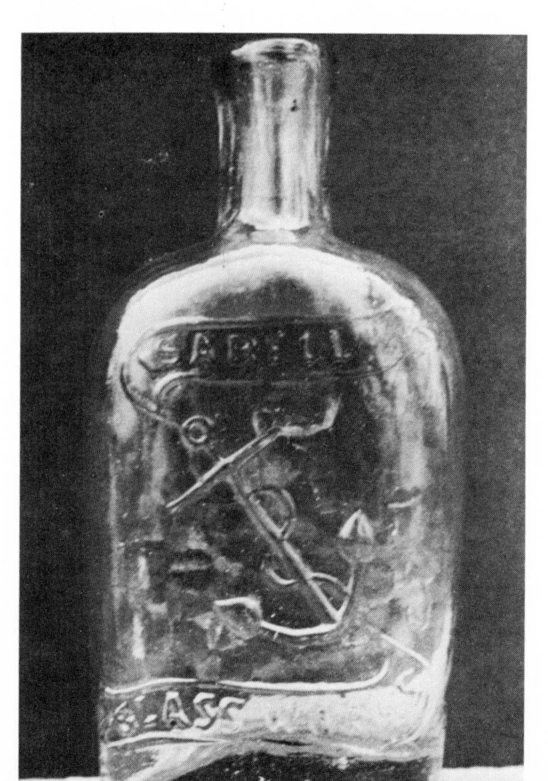

Fig. 44 ISABELLA GLASS WORKS at New Brooklyn made aqua quart, pint and ½-pint flasks with an anchor, ribbons above embossed with ISABELLA and below GLASS WORKS. Reverse shows glasshouse; some pints have a sheaf of rye on the reverse. C. 1850s. *Charles F. Carr collection.* Not listed by McKearin.

Stanger and Whitney Ware at Malaga

A SECOND GENERATION Stanger—Christian L.,—a son of the original Christian who came with a large family from Dornhagen in 1768 to make glass at Wistarberg, founded a bottle works at Malaga near Glassboro in 1810. This was a period when the Stangers and the Marshalls and other glassmen seemed to be having problems at Port Elizabeth and were casting about for greener fields. Others of the seven Stanger brothers had had financial troubles in the works they founded at Glassboro, and some of them and their in-laws from Wistarberg may have joined Christian at Malaga.

The junior Christian Stanger kept a now rare "Receipt" book dated September 6, 1828, in which he noted down not only the "bach" formula at Malaga but apparently from every place he had blown glass. That he took great pride and interest in his craft is evident from the numerous formulas for both window-glass and bottle glass. Of the latter he labeled "Joseph Porter's Bach at Waterford" as "Best," but he also collected recipes from Winslow, Hammonton, Millville, even from Henry Bostwick of Pittsburgh. A firm believer in glasshouse tradition, even while building new style furnaces, Christian L. Stanger made precise drawings of furnace plans used by his father Christian Sr., in 1800 and 1806 (see Port Elizabeth).

By 1820 the junior Stanger may have been off to see what he could learn from other glassworks. At any rate, that was the year when Daniel H. Miller bought the Malaga furnace and named it the Franklin Glass Works. Nine years later he sold it to John G. Rosenbaum who joined with the Whitney brothers of Glassboro in 1830 for a stable period of some 25 years. However, when Rosenbaum advertised the Malaga works for sale in 1857, through the *Woodbury Constitution,* there was no mention of the Whitneys. Rosenbaum was selling not only two glass factories, described as in full operation, but also 9,000 acres of timber land, 40 dwelling and grist and sawmills. With the death of Rosenbaum the furnace went out of blast in 1859 but the *Constitution* announced that Whitney Brothers and Warrick leased the works in 1860. Then in 1861 heirs of Rosenbaum rebuilt the plant as a window-glass house, which in 1873 was incorporated as the Malaga Glass and Manufacturing Company with William B. Rosenbaum as one of the organizers. At that time Malaga employed some 80 workers. The plant was still in operation in 1883.

With the Stanger and Whitney influence strong at Malaga the quality of metal available for offhand glass must have been high but authenticated examples have not come to light.

The Window-Light Workers

A CASUAL "ANTIQUER" seeing bull's-eye window panes, with their center swirl of dense green glass, can't be blamed for assuming that these decorative bits were intentionally made that way. Actually, bull's eye panes are castoffs put to good use by thrifty pioneer settlers.

CROWN GLASS

The first American window glass, a great advance over hides or sheets of mica at the windows, was nevertheless most primitively made, by the crown method. The blower would form a pear-shaped globule of glass which he then moved down to the "bottoming" hole, in front of which was a low wall to protect the man against the heat, where he twirled the parison which caused it to spread out. A helper then stepped up with a small gather of glass on a punty rod that he attached to the opposite side of the "blow." Then another workman touched a cold iron dipped in water to the blowpipe side, causing the pipe to separate. With one end of the parison now open, more twirling before the fire made the object basket-shaped.

Suddenly the blower would twirl the punty rod so fast that the basket, with a loud ruffling noise like the snap of a flag in the breeze, would flatten into a smooth round plate. This process, described in an 1837 pamphlet, "Conversations on the Art of Glass-Blowing," printed by Mahlon Day at 374 Pearl Street, Manhattan, was called flashing. The disk, about 36 inches in diameter, was moved to a flat surface, separated from the rod and placed in annealing ovens, warmed only to red heat. Sometimes the cooling process took two to three weeks.

Small square or diamond panes were cut from the circle of glass, to be fitted into mullioned frames. The thick knot where the rod had been detached was excellent for panes around doors as the glass was translucent but not transparent. The legend that the bull's-eye panes were installed in order to deflect Indian arrows is—well, just legend.

There is substance for believing, though, that bull's-eyes in Jersey and Delaware houses built from 1740 to 1780 were made at Wistarberg, for there was no other window-light place operating then in those rather isolated colonies and Wistarberg certainly was using the crown method, as the cylinder process was a 19th century development.

The Hon. John T. Bodine who supplied most of the data on Jersey for Weeks' 1884 U.S. census *Report on the Manufacture of Glass* stated he believed that Columbia on the Delaware which operated from 1812 to about 1838 was a crown glass works. This seems unlikely as the glasshouse depicted in the Thomas Birch painting is two stories high, needed for cylinder glassmaking but unnecessary for the early bottle works or crown glass blowing. Some sizes of glass advertised for Columbia, moreover, were much larger than could usually be cut from a disk of crown glass.

THE CYLINDER METHOD

Window-glass made from handblown cylinders or rollers was a transformation of the early 19th century, one that opened the way for large panes and clearer, eventually nearly flawless, glass. Cylinder glass was as revolutionary for its time as the continuous-tank method and machine-made window-glass which were in the agonies of creation at the close of the 19th century.

Some of the greatest showmen and unsung heroes of the glass industry were the men who blew, entirely without machines, window panes by the cylinder method prevalent from the 1830s to the early 1900s.*

Their story, rarely told, comes alive in the words of Charles Westcott, Jerseyan and 76-year-old blower of precision laboratory glass, whose father, grandfather and great-grandfather were window-light blowers. (Old-timers never speak of window *pane* blowers.) The sojourns of these four generations show, like the travels of Samuel Huffsey, how far afield Jersey glassblowers ranged, and accordingly how difficult it is to affix the provenance of many collectors' wares made in the Jersey tradition.

Jesse Wescoat, Sr., grandfather of Charles Westcott who changed the spelling of the family name, began blowing cylinders of glass at the Batsto Works established in September 1846 by the Richards family when they saw the fortunes of their iron empire toppling.

An iron blowpipe and two iron blocks or molds for shaping window-glass parisons, now owned by Charles Westcott and on exhibit in the Batsto Museum, were the tools of Jesse Wescoat, Sr., and his descendants. When the glass project ended in 1867 and Batsto became a ghost town, the senior Wescoat packed up his tools and went to blow at nearby Waterford, noted for good workmanship, then later at Winslow, also of high repute, on the same stage road.

These tools descended to Jesse Wescoat, Jr., who as a window-glass blower used them at Glassboro while working there. Daniel Wescoat, born at Waterford in 1859 in a white house still standing on the main road, and father of Charles, also used the tools at Glassboro. Charlie recalls as the happiest days of his life his early childhood in Magnolia where his father in 1901 was a windowpane blower for the Magnolia Glass Company, an outfit unrecorded in any standard works on glass.

From Magnolia, Daniel moved to Shingle House in northwest Pennsylvania to blow for the window-light furnace in this little town. Finding blowing too strenuous he became a flattener. When a union dispute about 1907 caused a work stoppage, Daniel left his tools on the premises in expectation of being called back shortly. Blowing did not resume and

* *Conversations on the Art of Glassblowing,* printed in 1837 in New York City, is written for the laity, so the cylinder method described must have been well established by then.

Daniel moved his family back to Vineland. Years later Charles retrieved the blocks and pipes from a blower at Shingle House.

"When I went to look for the tools no one even knew where the window-light factory had been but I recognized it right away. They're usually 1½-story frame buildings," Westcott said. The Mahlon Day pamphlet describes the furnaces of crown works as conical. Those of cylinder works were generally bottle-shaped, with a powerful draft. Even a bottle-glass furnace needed a fearful draft. Ernest C. Stanmire, Jersey glassworker and antiques dealer, recalls seeing a man at Moore Brothers in Clayton sit down to eat a sandwich, only to have it whisked irretrievably up the chimney.

It took a certain constitution and co-ordination to be a proficient window-light blower, and not many men could qualify.

"Those old window-light blowers were the proudest people in the world," Charles Westcott recalls. "Everybody realized how highly skilled they were, and the blowers took exceptional pride in their talent. They had to be real men. They combined fast thinking with brawn."

Brawn the trade certainly demanded. For the iron blowpipe hefts about 30 pounds, and the glass gather added about another 50 or 70 pounds. All told, the blower not only had to lift at least 80 pounds of pipe and lethally hot molten glass but also had to manipulate all swiftly, adroitly, so as to avoid breaking the glass and burning himself and his fellow workers. A split-second lag in reaction could mean disaster for the whole shop.

Window-glass blowers usually worked at a 4-pot furnace, two men to a pot. At peak operation, white-hot fires blazing and a dozen men and small boys rushing about in dangerous proximity, the scene was a confused inferno.

The blower, wearing boots and stripped to the waist, ascended a ramp or steps to a platform where he could work on a level with furnace doors. Below him was a pit. On a string around his neck, the blower usually wore a cowl board, a face-shaped wooden mask, eye-slits fitted with amber or blue glass. Ready to approach the searing flames, the blower clamped the mouthpiece of the cowl board between his teeth, his sole protection against the murderous heat.

His smaller or dipper-shaped iron block, though used first, was called the "second glass block." The gatherer, not the blower, picked up a blob of liquid glass on the end of the pipe, turned it in the smaller block to give some slight form, then kept adding more metal in about three or four trips to the furnace until he had about 60 pounds of white-hot glass which he had in the meantime expanded to rude shape.

The blower now began blowing this parison into an iron block of about 18 inches diameter, until the parison seemed to shape to a similar diameter. The "blow block" had meantime been placed a-tilt in a wooden tub or barrel cut down to a height comfortable for the blower. Sawdust was usually sprinkled in the block to keep the glass from adhering to the iron, and the block was set in water as a coolant. By the end of this process the water was usually boiling.

Now with the block as a guide the blower blew the glass balloon until it was several feet long. Then he took this fragile roller to the swing-hole, a drop-off of at least 9 feet below the platform or foot-bench where the worker stood. While swinging the blowpipe like a

Fig. 45 WINDOWLIGHT GNOMES in fiery Pittsburgh scene of 1876. Note cowl boards used by five workmen; trimmed cylinders on cradle in foreground. From *Every Saturday*, March, 1967. *Courtesy of Corning Museum of Glass.*

pendulum, the crouched blower stretched the glass cocoon to the wanted length, about six feet, sometimes more.

Pull of the iron and weight of the glass were so great that many of the men wore a chain, one end attached to their belts, the other to a post, so that they would not be dragged head first into the swing-hole filled with the broken glass of rejects. Blowers who scorned to wear a chain were often pulled forward and crashed into the hot metal and broken glass in the pit below. Some never came out alive.

Window-light blowers wore heavy stripping around their wrists to give them steel-like control of the great weight. The longer they manipulated the parison "the heavier it got." The blower could not relax for an instant before the roller was deposited in a wooden cradle on a sawhorse to cool.

The critical point, however, came before that stage. It was the opening of the far end of the roller, in this ingenious manner. When the roller was the proper shape and length, the blower gave it a mighty heave up to an iron crane in front of the furnace so as to reheat the cylinder. With both his thumb and the blowpipe in his mouth, the worker blew an extra puff that trapped air inside, as he immediately capped the pipe with his thumb. The expanding hot air forced open the far end of the roller. It was now ready to transport to the cradle. Some of the showmen—and there was often a cluster of visitors—would swing the roller and blowpipe over their heads in a great virtuoso display of strength and skill. But sometimes things went awry and the hot glass broke into myriads of fragments that showered down on the workers.

When a roller had been carefully deposited on the cradle a helper touched the glass near the blowpipe-end with a wet iron and this magically released the cylinder from the pipe. The roller was now a long pale aquamarine pod with rounded ends. After the glass cooled a bit these ends were cracked off. To do this a thin strip of molten glass was laid on so as to encircle the cylinder where separation was wanted. Again the ends were touched with wet metal and the tops fell off, leaving an open-end glass cylinder. Usually retrieved, the caps were prized as bells under which to display wax fruit.

Next, a workman threw a handful of sawdust the length of the cylinder, the curved surface of which caused the sawdust to fall to the bottom. Then a hot iron rod was run back and forth along the bottom of the roller until it was grooved. Once more, the glass was touched with a wet iron for an instant and, lo, the cylinder split neatly down its entire length. Now a curved sheet, it was carried to the flattening ovens where renewed heat made it flexible, so that it could be leveled to a plane surface. In the final step before cutting into panes, the large sheets were placed in a "dip," a barrel-like container full of boiling water, to be tempered for a half hour or so.

Window-light blowing was so well paid in relation to other glassblowing that a man couldn't get into the trade unless he was the son or the brother of one of these vastly proficient craftsmen who, the theory was, would teach his relatives the secrets. No doubt about it, window-light blowers had status.

Yet it was the *cutters* who were the only glassmen who came to work wearing a collar and tie. Their skill was so essential to high production that they were paid even better than the blowers.

The cutter, with both arms outspread to hold the large oblong of glass, would stand the pane upright on the cutting table. Then, to the consternation of small boys and other uninitiated souls, the cutter would let the sheet of glass fall to the table, which it did without breaking. An air cushion protected it—usually. Cutting into small panes was done in the 1850s or so with a pencil-shaped tool that was diamond-tipped. Harder than glass, the diamond was simply drawn alongside a ruler and neatly cut out panes, provided the sheet did not have too many "stones" and air bubbles. "The job looked as easy as separating a soda cracker from its mate," said Westcott.

Because window-light work was so strenuous, union rules in the early 1900s provided that blowers were not allowed to make over eight cylinders an hour. A day's work was 64 cylinders, but many men could not turn out that number. About 1902 a window-light blower could earn $90 a week, but the average was more like $60, still high for the times when unskilled labor was paid about a dollar a day. Blowers were paid $20 a week market money. The balance due was paid at the end of the month, a practice which allowed the employer time to meet his bills. How the blower met his creditors evidently was his own worry. His monthly pay was determined by the number of boxes of lights that could be cut from cylinders he blew. If his cylinder output was low, if the glass was badly flawed, if the cutter was inept, that was the blower's hard luck.

Yet the time was approaching when the proud window-light blowers would be pleading for work: the incubus of The Machine began to loom large and ominous. As early as 1874 the Window Glass Workers Union had forbidden its members to work a cylinder machine invented by Ralph Gray, but it was evidently no match for men. Not until a cylinder-inflating machine was perfected in 1903 by J. H. Lubbers, a flattener, did the menace seem real.

The true mechanical revolution in window-glass, however, came from a totally new approach, that of drawing out flat sheets of glass instead of using the roundabout way of inflating cylinders and then splitting them. Irving W. Colburn, who had tried the latter method in 1898 at Blackford, Pa., then after some years of costly experiments produced the first workable machine for making flat drawn glass. But with a high overhead expense, by 1911 the Colburn Machine Glass Company failed. Michael J. Owens of the Toledo Glass Company then bought Colburn's patents and with corporate financing and capacities eventually produced commercially successful equipment that displaced all window-light blowers. After considerable litigation an award was made to Colburn, but too late for him to enjoy any financial success for he died soon after.

The first machine for making window-glass was used at Jeanette, Pa. The last hand-made window-glass in the United States was blown at Bridgeton in 1926 by the LeFevre Glass Company, using a tank furnace. The owner thought he could compete with machines. He couldn't.

Why would glass collectors be interested in window-glass factories which were in business solely to produce sheets of flat glass of nondescript or no color?

The reason is that some of the most highly collectible sugarbowls, jam jars, pitchers and milk pans were made of remarkably clear and brilliant aquamarine glass that was the stuff for making window-lights. Although many persons assume that bottle glass from which many unusual original creations were blown is the finer of the two early 19th century metals, the fact is that then standards for window-glass were much higher than for bottle glass. The proprietors insisted on glass free from stones, streaks and spots of impurities such as that caused by oxide of iron. As early as 1842 the Franklin Institute awarded honorable mention to Coffin, Hay & Bowdle for the good quality of their window-glass, and in 1851 gave a silver medal to the New Columbia Glass Company (near Batsto) for the best color in window-glass and also to the Jackson Glass Works for the best surface in window-lights.

With such high grade metal accessible even in the 18th century, skilled Jersey gaffers like Kreismayer, Wentzel, and Caspar and Johan Halter at Wistarberg and the Stangers at Glassboro and Port Elizabeth could easily have fashioned the clear, thin-walled, sparkling pitchers, goblets and other household ware so often attributed to later periods.

The excellent clarity and surface of early Jersey window glass dispel the notion that Jersey table glass of 1800 must have been thick and dark brown, like that made at Ellenville, N.Y. before the glassworks there started importing Jersey sand.

Columbia . . .
Gem of the Delaware

Columbia Glass works built on the east bank of the upper Delaware River in 1812 is probably the only American glasshouse to have been painted in oil by a distinguished artist, Thomas Birch, who visited the *Cape* of Delaware in 1807. The painting, titled "Columbia Glass Works," was later rendered as an aquatint by William Strickland (1787–1854).

There is even reason to believe that Birch might have been commissioned to depict the Columbia Glass Works, for although the scene includes that renowned landmark, Delaware Water Gap, the painter could have had a better view of it farther upstream.

Columbia remains the most mysterious of the Jersey glasshouses, a subject for speculation. Despite its early fame, remarkably little has been documented about the original settlement and its industry which flowered with the War of 1812. Hence it has been gratifying to assemble some new facts about Columbia and to present two disparate examples of glass from the area, with meaningful histories.

Today Columbia is a sweet little village, described even in 1881 as quaint, on high bluffs overlooking the fast-flowing river, a few miles south of Delaware Water Gap, gateway to the road west in covered-wagon days. Many dwellings in Columbia, ignored by zooming highways just to the east, look like vintage early Jersey, but few are known to have been standing when the glassworks was built.

The site of the glassworks, however, now covered by private residences, is well known even without documentation from the Strickland engraving. Householders are still continually spading up large chunks of glass in their gardens, and usually of the same bright unclouded aquamarine that signifies South Jersey sand.

Information about the life-span of the Columbia works has been vague: 1815 to 1844, writes one author; 1812 to 1833 says another. But here is incontrovertible fact about the beginning: a map drawn by Adolphus Loss in 1813 shows that in November of that year Francis Mayerhoff was the owner of a carefully plotted Town of Columbia, embracing some 30 acres. Even at that early date the map showed the glasshouse location, as well as tempering ovens, in a separate building. This last is highly significant as it shows that the Columbia Glass Works was intended for the making of window-glass.

Exact site of the Columbia Works is easy to ascertain from the Loss map which shows that the property faces the present riverside street and extends at least to the entrance of the footbridge which spans the Delaware between Columbia and Portland, Pa. Much of the property is now owned by Mrs. Carl W. Simpson, a life-time resident here, who believes that the glassworks foundations are beneath the large block of residences. The map lists among various lot holders in the new town (it had previously been a settlement known as Kirkbride's) the names of John Van Kirk and William Heyberger who figured also in a later stage of the history.

Snell's *History of Sussex and Warren County*, published in 1881, states that in 1812 Francis Myerhoff (sic) with a colony of Germans located at Columbia to engage in manufacturing glassware. These were not necessarily the type of Germans who came from the Rhenish Palatine to South Jersey in the mid-1700s, with virtuosity at glassblowing their only means of making a living. Francis Mayerhoff, I find from Longworth's New York City Directory for 1810, 1811 and 1812, was a merchant at 351 Pearl Street. That he was a successful businessman is indicated by Newton courthouse records showing that in 1812 he was able to pay the then impressive sum of $20,000 to John Nyce for the Columbia frontage with a commanding view of the Delaware River, a prospect both pleasing and destined for profit. After an outlay of more thousands of dollars, Mayerhoff by 1813 had not only plotted his town of Columbia and assigned lots to various associates but also put the glassworks and tempering ovens into operation. An early sawmill at the mouth of the Paulins Kill which flows into the Delaware was taken over by Mayerhoff and was used as a stamping mill to pulverize clay needed for glass-furnace pots.

Even in 1812 Mayerhoff had already bought the ferry operating to the Pennsylvania shore, which a William Able had started in 1800. There evidently had been still another owner, however, for Kirkbride's had an alternate name of Dill's Ferry.*

Historian Snell reported that wood and flint for the glassworks were obtained in Knowlton township where Columbia is located. The reference to flint is obviously in error as this mineral is not used in making "flint" glass. There is no information to support the idea that Mayerhoff was making flint glass even with oxide of lead.

Mayerhoff had sand for glassmaking hauled in from Sand Lake, 12 miles away, at the extreme north end of Hardwick township. This sand, described as rather coarse and yellow, doubtless contains more iron than the fine white sea-sand underlying so much of South Jersey, which when not mixed with extraneous chemicals usually produces a clear glass whose broken edges are aquamarine of varying shades.

The northern sand proved to be unsatisfactory for the quality of glass Mayerhoff demanded and he soon found himself driven to the expense of importing South Jersey sand by way of Philadelphia. Why this roundabout route? The problem—lack of other suitable transportation—probably doomed Mayerhoff's glassworks and definitely affected the slow settlement of Sussex and Warren counties. Columbia was tucked away below heavily forested Kittatinny mountains, where black bear and wildcats prowled (there is still a bear-hunting season in northwest Jersey). From this isolated region there was no through road on the east side of the Delaware to South Jersey sand. Rapids in the Delaware, one stretch still known today as Foul Rift, made navigation upstream to Water Gap all but

*The odd long craft, seen in the aquatint (Plate 4), which is being poled by four pikemen guided by a captain with tiller in hand, may or may not have been the ferry, but being a Durham ore boat it has a long history of having been the type used regularly to transport iron from Durham Furnace established about 1750 some 12 miles south of Easton, Pa. George Washington commandeered Durham boats to move his troops secretly across the Delaware on Christmas night of 1776 for the surprise capture of Trenton.

impossible during the lifetime of the Columbia glassworks. Downstream, lumberjacks piloted cargoes of logs strapped to huge rafts which were often dashed up on shore, though Durham boats laden with pig iron frequently succeeded in making the perilous ride to Philadelphia and Trenton markets. But this was no route for fragile window-glass. Mayerhoff had no alternative but to have South Jersey sand hauled up in wagons along roads west of the Delaware.

Having then almost no communication with southern New Jersey this part of Warren (formerly Sussex) county lay in an east-west travel pattern; a main stage route in the early 1800s ran from Elizabeth to Easton; another, from Morristown to Newton and thence to Columbia. It is surprising to note that even today Columbians and their neighbors are oriented to Easton and Bethlehem, Pa., rather than to Jersey towns of similar size. This brings up a very significant bias when it comes to the attribution of glass from this factory. Undoubtedly much table ware, which certainly was blown here in a region "hurting" for glass utensils, found its way to thickly settled centers like Bethlehem and Nazareth, then later was ascribed to Pennsylvania furnaces, possibly even to Stiegel.

Whatever its later disasters, the Mayerhoff glassworks basked in quick prosperity. By 1817 Columbia had the astonishing number of four hotels. As visitors came from far and wide, in spite of bad roads, to view the novel sight of glassblowers at work, some hotels may have opened for the accommodation of these early tourists who coincidentally found the mountain climate of Delaware Water Gap salubrious. A tavern was located close to the river, near the piers built in 1869 for the 796-foot covered bridge which spanned the Delaware here until destroyed by flash floods of the 1960s.

Whether or not Mayerhoff sold to New Yorkers is not known, but he did have an agent in Philadelphia, named William Geisse, as noted in advertisements of the Philadelphia *General Advertiser* of 1815. The Geisses, a well known family and landowners in early Columbia, were Moravians, the German religious sect who founded Salem, N.C., and Nazareth and Bethlehem, Pa. As the Moravians or United Brethren also founded, back in 1769, the charming village of Hope, about eight miles southeast of Columbia, and have left such striking monuments as a great stone gristmill which ground grain for Washington during the American Revolution, it would be fascinating to know, because of the sect's distinctive folk-art, if any or most of Mayerhoff's colony belonged to it. In my research I enjoyed meeting Mrs. Hester Van Horn of Hope whose great uncle was the John Van Kirk who was an owner of Columbia. Though having no information at all about Columbia works, she does not believe that this glasshouse was founded by Moravians, though admitting that they may have participated.

Still, in Columbia, and even across the river in Portland—not even born in Birch's painting—the Moravian tradition persists. From the late Mrs. C. Beck of Portland I first heard the theory that the reason for the abrupt departure of Moravians from Hope and nearby places such as Columbia was a smallpox epidemic. Most of the Moravians left for Nazareth and Bethlehem, and the riddle may still be in the well-kept archives there, beyond the scope of this book.

Mayerhoff, wrote Snell, was spoken of as a gentleman of education and refinement,

GREEN FOR MONEY is the 8-looped topping of this unusual bank. Centers of loops are crimped with an iron and the crown is superimposed on a clear jelly glass which has been blown in a 12-rib mold. Rough pontil. H. 4 inches.

JERSEY BANK. A one-of-a-kind folk art object, such as may have originated the custom of putting the butter-and-egg money in the family sugar bowl. Of bottle green non-lead glass, the bank has a crimped applied foot and graceful applied handle with leaf curl. Early 19th century. H. 5 3/8 inches. *Chrysler Art Museum, Provincetown, Mass.*

PLATE 4

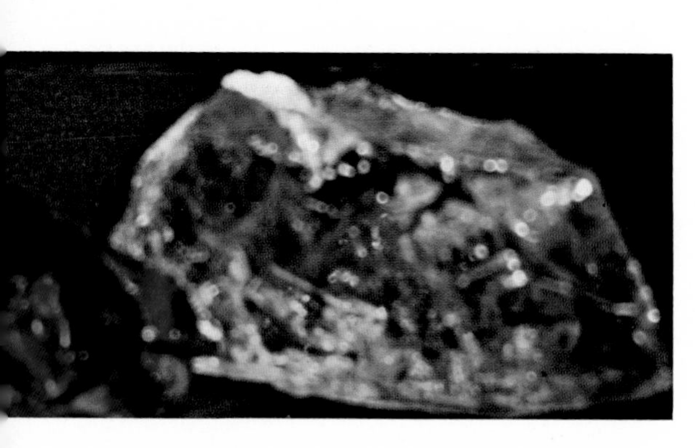

EMERALD AND CANARY SLAG from Eagle Glassworks site, Port Elizabeth, 1960s.

"View of Water Gap and Columbia Glassworks—River Delaware" is title of this *aquatint by William Strickland, from an oil by Thomas Birch.* Glassworks founded 1812 by Francis Mayerhoff, Manhattan merchant.

THREE TYPES OF LILYPAD decoration. Two aqua pitchers at left are casually made, whereas sapphire creamer at right is executed with precision. All have handles crimped at base. From left, H. 4½ 7½ and 4 inches. *George Horace Lorimer collection. Philadelphia Museum of Art.*

PLATE 5

18TH CENTURY JERSEY, possibly Wistar or Stanger; from Glassboro area. Vivid grass green; small pinched handles with thumb and finger rests; flanged set-in flattened cover with ball-on-button finial. Reproduced for Corning Glass Center but no longer available. H. 3 3/4 inches. *Ex-McKearin collection. Courtesy, Corning Museum of Glass.*

INTERLACED WAVES of golden amber and white create a rare mug, its colors suggesting Whitney Works. C. 1835–50. H. 5¼ inches. *Ex-McKearin collection. Courtesy, Corning Museum of Glass.*

and naturally appeared to some as rather aristocratic. To use that word in describing anyone of the early 1800s, it was well to smile when you said it. In that day of ebullient egalitarianism, no one in the young nation wished to be called aristocratic, as Mrs. Frances Trollope constantly reminded Americans, to the point of irritation.

After a decade Columbia appeared to be thriving. An advertisement of July 21, 1833, in the Easton *Centinel* gave notice:

> The Columbia Glass Works will continue the blast in the month of August next, when orders will be received for all sizes of *Window Glass* and executed by
>
> Abraham Piesch

Piesch was then manager of the works. John T. Bodine, an experienced glassworks owner who furnished information on Jersey glassmaking for the 1884 census report by Weeks, stated he believed Columbia made window-lights by the crown method, and Snell wrote that the works made "crown glass of superior value." If the crown method was used the panes would necessarily have been much smaller than if cut from cylinders of glass (see window-glass making). Oddly, the 2-story look of the glasshouse as shown at the right in Strickland's engraving is characteristic of cylinder works, where swing-pits were built. The Geisse advertisement of 1815, aforementioned, surely confirms that this was an early cylinder glass plant. The agent for Columbia advertises for sale 300 boxes of glass in 27 different sizes from 6 by 8 to 26 by 36 inches. A size of 36 inches is incredibly large for crown glass.

By 1825 tragedy had come to Mayerhoff. He had lost his fortune in Columbia and was forced to suspend glassblowing. That same year he was sold out by the sheriff. Piesch, the manager, became the next owner but he too was soon forced to close down. He was succeeded by O. D. William Lilliendahl, who in turn was followed by S. Smouth. Then on February 12, 1833, the glassworks was sold to a group, including Lilliendahl, John Beck, Frederick Salade, William Heyberger and John Van Kirk, both of the latter shown as owning lots in 1812. This company was incorporated with the then huge capital of $100,000, according to Gordon's *Gazeteer of New Jersey,* which in 1834 reported Columbia as a "prettily situated" town with two taverns, a store, a Presbyterian church, a sawmill and 20 dwellings, as well as the glasshouse.

How long Columbia continued after the 1833 reorganization is not positively known. Van Rensselaer placed the tentative date as "prior to 1844" because Barber and Howe did not mention a glassworks at Columbia in their 1842 edition of *Historical Collections of New Jersey.* This reasoning is not a reliable guide, however, for their book did not even mention a glass factory at Bridgeton, though one definitely was in operation then.

Among longtime residents of Portland, Pa., Columbia and Hope there is accepted agreement that the panes for St. Luke's Protestant Episcopal Church at Hope were blown at Columbia. As this edifice was begun in 1832 and not fully completed until 1839, when it was consecrated in October by the celebrated Bishop George Washington Doane, the myriad of small panes for the distinctively shaped gothic windows of this charming country church were presumably made in the late 1830s.

Fig. 46 COLUMBIA GLASS WORKS PRESERVE JAR purchased by collector Asher J. Odenwelder at Oxford Furnace, N. J., 12 miles southeast of Columbia. Bubbly medium green, c. 1815. Foldover neck; 8 inches high. *Private collection.*

The bubbly, green preserve-jar with a raindrop shape, shown above, bears strong evidence of having been blown at Columbia. The jar was first purchased from an individual in Oxford, N.J., in 1936 by Asher J. Odenwelder, Jr., of Easton, Pa. His collection of Pennsylvania German antiques and other primitives was so famous, so knowledgeably selected, that after his death dealers came from all over the nation to bid at the sale which took place in 1958.

This preserve jar is illustrated in a booklet which Odenwelder had had printed in 1948 called *The Collector's Art, A and Z.* Pictured resting atop a Pennsylvania dower chest, the preserve jar never reached the public sale.

Instead, the glass was bought just in advance of the sale by a woman who had seen the jar several years earlier when she was a member of a party making a tour of the Odenwelder house, described as full of treasures. A label then attributed the jar to the Columbia Glass Works. The woman, who is the present owner, has lived long in the Columbia region, as did her relatives by marriage, and had been intrigued by unrecorded stories of the glassworks that was unique in northwest Jersey. Seized with collector's fever, the woman felt she must own the jar, and so when the Odenwelder sale was announced she went personally to inspect the glass and then was able to purchase it ahead of the sale. It was then she learned that Mr. Odenwelder had bought the jar at Oxford Furnace. The iron-smelting furnace there, state-owned ruins of which still remain, was first built in 1742 and operations continued until 1884. Only 12 miles from Columbia, a thriving iron center like Oxford would surely have had need of such glassware as this jar. The definite green color is the kind that could have been blown when Mayerhoff was using north Jersey sand.

The aqua threaded pitcher with handsome strap handle (Plate 3) is a perfect match for large glass fragments found in great numbers at the Columbia site, but this by itself would not document the provenance. What is unusual is that the well-formed pitcher has never been in the hands of dealers or collectors but has been owned by members of the Hartung-Brughler family who lived at Delaware, a village two miles from Columbia. Mrs. William Cummiskey, née Minnie Hartung, who was born at Delaware, owned the pitcher for most of her life, which ended in 1967 at the age of 90. Her mother, of the Brughler family, is said to have received the pitcher when she was a young girl visiting the glassworks, a gift because of a heat crack at the handle. There is now a half-inch hole beside the handle.

As there never was another glassworks in northwest Jersey except for the once-famous one of Columbia, the provenance here is far better documented than that of much early glass. Because of the aqua color, the pitcher was no doubt blown when South Jersey sand was being imported.

The late George W. Cummins of Belvidere, whose *History of Warren County, N.J.* was published in 1911 and who had an M.D. degree from Columbia College and a Ph.D. from Yale, as well as a reputation of being a careful recorder of the history of his region, is reported by Mrs. Knittle to have owned tumblers blown at Columbia. I have been unable to trace them, however. Without presenting documentation or further details, Mrs. Knittle stated that A. H. Rice of Bethlehem owned a Columbia plate and that Willoughby Farr owned a footed bowl made there. All of this glass was reported as being light green.

The Belvidere *Apollo* for Jan. 3, 1829, announced a regular meeting of the Hot Rum Society. It is pleasant to imagine that the rummers used were tumblers like those Dr. Cummins owned and were made at Columbia Glass Works.

"Dr." Dyott of Dyottville, Philadelphia County

ONE OF THE MOST flamboyant figures in the story of American glass, "Doctor" Thomas W. Dyott, minister to man's pains, has been neglected in favor of "Baron" Stiegel. Yet not for want of self-advertising. Among the many historical flasks produced in Dyott's Kensington factory were three that bore a portrait of Benjamin Franklin on one side and of the illustrious Dyott on the other.

But the story of Thomas W. Dyott is best told from his own publications and the report of the committee sent to investigate his affluent Kensington Glass Works. As he described them in 1833 they were located between Kensington and Richmond in the extreme northern suburbs of Philadelphia. "The prospect on the river north and south, as well as the Jersey shore, is here the most beautiful and striking of any other on this part of the Delaware. Owing to a crescent bend of the river, a full view of the city as it extends down the curving bank is beautifully displayed; while the gaze is lost in the haze and verdure of the undulating surface of the Jerseys." "Dr." Dyott had reason to think fondly of Jersey, as we shall see.

When the committee of Eminent Philadelphians had come to inspect his glassworks Thomas Dyott reported that the first bell rings at daylight. Blowing begins at 7—and then goes on till noon. There is a rest for dinner. Then blowing from 1 till 6. But—how modern—in both morning and midafternoon there is a rest for crackers or biscuits. But entirely unmodern, after the evening meal there is prayer and singing. If you are a small boy, bed at 8. Little bit older, up till 9:30. Then "lights out."

This is how Thomas Dyott described his accession to the Kensington Glass Works: "During the war [of 1812], I became interested in a factory in New Jersey, which was the first establishment that continued in operation for any number of years, and which afterwards became the principal school of instruction to the workmen who were subsequently employed in the business.

"At a later period two other factories were established; and were in successful operation, until after the conclusion of the Treaty of Peace, when they were compelled to suspend business owing to the importation of the foreign article, which was designedly sacrificed at auction by the British agents, who publicly acknowledged at the time that they were instructed to sell at any prices, for the purpose of breaking up our manufactories.

"For a number of years, by persevering through the most formidable difficulties I continued my establishment with indifferent success; and afterwards located it in the county of Philadelphia in the situation just described, where I could give it my personal attention and introduce such reforms and alterations into the system, as reason . . . dictated; confining my operations principally to the common articles of Glass Ware; but with occasional encouragement from individuals to extend it to the manufacture of every description of Druggists' and Chemists' Ware."

When Dyott tells, as above, that during the War of 1812 he had an interest in an early

Jersey glasshouse we know he meant the one started by the Stangers at Glassboro in 1779 which became known about 1816 as the Olive Works. In 1817 the owners advertised that the entire output would regularly be sold through Dyott's Philadelphia warehouse. What has not been noted before is that even during the War of 1812, as Dyott tells us above, he had a financial interest in certain other Jersey factories.

Another Jersey furnace from whom Dyott bought bottles made to his specifications was that at Clementon, as he announced in the *American Centinel and Mercantile Advertiser* for Dec. 23, 1819. This advertisement listed over 60 types of bottles, jars and vials which Dyott offered for sale. Excavations made at Clementon by A. Richmond Morcom, beginning in 1965 and reported in the *Journal of Glass Studies* for 1968 reveal the hitherto unknown fact that Pitkin-type flasks were made in New Jersey. Morcom also proved that many other bottle fragments he found matched those named in Dyott's advertisements.

Dyott consistently advertised for sale such historical and pictorial flasks as Washington & Eagle, LaFayette & Eagle, Eagle & Cornucopia, Dyott & Franklin, Ship Franklin & Agriculture, so it is reasonable to assume that some of these were made in Glassboro and Clementon instead of only at Kensington as is the prevailing opinion. Morcom found no fragments of historical flasks, but the glassworks site had been largely removed for fill when he began his research. The site of the Olive Works has had no professional excavation. (See Pitkin Flasks at Clementon.)

It is worthy of note that two New Jersey factories, Samuel Huffsey of Millford and Hall, Pancoast & Craven of Salem, had some molds made by the same excellent moldmaker whom Dyott employed: Philip Doflein of Philadelphia.

Born in the British Isles, Thomas W. Dyott, who arrived in Philadelphia about 1795, and rose from a shoeshine boy who manufactured his own blacking to become the owner of a large and prosperous glassmaking village, owed much of his meteoric success to the gullibility of human nature. Very early he discovered that surefire medical "cures" were far more profitable than shoe polish. By 1807 he was listed in the Philadelphia Directory as owner of a Patent Medicine Warehouse at 57 South Second Street, and in 1809 as a medical dispenser, equivalent to apothecary, and owner of Robertson's Family Medicine, at 116 North Second Street.

Much of Dyott's early life is apocryphal but he soon began documenting his moves, in frequent advertisements not only in Philadelphia and New Jersey newspapers but others as far west as Pittsburgh and Tennessee. Evidently during the confusion of the War of 1812 Dyott had managed to attach unobtrusively to his name the two important letters of "M.D.," and by 1815 he was boasting in the Philadelphia *General Advertiser* of July 1 about "Long experience and extensive practice in the city of London, the West Indies, and for the last nine years in the city of Philadelphia." As of 1815 he already owned a wholesale and retail drug business at Second and Race streets.

In advertisements in the Pittsburgh *Mercury* and other 1826 newspapers he was describing himself as "Grandson of the celebrated Dr. Robertson, of Edinburgh," and under the headline of "Approved Family Medicines" he featured, Vegetable Nervous Cordial, Infallible Tooth Ache Drops, Anti Bilious Pills, Stomach Elixir of Health, Infallible Worm Destroying Lozenges, Stomachic Bitters, and Celebrated Gout Drops, all of which he said were prepared only by himself, T. W. Dyott, M.D.

The patent-medicine king of his times also claimed to sell effective remedies compounded by noted M.D.s. One such incident revealed a court record in Dyott's past. A Dr. H. P. Lee of New London, who was a Fellow of the Connecticut Medical Convention, in 1820 issues of the New York *Commercial Advertiser* had been offering a $40 reward for information leading to "vendors of spurious pills purporting to be the same as my genuine pills." Then Dr. Lee added, "T. W. Dyott having already been convicted and advertised . . . is an exception to the information requested."

Now in 1833 after having bought the Kensington Glass Works and renamed it Dyottville, "Dr." Dyott seemed headed for trouble again. A committee of Philadelphians —John Sergeant, Horace Binney, J. R. Ingersoll, C. A. Chauncey, A. D. Bache, Jonathan Goodman and Thomas P. Cope—had been chosen to make a discreet tour of the town he owned, though the purpose was actually to check on reports of Dyott's autocratic control of his "citizens." The now famous doctor not only gave the committee the keys to his village but even prepared for them a circular showing how paternalistic was his concern for his workers.

Dyott himself has left a positively Dickensian record of Dyottville life, in the 1833 printed report to the Philadelphia committee appointed to investigate him and his works.

"My glass establishment is located on the Delaware about two miles above the city of Philadelphia and comprises four factories of ten pots each, melting daily nearly 8000 pounds of Glass, or on an average about 1100 tons per year.

"The number of hands employed at the present time, including men and boys, varies from 280-300 persons."

Besides glassblowers of whom there were 50, and 130 apprentices, about 200 persons were occupied as "Teachers, Superintendents, Clerks, Fire tenders, Wood choppers, Rosin Pounders, Batch Makers, Sand washers, Clay pickers, Bottle grinders, Basket makers, Wheelwrights, Bricklayers, Shoemakers, Tailors, Farmers, Baker, Butcher, Boat and Scowmen, &c., &c."

In addition about 15 to 20 "females" were also engaged in cooking, tailoring, dairying and laundering. These females lived in apartments in the house of the superintendent, Mr. Dyott, brother of the proprietor, "where every regard to morality, decorum and piety is strictly observed and mildly enforced."

Boys of six to 16 years were hired as apprentices, "generally children of the poorer classes, many of them orphans, or having parents unfit or unable to provide them with instruction, they are, when received into the establishment, destitute of all Education, and in some instances of even a knowledge of the alphabet."

Dyott said he had set up a night school for these children and provided such recreation as shinney parties, football and sky rocket (whatever that might have been). Flutes and "note" books were given to those children who wanted to learn music. "In this manner, too, all vile and obscene songs have been superseded; which in former times, the workmen and apprentices were accustomed to indulge in when at their labor."

"Whilst at their pleasing task, they frequently raise the heart-cheering song, in which all join in full chorus—mirthful, innocent and happy, safe from the winter's blast, and hunger's pinching pang. A little boy of seven years old will construct the wicker work of a demijohn, with as much neatness as a veteran journeyman of fifty."

A continuous record was kept of the daily labor of each man and boy. Industrious journeymen—skilled blowers—could earn by extra work from 12½ to 50¢ a day. It was not uncommon for them to earn $1 to $1.50 a day, wrote their employer. They were given only pocket money and the remainder due was passed to the credit of their account. (How this worked out for the employee can be learned from the diary of Samuel Huffsey.) If the workers were industrious, said Dyott, they might acquire a small capital. All gambling such as card playing, lotteries and penny tossing was prohibited.

Pointing out that his community had a medical department and an apothecary and "Surgical Shop" in charge of a physician and a nurse, Dyott noted that there had been no cholera among his workers during the Philadelphia epidemic of 1832. He had evidently been questioned by the committee about health conditions for he said, "The instance of a consumptive Glass Blower is so very rare that it may be doubted whether the exertion of blowing does not, by giving a slight and healthy expansion to the chest and lungs, add vigor and energy to the whole frame." He had never known, he said, of a glassblower becoming blind or developing diseased eyes. (As time went on, glassblowers' cataract was recognized as an occupational hazard.)

Once again Dyott tells the committee and the modern reader that as early as the War of 1812 he was directly involved in the manufacture of glass and we know from his own advertisements and other sources that these furnaces were the Olive Glass Works at Glassboro and the Clementon (or Gloucester) Glass Works. In the following passages Dyott tells the committee how he happened to set up his fief of Dyottville.

"So early as the year 1815, I first became interested in glass works. I soon discovered that the workmen were more immoral and intemperate in their habits than most classes of artisans." There were several causes for this fact, Dyott told the investigators; mainly, that half the glassblowers' time was spent in idleness as the furnaces ran only about six months of the year. As the workers were hired in the idle season, employers were compelled to advance funds "out of the high wages" allowed the men. Another cause of intemperance, Dyott said, was "a vulgar notion" that as the blowers' work exposed them

Fig. 47 BENJAMIN FRANKLIN-T. W. Dyott flasks like this were advertised in the Bridgeton *Observer* in 1819, the same year when he advertised that he was buying the entire output of the Olive Glassworks, Glassboro, and the Gloucester Glass Works, Clementon. Franklin flask GI-95, similar to this but without a Kensington attribution on the edges, probably was blown at the two Jersey glassworks named above. *Philadelphia Museum of Art.*

to intense heat, "thereby producing perspiration and thirst that it was necessary that the latter should be quenched with an addition of spirits, to prevent the weakening effects of water."

"Finding it impossible to reform the older workmen," Dyott goes on, "I conceived the idea of producing a new set with entirely different habits." He admitted he had met with opposition but claimed to have succeeded, and had entirely abolished the use of "ardent spirits."

By building a new type of furnace so as to run from one to two years, Dyott told the committee, there was no idle time; he added that if there happened to be (such as for furnace breakdowns, which he did not mention) all hands were put on wicker work.

What Dyott did not reckon with when ingeniously devising a 12-month furnace was the perishability of the human "frame." In the hot, humid summers of Philadelphia blowers and gatherers exposed additionally to the fiery blasts of furnaces were wont to collapse from heat stroke. As the concept of administering water-soluble vitamins, salt tablets and other minerals was not discovered until well into the 20th century, untreated heat prostration was often fatal. During the 19th century most owners of South Jersey glasshouses found it necessary to close down at least during July and August and to use that time for repairing furnaces and building new melting pots.

Some persons who have evidently not read the 1833 report have referred to Dyott's glassmaking village as an idealistic venture. But to the apprentices the system must have seemed like involuntary servitude and to those who managed to graduate from apprenticeship the work could be said to be voluntary servitude, for lack of alternative employment. Rebellion against Dyott's type of exploitation inevitably created glassmakers' unions and agitation for them began about 1838.

When Dyott wrote that "The idea of *constraint*, which a stranger is apt to form is entirely erroneous," the committee evidently judged him by his own words for they commented on the "Kind but attentive vigilant guardians." Having come prepared to criticize they closed the case by saying "Dr. Dyott has rendered a service of keeping up his blasts at all seasons."

Even as Dyott was writing his favorable report on himself he was exploiting his adult workers. At the end of the 1834 spring blast, Sam Huffsey, one of Dyottville's most proficient blowers, recorded that he had had to accept Dyott's note for $100 in lieu of cash. (See The Saga of Samuel Huffsey.)

Dyott had set up his own "Manual Labor Bank," at the corner of Race and Second streets, for which he claimed a capitalization of half a million dollars, based on real estate (Dyottville?). His private bank issued its own paper money, signed by himself, which depicted a glassworks in full blast. Then abruptly in 1838 Dyott's career of euphoric expansion was terminated. His Manual Labor Bank had failed and he was later convicted and sent to Pennsylvania's Eastern Penitentiary. Yet once again he was able to talk himself out of a tight spot. In 1841 he was pardoned on condition that he make an assignment for the benefit of his creditors.

Never again did the promoter go back to the glass business but in later life he was again selling nostrums, where the deficiencies were less obvious than in the counting-houses.

Fig. 48 ODD PINCHED HANDLES, irregular applied foot, and grayed clear glass date this vase about 1800; H. 5½ inches. Opal pitcher has a curled handle drawn with a sure flourish. C. 1830. H. 4½ inches.

Fig. 49 PEDESTAL ENTIRELY HAND-TOOLED is applied to font of rare Jersey lamp blown in reddish amber glass; hollow foot, first quarter 19th century. H. 7 inches.

Fig. 50 THE HAND-TOOLED STEMS OF CORDIALS AND COPPERWHEEL engraving of wine glass indicate early period. Stem of goblet is applied. All in clear glass, engraved cordial with greenish tinge.

Fig. 51 EARLY JERSEY CANDLE-STICK of impressive design: especially the double-baluster stem topped by gadrooning, the whole resting on a well-balanced circular foot. Light green. H. 8⅞ inches. *Courtesy, The Henry Francis du Pont Winterthur Museum.*

Fig. 54 A DEEP RUBY TUMBLE made in South Jersey has applied aq foot. (RIGHT) H. 5 inches. *Crawfo Wettlaufer collection. Photo by Jo De Bus.*

Fig. 52 MATCHLESS PAIR, alike in sweeping handles and wave-like lilypad decoration. Sugar bowl with lilypad on the cover as well is exceedingly rare; it has a galleried rim. Clear aqua, first half of 19th century. Bowl, H. 5½ inches; creamer 5 inches. *Crawford Wettlaufer collection. Photo by John De Bus.*

Fig. 53 EARLY CARAFES, probably used for water as necks show no marks of stoppers. Soft deep cerulean blue, not cobalt. Pontils ground but not polished. H. 6 inches. Blown-molded, paneled whiskey glass.

Fig. 55 WEIGHT 5 POUNDS, this massive chalice is 11½ inches high yet is extraordinarily well proportioned and looks as if carved from ice. Probably made for church communion service: base is heavily scratched as if moved over marble altar.

Fig. 56 CLEMENTON STYLE FLASKS match, in dark green color and finely spaced, swirled ribbing, the numerous bottle fragments found at Clementon Glass Works site by T. Richmond Morcom in 1967, the first such reported in New Jersey. Flasks illustrated are likewise made by the half-post method, a second dipping of glass which leaves a ridge below the neck. *H. M. Smith collection.*

Fig. 57 CHESTNUT FLASK or pocket bottle of the type blown at Stangers' at Glassboro in the late 18th century. Flat sided and blown in a dip mold to create ribbing at the base of the neck. Reddish amber, ½ pint.

Fig. 58 CLASPED HANDS and square-and-compass design within a large shield were insignia, about Civil War times, of Junior Order of United American Mechanics, and this flask may have been made to honor them, not being a Masonic bottle as commonly supposed; cartouche below shield has word UNION. Reverse, not shown, has eagle flying to right, with ribbon in its beak; below eagle, some flasks have initials A.R.S. for A. R. Samuels described as a manufacturer of glass, particularly patent fruit jars, as early as 1855. McK.G. IV-42. Aqua quart.

Fig. 59 DANISH, 1825. Hip flask in clear soda glass blown at the noted Holmgaard Glass Works near Copenhagen is similar to the ribbed pocket bottles made in South Jersey and at Stiegel's glass works. H. 5 inches. Also made in cobalt. *Ex-collection Peter F. Heering.*

Pitkin Flasks at Clementon

In the years after the War of 1812, when the Clementon or Gloucester Glass Works was in full fire, a popular entertainment was sleighing parties to watch the glassmakers at work. Competing entertainments were a zoo of "7 beasts" at nearby Woodbury, among them "one very Antick Baboon," the July Fourth "Jubilee of Independence," and an advertised hanging that never took place as scheduled. Judging from Samuel Mickle's diary, extracted by historian Frank H. Stewart, the glasshouse was a social center of its region. A diary entry of Jan. 22, 1811, records a tragedy along with the merriment: "Trial Westcott dec'd last night at dance at Clements Glass Works."

With so much extra-curricular activity going on at Gloucester Glass Works can anyone doubt that offhand ware was blown on exhibition nights? And as Clementon was the fourth Jersey glassworks (after Wistarberg, the Stangers' at Glassboro and the Stangers' at Port Elizabeth), built about 1804 amid primitive surroundings, the first glass articles welcomed would certainly have been bowls and pitchers.

The stunning surprise about Clementon, not revealed until 1968, is that Pitkin flasks were blown here for the Philadelphia trade in the second decade of the 19th century, and probably in the first one.

Prized collector's items when well formed and richly colored, these swirled flasks are now known to have been incorrectly attributed to the Pitkin Glass Works, in existence at East Manchester, Conn., from 1783 to about 1830. No documented examples of Pitkin-made flasks are known nor have excavations revealed even swirled shards there. Fragments of this type of ribbed flask have been found, however, at the site of the glasshouses at Glastonbury and Coventry, Conn. Later, somewhat similar flasks were made in quantity at Ohio factories. But apparently no one suspected that Pitkin flasks were made in New Jersey until A. Richmond Morcom, former track star and now a coach at the University of Pennsylvania, whose avocations are glass collecting and archeology, began a detective search.

Like many a serious collector Morcom had read that T.W. Dyott, who gets credit for originating many of the best historical flasks, advertised in papers such as the *American Centinel and Mercantile Advertiser* of Dec. 23, 1819 that he was buying and selling all the bottles being blown at the Olive and the Gloucester Glass Works in New Jersey and the Kensington factory just north of Philadelphia then. Dyott offered more than 60 types of bottles and jars, among them, cologne bottles, snuff and mustard jars, "common ribbed flasks." In other advertisements he listed by name some of his historical flasks, such as Washington & Eagle, Dyott & Franklin. But modern collectors had no way of determining which articles were made at the two New Jersey factories. As the site of the Olive Works has long been built over, that left Clementon, a small town, as a more likely prospect for archeological digging. The problem was that because the Gloucester Glass Works closed down about 1825 no one was alive to tell where it had been.

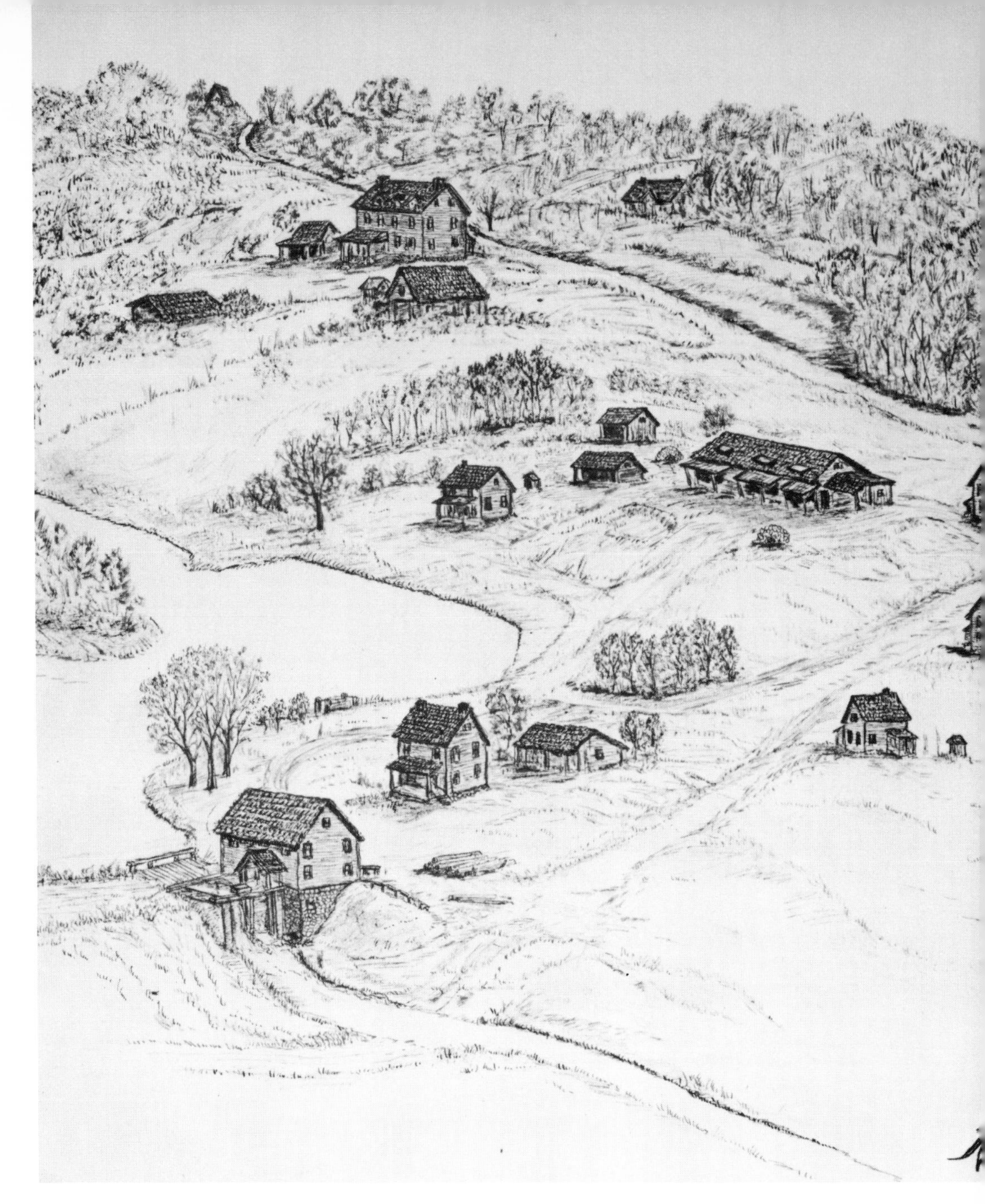

Fig. 60 CLEMENTON OR GLOUCESTER GLASSWORKS, long low building in CENTER. To right of it is operator's house in front of which runs White Horse road, today "avenue." Road going up hill was stage route to Long-a-Coming or Berlin, 3 miles east. FAR RIGHT, be-

Fortunately, Morcom was referred to a Clementon history buff, John H. Fisher, an electronics engineer, one of whose avocations is painting. When his children were still in school, he recalls, they used to bring home what they called "jewelry," bright chunks of glass which they had found on a hill a few blocks away. Their father recognized the pieces

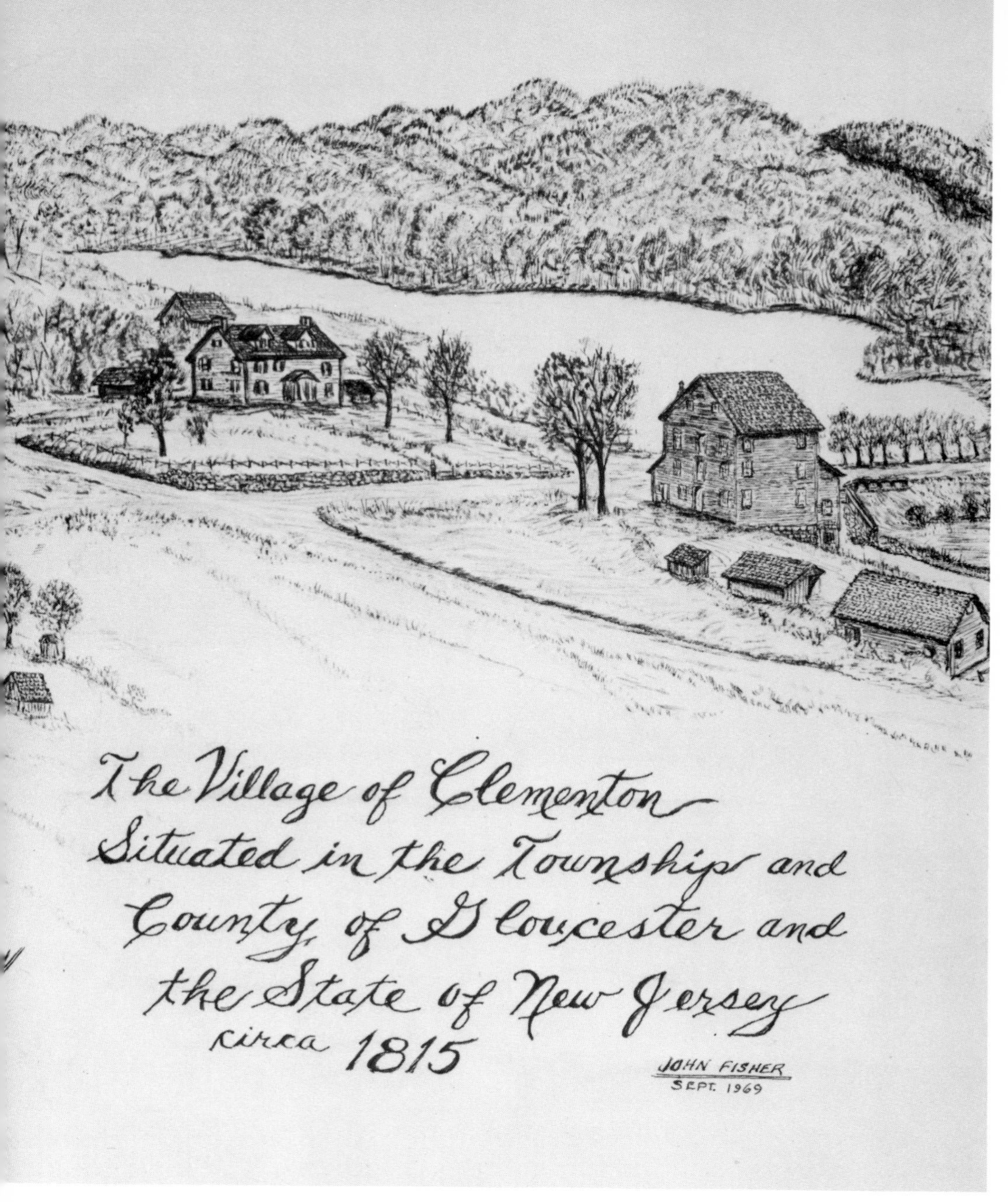

low Clementon lake is gristmill and to left of it, the miller's house. TOP LEFT, the tavern. LOWER LEFT, the sawmill and operator's house. *Drawing made especially for "The Glass Gaffers of New Jersey" by John Fisher, from his research.*

as glasshouse slag but though a lifelong resident of Clementon he did not know where the Gloucester Glass Works had been, nor did anyone else seem to know. Then he located descendants of a glassblower who had worked at the Batsto and the Atco windowlight furnaces and through them was able to confirm that the hill on White Horse Avenue near the Berlin road was indeed the site of Clementon's glassworks. From subsequent research, artist Fisher made the accompanying drawing, especially for this book, which shows the terrain and locations of main structures of Gloucester Glass Works about 1815.

Before Morcom arrived in Clementon to dig, most of the hill had been removed for fill and by May 1961 the area remaining was only about 12 by 50 yards. Yet this small plot yielded many historically rich finds, as revealed in Morcom's report which was condensed for the 1968 *Journal of Glass Studies* by Kenneth M. Wilson, assistant director and curator at the Corning Museum of Glass. That this site was no mere cullet dump was proved over and over by findings of numerous moiles or "knock-offs" from the blowpipe.

Over 300 fragments of Pitkin flasks were recovered, in the classic ribbing of right and left swirls and also "broken swirls." All Pitkins are made by setting the ribbed pattern in a ribbed dip mold, then expanding the pattern by blowing the parison and twirling the blowpipe to the right or left. The broken swirl pattern, resembling the texture of an ear of popping corn, was created by the half-post method; after the flask had been swirled in one direction it was dipped in a second gather and patterned in the mold, then twirled in the opposite direction. The second gather is visible in a line of demarcation near the neck. This technic is of Continental origin and as most of New Jersey's early blowers were Palatine Germans it is natural that they would have introduced this traditional method to their new homeland. One can only speculate on how many New Jersey swirled flasks have been attributed to New England, Stiegel or Ohio factories. The colors of Pitkin shards from Clementon range from golden to deep amber, aqua and numerous shades of green. Many fragments of plain, flattened "chestnut" flasks were also found.

A finding as astonishing as the Pitkin shards were fragments of clear or flint glass. Six of these were moiles, indicating that they were part of Clementon's production, a view supported by the fact that decanter bases showed no signs of wear. Fragments of additional objects in colorless glass were goblets and other drinking glasses and vials. Two small fragments of deep blue glass were found and two vials in light blue.

Numerous nearly whole vials as well as necks and bases of a wide variety of bottles were excavated. One pale amber bottle bears the words "Essence of Peppermint Made By The King's Pat" and the bottle is lettered "True Oephalick Snuff by the King's Patent." Many other bottles typical of the period were identified by shape such as the square containers for London Mustard. Dark olive-amber, called "black" glass, was used for gin bottles.

Equally fascinating are Clementon furnace artifacts, giving evidence that this is indeed the glasshouse site. Strongest proof is two clay covers to plug the eye of a furnace while a batch was being melted. These closures were discovered to be nearly identical in form and substance with one found during archeological research in 1962 and 1963 at a furnace of Amelung's "glass manufactory" organized with German blowers in 1784 at New Bremen, near Frederick, Md. Parts of blowpipes, pontils and glasspots were also found.

Portions of household glass recovered at Clementon indicate how indispensable such ware was in early villages. Among artifacts collected were fragments of bowls with threaded decoration, green and clear tumblers, decanters, and vessels with handles, such as mugs. And confirming those reports of exhibition blowing for sleighing parties, fragments of glass canes turned up!

Strangely, no shards of Dyott's famous historical flasks were found and it may be that

JAM POT in cobalt flint glass has a bell-shaped cover, set in flanged rim, to hold spoon. Wafer knob, though English in origin, was much used later at Whitall Tatum. Inverted foot. H. 6½ inches. MINIATURE aqua pitcher with melon-shaped base may be Clevenger as it is similar to full-size pattern-molded pitchers they made in the 1930s. H. 2 inches.

AN ARTIST IN CONTROL of his medium created this amber pitcher which has white swirls flowed on in unusual free-form design. The vigorous simplicity of the ear-shaped handle and circular foot lends a sculptured quality. H. 6 3/4 inches. *Crawford Wettlaufer collection.*

PLATE 6

NO KNOWN COUNTERPART. Very rare aqua sugarbowl, from a private home near Glassboro. Deeply swirled globular body is topped by heavy ring on which rests matching cover with applied ball-on-button finial. Crimped circular foot, applied. Late 18th century H. 8½ inches. *Ex-McKearin collection. Courtesy, Corning Museum of Glass.*

PLATE 7

JOEL DUFFIELD, BLOWER, Whitney Works, Glassboro. Cobalt bubbled glass with typical South Jersey globular body. Threaded neck, ear handle, crimped foot. C. 1835–40. H. 6 7/8 inches. *Ex-McKearin collection. Courtesy, Corning Museum of Glass.*

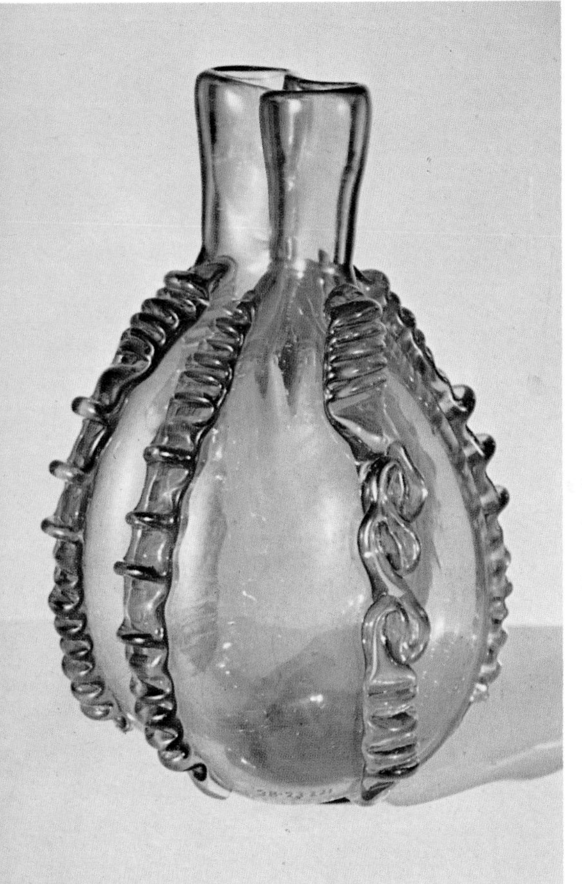

DOUBLE FLASK or gimmal bottle with rigaree decoration in the Venetian manner but attributed to South Jersey C. 1840–1860. H. 7½ inches. *George Horace Lorimer collection. Philadelphia Museum of Art.*

SAPPHIRE BLUE, DISTINCTIVE JERSEY COLOR, forms a pitcher of matchless design, a column rising from a globe, the flared rim tooled. The graceful question-mark handle is symbolic of the provenance, but the color matches a handle fragment found by the author at Waterford. Applied, crimped foot. H. 7 inches. C. 1825–1850. *Ex-collection Peter Tillou.*

some could have been discovered in the fill removed to the Clementon post office site. As I retrieved a large fragment of a cornucopia flask on the site of Waterford Glass Works which Jonathan Haines built about 1822 and whom Dyott listed as proprietor of Gloucester in 1819, I believe that Dyott-styled pictorials must have been made at Clementon as well.

Although Jonathan Haines, born at Mansfield in 1791, operated the 21-pot furnace at Clementon, the village, its structures and surrounding timberland were owned by Samuel Clement whose address in 1815 was Haddonfield. The glass works is shown on Watson's 1812 map of New Jersey but there is little tangible prior history.

Then on June 6, 1815, Clement, Hawson & Company, owners of the settlement, announced in the *United States Gazette* a proposed private sale of the entire village of Clementon. The advertisement gives a clear picture of the simplicity of those early Jersey communities: "a grist mill, worked by one of the best streams of water in the state. . . . capable of grinding from thirty to forty thousand bushels of grain per year." Near the mill was "a comfortable dwelling for the miller and a large capacious two story house well built and furnished in modern style, a commodious carriage house, stable and barn, a handsome garden and yard well fenced in and painted, ice and smoke house, a store so situated as to be capable of vending from forty to fifty thousand dollars worth of goods per year."

The glass house was reported as in full operation, with an unusual kind of furnace "built upon a new plan to contain nine melting pots and includes twelve others which one cord of wood renders the glass made from the batch so pure and fine as to be fit to work." Nearby were the grinding, pot, clay, packing and sand houses.

A large 2-story building housed a tavern, a nearly new sawmill was on "an excellent stream of water, having a head of from 18 to 20 feet fall," and the village was in the center of 280 acres partly covered with young oak and pine and an apple orchard of 300 grafted trees. Adjoining the store tract were 1500 acres of prime timber land with another stream of water and a new sawmill.

The sellers besides Clement were Caldwell S. Fisher of Woodbury, Samuel W. Hawson, Gloucester, and Josiah F. Clement who resided in the village.

The buyers are today unknown but as only part of the total price was required, Jonathan Haines may well have been a purchaser. At any rate, Jonathan Haines signed his name to "shinplasters" issued June 26, 1817, for the company store which he then owned jointly with Samuel Shreve.

Haines was a busy glassmaker in 1817, a year in which he also became a partner with William Coffin, Sr., at his Hammonton works, a joint venture that lasted until about 1820 when Haines was building his own hollow ware furnace at Waterford. His death in 1828 cut short a career that we now belatedly know was one of fine glassmaking.

The Woodbury *Columbian Herald* of Feb. 20, 1822, carried an announcement of a sawmill and 1200 acres of land for sale in Gloucester township near Clementon Glass Works, by John Woodward, Joseph Monroe, James W. Caldwell, and Michael C. Fisher. This advertisement is the last documentation we have of the Gloucester Glass Works which is thought to have closed down about 1825.

The White Horse tavern near Clementon Glass Works, historian Frank Stewart discovered, sold such drinks as madeira, claret, toddy, rum, Geneva, brandy, cider, beer, porter—all of which would have required special glasses as well as decanters, jugs and demijohns.

Fig. 61 BOLDLY DESIGNED light aqua pitcher, remarkably clear; one of a pair. Wide neck has tooled rim. Ribbed loop handle ends in vigorous crimp. Small circular applied base. H. 6½ inches. *George Horace Lorimer collection. Philadelphia Museum of Art. Photo by A. J. Wyatt, Staff Photographer.*

Fig. 62 EMERALD GREEN LILYPAD pitcher has widely threaded neck, sheared lip, handle ending in crimps. Lilypad design Type III; applied foot. Early 19th century. H. 8¾ inches. *George Horace Lorimer collection. Philadelphia Museum of Art. Photo by A. J. Wyatt, Staff Photographer.*

Fig. 63 JENY LIND is misspelling of noted Swedish singer's name above her portrait wreathed in laurel. McK. GI-105, quite similar to Whitney Brothers calabashes McK. GI-103 and 104 which have a period after Jeny. Reverse shows glasshouse differing from known Whitney bottles, as the smoke rises upward in 105. Definite source not known. As in Whitney Lind calabashes, 11 heavy vertical ribs, rounded collar. Quart aqua calabash listed as rare by McKearins. *Crawford Wettlaufer collection. Photo by John De Bus.*

Fig. 64 BRIDGETOWN embossed on this flask was the early name for Bridgeton. Portrait of Washington on observe and of Henry Clay on reverse. Each side embossed BRIDGETOWN/NEW JERSEY. Probably made by Joel Bodine & Son for Clay's 1847 vacation at Cape May. Aqua, quart. McK. GI-25.

Fig. 65 CLASSICAL PORTRAITS, sometimes said to be of Sir Walter Scott, LEFT, and Lord Byron (subject shown wears a Byronic collar). Flask is in the style of other ½-pints from Bridgeton, particularly Stratton, Buck and Company, founded 1837, a few years after the deaths of Scott and Byron. *Photo, Corning Museum of Glass.*

Fig. 66 WASHINGTON-JACKSON portraits are impressed on obverse and reverse of this golden amber ½-pint flask. Although the McKearins attributed it to Coventry, the flask is nearly identical in design with the Scott-Byron and other Bridgeton ½-pint. McK. GI-34.

Fig. 67 WASHINGTON-TAYLOR ½-pint flask is embossed WASHINGTON on the obverse; reverse shows bust of Gen. Zachary Taylor in uniform, above him the words BRIDGETON*NEW JERSEY. Made by either Stratton-Buck or by their successors, the Bodines of Bridgeton. McK. GI-24, amber.

Fig. 68 PORTRAIT·FLASK said to honor Louis Kossuth has lettering BRIDGETON. NEW JERSEY in arcs on sides of bust. As the Hungarian patriot visited America in 1851, the flask would have been made by Joel Bodine & Sons. Reverse shows sloop sailing left with pennant flying. McK. GI-III, pint aqua, listed as scarce. *Crawford Wettlaufer collection. Photo by John De Bus.*

Fig. 69 LEFT: TOP-HATTED HUNTER blazes away at two birds in flight, with two hounds on point, in Hunter-Fisherman calabash believed to be uniquely Jersey. Not listed in McKearin. Quart, deep aqua. RIGHT: on reverse ANGLER with creel holds fish at end of line, in background a mill and waterwheel. Scalloped neck line, ribbed sides and height similar to Fislerville calabashes. Variations of Hunter-Fisherman bottles attributed to also Whitney Works and Holz, Clark and Taylor of Salem.

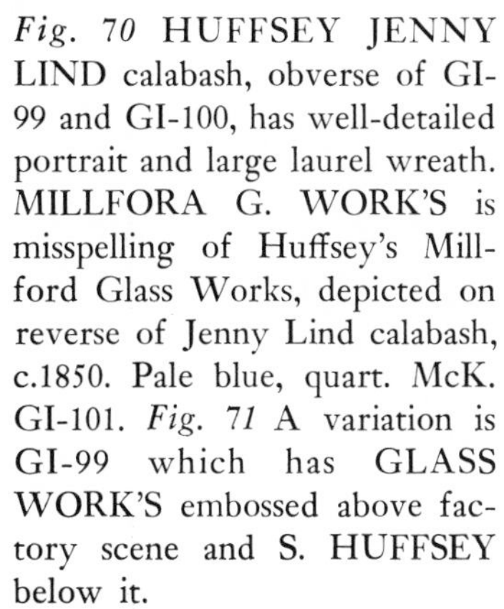

Fig. 70 HUFFSEY JENNY LIND calabash, obverse of GI-99 and GI-100, has well-detailed portrait and large laurel wreath. MILLFORA G. WORK'S is misspelling of Huffsey's Millford Glass Works, depicted on reverse of Jenny Lind calabash, c.1850. Pale blue, quart. McK. GI-101. *Fig. 71* A variation is GI-99 which has GLASS WORK'S embossed above factory scene and S. HUFFSEY below it.

Fig. 72 GOOD GAME is lettered beneath antlered stag facing right on Coffin & Hay pint aqua flask, McK. GI-1, listed as comparatively scarce. Reverse shows stylized weeping willow tree in oval panel. *Crawford Wettlaufer collection. Photo by John De Bus.*

Fig. 73 COFFIN & HAY Eagle and Stag flask, McK. GII-49. Eagle perched on panel has six arrows in right talons, olive branch in left; sun rays around head; shield has seven vertical and four horizontal bars. Reverse shows antlered stag, above it in arc COFFIN & HAY; below, HAMMONTON; aqua ½-pint, listed by McKearins as scarce. *Crawford Wettlaufer collection. Photo by John De Bus.*

Fig. 74 FOR OUR COUNTRY is embossed below 20-star American flag on Coffin & Hay pint flask. Reverse shows wings and head of eagle facing left and topped by sun rays; below, a shield with six vertical bars set above crossed laurel branches, Aqua. McK. GII-54; variants, GII-52 and 53. Charles F. Carr collection.

Fig. 75 RARE COFFIN & HAY ½-pint flask: eagle and bunch of grapes (McK. GII-56) in bubbly golden amber. Obverse shows 13 stars above an eagle with head and wings surmounting a shield having five broad vertical bars and six narrow horizontal bars. Rising from base, a palm and an olive branch crossed.

Coffin & Hay— Flask Makers

COFFIN & HAY / HAMMONTON are words that bring joy to knowledgeable bottle collectors, when the words are blown into historical flasks. These Jersey flasks are desirable because they not only are highly original but also show a sense of excellent design uncommon in a field where pictorical effects are likely to be primitive. As might be expected, the "name" flasks are not the only ones made by Coffin & Hay at Hammonton.

The words "Coffin & Hay, Winslow, N.J." in old records indicate continuity of the former firm but give no hint of the turmoil and change that went on in a lifetime ranging from 1817 to 1892 and covering two neighboring New Jersey towns.

Pioneering flask collector Edwin Atlee Barber wrote that Hammonton historical flasks were blown only between the years 1836 and 1838, but in light of the fact that his sketchy account of the firm has had to be drastically revised and from new evidence cited below, not to mention the quantity of Hammonton flasks extant, it seems likely they were made for a much longer period, and considerably earlier.

The numerous changes in firm names and their dates will be given in as much detail as known, in hopes that new facts will come to light from old letters and ledgers. The story of the Winslow Glass Works will be covered in a later chapter. Hammonton-Winslow glassmaking was essentially a family affair of the Coffins and the Hays and men who married into those families.

Born in Green Bank in 1775, about 1812 William Coffin, Sr.—whose father, a native of Newbury, Mass., and a resident of Philadelphia, had settled in Green Bank on the Mullica river—built a sawmill at the request of Dr. John R. Coates, over a stream flowing into what is now Hammonton lake. The mill has long since vanished but the site is known to be at the culvert bridge on Route 30 where it passes the east end of Hammonton lake.

Coffin ran the sawmill for two years and then in 1814 bought it and 1,598 acres which included the lake, a heavily forested region without settlements. The prospects should have discouraged anyone who didn't realize that "The Forks" of the Mullica, a tidewater river, was only a few miles away and that the whole wooded area was underlaid with glass-sand.

William Coffin must have realized the potentialities, for by 1817* he had built a glass furnace opposite the mill. He named the settlement Hammondtown (now Hammonton) after one of his sons, John Hammond Coffin, born in 1816 to Ann Bodine Coffin.

Although Coffin was not a glassblower at the start of what became his major career by 1819 he had taken into partnership Jonathan Haines who was indeed an experienced

*This date, from Wilbur and Hand, who, as newspaper publishers in Hammonton, printed in 1899 a history of the town, is two or three years earlier than that quoted by some other historians but Wilbur and Hand researched the property transfers and gave other evidence of careful study of Hammonton's history and are regarded as accurate sources.

Fig. 76 Hay & Co.'s Glass Works, at Winslow, Camden Co.

glassmaker. From about 1804 he had been manager of the Clementon or Gloucester bottle works, a furnace where A. Richmond Morcom in 1968 reported excavating numerous fragments of Pitkin-type flasks. Clementon was a glasshouse where the bottles were so excellent that "Dr." T. W. Dyott had hired the entire output to make historical and other flasks, as well as medicine bottles. If historical flasks were not being made at Hammonton at this early date, the swirled Pitkin types could easily have been made, as the molds were so simple to produce as compared with pictorial ones.

Coffin and Haines ended their partnership about 1822 when Haines made ready to set up his own furnace in nearby Waterford township, Camden county.

Continuing a profitable lumber and glass business, which included both window-lights and hollow ware, Coffin in 1823 made his son William, Jr., a partner. About 1828 the latter became a member of a new firm, Coffin, Pearsall & Company, which erected a glassworks at Millville but after about two years Coffin withdrew, in order to give full attention to a glassworks that his father was organizing at a new place to be called Winslow, as described in the following chapter.

The elder Coffin continued running the Hammonton Works until 1836 when he leased it to another son, Bodine Coffin, and to his son-in-law Andrew K. Hay who had married Coffin's daughter Jerusha.

Hay, a Scotsman from Massachusetts, is described as a "practical glassman," but if so he also held the job of bookkeeper for the senior Coffin. Hay is sometimes credited with designing the molds for Coffin-Hay historical flasks, but so far no shred of documentation has been presented. The idea may have sprung from the fact that in later life Hay proved himself talented and dynamic in such other arenas as railroading and politics, but the

Coffins were equally prominent in their own special fields. Mold-designing in that day was more likely to be the creation of a skilled craftsman rather than of a community leader or successful entrepreneur.

After a couple of years the partnership of Bodine Coffin and Hay was dissolved, which may have given rise to the opinion that historical flasks were blown here for only two years. But there were other "Coffin & Hay" associations soon after. Moreover, it is unlikely that so many varied molds would have been made during such brief time. The flasks which bear no name but are similar to the name-embossed ones may well have been made later for Coffin & Hay at Winslow.

Taking charge again at Hammonton, which was now concentrating on hollow ware, the eldest Coffin ran the glasshouse until 1840 when fire consumed it. Suspicious of arson, Coffin discharged his glassmakers, imported a new crew from Massachusetts and rebuilt the furnace.

The heart of his community was at the crossroads now marked by the White Horse Pike (Route 30) and Central Avenue, Hammonton. Before and during the bulldozing which took place in the building of Kessler Memorial Hospital at this location, I did some searching for fragments of early glass. A site often disturbed, there was some modern glass but still plenty of green-glass in aquamarine to indicate that this had been a glassworks slag heap. Especially interesting are bases and necks of small aqua vials, some only ¾ inch in diameter, such as were once used for expensive medicinals. As there was considerable dark olive slag, not natural for the white local sand, this might indicate iron oxides were being added to make lightproof demijohns, or simply that these New Englanders preferred the dark bottles they were accustomed to.

The glass furnaces were opposite and north of the modern hospital. The Coffin house, small when built about 1812, but with a large addition made in 1825, none of it existing now, was on the edge of the lake. The flattening ovens for window-glass were diagonally opposite the Kessler Hospital. The company store was near the lake, on the present hospital site.

This settlement had a combined church and school, one where the Coffin children

Fig. 77 WILLIAM COFFIN HOUSE built about 1825 on Hammonton lake. Road in foreground is now White Horse Pike, route 30. *Photo, courtesy of Mrs. William Coffin and Mrs. J. R. de Arellano.*

Fig. 78 FAMED COFFIN FAMILY. Three sons of William Coffin who founded Coffin & Hay Glassworks; LOWER LEFT, Bodine Coffin; holding child, Edward Winslow Coffin; RIGHT, John Hammond Coffin for whom Hammonton was named. TOP LEFT, William Coffin, grandson of first William Coffin in New Jersey. *Photo, courtesy of Mrs. William Coffin and Mrs. J. R. de Arellano.*

were educated. A circuit-riding preacher came to the village about every fortnight and was "hospitably received at the Coffin manor."

In later days Hammonton was served by the fast mail route, a stagecoach from Camden, traveling through "the deer woods" to Leeds Point on the Jersey coast, every Wednesday and Saturday and returning Monday and Thursday.

Finished glass was carted, along a road approximately that of Route 542, to "The Forks," about 1½ miles below Pleasant Mills, to what was probably the Batsto iron docks, and there awaited sailing vessels bound for New York and Philadelphia. Wagons also moved glass to Camden.

In retrospect we know that William Coffin's life was drawing to a close, yet in 1840, the year of the destructive fire, he returned to Green Bank to set up a small furnace later managed by his son Bodine. Soon after that Hammonton was named a federal post office, with Coffin as postmaster.

A direct descendant of Tristram Coffin who settled on Nantucket about 1642, William Coffin had disciplined his sons to become industrious efficient glassmakers, and when he died in 1844 William Jr. and Edward Winslow were ready to take over the Hammonton Works. In 1851 Edward sold out to his brother who conducted a profitable business until 1857 when a financial panic burst, in which some 6,000 firms failed. Hammonton Works never operated again, but Winslow more than made up for the loss.

Winslow and Squire Hay's Prosperity

NO EARLY HISTORY of New Jersey gives such a human picture of a 19th century glasstown as the story told by The Old Settler, an 82-year-old woman who lived her entire life from the age of three in Winslow, in a lively interview by a reporter from the *Hammonton News* in 1928.

Why The Old Settler wished to remain anonymous is not clear, for she had nothing but good to say about her father's bosses at the Winslow Glass Works.

"Winslow was a prosperous place," said this immigrant from Germany whose father came ahead of the family to see if America was what it was billed to be. Arriving in 1849, they all stayed.

"Squire Hay was such a fine man and loved Winslow and so did his children. They grew up in Winslow, then went to boarding school and were 'finished off' in France. But they built their homes in Winslow. Mrs. Cochrane (one of Andrew K. Hay's daughters) had a cabinet maker come from Philadelphia to make her furniture, and then the house was open to the public for a day before they moved in . . .

"Mrs. Bernadoux—one of the girls married a Frenchman—named her son Winslow Bernadoux. He grew up and joined the navy . . ." In the Spanish American War this John B. Bernadou was famed for bravery in his command of a torpedo boat named the *Winslow.* He is credited with being the pioneer inventor of smokeless powder.

Recounting that her family lived first in a frame house, then moved into a log cabin on the edge of the woods, The Old Settler said, "Winslow was full of real old-fashioned log cabins. Then there were 'pigeon houses,' that is what we called the two-family frame houses. Nearly everyone worked in the glass factory, and Squire Hay owned the houses where the people lived. Every spring he had the houses whitewashed so that they looked nice and neat, and they were surrounded by beautiful gardens. . . .

"Squire Hay had worked as head bookkeeper for Mr. Coffin when Mr. Coffin had the glass factory in Old Hammonton . . . Squire Hay got Mr. Coffin to establish glass works in Winslow, and then he married Mr. Coffin's (Wm. Jr.) sister, and Squire Hay eventually obtained control of the factory. He was a practical man, and his wife was a beautiful woman and good."

The formal history of the Winslow Glass Works was not quite so simplistic as described by The Old Settler. The story begins in 1829 when William Coffin, Sr., of Hammonton bought tracts of timber in Camden county about six miles west of Hammonton and with his son-in-law Thomas Jefferson Perce and William Coffin, Jr., built a glass factory in the midst of a thick pine forest. William, Jr., was the first to fell a tree for the site, but the locale was named for the senior Coffin's youngest son, Edward Winslow. The firm name, however, was William Coffin, Jr., & Company. In 1833 the elder Coffin retired and the firm became Coffin & Perce. The latter died two years later, leaving William, Jr., sole owner. In 1838 he sold a half interest to his brother-in-law Andrew K. Hay. Before long a third partner, Tristram Bowdle, was admitted. Coffin, Hay & Bowdle continued to 1847 when William Coffin sold his interest to his brother Edward and to John B. Hay, Squire Hay's nephew. In 1850 Bowdle retired, and a year later Edward Coffin sold his share to Andrew Hay who with his nephew became sole owners at Winslow.

The Hays at once made many improvements. In 1852 a deep artesian well was driven to supply steam to the grist and sawmills. Glassmaking continued under control of Squire Hay until his death on Feb. 17, 1881, at the age of 72. At that time the works consisted of two window-light plants and a hollow ware furnace.

John Hay and other heirs continued glass production until 1884 when the Tillyer Brothers of Philadelphia, also residents of Winslow, took over. At that time several hundred men and boys were employed and the firm owned, besides the factories, a large store and about 100 houses. The quality of the glass, wrote Prowell,* was superior.

The Tillyers leased the Winslow Glass Manufacturing Company from William Coffin Hay, who was Andrew's son, and George Cochran, his son-in-law, and continued making window-glass and bottles. Then on Decoration Day of 1892 a raging fire swept the three glass plants and many houses, beyond hope of repair. The Tillyer house was spared as was the Hay mansion, a huge white house with fluted columns, still occupied today, seedy and sad looking.

And what of Andrew K. Hay who, with his family, prospered in Winslow and brought a relative prosperity to the workmen there? Of Scottish descent, he is said to have come from Massachusetts. That he ever had time to sit down and carve mold designs for Coffin & Hay whiskey flasks, as is claimed, seems unlikely in view of his lively temperament and the much larger irons he had in the fire.

His view was definitely not toward the miniscule. He and Samuel Richards of the Jackson-Atco Works, Enoch Doughty, Dr. Jonathan Pitney, and Judge Joseph Porter were hatching plans for a railroad from Camden to Absecon Island (now Atlantic City), which would transport glass from towns like Waterford, Hammonton and Winslow. By 1849 Andrew K. Hay had graduated from local politics and had become a Republican Congressman. In 1850 the railroad's charter was granted and on July 1, 1854, the locomotive *Atsion* of the Camden & Atlantic's single track railroad chugged from the Delaware through the pines to what was named that day: Atlantic City. Along the triumphal way the train of nine coaches filled with 600 prominent guests stopped at the junction near Jackson where the Richards' glassblowers cheered; at Waterford Glass Works Joseph Porter, the owner and a member of the railroad's board of directors, received a gun salute and a wreath that read "Welcome to Waterford," and at Winslow the chairman of the board of directors, Andrew K. Hay, took bows from the rear platform.

A locomotive was later named for Hay and when one of his daughters was married this engine pulled two coachfuls of guests from Winslow Junction to the village. When he died in 1881 the same train bore him and the mourners to Colestown where he is buried.

* *History of Camden County,* 1886.

For its day the speed-up in time effected by the railroad in moving glass to the broad Philadelphia market wrought a near miracle that may explain why Winslow and others along the route survived the Panic of '57 and the depression of the Civil War.

The Old Settler describes the contrast: "Before the railroad came, the glass was taken over the stage road to Camden in wagons like the covered wagons of the West by four and six mule teams." These were indeed canvas-topped wagons, Jersey's own version of the old Conestogas.

It is usual to assume that the Civil War had little direct effect on New Jersey but the story told by The Old Settler gives a grimmer reality to what happened in glass towns during that conflict:

> "Winslow was a thriving hamlet and everyone was happy and got along well when there came rumors of war, only no one thought they were serious. Then one day the bell that hung on one of the factory buildings and rung in case of fire, rang. All of the people went to see what was wrong, and there they found a military recruit officer standing by the flag pole in front of the boarding house.
>
> " 'S. Carolina has seceded from the Union,' he said, 'and the president is calling for volunteers to defend the Constitution.'
>
> "Those were sad, sad days in Winslow. Men would leave their ploughs in the field and their scythes hanging on the trees and send word that they had run away to enlist. Only the middle-aged and old-aged men were left in the factory. There were three and four gone from many a home. I remember there were a number of young married German couples there living in a row. Some of them had small children. The men all went to war.
>
> "The middle-aged people tried to keep the factory going, and Squire Hay brought in blowers from Belgium, but they were a rough sort, and we did not want them in Winslow, so they had to leave.
>
> "Those were sad, sad times for us. Every Sunday we went to church—there was an American flag draped across the front—and we earnestly prayed to God to save our country. Our country needed so much and was so poor, and there seemed to be no one to help her, and we were afraid of what might happen if the South won the war.
>
> "Everybody was poor—and finally after four years the war was over. Some of the men never came back, and some of them came back—worn and shattered."

To anyone who thinks that the name "Coffin & Hay" pertains only to Hammonton an award that the Winslow Works won in 1840 from the Franklin Institute of Philadelphia is revealing because this honorable mention or third prize was given to "Coffin & Hay of Winslow, N.J." The articles were "two glass shades for flowers," which probably meant large glass bells for wax flowers and fruit. The comment was "This article has a slightly greenish tinge, which no doubt may be avoided; the shape is good, and the whole effort successful."

Two years later the Franklin Institute awarded its third prize to Coffin, Hay and Bowdle.

In 1845 the American Institute of New York presented a diploma to Coffin, Hay and Bowdle as the American Cylinder Glass award at the 18th annual fair. That same year the Franklin Institute commented on but did not present an award for "large lights of glass" exhibited by the firm: "Lights of glass of American manufacture of this size are rare. The glass is not inferior in color to the best foreign, but is not so free from specks and waves as is desirable for the purpose for which large lights are used."

PLATE 8

MATCHED PAIR, EXCEPTIONALLY FINE IN COBALT. Sugar bowl has galleried rim with tooled cover inset. Applied finial is tooled, has rough pontil mark; applied circular foot. H. 6¼ inches. Pitcher has bulbous base, low-set handle with end turned up. Rim has three rows of tooling. Applied circular foot. H. 7 inches.

SCARLET PITCHER of 2-quart size posed problems in blowing as did claw handle of contrasting clear glass and flaring pleated rim. Absence of amber shows Hofbauer skill in formulas and in fire-polishing. *Barbetti collection.*

DEEP AMBER pitcher shows fine control of the metal in the harmony of proportions and meticulous lily-pad decoration. Ear handle, wide flaring lip, applied foot. C. 1840. H. 7 inches. *George Horace Lorimer collection. Philadelphia Museum of Art.*

PLATE 9

STIEGEL-TYPE COLOGNE BOTTLE blown by Emil J. Larson, 1930s, from 18-rib mold. Applied ring. Stopper also blown in a mold. Grape-colored, 6½ inches high, non-lead glass. FREEBLOWN AQUA PITCHER with threaded neck and configuration similar to Columbia pitcher. Double strap handle. H. 7½ inches. C. 1810.

ONE OF FOUR KNOWN cobalt blue, 1-quart Mason jars blown at Moore Brothers, Clayton. Embossed: MASON'S FRUIT JAR/-PATENTED/NOV 1858. *Collection of Lewis De Eugenio.*

WHITE WAVES ON DEEP AQUAMARINE seem to symbolize the South Jersey coast where glasshouses abounded. Although obtained from widely separated sources these mugs appear to have been fashioned by the same blower. H. 6 inches and 3 7/8 inches, respectively. *Courtesy of the Ruth Bryan Strauss Memorial Foundation.*

"Christian L. Stanger's Book Sepr. 6th 1828" is the title, in even slanted handwriting, of a worn and now well-cared-for notebook that sends a cryptic message from the past. Through the generosity of the owner, A. L. Smith, I am permitted to quote from this rare volume. The subject is partly "Receipts of Window Glafs," and Stanger, son of the Christian Stanger who was one of the original seven brothers at Wistarberg, appears to have collected batch recipes at nearly every furnace where he had blown glass. One of these places was Winslow where Stanger obviously was working in 1838, for he records:

"French bach given by a french man at Winslow October 7th 1838

3000 b Sand
550 b Salt
1100 b Soda
1200 b Chalk or Lime
80 b Charcoal"

If anyone doubts that the Coffin & Hay name of the embossed Hammonton flasks continued at Winslow one need only peruse the absorbing pages of the Stanger notebook. On one page, for instance, he jots down three different recipes: "Wm Coffin Jr & Hay bach at Winslow obtained from James Githin maker of the bach.

100 b Sand	100 b Sand	100 b Sand
33 b Lime	35 b Lime	35 b Soda
30 b Soda	37 b Soda	35 b Lime
10 b Salt	20 Marl	15 b Salt
for Window Glafs	15 Salt	for Vials & bottles of Different Sizes
	for Carboys Green	

On other pages Stanger lists a recipe as "William Coffans Pot Mixens" and another as "William Coffan Jr Pot Mixens" and still another as "Wm Coffin Jr at Winslow."

That Christian Stanger Jr., had a supervisory position at Winslow seems evident from his letter of April 29, 1845, to Benjamin Riggins at "Estells Glafs Works" about cutters' wages. In his usual exquisite handwriting, the letter indicates that at this period the cutting shop for Winslow window-light furnace was called Albertson & Hay, a name not hitherto recorded in modern chronology. Nor has there been mention before of children learning to cut window-glass.

Gentlemen: I received your letter in regards to the Cutters wages and should have answered it before this but i read it at a time i was very much hurried and laid it away and it slipped my mind until today i saw it again. You wished me to send the price of cutting. James Hay and Samuel Albertson has all the cutting for the twenty four blowers for which they get 20 cents per box without any discount and have their houses rent free. This year they paid rent i believe for the previous years they cut but it is taken off this present season, and they hire their under cutters themselves. i believe Albertson & Hay pays fifteen cents to hands they hire. They also have some children of their own learning to cut, Apprentices. You must excuse me for not writing sooner as i entire forgot it.

from your fr
C L Stanger

Lobbyists to Washington

Phila. April 21, 1842

Mr. Daniel E. Estell
Mays Landing
Dr. Sir

Mr. Porter* and our Mr. Coffin have been twice to Washington at their own expense in relation to business affecting the interests of all the Glass-makers, and intelligence just received makes it necessary for them to go on again—they propose to go next week, but they think it right that their brother manufacturers should pay a portion of the expenses incurred in these journeys, to be estimated according to the number of Furnaces employed by each Factory—

As the new Tariff will raise the price of labour, if we do not get our share of protection we shall suffer more than we should under the Compromise Act.—Please give us your views on the subject.

Respectfully yours
Coffin, Hay & Bowdle

A fascinating document, also owned by A. L. Smith, consists of two 7½ by 12 inch pages, with exquisite calligraphy, covered with the precise "Dimentions" of both window-glass furnaces at Winslow for the seasons of 1838-39 and 1839-40, and for the "Old House" in 1843. Measurements cover such details as the size of the arch, the size of the keystone, size of the lock or shear hole, and the spring of the cap.

Recipes are given too for making clay caps at the old and new houses. One for the "New House" in 1840-41 reads as follows:

6 measures Old burnt cap
4 measures New Castle raw—
ten rounds put on in this way together with some
new hard burnt New Castle Clay
the burnt heaped a little more than the raw

At the top of one page is "Dyott's Mixen for Flint Glafs":

160 lb. Sand
28 lb. Lime
200 lb. Pearl Ashes
36 lb. Salt
5 lb. Arsenic
8 oz. Manganese
50 lb. Cullet

As all else on these pages is about Winslow, could it be that Dyott was buying glass from the Coffins and the Hays as he had from Clementon and Olive Glass Works in New Jersey?

On a slant in one corner is the word "James." Near it and somewhat doodled "Pd. me 5.4." The word "Camden" is visible, preceded by an illegible word.

*Undoubtedly Joseph Porter, owner of Waterford Works

Because handsome—and now eminently collectible—flasks are known to have been blown at Hammonton, it is reasonable to suppose that similar historicals were made under related managers at Winslow. Yet Mrs. Knittle wrote that many of the flasks stamped "Hammonton" are thought to have been made at Winslow. As she gave no evidence whatsoever, this seems to be an indefensible statement.

At least 13 different designs of flasks have been attributed to the Coffins and the Hays. To this list should probably be added GENERAL TAYLOR NEVER SURRENDERS, a Washington, and the ubiquitous cornucopia.

The Old Settler injects a surprise, however, when she states, "I can remember when they [at Winslow] made glass bottles ornamented with a picture of Jenny Lind on one side and Kossuth, the Hungarian patriot, on the other."

This could be none other than a hitherto unidentified calabash, No. 100-GI-100 in McKearins' chart of historicals. They describe it as comparatively scarce, meaning only 75 to 150 extant, and do not illustrate the Kossuth portrait. As the first Jenny Lind calabash did not appear before 1850 when the "Swedish nightingale" made her triumphal tour of the United States, and the Kossuth calabash was made a year or two later, it seems likely that the combination Lind-Kossuth was a late bloomer sold in the early 1850s.

The Old Settler, I find was "Granny" Sutts, widow of Manas Sutts, a gatherer at the Winslow works. As she was interviewed in 1928, long before collecting of flasks became widespread, her information and recollection that a Jenny Lind calabash was made at Winslow must have been correct.

When the Old Settler's parents came to Winslow in 1849 dense forests with tall pines, sometimes four feet thick, stretched for miles. "We didn't have coal then and we used wood for everything, even to the fires in the glass factory." That was the rub, Andrew K. Hay must have been thinking, for wood fires were not hot enough to make clear bubble-free glass. Hay's railroad soon brought in Pennsylvania coal and in 1854 he obtained a patent for an improved way to use anthracite in a glassworks.

In the 1870s business was booming at Winslow as it was for most South Jersey glass

Fig. 79 An early Jersey covered wagon.

Fig. 80 THIN AND SAD-FACED, the glass men of Winslow Works, owned mainly by the Coffins and the Hays, were photographed in 1875. *Photo courtesy of Jesse Ford.*

manufacturers who survived the dislocations of the Civil War and its aftermaths. The Hays patented a fruit jar which, though it appeared long after Mason's early patents, sold well. Patented Jan. 5, 1875, June 5, 1877, and April 25, 1882, the container had a glass top closure with a single wire bailer and is embossed in mid-section with the words WINSLOW JAR.

In 1879 the Mt. Holly *New Jersey Mirror* of Aug. 28 reported that 6,000 gross of the Winslow jars were blown annually, besides all sizes of bottles to 5-gallon demijohns. Window-glass of the best quality, this publication stated, "was flattened in the French and

Belgian manner and entirely free from stain, the great bugbear." The capacity was 6,400 boxes a month.

From 225 to 250 persons were employed in that year of 1879 at the hollow ware plant and the two window-glass furnaces which covered 15 acres. These were "large and convenient buildings," with modern equipment. In addition the Hays owned a steam sawmill and flouring mill, wheelwright and blacksmith shops, a large store, about 50 houses, 700 acres of farms, and 5,000 acres of timber, not to mention a mile of railroad spur to Winslow Junction.

Harry Sampson of Winslow, who was 80 when interviewed in 1962, in his youth became a window-light gatherer at the Winslow Works, then later a blower there and in West Virginia. He still refers to Andrew K. Hay as Squire Hay.

When other skilled laborers were getting $1.25 an hour, seasoned window-light blowers were earning $12 an hour. But they worked only six months of the year, and breakage cut down the earnings. The Winslow men were paid $20 "market money" for the first week of the month, then $20 to cover the next two weeks, and finally in the fourth week the balance due, in cash. Some blowers owned their tools but Harry Sampson rented his, as many others did, for 25 cents a month, which covered repairs by the company. Periodically the pipes would get iron scales inside which damaged glass; a blacksmith would then rehead the pipes with new iron. Later, some observant individual noted that the scale was caused by condensation of moisture on cooling pipes, so the secret was to keep the pipes near the furnace.

The union allowed workers to blow only 40 feet of single strength glass a week or 30 feet of double strength (it took 11 panes of single strength and 6 panes of double to equal an inch). Day work was regulated by number of cylinders allowed and the week's work by feet of glass obtained. Before the continuous tank process was adopted, window-glass blowers here worked seven to eight hours, then rested about 16 hours, while the mix was made ready and melted in the furnace. Then again men worked until all the metal was used up, a continuing cycle. Cylinders of glass were sometimes 70 inches long.

The window-glass furnace where Sampson worked, he recalls very definitely, had a swing-hole rather than a platform. The second and later furnace, which was built at a time when blowers were difficult to obtain was known as the "English house" (because workers were imported ?).

Only a small boy when the bottle works was operating, Sampson played and helped around the place. He remembers that large demijohns were made and many bottles, some so small that "only a gather as big as a chicken egg" was used to blow into the mold.

Harry Sampson gave up glassmaking at age 64 because "A window-light blower can't hardly work much after 65—it's hard work." During the next decade he was employed by a railroad and at a shipyard but had to retire at 74 though he still had "more strength and know-how than lots of the younger fellas."

In 1962 Harry Sampson said he was lazy and coddling his health. Reason? "I've seen some great things in my day. Now I want to see them put a man on the moon." His prescience has been rewarded. In 1969 he saw Neil Armstrong plant an American flag on the moon.

Fig. 81 GRACEFUL PROPORTIONS and hand-tooled leaf-like decoration on base and handle create a unique basket of clear, bubbled glass with greenish tinge. Attributed to South Jersey, early 19th century. H. 5½ inches. *The Melvin P. Billups collection, courtesy of the Isaac Delgado Museum of Art. Photo, courtesy of the Corning Museum of Glass.*

Fig. 82 THREADED MUG of green glass has unusually large thumb-rest, is typically 18th century but possibly made in early 19th century. South Jersey. H. 6⅛ inches. *The Melvin P. Billups collection, courtesy of the Isaac Delgado Museum of Art. Photo, courtesy of the Corning Museum of Glass.*

Fig. 83 GRACE of the ribbed, strap handle as it seems to flow from the exquisitely threaded neck of this pitcher and the perfection of the wave-like swag create an outstanding example of the South Jersey style of the 1825-1850 period. Blue-green aqua. H. 8¼ inches. *Courtesy, The Henry Francis du Pont Winterthur Museum.*

Fig. 84 SCULPTURED high swag decoration is superimposed on pitcher of exceptional form and color, a brilliant green. Fine ear-handle ends in leaf curl. Hand-tooled rim; applied circular foot. *Alfred B. Maclay sale of 1935, Anderson Galleries. Photo by Taylor and Dull.*

Fig. 85 OVERALL THREADING displays an unknown gaffer's art in forming this clear, pear-shaped sugar bowl of rare beauty. Bell-shaped cover, with applied button, is set into galleried rim, both cover and rim edged in blue. Diamond-point engraved "Prudence Goodall 1836", surrounded by tendrils. H. 6½ inches. *George Horace Lorimer collection. Philadelphia Museum of Art.*

Fig. 86 FORTHRIGHT CLARITY of design, with a bubble for accent, is exemplified in this light green vase characterized by vigorous curves. Probable period, 1825-1850. H. 5¼ inches. *Courtesy, The Henry Francis du Pont Winterthur Museum.*

Green Bank on the Mullica

William Coffin, Sr., who was born in Green Bank and who became a founder and successful co-owner of noted glassworks in Hammonton and Winslow in 1842 returned, with his son Bodine, to his native village to operate window-light and hollow ware furnaces.

Located opposite the north end of the present-day bridge across the Mullica, the Green Bank glasshouse was on land owned by Nicholas Sooy and his son-in-law Thompson, who leased the furnaces to glassmakers. Sooy & Thompson account books show that Boarden Westcott built the flattening house in 1842, evidently to Coffin specifications. From Sam Huffsey's diary we learn that Sooy and Thompson themselves were operating a bottle works here in 1837 and 1838.

After the senior Coffin's death in 1844 the works was continued by Bodine until just prior to 1850. The following letter of Feb. 27, 1848 indicates that layoffs were already in progress, for Coffin here writes to Daniel E. Estell, owner of the window-glass works near Mays Landing:

> "The bearer of this is Simon L. Wescoat a glafs cutter by trade and wishes to get cutting & if you are in want of a cutter for the next blast I can recommend him to be a good cutter and will cut to order & keep his work up & he is also a sober man but is a devil of a fellow for the womans, as the crutch man says.

The crutch man was the one who held a tool called a crutch (see Fig. 200), similar to a block or cup, for shaping the parison of glass; the tool had a short leg which was held by the crutchman while the blower created the initial shape.

From Mar. 1, 1850 to Mar. 1, 1852 E. L. Wells & Company of Philadelphia rented the glassworks. Then from May 1, 1852 to Aug. 1, 1853 D. O. Ketchum & Company undertook bottle-making. As neither firm used the flattening oven, this equipment was sold.

The bottle furnace appears to have been out of blast until about 1857 or 1858 when, during the glassmakers' strike of that time, Sooy & Thompson leased the works to some blowers from Glassboro. They made glass on the co-operative plan, with Sooy as their clerk, but the arrangement was short-lived.

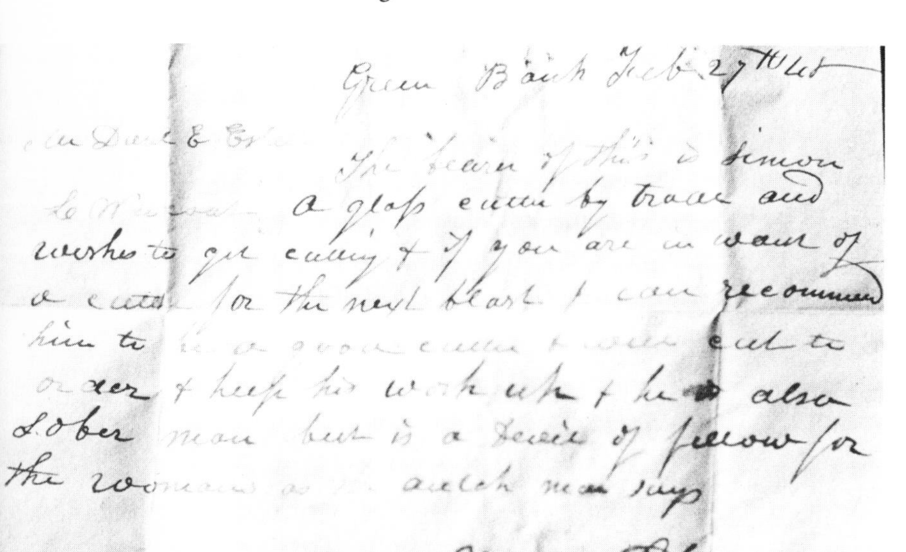

Green Bank Feb 27th 48

The bearer of this is Simon L Wescoat a glafs cutter by trade and wishes to get cutting & if you are in want of a cutter for the next blast I can recommend him to be a good cutter & will cut to order & keep his work up & he is also sober man but is a devil of a fellow for the womans as the crutch man says

Yours B Coffin

Fig. 87 LETTER OF RECOMMENDATION from no less than one of the famous Coffins who in 1848 was attending the demise of his glass works at Green Bank on the Mullica.

Waterford Works and "Waterford Wages"

Walt Whitman was here. The place impressed him. He wrote about it in notes he took while traveling by horse and buggy from his home in Camden (now a state historic site) to the Jersey shore: "Waterford Glass Works, nice little cottages here." Perhaps Whitman intended, judging from his numerous notes, to write some verses on the evanescent romance of the Jersey pine barrens around Waterford, but he never did.

Yet what he wrote about Waterford is significant: "Nice little cottages." Few glassworkers of that day had nice little cottages. Just prior to the Civil War when Joseph Porter was a principal owner of the Waterford Glass Works, glassmen were well paid by standards then current. Making handsome glass for the Philadelphia trade, Porter sought to attract expert blowers and paid them according to their skill. "Waterford wages" became an old-time phrase that signified something like glassblowers' heaven.

Listening to some amateur sages one hears that Waterford Works was named for Ireland's famed Waterford glass, noted for exquisite cutting. There is no evidence whatsoever that such exquisite cutting was ever done here. The township has long had the name of Waterford, probably given by some homesick Irishman.

New Jersey's Waterford was fortunate in having at least two creative glass entrepreneurs. Joseph Porter, in the middle period, was one. Jonathan Haines, an Irishman, was the leader.

As late as 1886 when Prowell's "History of Camden County" was published he described Waterford as having surrounding forests where "many native pines are still growing, whose odors contribute to the salubrity of the village." When Haines set up his Waterford Glass Works in Camden County in 1822, the region was unbroken woodland, wrote Prowell, and, he might have added, one springing from clean white sand.

We first hear of Jonathan Haines as the original operator of the glassworks which Samuel Clement built about 1804 at what is now Clementon. Also known as Gloucester Glass Works, this was undoubtedly the fourth glass center erected in New Jersey. Archeological research reported in 1968 revealed the startling finding that Pitkin-style flasks were made here. In 1819, the year in which Thomas W. Dyott announced he was buying the entire output of Gloucester works, Haines left Clementon to join with William Coffin, Sr., in creating the Hammonton furnace, now famed for its handsome and varied historical flasks in such a range of colors as emerald, sapphire blue, citron, golden amber and milk white.

In his years at Hammonton anyone as enterprising as Haines is known to have been would have mastered the art of producing these mold-blown flasks. Only one flask marked Waterford is known, however, first reported by Van Rensselaer and not noted by the McKearins. Van Rensselaer attributed the flask to Haines' successors. Pint size in a bluish

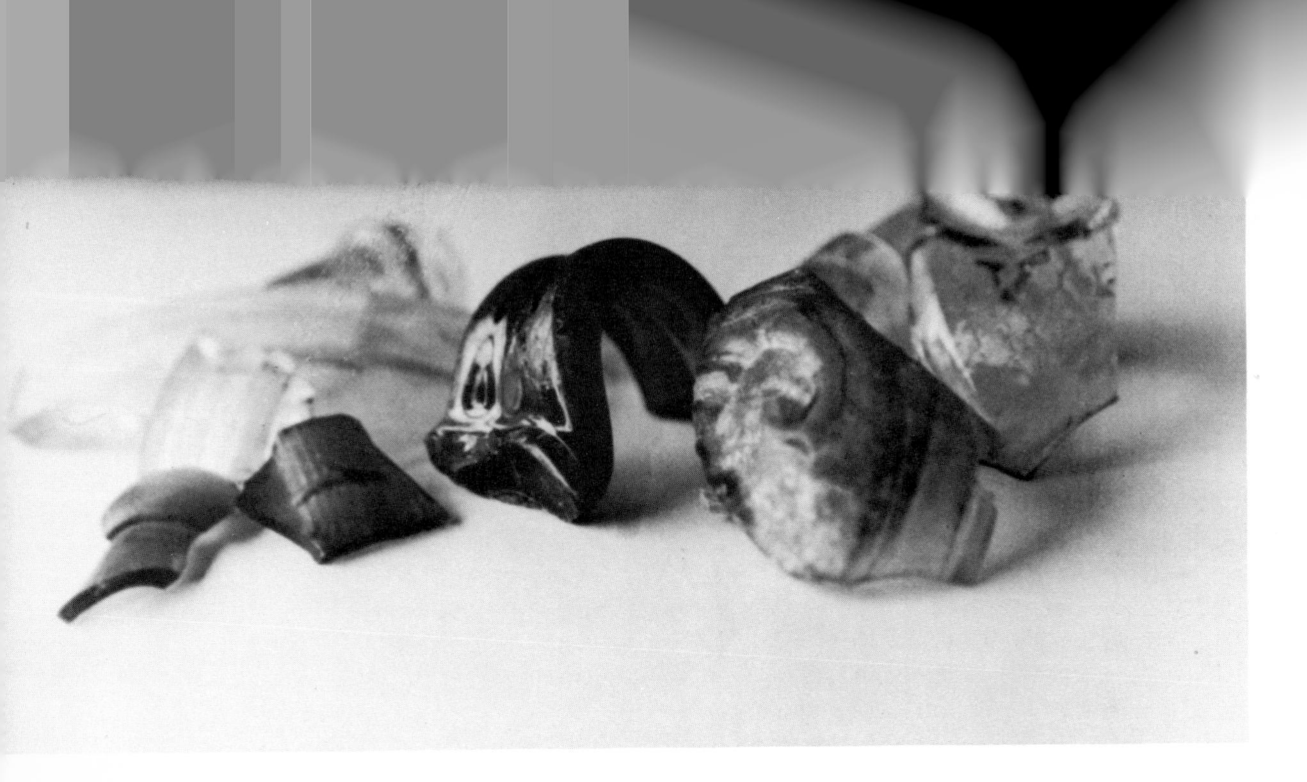

Fig. 88 JERSEY CORNUCOPIA FLASK fragment, first time reported, excavated at Waterford as are other early shards. Remarkable too is portion of double strap-handle of sapphire pitcher. IN BACKGROUND, top edge of large aqua bowl with wide folded rim. IN FOREGROUND, green fragment in fasces pattern, as if for border of flask. AT RIGHT, patterned fragment of bottle, unknown.

aqua, the flask shows a spread eagle with a ribbon, above arrows and an olive branch. The reverse contains a large shield, clasped hands, seven flat bars, a shield-shaped oval and 13 stars. The design is topped by the name "Waterford" and there is a branch on either side. The bottle has a double-collared mouth. In view of the numerous designs of Hammonton flasks it is likely that Waterford also had others, not marked, such as one of the non-attributed Washingtons.

From limited digging I have done at the Waterford site (since bulldozed) I have found the lower fourth of an aqua cornucopia flask and its base with a pontil scar. Very significant also are shards of other vessels in colors corresponding to those at Hammonton rather than the limited range of Clementon. One of the most interesting fragments is part of an early ribbed strap-handle of a sapphire pitcher like that on Plate 7.

Having already accomplished much, Haines died prematurely at the age of 37, the cause unknown today. The works were sold to Thomas Evans, Samuel Shreve and Jacob Roberts. When the latter died the firm became Porter, Shreve & Company, with John Evans having bought a sixth interest. Joseph Porter was known as an active resident manager under whom the works prospered in the making of window-glass, hollow ware and tableware of high quality. The firm had sales offices in Philadelphia.

Soon after the glassworks was functioning the Waterford Methodist Episcopal church was established and was encouraged by Joseph Porter and his associates. Shreve and the Porters donated a lot for the church and conveyed the title to Daniel W. Westcott, Brazier

Wescoat and Arthur Wescoat, who were among the glassworkers. The Porter mansion was located near the church.

Joseph Porter not only pioneered in paying higher wages to glassmen, generally underpaid in the decades before the Civil War, and in building nice little cottages, but he also instituted an industry-wide revolutionary change when he provided a weekly day of rest for his workmen. Until then it had been an inviolable rule that glass furnaces could not close down on Sundays as long as there was metal in the pots. Porter's new system proved so workable that soon other owners of furnaces had to adopt the plan.

When Porter died in 1862 his death must have been mourned by many a glassblower. A son, William C. Porter, who had been running a glass plant at Medford in the 1850s took charge, but in 1863 sold out to Maurice Raleigh, not a glass entrepreneur but owner of about 10,000 acres that included the Atsion Furnace estate. At the time of sale Waterford consisted of two window-glass furnaces and a third for hollow ware.

All three furnaces went out of blast during the Civil War and in 1870 many of the clay molds were sold at a sheriff's sale to R. H. Tice who purchased them for his son Clayton B. Tice, then operating Isabella furnace at New Brooklyn.

Not recorded in Jersey histories or those on glass is that this works had a final unusual phase when it was organized in 1874 as the Waterford Glass Company with Maurice Raleigh as president and John Gayner as superintendent, a post he had held at the Norris-

Fig. 89 WATERFORD FLASK shows name enveloped by ribbon and 13 stars above large shield with clasped hands; seven bars above an oval medallion have a laurel branch on each side. Obverse: spread eagle with ribbon, on arrows and olive branch. Pint aqua with collared mouth. C. 1865. *Courtesy, The Corning Museum of Glass.*

Fig. 90 MASTER hands of unknown gaffers fashioned these pitchers, notable for flaring handles, graceful curves and symmetry. Large pitcher is deep aqua with white swirls. Lilypad pitcher in lighter aqua. *H. M. Smith collection.*

town, Pa., Glass Works. A year later, as reported in the *Crockery Journal* of Aug. 19, 1875, the firm was blowing glass lamp shades, round, square and oval, "quite equal to the imported French stock," the only such establishment in New Jersey.

Most intriguing of all is the account of exceptional stained glass which was being blown here in the 1870s, not merely the usual square panes for country churches but pictorial scenes and figures, with a new process of coloration that captured the brilliancy of antique glass. That this was no reckless boast was indicated by the examples "of the fine work that has emanated from this establishment," that could be seen at the National Capitol in Washington, D.C., the Pennsylvania Capitol, the St. Louis Court House, Philadelphia's Episcopal Church of All Saints, some half dozen churches in Baltimore, as well as many other metropolitan churches and synagogues, and private residences such as those of F. A. Drexel, Matthew Baird and Theodore Cuyler in Philadelphia.

The firm's agent, with an office at 124 North Fourth Street, Philadelphia, was Thomas J. Stewart who had previously been agent for Norristown glassworks. George A. Russell, also with an office in Philadelphia, was treasurer. The company was geared to produce also some 2800 boxes of single and double thick window-glass each week, made by a process guaranteed against staining and rusting.

In 1879 John Gaynor went to Salem, N.J., to set up a new glass works intended as a continuation of the Waterford Works. A bottle factory, Gayner Glass Works, prospered down to modern times (see Salem) but by 1880 Waterford was out of blast, and in May of 1882 a fire destroyed most of the structures.

The Saga of Samuel Huffsey

A MYSTERY RANKING with the secret formulas of some of the old glass gaffers is "What became of the journal of Samuel Huffsey, glassblower?"

The Huffsey journal once reposed in the archives of the Gloucester County Historical Society in the history-redolent town of Woodbury, New Jersey. But the present archivists of the museum are about ready to concede defeat in locating this important record of the early days of glassblowing in the United States. Luckily, Frank H. Stewart, late curator of the Gloucester County Historical Society, compiled an abstract of much of Samuel Huffsey's diary, which was published in the 1930 Yearbook of the New Jersey Society of Pennsylvania.

Sparse though this account is, it offers a rewarding look down the telescope of history at the Stanger brothers, that most durable family of early Jersey glassblowers, and the harsh lot of the workers during the first half of the 19th century.

Like the tides along the Jersey shore, glasshouses rose and fell, but with irregular regularity, when gutted by fire or drained of dollars. If a glasshouse collapsed, the way of life of the worker usually collapsed too and he was compelled to pile his family and their meager belongings on a wagon-team to journey to another village in search of a new job.

In the course of some 30 years Samuel Huffsey moved from town to town in a veritable odyssey of glassmaking: from Port Elizabeth in "down Jersey" where he was born, to Hammonton, N.J.; to Philadelphia; back to Hammonton, then to Kensington near Philadelphia; to Millville; to Philadelphia again, then back to Millville; next to Pittsburgh; again to Kensington; once more to Millville; from there to Bridgeton, N.J., and still another time to Philadelphia and adjacent Dyottville, Pa. Nor was Huffsey unique in undertaking these Flying-Dutchman travels, for many of his contemporaries journeyed even farther afield: to Cape Cod, to New York, to Ohio, to Kentucky, to Maryland and West Virginia.

Within this pattern of wanderings down the years was an annual rhythm, one that rose to a crescendo in September when the furnaces blazed up all over South Jersey, and then subsided as the fires were doused in May, to be followed by a new theme as workers sought other and cooler employment during the summer. Whatever it was, the life of a glassmaker was scarcely monotonous.

To collectors of glass, Samuel Huffsey is invaluable as a name-dropper. His journal is studded with references to men who created glassmaking history: among them, the original Stanger brothers, Daniel Focer, Joel Bodine, Thomas W. Dyott, William Coffin and Jonathan Haines. Factories owned by the last four men turned out some of the most famous historical flasks, and undoubtedly Samuel Huffsey blew many of these now rare liquor bottles. Because most of the names noted by Huffsey are patronyms still common in New Jersey, Pennsylvania, and some other eastern states, many are listed here as they may offer clues to collectors in tracking down new examples of old Jersey glass or in determining the provenance of specimens already in collections.

The bread-and-butter jobs of Sam Huffsey and his co-workers were most often the blowing of bottles of all kinds, but at such pitifully small wages as to furnish bread with no butter. Judging by Sam's journal, the peak of wages for blowers, the elite of the industry, was during the War of 1812. The rate then for blowing 1-ounce vials was $1.00 per gross, and this meant 144 usable bottles, never any rejects. Before the machine age, spoilage was high in glassblowing, and there was a lot of unremunerative breath expended. Small wonder that bottle-blowers and window-pane makers fashioned end-of-day glassware to sell on the side or to eke out their families' scanty supply of tableware.

Like many another American glassblower, Samuel Huffsey's ancestors arrived in the New World by way of Holland, although whether his family were Dutch or German is not clear. Immigrating from Amsterdam, Sam's grandfather George Huffsey, Sr., came to Philadelphia and served an apprenticeship as a tanner with one Ashberton, at the southeast corner of Third and Dock streets. George was "set free" in 1770 and thereupon went to Mt. Holly, N.J., where he married a young widow, Margaret Brandinburgh, with a son named John. The couple had three children, Hetty, Meaily and George, Jr. About 1772 the family moved, with "other Germans," as Stewart writes, to Maurice River, N.J., an oyster-dredging settlement opposite Bivalve, N.J., on Delaware Bay.

George Huffsey, Jr., father of Sam, as a young man was employed by Randall Marshall, partner in a glassworks and owner of a tannery in Port Elizabeth, about six miles upriver from Bivalve,—and not to be confused with Elizabethport, now Elizabeth in Union County. Sam Huffsey's father married in 1799 and by 1807 was settled permanently in Port Elizabeth as owner of a tanyard.

Young Sam, born April 5, 1801, went to school to a Mrs. Gaskell until he was about 10 years old, not long enough to change his penchant for phonetic spelling. In the autumn of 1811 at his green age he went to work as tender for two glassblowers, Oliver Smith and Christian Hinds, at the Union Glass Works, on the northwest bank of Port Elizabeth Creek near the dam.

This glassworks, which made history though its origin is somewhat nebulous, was established soon after 1800 by those accomplished artisans, the Stanger brothers. The owners were none other than Jacob Stanger, Philip Stanger and William Shuff (so spelled by Huffsey, but correctly: Shough), all of Glassboro. The first three partners were also gaffers here and, Huffsey records, had brought with them from Glassboro these other talented wielders of the blowpipe: Frank Stanger, Solomon Stanger, Philip Stanger, Daniel Focer, a Stanger relative by marriage, and Daniel Shough.

In the fall of 1811 the Union Glass Works was going great guns. This was the troublesome time when, as John Randolph thundered, the United States was being "embargoed and non-intercoursed almost into a consumption." It was true that America's foreign trade was nearly dead of attrition because of English and French embargoes against United States trading vessels. Ships were rotting in the harbors of New York's East River, at Philadelphia and in Delaware Bay, their masters not daring to venture into open ocean for fear of seizure. Hungry unemployed sailors had been rioting in the streets of Manhattan as early as 1807. Soon their plight became a rallying cry for the whole country: "FREE TRADE AND SAILORS' RIGHTS!" A slogan so popular that later it appeared on Dyottville flasks, as we shall see.

But the various embargoes, starting in 1807, eventually acted like energizers on some American industries, those that could get raw materials. In South Jersey glass-sand was one of the few commodities in bountiful supply.

The furnace of the Union Glass Works was evidently being fired to the limit, for in December of 1811 the building burned down. It was not rebuilt until 1812 and the 8-pot furnace did not go into blast until March. It was at this time that piece-work wages were $1.00 for 144 1-ounce vials, as high as Samuel Huffsey appears to have recorded. In the summer of 1812 Sam went to school for a while and then helped his father in the tanyard, but by September he was working as a tender at the factory where the five Stangers and the two Shoughs still were the blowers. William Linthicum and John Keen, who later became blowers, now were only apprentices.

To many Americans the War of 1812 was a remote event, with no threat of personal danger. But not so to 12-year-old Sam. In 1813 the British blockaded Delaware Bay with a dragnet to keep American vessels from Philadelphia and Jersey ports from trading with Napoleon's France and its satellites. So close were the English to Port Elizabeth that Sam heard the guns of their ships roar. Not only that, the enemy swooped down in landing-party raids and carried off neighboring cattle and fowl. Jerseyans became as jittery as they had been over Tory and Refugee guerrilla attacks during the Revolution, in 1813 a fresh raw memory along the Delaware. A cry went out for succor, and Gloucester County sent down a whole army of militiamen to drive the hated English from the South Jersey coast. Quickly, depredations ceased.

But trouble of another sort loomed at Port Elizabeth. In retrospect we know that on November 5, 1814, a Bridgeton court ordered division of the Union Glass Works into four equal shares. But it must have come as a shock to young Sam to learn in June of 1814 that the company, which for some time had had a change in ownership, was being dissolved. As to causes, we need scarcely seek beyond fire losses, costs of rebuilding, and the wartime depreciation of American currency. This was the second time the Stangers had endured the panic of currency inflation.

Workers now left for other jobs; some of the Stangers may have gone to Malaga where Christian Stanger had started a glassworks in 1810. But Jacob Stanger and William Shough retained one part of the Union Glass Works and built a small furnace of four pots. The two partners and Shough's son Daniel were the only blowers in the autumn of 1814. Young Huffsey must have considered himself lucky to be included as helper.

But disaster descended with the new year. Late in January of 1815 Sam's father died of typhus. His wife Sarah, in delicate health herself, was left with five young children to support, none of them old enough to run the tanyard. In desperation Sarah offered three of her children to be bound out: Rebecca and John to Jonathan Dallas, and Margaret to Job Hugh. Sam, more fortunate, was at last apprenticed to the factory to learn "the art and mystery of blowing hollow ware glass."

During the ensuing year, however, he must have been absent often because of illness, for in February of 1816 he was discharged, the reason stated as sickness. William Linthicum was given Sam's job and his apprenticeship forfeited, with a penalty of $500, a terrible blow to a poverty-stricken family.

At this time the Union Works had become two separately owned furnaces, both of six pots, *under one roof.* Abraham Reeves, Randall Marshall's father-in-law, had been taken into the Stanger-Shough partnership and the blowers were Samuel Focer, Adolph Button, Daniel and Samuel Lutz and Stephen Reeves. The other furnace was owned by Randall Marshall, who had as blowers his son Thomas Marshall, John Turner, John Collect, Jeremiah Carter and John Keen, Sam's special friend. In true Alger tradition, Sam, out of desperate courage after his discharge, got a job at the Marshall furnace, not as apprentice but as blower. Marshall, however, drove a stiff bargain, Stewart notes: the pay was 75 cents a gross.

The year 1816 must have been a terrifying one for the sickly Widow Huffsey. "There was a spot on the sun and frost every month throughout that summer. The crops failed, the people were alarmed, and corn was worth $1.75 to $2.00 a bushel." But in September Sam was back working for Marshall, at the same wages.

During this period Marshall had also moved one of the original furnaces to the edge of Tuckahoe, 12 miles east, a place that soon prospered and came to be known as Marshallville Glass Works. At least two Stangers—Frederick and Philip—became associated with it, and Frederick married Marshall's daughter Ann, who lived for only three years after the marriage.

In the summer of 1817 a new company was formed at Port Elizabeth, the Eagle Glass Factory, destined to become a famous name in South Jersey glass because of the Getsinger brothers who owned it from 1831 to 1846. But in 1817 the glassmen were William Shough, William Riggins and Ollie Parks.

At a still lower wage, 62½ cents a gross, Sam Huffsey went to work for the Eagle Glass Company, but as winter approached the place had gone out of business under that management. Sam then went to blow at an 8-pot furnace, the name not mentioned.

Great Britain's trade policies were now wreaking as much havoc with the American economy as her guns had upon the national capital in the War of 1812. The rejected mother-country was flooding the United States with well made, low priced, irresistible merchandise of every kind. Home industry, having expanded tremendously during the war, was demoralized by this glut of goods. No Americans now wanted "free trade" if it meant free entry of English articles. At last recognizing the danger, Washington lawmakers by April of 1816 had established tariffs, moderate for the most part, on many English imports. But the glass business was doomed, for lack of a protective tariff, Stewart notes. One by one, the fires in the marginal glasshouses were quenched.

The year 1818 undoubtedly marked the closing of one era of virtuoso glassmaking that began with the first four skilled gaffers imported by the Wistars—Johan Wentzel, Caspar and Johan Halter and Simeon Kreismayer—and continued as the Stanger family flourished at Glassboro after the Revolution, then rose to new heights at Port Elizabeth as the Stangers, whose whole life was glassblowing, taught their sons and grandsons the

PLATE 10

TRUMPET-SHAPED amber vases with light green pedestals, applied and tooled. H. 6 3/4 inches. *George Horace Lorimer collection. Philadelphia Museum of Art.*

STIEGEL-TYPE FLASKS of non-lead glass. Blue pocket-bottle has 18 swirled rib, shows much wear. H. 4 3/4 inches. Swirled amethyst flask also has inverted diamond pattern; attributed to Emil J. Larson, Vineland, 1930s. H. 5 5/8 inches.

CEREMONIAL GOBLET, emerald green, has scattered bubbles and striae. Remarkably harmonious proportions. Applied baluster stem has two entrapped air bubbles and a hollow knop. Circular foot with edge folded upward. H. 11 3/4 inches. MINISCULE GOBLET, lampwork by Walter Breeden.

UNIQUE PAIR of South Jersey style candlesticks are aqua with sapphire bases, their intricately tooled stems set on a wide inverted foot. C. 1850–1860. *George Horace Lorimer collection. Philadelphia Museum of Art.*

PLATE 11

FINESSE is displayed by an unknown gaffer who combined rich amber with clear glass for handle, lilypad decoration, crimped foot and rings of this impressive pitcher. H. 7 3/8 inches.

TRANSMUTED from molten glass to ice-like sculpture, this white-looped aquamarine pitcher conveys strength in every aspect, from the curving sheared lip and arching handle to the platform base. H. 7½ inches. *Crawford Wettlaufer collection.*

secrets of the old-world art. Sam Huffsey was indeed fortunate to have been apprenticed to those great gaffers—the Stangers.

But proficient though he had become, by 1818 Sam was ready to concede defeat: there were no jobs for glassblowers; so, like his brother and his sister Becky, he went to work as "help" for Jonathan Dallas. Although he received no wages, only bed, board, clothing, and his mother's house rent, Sam, apparently having no choice, stayed on here until he came of age,—April 5, 1822. Dallas, a Quaker of fine character, gave Sam "good advice and example."

Eager to try a new vocation, the youth now shipped for two months with a Captain Chance who sailed between Port Elizabeth and Philadelphia. Then the boy did a stint as team-driver for the Widow Sanders near Tuckahoe. But as hoar-frost settled on the cranberry bogs, almost a signal for the start-up of glass fires, Sam and his friend John Collect were lured to the Hammonton Glassworks where William Coffin, Sr., and Jonathan Haines operated a 6-pot hollow-ware furnace and an 8-pot window-light furnace.

Coffin had come to this piney wilderness in 1812 from Green Bank on the Mullica and out of wartime success had created the flourishing settlement of Hammonton. But in 1822 he and his partner Haines were paying blowers only 25 cents a gross, the lowest wage that Huffsey seems to have recorded. His friend John Keen was blowing bottles here but the names of other workmen are new to us: Jesse Zane, John Able, William Wallace, Joseph Able, Frederick Stockley and William Woodward.

In the excess production as a result of the War of 1812, there arose a veritable tidal wave of whiskey and other distilled liquors, so great that the problem became one of blowing enough demijohns and flasks to hold the potent liquids. Of customers there was no shortage, especially when the flasks were made alluring with fighting slogans and faces of virile patriots.

Some of the most artistically designed bottles in the entire roster of American collectors' flasks came from the Hammonton Glassworks. It is reasonable to assume that the comradely trio, Sam Huffsey, John Keen and John Collect, experienced bottle-blowers as they had become, fashioned some of the mold-blown Hammonton flasks now among historic rarities.

As Huffsey's mother had a few months earlier moved to Philadelphia, on Front Street below Vine, he joined her there in the summer of 1823, doing such odd jobs as mowing grass on Hog Island and working in a lumberyard. But in autumn he returned to bottle-blowing at Hammonton, where he stayed until May, 1824. That summer he worked on vessels in the port of Philadelphia and in August took passage on one to visit his brother in Port Elizabeth.

Perhaps out of that brotherly confab arose an important decision. For on his return to Philadelphia Sam went to work as a blower for the bottle tycoon—"Dr." Thomas W. Dyott of Dyottville in Kensington, Pa.,—and by December Brother John was working there too.

That incredible personage Dr. Dyott tacked an M.D. after his name to make the pharmaceutical contents of his vials seem more therapeutic. He was primarily in the drug business and only secondarily in the bottle business, but for a time he did astonishingly well on both counts, and even on a third, the manufacture of fancy liquor flasks.

Today the initials "T.W.D." on the bottom of a flask will put a covetous glitter in the eyes of a collector, but "T.W.D." was the mark of the seller. Likely as not the maker was Sam Huffsey or John Collect or John Keen or Sam Lutz or Frederick Stockley, all of whom followed Sam to work as blowers at Dyottville, then a humming model town of two glass factories with eight pots in each. Other Huffsey associates, presumably Jerseyans, were Johnson Beckett, James Hay, John Sutton, Christian Pot, and Daniel Lutz.

These blowers, not to mention the famous Dr. Dyott, were all set for a great event that took place on September 27, 1824, in nearby Philadelphia—the return of America's hero, General Lafayette, to receive his due as the savior of the newborn republic. The blowers dropped their pipes and to a man joined the crowd on Frankford road to hail the procession headed by Lafayette and his son. Samuel Huffsey wrote that he had a good view. He and his fellow workers must have puffed with pride as they thought of the Lafayette flasks blown for the state occasion.

Fleeting was the glassblowers' fame, though, for one of these historic Dyottville flasks with Lafayette's portrait on one side and an eagle on the reverse bears the mark "T.W.D." This bottle Dyott advertised in September, 1824. Another Lafayette-eagle pint flask (both are now comparatively scarce) has the impressed words "Republican Gratitude" and "E Pluribus Unum." Here T.W.D.'s fame is cemented with the words "Kensington Glass Works Philadelphia."

The first known advertisement in which American flasks can be identified appeared in Philadelphia newspapers in March 1822 and, according to Helen McKearin, featured three of Dyott's bottles: one showing an American eagle on both sides; another, a Masonic-agricultural flask; and a third flask with the 74-gun frigate *Franklin,* and the pre-war slogan, FREE TRADE AND SAILORS' RIGHTS.

Surely, the latter Dyott bottle is proof that he was selling historic flasks long before 1822, more likely in 1815, for that was the year the ship *Franklin* was launched at Philadelphia and "Free Trade" was still a rallying cry. Even in 1815 when the war had come to a close and trade *was* free again the phrase was obsolete and in another year had become anathema because by then "free trade" signified British goods coming in free of duty at American ports and hurting American manufactures. When Dyott advertised these flasks as late as 1822 he was probably hoping to unload war-surplus on the uninformed but thirsty.

From this distance, the year that Sam Huffsey spent at Dyottville appears to have been one of his happiest. He stayed there until 1827 and then left only because Solomon Stanger brought up a thorny problem. But to go back a bit . . .

In March of 1825 one Theopholis Holmes showed three young ladies the process of glassmaking at the celebrated community of Dyottville. Was Sam Huffsey a star blower on this tour? It's pleasant to think that he was, for about a year later, June 8, 1826, he married one of the patently impressed young ladies—Mary A. Hoffman.

Pharmaceutical vials were still the staple, and for blowing these Sam was receiving 40 cents a gross. But, accomplished as he was, during the summer of '26 he built an 8-pot furnace, let's hope at extra compensation, for Dyott.

Blowers now besides Sam and his brother, who had moved ahead rapidly, were

Johnson and William Beckett, John Collect, David Focer, William and Robert Wallace, John Laden, Joseph Linthicum, Adam Baldwin, and, surprisingly, Solomon Stanger.

For about two and a half years Sam Huffsey had apparently been blowing glass agreeably enough every day of the week while the Dyottville furnaces were in seasonal blast—September to June 1. But now in March of 1827 Solomon Stanger and he called a meeting to discuss the impropriety of blowing glass on Sunday as was the prevailing custom—except where the religious Stangers blew. Tycoon Dyott was adamant, and with some reason, for no one had devised a way to bank the fires for so long a time. As frequent start-ups from a cold furnace could bankrupt a glassworks, Dyott refused to change the custom, and eight of the 30 employees, including Solomon and Sam, felt obliged to leave.

By this time Huffsey evidently had considerable reputation as a glass gaffer, for two months later he was offered a silent partnership in a going concern at Millville owned by Dr. George Burgin, a Philadelphian, Richard L. Wood, a leading industrialist of Millville, and Joel Bodine, who would become one of New Jersey's most successful glass manufacturers. Sam accepted with the proviso that glass would not be blown on Sundays.

Like a Pied Piper he brought with him good Jersey blowers he had known elsewhere: John Collect, of course, and Johnson Beckett with his son William, David Focer, William and Robert Wallace, Joseph D. Able, Thomas Haines, Jeremiah Carter, William Woodward and William Smith. A new 8-pot furnace was set up and went into blast by Sept. 1, 1827.

A week later came a crushing blow. Sam's younger sister Sarah was dead. In November Sam himself was taken deathly sick. His doctor advised him to wind up all his earthly affairs. Fearing the worst, Sam did so, making an agreement with Dr. Burgin to sell his interest at the close of the blast. Miraculously, Sam began to improve and by January was at work again. Perhaps feeling that a miracle had indeed occurred, he began to attend the Methodist church and was converted to Methodism by a local clergyman named Josiah Shaw. From this time on Huffsey's diary is much concerned with religion.

In June of 1828 he received $400—no small sum then—for his interest in the Millville factory, which he loaned to his mother-in-law in Philadelphia. Inexplicably, he returned to Millville to blow glass at 48 cents a gross.

In the summer of 1829 he and some friends made a trip to New York in a sailing vessel, a voyage of three days. That September he was blowing for William Coffin, Jr., Dr. Burgin and R.L. Wood at Millville.

Perhaps recalling happier years, he moved back to Kensington in June of 1830 to work for Dyott again. Here he joined the Old Brick Church, became a class leader and was prospering enough to build himself a house on Wood Street.

No doubt about it: life in Philadelphia then was more exciting than in South Jersey. In June of 1832 President Andrew Jackson rode through the city in a frenetic re-election campaign. Although none of the known Andrew Jackson flasks bears the Dyottville or Kensington imprints, it seems unlikely that Dr. Dyott, catering to a mass market as he did, would have passed up a chance to honor the Hero of New Orleans and spokesman for the people.

A few days after Old Hickory had stirred up the town the Indian war prisoners, Chief Black Hawk and his son, sparked even more excitement. Far from acting or being treated like the prisoner he was, Black Hawk, in the words of New York's sophisticated ex-Mayor Philip Hone, "was the order of the day." In Manhattan the Indians arrived by steamboat and there had marveled at a balloon ascension. In Philadelphia Black Hawk and his entourage were privileged to witness the mysteries of glassblowing at Dyottville and were given some glass bottles.

The summer offered further attractions for Sam. In July he attended a Methodist camp meeting at Vincentown, N.J., whither he went by small boat, ascending Rancocas Creek. Arrived there he lived in a tent. By September he was ready to report again for duty with Dyott, at 45 cents a gross. Glasshouse No. 2 where he worked with 15 other blowers was one of four which, together with tenants' houses, stores, schools and other buildings, were spread over nearly 400 acres along the Delaware. Dyottville was now famous as a model town.

Again in September of 1833 Huffsey was working for the patent-medicine king. But now blowing at the No. 1 glasshouse, Sam found that most of his fellow workers were boy apprentices, a foretaste of gloom to come. In December Dyott called all hands together at the schoolhouse and announced dire news: he was having financial troubles. Money was tight and there was no market for glass.

Dyott was not the only one financially embarrassed. Nationwide, business was beginning to feel the pincers, for this was the prelude to the dreadful Panic of 1837. Even now, on December 27, 1833, rich Philip Hone wrote with prescience in *his* diary: "The holidays are gloomy; the weather is bad; the times are bad; stocks are falling; and a panic prevails which will result in bankruptcies and ruin in many quarters where a few short weeks since, the sun of prosperity shone with unusual brightness. It will be worse before it is better."

Promoter Dyott apparently made working for him without cash wages seem more attractive than looking for work elsewhere; or perhaps he offered the men credit at the company store, as was customary when glassmen were short of cash and "shinplasters." For a while most of the hands stayed on. But the situation soon became intolerable. At the end of the spring blast Huffsey received Dyott's note for $100 in lieu of cash. As Dyott's paper money stated that his Manual Labor Bank was backed by capital of $500,000 his note must have seemed secure, but one doubts if Sam ever collected. Dyott, nevertheless, went right on expanding, on credit.

In 1838 after the terrible panic. Dyott was convicted of fraudulent bankruptcy. The resilient type, he later got back into the tonic business, despite a previous prison term.

Now in July of 1834 Sam Huffsey and his brother-in-law Joseph Linthicum made the momentous decision to cross the Alleghenies and go to Pittsburgh, to blow glass for William McCully who today is noted as a manufacturer of historical flasks and medicine bottles.

The unbelievable ordeal in 1834 of moving from Philadelphia to Pittsburgh, a distance of 300 miles across the Alleghenies today, comes through in Huffsey's notes of his journey over the "Main Line of Public Works of Pennsylvania," predecessor of the Pennsylvania Railroad. A bizarre system of transport but a daring conception for its day, it required frequent transfers between mule-drawn canal boats and fragile railroad cars looking like stagecoaches. The latter had to be hauled up and down, by cables and a stationary steam

Fig. 91 Canal boats transfer at Hollidaysburg, Pa., 1840.

engine, over frightening inclined planes in order to cross the mountains. Barber and Howe record that the first canal boat did not travel over the inclined planes of the Portage Railroad until October of 1834. Yet here in mid-July Sam and his party of seven were preparing to embark on the hazardous trip.

On Monday July 14 the travelers shipped their household goods out on the Schuylkill river via canal boat. At six the next morning Sam and his wife Mary were at the Columbia Railroad Hotel near Fairmount Park where the train for the west left at 9 a.m. The cars moved rapidly and when they reached the Columbia inclined plane were drawn up it by steam power. At the plane's summit the carriages traveled with great speed to Lancaster, then clattered on to Columbia which they reached at 7 p.m. After stopping here for supper, at 8:30 of a bright pleasant evening the travelers boarded a canal boat drawn by two mules driven by a boy on the towpath. At six the next morning they arrived at the Harrisburg dock and had time to tour the state capitol buildings before their boat left at 10 a.m.

For a couple of days Huffsey neglected his journal but on July 19 he noted that at 7 a.m. they had arrived at Hollidaysburg, with time to leave the boat and get into railroad cars that would take them across the mountains. When the cars reached the foot of the first inclined plane the conductor informed passengers that there had recently been several serious accidents. These were indeed serious; cables sometimes broke and cars were hurtled down the steep slopes. Some travelers got out and climbed to the summit on learning of the danger. But the members of Huffsey's party decided to take the risk and remained in the cars.

Fig. 92 The railroad through Lancaster, Pa., when Sam Huffsey journeyed to Pittsburgh.

After successfully traveling up and down five inclined planes the group reached the crest of the Alleghenies about 1 p.m. Here they took dinner and admired the view at the Summit House, then returned to the cars to face five more inclined planes on the west side of the mountains. These too were crossed without mishap and by 7 p.m. the passengers were safe in Johnstown, 104 miles from Pittsburgh, Sam noted. That same evening they embarked on the final canal boat.

Sunday morning the Huffseys arose at 5 a.m. and gave thanks to the Almighty. That night after prayer they retired at 9 p.m. And lo, the next morning at 10 a.m. July 21 they were in Pittsburgh. A 6-day journey from Philadelphia!

The prospect seems to have pleased. The household goods arrived five days later, and Sam rented part of a house from William McCalvey of Bayardstown. Blowing started earlier, August 18, in this cooler climate.

Of the names of 15 blowers listed by Huffsey as working at McCully's 7-pot furnace, at least five—Huffsey and his brother John, his brother-in-law Joseph Linthicum, David Focer and James Foicer—point directly to the influence of the Glassboro-Stanger tradition on Pittsburgh glass, which in turn spread down the Ohio and Mississippi valleys where their wares were marketed. David Focer who had worked with Sam in Dyottville was a member of the Stanger clan, and Foicer was a variation of the name. Other blowers listed may also have been Jerseyans: Daniel Evans, George Anffort, George Upperman, Benjamin Hess, John Hagna, Daniel Sheppard, James McCurdy, William Duffy, Joseph Davis and Charles Spencer.

When the furnace went out of blast in May, 1835, Sam contracted to blow vials for another season at 50 cents a gross but his brother returned to Philadelphia. In the fruit-basket-upset procedure of glassmaking then, another Jerseyman Joseph D. Able (whom we met at Millville) joined the Pittsburgh group, as did David Springer.

By spring of 1836 the cost of living had become exorbitant. In Manhattan rents rose 50 per cent, Mayor Philip Hone wrote; beef was 25 cents a pound, small turkeys cost $1.50 a piece. The combination of high prices and low fixed wages prevailed as well in cities like Pittsburgh and Philadelphia. The plight of workers and the unemployed became so desperate that in February there were violent riots in New York City where stevedores and other waterfront workers struck for higher wages. They were quickly joined by mobs of hungry men from other occupations. Manhattan's mayor responded swiftly by calling out armed troops who carted ringleaders off to jail.

In May the kettle was about to bubble over again and in June even journeymen tailors, reaching the boiling point, tried to organize a trade-union. At City Hall Park on June 6 a vast crowd of New Yorkers assembled in response to an anonymous handbill depicting a coffin:

> THE RICH AGAINST THE POOR . . . the freemen of the North are now on a level with the slaves of the South! Twenty of your brethren have been found guilty for presuming to resist reduction of their wages ! and Judge Edwards has charged an American jury, and agreeably to that charge, they have established the precedent that workingmen have no right to regulate the price of labour, or in other words, the rich are the only judges of the wants of the poor man . . . On Monday, the liberty of the workingmen will be interred . . . Let the courtroom, the City Hall, yea ! the whole park, be filled with *mourners;* but remember, offer no violence to Judge Edwards, bend meekly, and receive the chain wherewith you are to be bound. Keep the peace! Above all things, keep the peace!

Glass gaffers did not have even such seeds of union plants until the late 19th century. In Huffsey's day a glassblower's only alternative to low pay and long hours of hazardous work was to change jobs. On the very day of the New York "union" meeting, one of the earliest, Sam Huffsey left Pittsburgh and took the slow canal boat back to Kensington on the Delaware.

But not to blow glass. To open a grocery store in his own house. To change an occupation that he had struggled so hard to master must have meant that Huffsey was thoroughly disillusioned with its rewards. It is probable too that his health, delicate like that of his mother and sisters, was declining.

The opening of the new year, 1837, was bitter. Sam's longtime friend John Keen was buried that day. This was the year of the Great Panic that toppled fabulous fortunes. By May the New York and Philadelphia banks had suspended payment to their depositors, as raging crowds milled around the barred doors. Of 850 United States banks, 343 closed their doors permanently, swallowing up the capital of rich and poor alike. Suffering was intense among the unemployed and those whose savings had been wiped out.

Even the Huffsey grocery store did not furnish a living, and so that year Sam bought a horse and market-wagon to peddle food from door to door. But people just weren't eating, that is, not to amount to anything. In December of the dreadful year of 1837, Sam sold his team.

Just when times could not get any worse, Sam and his brother-in-law Linthicum were offered the chance, no doubt because they were excellent craftsmen, to blow glass at Green Bank, for Nicholas Sooy and Sooy Thompson, at a wage of 50 cents a gross. At this 8-pot furnace Sam's colleagues from happier days, William Woodward and John Collect, were with him again. Other blowers were Nicholas and Charles Griner, Bartly Rhinear, Noel Mesick, William Peacock, Mager Clark, and James and Michael Earley.

The depression carried over into 1838, but still, wages were not so low for Sam as they had been while working for the Coffins. October found him in Millville blowing at 45 cents a gross for William Scattergood, Haverstick & Co., predecessors of the famous Whitall Tatum & Co. Scattergood had more than one house, the 8-pot furnace of the one where Sam blew, having these other workers: William Reed, Joel and Every Mesick, Daniel Barrett, Isaac and Enos Sutton and Watson Gale.

Times in 1839 weren't much more promising when Sam and his wife Mary moved in with his uncle George Gale at nearby Bridgeton. Here Sam got a job with the important glass factory of Stratton, Buck & Co. Working at 40 cents a gross, Joseph and William Linthicum joined Sam, but otherwise the blowers are new names: Samuel Dotton, Thomas Read, James Cox, John Christ, Hiram Duffel, Thomas Broadwater and Thomas Kingkade.

In April of 1840 Sam's only remaining sister, Margaret Faunce, was buried in Kensington. Sam stayed on at Stratton Buck for the 1840-1 blast, for which new blowers were Daniel and Samuel Dawson and Nuh (sic) Early.

The year, 1841-1842 marked not only the death of John Buck but also of his glassworks. On March 1 a fire in the packing house made a molten worthless mass of about $10,000 of finished glassware. The fire finished Sam Huffsey's job as well. He moved back to Philadelphia, into a new frame house.

Sam's fortunes, though, were on the toboggan. He went to work again for his one-time partner, Dr. Burgin (where, we do not know, but probably in the Philadelphia area) at the ignominious rate of 25 cents a gross. Other unlucky blowers at this wage were Henry Faunce, Nicholas Griner, William Young, Michael Christ, James Christy, Robert McCurdy, George Heffer, Daniel Hill, Jacob Smith and John Johnson.

Though plainly a seasoned gaffer by this time Sam in the summer of 1842 had to make do with odd jobs. He fashioned some tools for Henry B. Rapp at Dyottville, after Dyott had failed.

At age 42 Sam must have felt he was growing old for that was when he bought his first pair of spectacles, silver, which cost him $1.50. At that time he was reduced to making packing boxes for Rapp.

In June of 1844 Huffsey joined the Native American Party, a fateful step. Meantime, a proficient furnace-builder, he built one in July of 1845 for John M. Scott & Company.

Once more Huffsey went to work for Dr. Burgin in the autumn of 1846, at 30 cents a gross. But in April he had to give up glassblowing because of poor health.

The end of Samuel Huffsey's known journal is not sad, however. He went to a glassblowers' heaven: he was elected a tax collector in Kensington on the new party ticket!

Continuing his journal he records that his mother died September 15, 1848, and was buried in Kensington, that his brother-in-law and life-long friend Joseph Linthicum died at Millville July 26, 1852, and that the collapse of a hitherto unchronicled glass factory at Progress, N.J., in April, 1855, killed four blowers and injured others.

The rest of 400 pages of Huffsey's diary deal mostly with church affairs, Stewart writes, a statement that creates an intriguing mystery.

The astonishing fact is that although during the past century two quite different types of calabash flasks have turned up with the words S. HUFFSEY or GLASS WORK'S / S. HUFFSEY blown into the bottles, until now no writer about glass has named a definite locale for his furnace. One style of these 3-pint calabashes labeled S. HUFFSEY shows a bas-relief of an impressive 2-story factory, a symbolic portrait, though, for nearly the same design appears on authentic Whitney calabashes.

Just where was Sam Huffsey's glasshouse? From my research all signs point to Millford, N.J. But which Millford? In the 1850s there were two such hamlets (sometimes spelled Milford). The one with which Huffsey was concerned is surely that which straddled the borderline of Burlington and Camden counties—as there had been an earlier glasshouse here called the Pendleton Glass Works.*

As volume of mail multiplied in Jersey, the Federal post office decided that two Millfords were too many so the now historic one had its name changed to Kresson. On highway 73 about three miles south of Route 70, Kresson looks as modern as chrome, and as defiant to archeological research. But oldtime glassworkers in the Medford area staunchly assert that Millford was the site of Huffsey's works.

The Philadelphia directory of 1850 lists S. Huffsey as a glassblower, but two years later he is named as a seller of glassware. This, however, was probably only incidental to his association with John S. Huffsey & Company which had a sales office for glassware at 50 North Fourth Street, Philadelphia. An 1852 advertisement tells that they were agents for the Atlantic Glass Company at Crowleytown and the Millford Glass Works at Millford.

Because of the portraits on two S. Huffsey flasks we can pin down their dates as being between 1850 and about 1852. One, a 3-pint calabash showing a bust of Jenny Lind, "The Swedish Nightingale" whom that prince of pitchmen, P.T. Barnum, ballyhooed for an American tour, appeared no earlier than 1850. For six months before the singer arrived on September 4, to a tumultous welcome at Manhattan's Battery Park, Barnum was plastering her name and image all over the United States. To honor the occasion at least six glass-houses created flasks with Jenny Lind portraits.

The Jenny Lind calabash blown at the S. Huffsey works shows her in a three-quarter view, facing left and wearing a bertha or cape-like collar with a centered brooch. Surrounding her is a wreath of laurel and above, the words, JENNY LIND. After reading Sam Huffsey's journal of quaint spellings it is fascinating to discover that the famous Whitney Glass Works issued a similar calabash with the singer's name recorded for immortality as JENY LIND. The reverse of the Huffsey flask shows smoke pouring to the right from the chimney, a slanting tree to the right, and a shrub to the left of the building—not very different from the Whitney calabash. But the latter is *ribbed.* Above the glass house is the

*Named for the town of Pendleton, the previous name for Millford, Pendleton Glass Works was built by Matthias Simmerman and associates after their Free Will Manufactory at Williamstown changed hands in 1837. Just before Huffsey became the operator, about 1850, the owners were Lippincott, Wisham & Company.

Fig. 93 LOUIS KOSSUTH looking like a Spanish conquistador arises from four furled banners on this calabash (GI-112). Reverse shows a side-wheeler steaming left. Embossed on waves: U.S. STEAM / FRIGATE / MISSISSIPPI / S. HUFFSEY. Latter's name also on top arc of paddle-wheel. Oval on base names PH. DOFLEIN / MOULD MAKER / NTH. 5t St 84 (of Philadelphia). Quart, reported in aqua and dark olive, emerald and yellow greens. Huffsey Glass Works, Milford, c. 1851. *Photo, Corning Museum of Glass.*

Fig. 94 KOSSUTH calabash attributed to Huffsey Glass Works has portrait and name of Hungarian patriot of the 1850s. Medium green, quart. McK. GI-113. Tree in foliage is reverse of Kossuth GI-113.

name S. HUFFSEY. Below, are the words: GLASS WORK'S, a significant misspelling.

In 1941 the McKearins rated the S. Huffsey Lind flask as common, meaning that 150 or more were thought to exist then. Now, many of these calabashes have gone into private collections; today it would be rare to find one in the open market. Specimens have been found in deep blue-green, olive-yellow, light yellow-green, and dark yellow-green, as well as olive. Only one specimen is known in blue, in the Corning Museum of Glass.

The other marked S. HUFFSEY flask, comparatively scarce (75 to 150 believed to exist), bears the portrait of another nineteenth century celebrity, Louis Kossuth, a hero of the Hungarian Revolution of 1848 against Austria and her ally Czarist Russia, in some ways a counterpart of the Hungarian uprising against the Russian Communists a century later.

In the revolt of 1848-50 thousands of Magyars were executed or imprisoned, but many managed to flee to England or the United States. Still close to their own wars for freedom, Americans quickly identified with the oppressed Hungarians. When one of their leaders, Louis Kossuth, his family and some 50 other patriots took perilous refuge in Turkey, the Sultan threatened to hold them prisoner for a year, but the clamor from America was so strong that at length the Turkish despot changed his mind. The United States sent its frigate *Mississippi* steaming across the ocean to bring the refugees to a free climate. Kossuth himself stopped off in London for 10 months but by the time he landed at Staten Island for a hero's welcome, souvenir-makers were ready for the event. Strangely, only New Jersey glasshouses seem to have produced Kossuth mementoes, or at least only theirs are known to have survived.

Of the few types of Kossuth bottles, two of the most appealing are attributed to the S. Huffsey Glass Works. But the moldmaker of one calabash is definitely known, as he carved his oval trademark into the iron: PH. DOFLEIN MOULD MAKER NTH. 5t. St. 84. This was Philip Doflein, a German mold-maker, one of the best, at 84 N. Fifth St. Philadelphia. As Doflein made molds for many famous Kensington and Dyottville flasks and South Jersey glass it is easy to see how Huffsey obtained his services. The attractive design shows Kossuth, caped and epauletted, wearing a plumed hat in conquistador style, a fashion that really grabbed the youth of the day. The hero arises from four furled flags, one with seven stars. Above his dashing likeness are the words LOUIS KOSSUTH. The reverse depicts the rescue ship with both masts and paddle wheel, churning the waves; beneath the vessel, the words U.S. STEAM FRIGATE MISSISSIPPI / S. HUFFSEY. And lest we forget, on the upper curve of the ship's paddle wheel, again: S. HUFFSEY.

Sam was no longer just a blower. He was now a capitalist.

The pioneer in the lore of historical flasks, Edwin Atlee Barber, wrote that in 1896 he actually located Philip Doflein at the age of 80 in Philadelphia and he had shown the author the metal mold for Huffsey's Kossuth flask made in 1851. But having done this fine piece of detective work, Barber went on to state in error that Huffsey's glasshouse was in Camden, a misunderstanding that might have arisen if Doflein had said the location was Camden county, which was true.

There is a certain Jenny Lind calabash with blown-in lettering: MILLFORA G. WORK'S. Barber did not attribute it to Huffsey, but merely suggested the name might have been intended as Millford (with no reference to New Jersey). Nor do the McKearins relate the Millfora Jenny Lind to Huffsey.

Putting the Millfora calabash and the Huffsey flask side by side it is plain to see that the two are identical in size and design, except for the name of the works. Even the misspelling of WORK'S is identical, the only recorded flasks that match in this respect. After reading Huffsey's phonetic spelling, it's even likely that he heard "Millford" as "Millfora," then changed the name when the error was called to his attention.

On May 31, 1856, while Sam Huffsey may still have owned it, the Millford Glass Works was bought at sheriff's sale for $4,900 by Joseph Iszard. Under the name Samuel Iszard & Company, the plant operated for a brief period, then failed some time before 1860.

But if the "Millfora" glass works closed down after only a few years of production, this is not the last we hear of Sam Huffsey. In 1867 he was living at 2018 Belgrade Street in Philadelphia where a directory lists him as a glass dealer.

Then approaching "threescore and ten," he had survived disheartening times, both national and personal, and could congratulate himself as a seasoned glass gaffer whose name was emblazoned on historic flasks.

The Estells of Estell Manor

LIKE NOCTURNAL MISTS rising from South Jersey's iron bogs and salt marshes, the aura of early times transpires from yellowed letters to Daniel E. Estell, who was a seventh generation of Huguenot Estells in America and who owned Estellville Glass Works and made it prosper from 1834 for some two decades.

John H. Scott, a landowner in the coastal region of what was then Gloucester county, in 1825 built this works on Stephens branch of the Great Egg Harbor river, for the purpose of making hollow ware and window-glass but by 1834 he had sold out to Estell.

Owning thousands of acres of woodlands, even much-prized cedar, the Estells were deemed rich by the lesser folk. But to own and to profit from were two different states, as this letter of "11 month 13. 1824" from Salem, N.J., indicates:

> Respt Friend:
> Danl E Estell
> Your favour 11th is now before me and I can only say in reply that sap lumber is one of the greatest *drugs* in our market. If you could make it convenient to send us a load of Hard boards of good quality we should be pleased to exchange corn for them—Corn (old) is worth 37½ to 40 cts, new—35 cts. The last hard board we paid 18$ for but at that price they must be good—Danny how goes the Election—After all our exertions for John Quincy the labour was fruitless—owing to the stupidity of eastern citizens. I know not what your sentiments may be but *Huzza* for *Old Hickory* let him go—from late accts in *he goes* by the people
> Yours in haist
> Joseph E. P. Rowe

Clearly the writer was satirical in his huzzahs for the people's hero, Andrew Jackson.

Like many another Huguenot the original Estells were French Protestants who had been driven out of France to safety in England from persecution by Catholics. The first Estell in America was more fortunate than most of his compatriots in receiving as an individual, rather than for a colony, huge land grants from the English Crown. Documents attest to such grants from George I and Queen Anne to Estells in the Great Egg Harbor region and George II is said to have dispensed still more land to the family. By Daniel Estell's time the property was a vast estate of 6,000 to 8,000 acres. Reason for the imprecise figure is that the English kings had no conception of the country they were giving away to speed settlement. Grants often overlapped leading to lawsuits, as occurred early in the 20th century over hundreds of acres once in the Estell domain.

As early as the mid-1700s the Estells had built an impressive 2-story house that still today is in use, as the clubhouse for the privately owned South River Game Preserve in the modern village of Estell Manor.

As is obvious from old letters, Daniel was an energetic and successful businessman, often addressed as "merchant", even before he owned the glassworks. His half brother John, who soon bought a share in the furnace, had already established a thriving trade, as John Estell & Son, in whatever the coastal area needed, a region including two other glassmaking towns: Marshallville and Port Elizabeth.

A billhead shows John Estell & Son buying iron pots from nearby Etna Furnace, for which the following prices were paid: $4.08 for each 34-inch iron kettle, $2.64 each for 22-inch pot, and $1.08 each for 9-inch pots.

Iron blowpipes were not made, evidently, at furnaces like nearby Weymouth and Etna, but by itinerant blacksmiths, as this letter tells, from Winslow, August 27, 1839. The writer is a dropper of then famous names: J. R. Stanger. Addressed to Daniel Estell at Stephens Creek, the letter reads:

> Dear Sir: I understood a few days ago you wanted a Blacksmith to do your glafs house work and if you do i wish you would write and let me know immediately and i will come down and see you as i expect to move in about ten days and have not made up my mind where i shall go to any certainty. I am particularly acquainted with your kind of work as i have worked about a glafs house several years. For reference call on J R Stanger as he is well acquainted with me and worked on pipes of my make
>
> from your fr
> Jacob Sailer

By the next year Daniel Estell must have been discouraged, for there was this letter, and after all, the period was after the grim Panic of 1837. The letter of April 21, 1840, came from John Hartman of Philadelphia:

> Mr. Daniel Estell, Stephens Creek, N.J.
> Dr. Sir: You told me when I saw you last that you would rent your factory. If you are still in the same mind I wish you would let me know the conditions. If you rent the factory I suppose you will let the store with it. I have some idea of going into the business and I see no disadvantage in . . . your factory for making Glafs. Write when you receive this.

Daniel Estell's answer assuredly was no, because the glassworks continued, albeit in a state where there was almost no exchange of cash. In its more successful days, the Estellville Glass Works issued printed "shinplasters" like those of other South Jersey glass factories, but for a long period there are quantities of notes for bushels of corn, indicating that the people depended largely on cornmeal and suppawn, a cornmeal mush, instead of wheat as a staple.

Random sampling of 36 such notes shows they were made out in amounts from 1 to 30 bushels of corn, and usually in this fashion to Mr. David P. Simkins, evidently the storekeeper:

> Pleas let the Bearer William Thomas have 6 and a half bush. of Corn and oblige yours for Daniel E Estell [initials of the agent].

Fig. 95 FIRST ESTELL MANOR HOUSE, built about 1750 and still in use, though modified, at Estell Manor, New Jersey. Daniel Estell was the seventh generation of Estells in America.

Fig. 96 Daniel E. Estell (1801-1858). *Collection of Dr. George A. Bourgeois.*

Among the names of others entitled to corn were Samuel P. Evans, Abraham Cowan, John Peterson, Joseph Cain, J. Steelman (also a storekeeper), Naomey Estell, (John Estell's mother) William Stewart, John Hann, William Hansill, David Steelman, and Edmund Scull. The latter, a blower, was frequently entitled to 20 to 25 bushels of corn.

Estellville did not live by corn alone, as witness this letter of July 25, 1839, from M.M. & D.R. Martin of Manhattan to Daniel Estell:

> Above we have your bill of pork shipt per order by Capn Smith the quantity that you ordered before. We had the other all ready to send but as Capt Smith did not exactly consent to take the other things you ordered viz. soda, clay [glass-making supplies] etc and while waiting to know what he was going to do the first thing we knew he was off and course we did not send it.
>
> Pork however is a little cheaper than it was when you ordered before & that's why we have sent you a little more than you ordered, fearing that before you could order again it might go up. If you think you will want any more this summer you had better order it immediately for pork will certainly advance again as soon as there is any relief in the money market.

Another bill, from John D. Cocks & Co. of New York City, shows that in August of 1841 Captain Smith brought back to Stephens Creek a cargo of codfish, rice, sugar, soap and rye flour to the value of $257.96. Supplier David Vickery of Philadelphia in August, 1830, charged John Estell & Son with two bags of coffee at $32.52, a barrel of French brandy at $32.87, five barrels of pork for $75.20, along with tobacco, cinnamon, cheese, chocolate, soap, and "1 doz Brooms and 4 Reams Wraping Paper." Clearly, the Estell Glass Works was prospering enough by its fifth year to permit some luxuries.

As ledgers of Marshallville works suggest, there was close contact between that glasshouse and Estellville. As of July 4, 1834, there is a bill from John Estell to Randal (sic) Marshall for 3 kegs of white lead, 5 gallons of paint oil, 2½ pounds of "verdigreese," and other painting supplies amounting to $28.70.

We can even visualize the costumes of the day from an invoice of Oct. 12, 1831, which shows that John Estell was replenishing his stock with Red Flannel and English Silk, Black and white Calico, ready-made vests and 2 doz. Super Cravats, as well as woolen shirts, for a total cost of $110.05.

From account books and letters carefully preserved by Estell descendants it is clear that the main product which made the Estell works successful up to the 1850s, when ownership changed, was window-glass. What might be thought of as a backwoods factory was producing an astonishing amount of glass that was in demand in Philadelphia, Baltimore, New York and Boston.

A ledger record of 1846 shows that the Estellville window-glass trade had been built up to the extent that the firm had four brand names: Greenwood and Extra Greenwood, the top grades; Weymouth, named for nearby Weymouth Iron Furnace; and Atlantic, the least expensive grade. Greenwood was then selling for $5.25 a box, less variable discounts. Sizes ranged from 4 x 9 to 24 x 30 inches or almost any measure in between that customers might specify. During a period of about one month the ledger shows sales of 473 boxes with receipts of $2,146.10, a considerable sum for those days.

With agents in all of the above cities, Daniel and John Estell depended on them not only to sell glass but to buy clay, potash, and store goods. This letter of Feb. 28, 1848, from one of their Manhattan agents, gives insight into the trading and also the problems of the times:

> Mr. Daniel E. Estell Mays Landing
>
> Dear Sir: Your favor of the 14th came safe to hand and have taken note of your order for Soda Ash, etc. to be sent per the Schr. "Ione;" but nothing of her as yet can be learnt. We will keep on the lookout and as soon as she arrives will make the arrangements for the shipment of the articles ordered.
>
> A customer is in want of 16 Boxes 12 x 24, Greenwood Extra, 50 feet each which please send as soon as possible. We have agreed to have this Glass here in *two weeks* from this time and if anything should prevent the fulfillment of this order please write on receipt of the

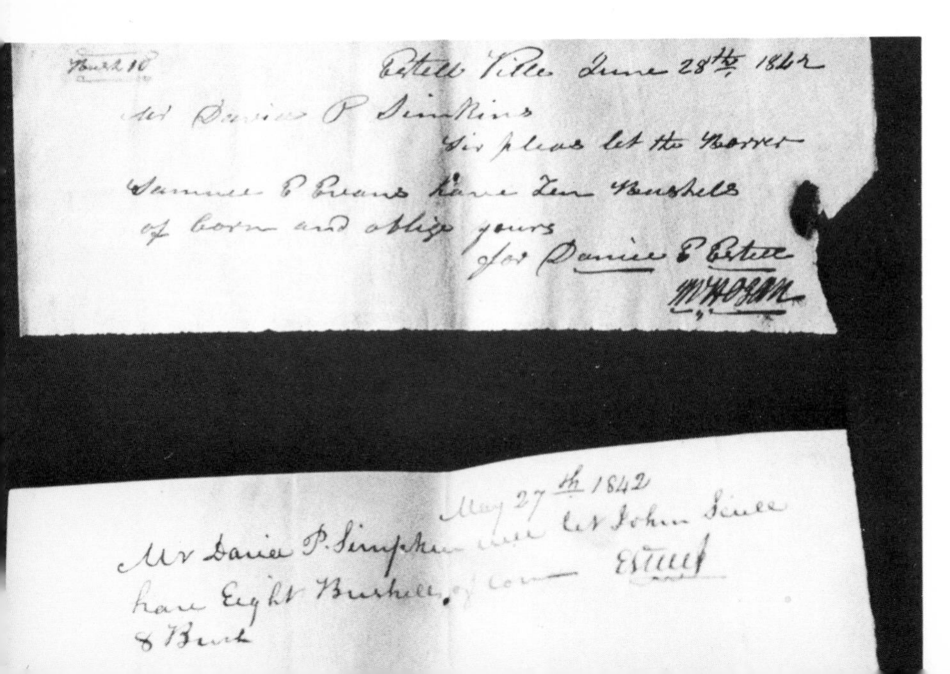
Estell Ville June 28th 1842
Mr Davies P Simkins
Sir please let the borrer
Samuel E Evans have Ten Bushels
of Corn and oblige yours
for Daniel E Estell

May 27th 1842
Mr Daniel P. Simpkins will let John [illegible]
have Eight Bushells of corn Estell
8 Bush

Fig. 97 CORN MONEY—"sir pleas let the borrer Samuel E Evans have Ten Bushels of Corn and oblige yours..................For Daniel E Estell." These corn receipts were frequent supplements to credit for wages.

Fig. 98 "Shinplasters" or company money used by Estellville workers at glassworks store.

enclosed and in either case will be glad to hear from you that we may know the enclosed has been safely received by yourself.

You are probably aware that we have about two thousand boxes of old glass on hand, which we were not fortunate enough to dispose of at the public sale last fall, the prices then ruling as we thought too low. Mess. Cooper & Townsend have also about the same quantity, in the same way, which they now propose to sell at auction as soon as the Spring trade fairly opens, say the last of March or the first of April, and we propose including yours in the same sale, disposing of the whole for the most that can be obtained, namely 4000 boxes. This Glass alone however would not do to put in a catalogue, as a great deal of it is made up in compacts of very indifferent sizes. It would be well therefore to include some of the new Glass in the sale to make up a good assortment of sizes. Otherwise it would be very difficult to get a good company to attend the sale & and even though we might stop the sale of the *new* it would be better to put some of it in the list.

We cannot but think . . . that there is going to be a good demand for window glass this year, yet we think the old Glass should be disposed of, as there seems to exist in the minds of the sashmakers a prejudice against it.

We remain, yours truly,
Pollen & Colgate

The Estells had a sailing vessel of their own but other ships, even such as the schooner *New Jersey,* largest one of its time to make the run between Boston and Philadelphia, often were no match for foul weather, as this letter dated Philadelphia July 24, 1835, shows:

Dear Sirs: I have the pleasure of informing you of the safe arrival of the Schooner New Jersey from Boston. She arrived yesterday after a severe pafsage without sustaining any injury.

Fig. 99 UNIQUE ARCHITECTURE for a glass works—Estellville—from an early 20th century postcard. Some walls with high arches still remain on private property at Estellville Manor, and nearby are ruins of the grinding shop.

The Maria sailed from here yesterday morning bound for New York. I was in hopes we should have had the New Jersey loaded and off by tomorrow night but she did not get her stone all out today and I am afraid we can't get her off before Monday. The Sloop Two Sisters has not yet arrived. Capt. Adams informed me yesterday that he was on board of her last Thursday week ago in the great Kiln [Kill] near New York, where they had put in for a harbour. The Two Sisters and two or three others draged ashore in the severe blow on Wednesday night but Capt Northrop expected to get off next high water. I have been looking for her for the last ten days but can get no further account from her.

I was in hopes that i should have been able to go down to your neibourhood by tomorrow's stage but i find I cannot rightly leave at present and I expect to have to go on to New York the beginning of next week. Capt West says the New Jersey leaks considerably in her bottom and he is afraid he will have to put her on the Screw Dock, as it keeps getting worse every trip

Respectfully yr Ob Sr
Armer Patton

Daniel Estell's correspondence shows a frequent exchange of letters among glassworks, both from owners and blowers looking for work, from such places as Winslow, Green Bank, Millville, Malaga, Schetterville, even Franklin Mills, Ohio. One of these letters dated only July 11 came by hand from Tuckahoe Bridge (the glasshouse at Marshallville) and was marked on the outside "in Haste, in care of A Stanger":

Mr. D. Estell: Since as I was informed you had not all of your Blowers engaged yet I would be most happy to accommodate you as I think I can suit. I have been at work at Canada last fire and since I came home father is anxious I shall stay about home and in Jersey and he is getting quite old. So I do not like to leave so far again. I can get a recommendation from good source if required. I would like to see and hear from you before you engage any others and my brother is also a wanting to place. We are both single men But if I had a place I think I would get married.

I am your most humble servant
John ?

The following recommendation dated Mar. 17, 1847, from Winslow Glass Works may have been written by a manager there.

Sir: By request I take this opertunity of writing to you that if you want a Blower to work a Pot & one to do Spare Blowing I can get them for you. The two men I speak of is by the name of Notts, Father & Son and from what I can learn the old man is a very good workman, he is a stout and able man & young. The blower he is with tells me that there is no fears but what next fire he will be capable of working anywhere. If you have the situation for them and see fit to give them work you will write to me shortly or Wm Notts at this place so that he write to his Father who is out west; for my part I think in all probability you would do well to give them work if you have vacancys. They have a family and expect to work the one pot between them and do the spare work when there is any to do. We are well, etc.

I am yours in the hands of friendship, etc.
Isaac L. Lowe

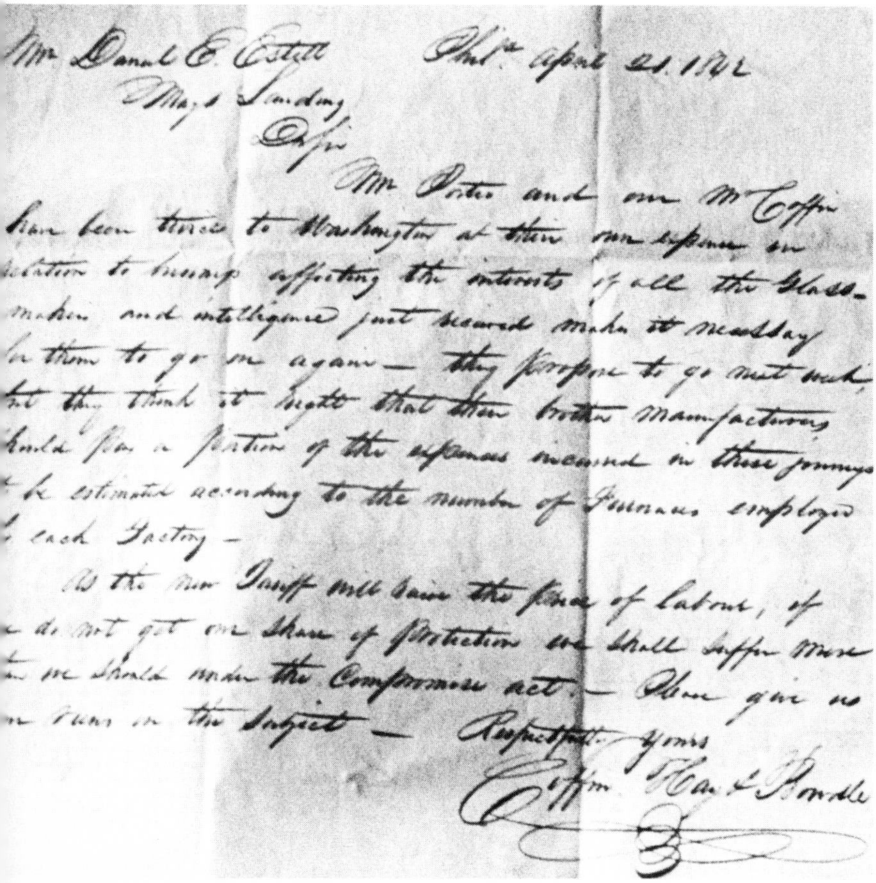

Mr Daniel E. Estell Phila April 21. 1842
Mays Landing
Dr Sir
Mr Porter and our Mr Coffin have been twice to Washington at their own expense in relation to business affecting the interests of all the Glass-makers and intelligence just received makes it necessary for them to go on again — they propose to go next week but they think it right that their brother Manufacturers should pay a portion of the expenses incurred in these journeys to be estimated according to the number of Furnaces employed at each Factory —
As the new Tariff will leave the price of labour, if we do not get our share of protection we shall suffer more than we should under the Compromise act — Please give us your views on the subject — Respectfully yours
Coffin Hay & Bowdle

Fig. 100 GLASSMAKERS OF AMERICA, UNITE! That is the gist of this 1842 letter from famous glass-works owners Coffin, Hay and Bowdle, who made some of the most interesting of all historical flasks, and here advise a firm stand against a destructive tariff. The appeal is to a fellow glasshouse owner Daniel E. Estell. Though the address is Philadelphia, the Coffin-Hay works were largely in Hammonton and Winslow.

A letter of Mar. 12, 1840, shows that New Castle, Del. was a preferred place for obtaining clay used in making pots. The letter also shows a hitherto unrecorded glassmakers' partnership of Stanger & Scattergood.

> Near New Castle
>
> Mr. Daniel Estte Sir
>
> per advice of Mr. William Coffin Jr. of Windslow I write a few lines to inform you that i work the old clay bank and am able to suply aney orders at the most reasonable price Mr. Coffin Sr. and Jun. getts. Clay from me Mr. Jacob Miller late of Glassboro and Stanger & Scattergood Booth &c of Milvill. and several others
>
> Yours, Respt. Edwin M. Nivin

In 1840 Daniel Estell received extremely bad news in a letter dated Jan. 15 from Caleb Parker & Son of Philadelphia:

> We loaded the Schooner Wm. Granger on the 18th Nov. 1839 for Boston with coal since which we have heard nothing of her untill last evening when we received a letter from the person she was consigned to stating that ther was verry little doubt but that she is lost together with her crew. Although we have no positive information to that effect it has been near 60 days since she left here. We understand from Mr. Armer Patton that you owned the vessel and our object in writing is to ask the favour of you to write and let us know whether you have any information about her that would aid us in obtaining the amt of insurance on the cargo. The cargo was insured in Boston.

Land grants or no, the Estells had shipping catastrophes that the Wistars never encountered on the placid waters of Alloway creek. The notarized document below signed by harbor officials of Norfolk, Va., on Jan. 27, 1831, shows how dependent Estellville's seaboard belt of sand and pine was for imported grain, of which a whole cargo here was lost and the vessel wrecked almost beyond repair:

> We the undersigned at the request of Capt William Phillips, attended a Survey on board the Schr, Benjamin S. Valentine of Great Egg Harbour, himself master. Laden with Meal & Rye Flour, bound from Philadelphia to New York and put into this Port in distress, make a report thereof, viz.
>
> On examination of the said Schr. we found that the head of her Rudder is split to pieces, her rudder case is cut away to secure the said Rudder, her waist board on both sides are partially damaged, and her upperworks and waterways are very much strained, her jolly boat and falls are lost, and her starboard anchor also. Her mainsail is partially damaged, the Gaff Topsail, Flying Jib & boom, with all the blocks, whiff, standing and running rigging appertaining to the same are lost . . .
>
> It appears that the said Schr. has been knocked down on her beam ends, at sea, and it is probable that some of her ground tier may be damaged. . . . Jacob Vickery, Isaac Talbot, B English

Examination by these officials showed that the vessel, blown so far off course, had to undergo extensive repairs before setting sail for New Jersey and that the many hogsheads and barrels of corn meal and rye flour were damaged, not by improper stowage, but from "Stress weather." The captain and the Estells must have been thankful that there was no loss of life.

Without railroads or passable stage roads to metropolitan markets such as Philadelphia and New York and with steamboats still a rarity, cargo space in sloops and schooners was sacred for raw materials and certain foods, and too precious to waste on housewares. Estellville's window-light blowers must therefore have made great quantities of aquamarine pitchers, bowls, or anything for which glass would serve. One thinks of the glorious array of aquamarine Jersey glass in the Billups collection, so much of which was garnered by the late David Hollander, and wonders how much came from Estellville workers blowing not for fun but out of real need.

A curious note is that the names of blowers applying for work or listed in the store books are rarely German, as were the earliest blowers in South Jersey, but most often stem from the British Isles, as Daniel Champion, Thomas R. Barrett of Gloucester City, and Daniel R. Lee of Gibson's Creek. In John Estell's account book bearing notations from 1828 to 1830 there are records of purchases by persons whose surnames make South Jersey glassworks history: James Stratton, John and Silas Wheaton, William Scott, Jeremiah Marshall, Randall Marshall, Constant Dennis, David Ford, Thomas Clevenger, and several Corsons and Vannemans. G. H. Abbott is also listed in the accounts; he was at one time postmaster of Etna Furnace, as Daniel E. Estell was for his town.

An interesting purchase from Manhattan in 1838 through C. W. Lilliendahl of 34 Maiden Lane were Diamond Sparks, at $1.50 each. These were real diamonds, though of low grade, to attach to handcutters for slicing glass.

Many agents seemed to be vying for the Estell trade, despite much bargaining to keep the price down. One of these agents was Morgan & Walker of 48 Cedar Street, Manhattan. In 1839 they wrote Daniel Estell, "We are selling and for several years have sold Mr. Rosenbaum's Glass [of Malaga] . . . but we do not receive one quarter part so much Glass as we want now from Mr. Rosenbaum. We have hitherto foreborne to write to you because we have been apprehensive to give offence to the agents above mentioned (whom we consider very correct and honourable men) [Squire and Merritt] but we have heard lately through Mr. Elsworth that you had proposed to him to take the agency. We would be pleased to have you give us a trial. . . ."

They seem not to have acquired the account. Instead, Bush & Hillyer of 178 Greenwich Street, Manhattan, were the Estell agents there during the 1840s. The Bush & Hillyer letterhead of 1840 (see Fig. 101) reveals for the first time that the Estell firm had the alternate name of Weymouth Window Glass Company. A letter from a customer for glass, which is postmarked Philadelphia, also has the address of Weymouth Glass Works, Stephens Creek, near Mays Landing. The Estells did much trading with Bush & Hillyer for bar and sheet iron, salt, soda for glassmaking, and paints. Judging from the lithograph of their 5-story building Bush & Hillyer were highly successful merchants. On another letterhead they stated they were "Agents for the Shakers."

Although doing a large volume of business in glass, timber and store supplies, apparently there was no sale, however small, that the Estells ignored, as this letter from a J. Beatty Jr. suggests:

> Dr. Sir Do me the favor to send me up a quarter box of good segars—what we get here are not fit to use—If you could also send me a few Irish potatoes, say ½ a bushell you'll oblige your 5$ enclosed
>
> Ob St.

(Notation on the envelope: "The goods sent by Stage")

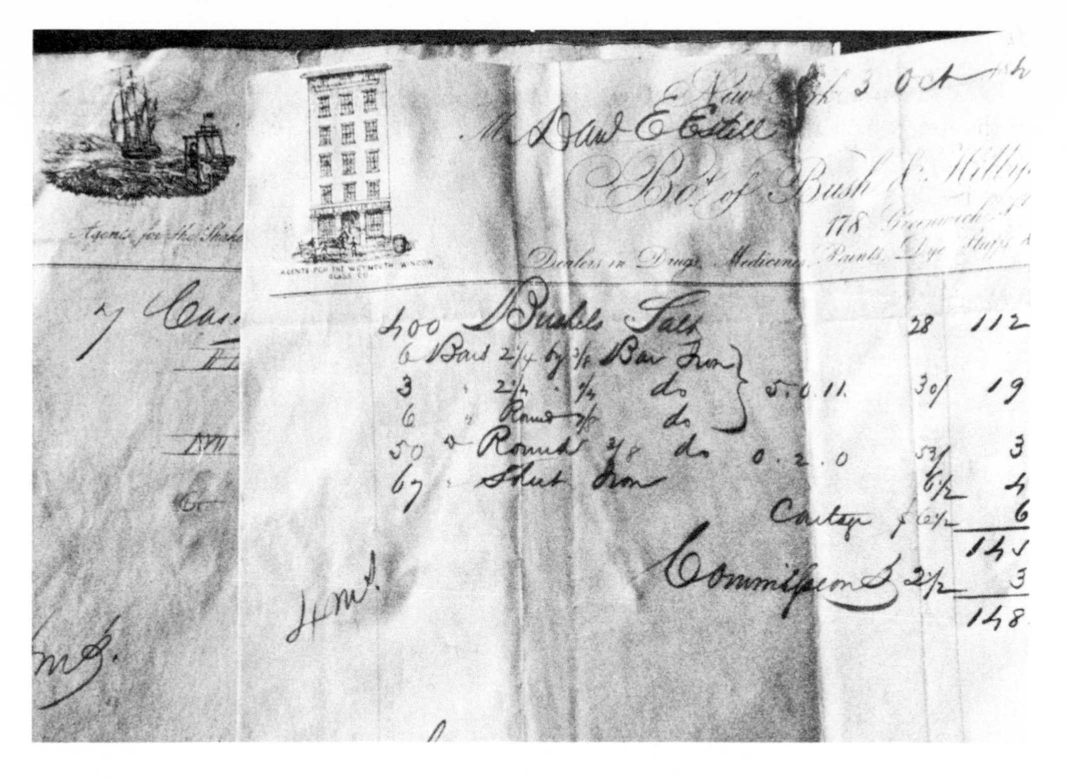
Mr Danl E Estell
Bot of Bush & Hillyer
178 Greenwich St
Dealers in Drugs, Medicines, Paints, Dye Stuffs &

400 Bushels Salt 28 112
6 Bars 2 1/4 by 3/4 Bar Iron
3 2 1/4 3/4 do 5.0.11. 30/ 19
6 Round do
50 Round 3/8 do 0.2.0 53/ 3
67 Sheet Iron 6/2 4
Cartage 6
141
Commission 2 1/2 3
148

Fig. 101 A NEW NAME: WEYMOUTH WINDOWGLASS CO. for Estellville Glass Works is revealed by this rare, quaint billhead for Bush & Hillyer, Manhattan, in 1840 one of Daniel Estell's several agents. Weymouth, a brand of Estell windowglass, had become a New York success and is featured on the letterhead, beneath the engraving of the 5-story building. The second billhead shows a ship sailing before the wind, usual method then for transporting glass to Manhattan from the Jersey coast.

At peak of activity in the late 1840s, the Estells' window-glass works employed about 80 persons and the village had the usual grist and saw mills as well as tenant houses and a Methodist church.

Soon after 1840 the Estellville works was taken over by Getsinger and Rosenbaum, according to Heston, writing in 1904. The early Getsingers were blowers from Port Elizabeth where they operated the Eagle works from 1818 to 1846. John G. Rosenbaum about 1850 was a joint owner with the Whitneys of the bottle works at Malaga. The new owners at Estellville converted the works to bottle-blowing.

In 1860 the Woodbury *Constitution* reported that the Estellville glassworks with 19 acres were sold for $1,500, but it is not known to whom. About 1875 the furnace was bought by Alexander H. Sharp, but partly due to shortage of local fuel and competition from coal-fueled plants in Pennsylvania the owner failed and the plant closed down in 1877.

For half a century the picturesque ruins of the Estellville furnace building have been part of a game preserve which is posted against trespassers. About 70 feet long, the structure is made of Jersey sandstone and has unusual arched windows and doors. Nearby are ruins of the grinding shop where necks of bottles and jars were ground.

A student group from Glassboro State College undertook some limited archeology of the site, which was reported by the late historian Dr. Harold F. Wilson in the *NJEA Review* for January 1961. Numerous fragments of handblown bottles were found but most surprising was a pile of cullet, sand, and ground limestone, all mixed and ready for firing. This raises a question of why glass production terminated so abruptly.

Some 40 years ago a former resident found on the preserve a cobalt rolling pin, undoubtedly made by an Estellville worker. One researcher reports finding a handblown champagne bottle.

Estellville today is a tiny settlement about five miles south of Mays Landing on Route 50. West of this is a new community, on Route 557, called Estell Manor in honor of the Greek Revival mansion which was built in 1832 by Joseph E. West for his young sister Maria Inglis West who became the bride of Daniel E. Estell. Maria had but a brief time to enjoy life in the handsome manor, as she died before she reached the age of 21. New light on her brother, long a figure of mystery in South Jersey history, is told in *Tall Pines at Catawba*, by Clark S. Barrett and Kenneth N. Scull. Somewhat modernized outside, the white pillared mansion, now on the highway, is a privately owned residence.

Fig. 102 RUINS OF ESTELLVILLE Glass Works, 1960s.

Fig. 103 ESTELL MANOR, 1832, the mansion built by Joseph E. West for his young sister, Maria, who, as Daniel Estell's bride died before she reached 21 years. The house is now a residence on Route 557 in the village of Estell Manor.

DENNISVILLE GLASS MANUFACTURING COMPANY 1836

On Dennis Creek which flows into Delaware Bay, Dennisville from Cape May County's early times was a shipbuilding center because the nearby cedar swamps yielded logs that were nearly rotproof, ideal for saltwater vessels.

One of the successful ship chandlers who lived in Dennisville built himself a fine house in 1822, with mantels and doorway carved by William Armstrong, much in demand for his unusual woodworking. This, the Nathaniel Holmes house, carefully preserved today, still stands in the hamlet of Dennisville skirting Route 47. Nathaniel Holmes is of special interest here because in 1836 he founded a glassworks on the north side of Dennis Creek near Dennisville. That is the only description left to us. Residents of Dennisville, many of whom are history buffs, collectors of antiques, and owners of charming early houses in the village, have no other clue as to the furnace site, much as they would like to know and have sought for it.

Members of the board of directors, besides Holmes, of the Dennisville works were Christopher and Richard S. Ludlam, Amos C. Moore, Samuel Mathews, Eleazer Crawford and Morris Beasley, well-known Cape May names. The product of the furnace is far from definitely known, however. Charles S. Boyer wrote that the output apparently was window-glass, and certainly there is a large amount of handmade small-paned window-glass in Dennisville. Without stating any sources, Mrs. Knittle wrote that Dennisville "has left splendid occasional specimens of 'offhand' blown glass," an unwarranted assumption. Nearby and contemporary with Estellville, Marshallville and Port Elizabeth, the product at Dennisville may have been similar, that is, green-glass used for windowlights, bottles and home utensils.

Fig. 104 PRIZED PRIMITIVE now but a kitchen bowl in the 18th century, typical also of later ones made at such early glassworks as Malaga, Estellville, Port Elizabeth, and Glassboro. Usual colors: aquamarine, amber, emerald and cobalt, such as this. D. 8 inches. Miniature Carboy in amber was probably made by Millville lamp-workers.

George Dummer & Co., Jersey City—Medal Winners

George Dummer sometime just prior to 1821 came from Albany, where he had apparently learned his trade as glass cutter at the Hamilton works there, and opened a glass retailing shop in Manhattan at 110 Broadway. By 1824 he had taken the bold step of setting up in Jersey a glass manufactory of broad scope: blowing, mold-blowing, engraving and cutting fine flintware. Under the name George Dummer & Company he took into the firm Joseph K. Milnor and William G. Bull, and P. C. Dummer, a brother, soon became active as well.

Within two years of its founding George Dummer & Company at the 1826 awards exhibit of the Franklin Institute, Philadelphia, shared "honorary mention for the splendid collection of cut glass," along with McCord & Shriner of Philadelphia, Jackson & Baggot of New York, the New England Glass Company of Boston, and Bakewell, Page & Bakewell of Pittsburgh.

The awards committee were so impressed that they stated in print, "The judges report that these articles are so well, and so extensively made, as to prove, beyond all question, that this country need not remain tributary to foreign manufacturers; and they state without hesitation that there was not an article exhibited that would not do credit to any foreign establishment."

Pressed ware, so little favored in New Jersey where glass workers and owners alike were proud to be a part of creative blowing, was added to the Dummer repertoire in 1827. But carriage-trade glass continued to be made in great quantity, with gilded and colored glass a part of the line. In the 1831 exhibit of the Franklin Institute five pieces of glass by Dummers' Jersey Glass Company were considered worthy of display.

Then in 1835 the Franklin Institute awarded George Dummer of Jersey City a certificate of honorable mention for astral lamp shades, some of them described as of extraordinary size.

Against competition from Pittsburgh, Philadelphia, New York and New England, the Dummers in 1838 won the Franklin Institute's silver medal, its first prize, for four pairs of fluted decanters, "the very best articles of Cut Glass exhibited, both for quality of the metal and beauty of the cutting."

Again in 1843, P. C. Dummer & Company (the same firm) placed first at the Franklin Institute with a silver medal for "a cut glass bowl, of graceful form and good finish, and of a superior quality of material," three vital points. This glassworks was cited as having "the best display of glassware in the exhibition." One of the choice items was a pair of "moulded and cut claret flagons."

A most coveted award came to the Dummers in 1837, no less than a gold medal for "the best specimens of cut and moulded glass" from the American Institute of the City of New York at its annual fair. Even in the depression year of 1838 the American Institute honored the Jersey Glass Company again with a silver medal. Then once more, in 1846, at this national competition Dummer cut glass won still another silver medal.

When the international exposition opened in October of 1853 at the Crystal Palace in Manhattan, glassmakers worldwide were alert for the awards, as here the 27th fair of the American Institute of New York was convening. From this far-flung competition the P. C. Dummer & Company ran off with a gold medal for "the best cut plain and colored glass." A quaint footnote is that at the same 1853 fair, Mrs. M. Dummer of Jersey City won a silver medal "for a knit quilt containing 700 pieces, by a lady 74 years of age."

When the Jersey Glass Company's sales office had moved to 61 Nassau street, Manhattan, the Dummers were advertising "All kinds of Cut Decanters, Tumblers & Wines, Champaignes, Jellies & Clarets, Liqueurs, Dishes in Sets, Centre Bowls, Celery Stands, Salts & Stands, Butter Coolers, Hall Lamps, Candle Shades." For the less affluent, the Dummers made "plain and moulded glass of all descriptions." From their advertising in 1846 it is apparent that they also made druggists' flint and green-glass ware and "chemical furniture, fancy bottles & vials." In brief, they were one of the rare Jersey factories in the first half of the 19th century that was producing both householders' fancy and utility ware, and trade glass.

That George Dummer must have been immediately successful in Jersey City can be seen from the fact that only two years after the glass works had been established at Communipaw Cove, west of Washington street, and south of the Morris Canal, the factory had 32 steam-powered cutting wheels in action and the owners were planning to install a dozen more.

Considering that so many honors were heaped upon the owners and there was such obvious demand for their creations, one might revise a cliché to ponder "Where have all the Dummers gone?" As there are scarcely more than a dozen pedigreed examples of Dummer glass in major or minor museums and this attribution rarely appears in auction catalogs of the 1900s, one can only hope that in time well documented objects will appear from private owners.

Although his once-famed glass is difficult to recognize, George Dummer was renowned and popular in his lifetime. A man of many-faceted interests and community spirit, only a year after building the glass works he established the Jersey Porcelain and Earthen Ware Company on adjacent property, and in this field of ceramics he both pioneered and won medals. Along with his business activities he took time to serve as chairman of the board of trustees of Paulus Hook (later Jersey City), and from 1826 to 1830 was president of Jersey City.

Born in New Haven in 1782, he died in Jersey City but for much of his life had had close associations with Manhattan. In 1840 he and his wife had their portraits painted by Samuel Lovett Waldo and William Jewett who jointly owned a fashionable portrait studio in New York City. Jewett, who lived in Bergen Hill, was a close friend of Dummer. The latter's portrait is an amazing character study revealing a man supremely confident but not smug, whose expression has been captured at the precise moment of some light banter with the painter. If he had been a general, Dummer could have been wearing all his medals but instead shows only a gold watch chain, discreetly tucked under a black, velvet-trimmed coat. A white shirt and a white stock set off his thick black hair and beard which merge to form a dark corona around a friendly 18th century face.

About 1830 the Jersey Glass Company became known, for George's brother Phineas, as P. C. Dummer & Company, but awards often continued to be made in the name of George Dummer. Although the firm underwent changes of name until its probable end in 1862, some member of the Dummer family was usually active, viz.: 1846, Dummer & Lyman (George Dummer, Jr., and George Dummer Lyman); 1848, George Dummer Lyman & Company; 1851, Geo. Dummer & Company (probably George Jr.); 1856 to 1862, August O. Dummer. In 1842 the glassworks location was described as Morris, Essex and Warren streets. In 1850 four of the family were listed as glass manufacturers: George Dummer at Essex and Green streets, near the factory; Phineas with a home at 52 Essex; George, Jr. and Augustus, listed as boarders, probably living at home. In 1844 Phineas had become mayor of Jersey City.

About 1862 the Jersey Glass Company was taken over by Reed and Moulds, of whom little is known. As the turmoil and the financial distress concurrent with the Civil War increased, all operations ceased. By 1867 all trace was obliterated by the construction of the huge sugar refinery of Matthiessen & Wiechers, the buildings and equipment for which cost a half million dollars.

By odd coincidence, when some eminent collectors began comparing notes on identical wine goblets this led to the discovery of what is surely Dummer glass. The McKearins had found five yellow-green wines and then learned that collector Arthur W. Clement had several matching ones which he had purchased from a dealer who had obtained them, along with an advertisement for the Jersey Glass Company, from a member of the Dummer family. The full account is given in the McKearins' *American Glass.* One of these wines, 4 inches high, is shown below.

Fig. 105 RARE GOBLET, attributed by collector Arthur W. Clement to the Jersey Glass Company (1824 to 1862), one of several obtained from the Dummer family. Tooled, applied stem; circular foot. H. 4 inches. *Corning collection. Photo, courtesy of the Corning Museum of Glass.*

Another wine glass blown in a similar graceful and simple form but in a grape-purple metal is also attributed to the Dummers. After I had given a lecture on glass, a member of the audience and a Jerseyan, showed me a goblet and a 7½-inch plate in the same rich color, which she said had come down in her family from Dummers' glass company.

For the first time collectors can now see in print what Dummer-Lyman cut glass looked like. Four unusual and authenticated pieces are shown (Figs. 106 and 107) through the kindness of Mrs. Henry C. Stockman and Mrs. H. Lawrence Whittemore, sisters who are great-grand-daughters of Luke C. Lyman (1792–1868) who married Sarah Dummer (1794–1868) and was associated with the Jersey Glass Company.

Even before this glass was cut, from lead glass, the blowers worked with a feel for proportion: the fruitbowl shallow but ample; the pitcher wide-mouthed but graceful; the condiment dishes with saucers carefully sized. Of the Middle Period of cut glass, before bad taste became rampant, these examples of Strawberry-Diamond and Fan cutting are handled in two quite different manners; the bowls with allover strawberry-diamonds and sawtooth edges, the pitcher with fans looking like maguey cactus. By 1900 these patterns had become blue-printed but here the look is lively and charming.

The Dummer pitcher and bowls illustrated bear a striking resemblance to English counterparts in Figs. 3A and 3B of Wakefield's volume, *Nineteenth Century British Glass*, which he ascribes to 1815 and 1820.

The hourglass, not usually thought of as 19th century, was one of many articles made by the Jersey Glass Company. Collector and writer Walter H. Van Hoesen stated that he had seen several sand glasses with the name of the Jersey Glass Company in the bottom wood frame.

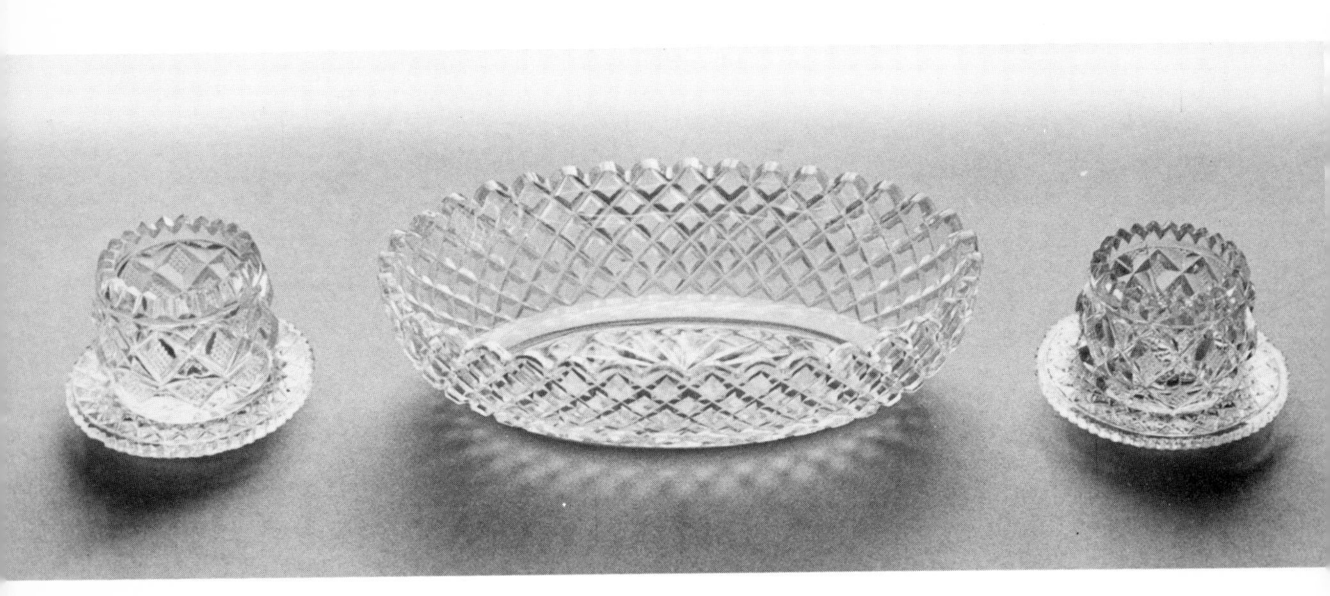

Fig. 107 RARE LYMAN-DUMMER cut glass, Strawberry-Diamond and Fan pattern. Until now no cut glass has been identified in print as from the Jersey Glass Company although the firm won many medals for excellence. Applied handle and circular foot; sheared lip. H. 7 inches. C. 1850s. *Collection of Mrs. H. Lawrence Whittemore, great-granddaughter of Luke C. Lyman. Photo by Lincoln McCabe.*

Fig. 106 STRAWBERRY-DIAMOND pattern in clear and heavy cut glass from the Jersey Glass Company of Jersey City. These rare pieces, a fruit bowl and a pair of condiment dishes with matching saucers, descended directly from Luke C. Lyman and his wife Sarah Dummer to their great-granddaughter. *Ex-collection Mrs. Henry C. Stockman. Courtesy of the New Jersey Historical Society. Photo by C. B. Crawford.*

Fig. 108 1853 PAPERWEIGHT from the Dummer Glass Company, Jersey City. A plaster of Paris "cast of the seal of the New Jersey Historical Society sunk in a ball of flint glass as a letterweight," reported the donor S. Alofsen in presenting the glass to the Society in 1868. *Courtesy of the New Jersey Historical Society. Photo by C. B. Crawford.*

The Dummer Glass Company was a pioneer in obtaining patents for pressed ware. Who was the first person to obtain an American patent for pressed glass will probably never be known because a fire in the U. S. Patent Office on Dec. 17, 1836 destroyed many records of the 1820s when this type of patent was being applied for. The first mention of making pressed glass is a patent granted Oct. 6, 1827, to John Robinson of Pittsburgh for "Making pressed glass door knobs." John P. Bakewell had earlier—Sept. 9, 1825—obtained a patent for "Glass Furniture (Knobs)." Only 10 days after the Robinson patent, Phineas C. Dummer was granted a patent "On the construction and use of moulds with a core, for pressing glass into various useful forms; called Dummer's scallop, or coverplate." Simultaneously, a patent was granted to George and Phineas Dummer and James Maxwell for "forming glass by the combination of moulds with mechanical powers."

The one type of pressed glass identified with a mark of the Dummer Glass Company is an oblong salt dish, nearly identical with one made and marked by the New England Glass Company, as N E Glass Company Boston. The Dummer salt is marked Jersey Glass Co Nr N. York. In *American Collector* for August 1939, Thomas Hamilton Ormsbee described minute differences between the two salt dishes. In 1970 similar oblong salts with differing pressed patterns of the Jersey Glass Company were exhibited at the New Jersey State Museum in Trenton. Greatest rarities for these pressed salts, usually clear, are some in apple-green glass.

Other Glassmakers in Jersey City

JERSEY CITY FLINT GLASS WORKS

Just when the Jersey Glass Company was preparing to shut down, H. O'Neill in 1861 opened the Jersey City Flint Glass Works, at a different site: Fairmount and Cornelison avenues. Its name leading to a fine confusion with the Dummer works, the O'Neill factory was listed as operating in Jersey City as late as 1883. Such long survival during the war and its subsequent upheavals might lead one to suppose that O'Neill had gone in for mass-market glass, but he continued to make blown flint glass in the face of competition from cheap and crude pressed glass.

His advertisement in the *Crockery & Glass Journal* for July 8, 1875, features FLINT GLASS WARE, in capitals, and though there is mention of such industrial glass as headlights and railroad chimneys, the text adds "Glassware of all Kinds" and private molds. Some fine glass may well have come from the Jersey City Flint Glass Works.

Jersey City Flint Glass Works,
Cor. Fairmount and Cornelison Avenues,
JERSEY CITY, N. J.
H. O'NEILL,
MANUFACTURER OF
FLINT GLASS WARE.
Particular attention paid to the Manufacturing of
Head Lights, Railroad Chimneys, Chimneys & Glassware of all Kinds
Private Moulds Carefully Attended to
To avoid delay, address orders to P. O. Box 214, Jersey City.

Fig. 109 Advertisement from the *Crockery and Glass Journal*, July 8, 1875.

HOMER BROOKE, MOLD MAKER

Homer Brooke advertising in the *Crockery & Glass Journal* for 1875 as "Glass Mould Maker," for 16 years at White, corner of Center Street, Manhattan, stated he had formerly been with the Jersey City Glass Works (this would have had to be the Dummers' factory). In 1875 he was offering to make every description of molds, including chimneys, lamps, mineral-water bottles, fruit jars, and patent medicine bottles,—molds for blowing, of course, not pressing.

TIFFANY GLASS AT JERSEY CITY AND HOBOKEN

Tiffany glass has become so firmly established in the minds of collectors as a New York product that few are aware Tiffany art glass was also blown at Jersey City and Hoboken. The first trademark, dating 1894, was granted the Tiffany Glass and Decorating Company then listed as located in Jersey City as well as New York. By 1904 when the firm was called Tiffany Furnaces there were workshops not only at Corona, L.I., but also in Hoboken.

As Tiffany glass has been comprehensively described (see Feld, Koch, and Revi in the bibliography) the story will not be repeated here; nevertheless, it is required reading for collectors seeking to distinguish between Tiffany and Durand.

A direct link between Durand and Tiffany designs was Harry Britton, a talented English gaffer brought to Tiffany Furnaces by Arthur J. Nash. When the Durand art glass shop opened in 1924 Harry Britton moved from Corona, L.I., to Vineland and became chief decorator for the Durand "fancy shop" during its entire life. Although the heads of this Durand shop strove to avoid duplication of Tiffany styles, the similarities and differences are numerous, and one of the pleasures of museum-going can be detecting the variations.

Another celebrated gaffer at the Corona furnaces was Arthur Saunders who had a close though brief influence on four younger artists of the blowpipe when he lived in Millville. At the turn of the century he set up a small furnace in Atlantic City where for a few weeks one summer, before the glassworks burned down, he worked with Ralph Barber, John Ruhlander, Marcus Kuntz and Emil Stanger—all of Whitall Tatum—in turning out fine art glass. In this instance, however, Saunders' influence was more that of the style at the Mt. Washington Glass Company of New Bedford, Mass., where his father had been superintendent.

The Freewill Glass Manufactory of Squankum

IT'S QUITE SAFE to say that no collector of blown glass ever boasted, "How do you like this flask from the Freewill Glass Manufactory of Squankum?" It's not a name to bandy about; indeed most collectors would think it a never-never name. But both the New Jersey hamlet and its glassworks were very real on June 23, 1835, the day the Woodbury *Constitution* reported:

> "With much pleasure we witnessed on Saturday last the raising of the 'Freewill Glass Manufactory,' in the thriving village of Squankum in this county. The main building is 44 feet square, Mill and Pot-House 50 by 22, erected in a beautiful and eligible situation . . . No accident occurred to mar the pleasure and good feeling in the large company of persons present."

By autumn the Freewill Glass Manufactory was fired up to make bottles of all sizes from ½-dram vials to 2-gallon demijohns, pint and ½-pint flasks, not to mention special containers for London Mustard, Turlington's Balsam (originally a London product), Godfrey's Cordial, and a durable favorite, Opodeldoc Bitters.

Accident did befall—what, we do not know—but the Freewill Glass Manufactory in the town of what is now Williamstown lasted for only one "firing." The founder, William Nicholson, and the other principal stockholders—Matthias Simmerman, Richard H. and Samuel P. Tice, John T. Brown, Jacob DeHart, Joseph L. Thomas, Richard Fordham, Israel Ewan, Isaiah Dill, Joshua Eldridge, Thomas Park, John E. Ayers—decided to dissolve the firm, and on May 2, 1836, they ran an advertisement in the Woodbury *Constitution* for their public sale, which today gives a picture of their situation.

At the sale on June 4, Nicholson bought the works for $5,700, paying $1,425 in cash and giving bonds to his former associates for their shares. Three weeks later John Swope, the glassworks storekeeper, bought a one-fourth interest for $1,425 and in September Nicholson sold another one-fourth at the same price to Benjamin Smith of Philadelphia. Woodward Warrick, a young school teacher, surveyor and owner of a country tavern, bought one-eighth of the factory, equipment and land for $712.50. The firm now went into another autumn-winter season as Nicholson, Warrick & Company.

When the spring blowing season ended, management shifted again, this time to include Gabriel Iszard, but the firm name remained as before. That is, one name did, but the company's announcement in the *Constitution* of July 11, 1837, concluded with the alternate name of Washington Glass Works. Surely this record refutes the prevailing opinion that the Washington Glass Works was not built at Squankum until 1839, by Joel Bodine.

It seems certain, in fact, that the Freewill glasshouse was known as the Washington Glass Works even by 1836. For in the *Constitution* of July 4, 1837, James L. Plummer announced that he had bought the Washington Glass Works Stage Line operating between Squankum and Camden; this would indicate an already well-established glasshouse and a stagecoach service named for it. Worth noting is Plummer's offer to transport coach passengers to nearby Brooklyn Glass Works as well, which was built by John Marshall and his son-in-law Frederick Stanger.

Inventories of the early public sales mention a group of 200 clay molds, a sizeable lot for a new furnace in those days. As the patterns included some for pint and ½ pint flasks, it is tantalizing to speculate that some may have been historical designs akin to those which were being made concurrently at New Brooklyn, Hammonton, Winslow, Bridgeton, Glassboro and Dyottsville, Pa. Surely a factory named the Washington Glass Works would have blown portrait flasks honoring the Father of His Country (or so one hopes !). The McKearins list 11 different Washington flasks with no definite provenance. But at Williamstown, archeologists, professional or would-be, have had no chance to explore for Washington flasks, because ever since 1835, glassworks structures, including tenant houses, have covered not only the original 6-acre tract, but streets and roads adjacent.

When William Nicholson at the age of 66 founded the Freewill-Washington Glass Works in 1835 he was the leading lumberman and farmer of the area, the fruit of 40 years' hard work since having come to Squankum as a 25-year-old blacksmith in 1784. Through the new glass factory Nicholson hoped to create a secure future for his children and add to the fortune of friends invited into the stock company.

Throughout the northeast states 1834-35 was a season of prosperity. Fortunes were being made in speculation in real estate, especially midwestern lands. Good times were creating an ebullient financial mood. Hindsight shows, however, that this was, in modern Wall Street jargon, "a super-heated economy."

The bubble burst with atomic thunder in the spring of 1837, the great northeastern banks failed, and financial markets were demoralized. Hard cash was virtually unobtainable, but William Nicholson, with faith in Freewill, mortgaged all his real estate, and so began the autumn firing. By spring the Panic of 1837 had become the Disaster of 1838, country-wide. Nicholson, "weak and sick in body," made his will on April 27, 1838, to which Joel Bodine was a witness. A month later William Nicholson was dead, and shortly his entire estate was absorbed by creditors. His children had to buy back what had been bequeathed to them. William Nicholson had willed the family homestead to his youngest son, Michael, but he, unable to buy it in at the forced sale, was left homeless and his family nearly destitute.

In 1839 Joel Bodine who had once been a stageline proprietor came to Squankum to re-organize the inoperative Freewill-Washington firm. Joining with Gabriel Iszard, he bought out previous owners. For a brief interval William Coffin, Jr., whose family had founded the successful Winslow glasshouse, then headed the firm, as William Coffin, Jr. & Company. But by 1842 Joel F. Bodine, who always took vigorous control, became sole owner. In 1846 he admitted as partners his three sons: John F., William H., and Joel A., two of whom had completed apprenticeships as glassblowers. Operating as Joel Bodine & Sons they built a second furnace in 1846. The father withdrew in 1855 but the sons continued as Bodine Brothers until 1864 when John Bodine and Walker R. Thomas took over as Bodine, Thomas & Company. About 1866 they incorporated as the Williamstown Glass Manufacturing Company which, under various managements, continued to make moldblown bottles as late as 1917.

A sign of the future success of the Bodine operation was that as early as 1843 this now little-known Jersey furnace had won an award from the American Institute of the City of New York for fine examples of druggists' glassware. The firm's advertising in 1850, from its Philadelphia address of Market and Water streets, featured "Cologne and Perfuming Vials, Porter, Mineral and Lemon Syrup Bottles, Jars, etc.," with apothecaries' ware as the staple. Like other major bottle works of the day, Williamstown advertised special attention to the making of private molds.

Unlucky was the youngster who dropped out of grammar school at the customary age of 11 to become a "carrying-in" or "snapping-up" boy at a glasshouse. Any future education was likely to be only in the school of hard knocks; few boys rose to become gaffers. But at Williamstown for a number of years in the 1870s a night school was conducted for children who worked at the furnace. Their wage of 50 cents a day was higher than at most comparable glassworks.

Another village improvement project, one to raise money for an iron fence around the cemetery, provided the whole town and countryside with one of its most joyful celebrations. The occasion was a "harvest-home," an *al fresco* festival in a nearby bosky dell. The *pièce de résistance* was no less than Horace Greeley, Manhattan's upright crusading newspaper editor. Jerseyans had a particular interest in Greeley (today perhaps best known for his advice, "Go West, young man!") because in 1846 he was a major investor in the North American Phalanx colony near Colt's Neck, N.J., which time has shown to have been the only financially successful socialistic settlement in the United States. The day's events at Williamstown produced a profit of $600, of which $50 was presented to Mr. Greeley for his stirring lecture.

Fortuitous also for Williamstown was that about 1865 the J. V. Sharp Canning Company burgeoned here, from the plentiful tomato crops. Tin-canning of some vegetables had been introduced to the United States as early as 1839, but consumers complained that the metallic taste was terrible for tomatoes. And so J.V. Sharp asked the Bodines to blow a glass container. The result is a highly collectible item, a high-shouldered whisky bottle with a large mouth to admit tomatoes. Impressed on one side the blown label reads J.V. SHARP / WILLIAMSTOWN/N.J. (See Fig. 110) Prospering with glass-packed produce, the company was incorporated in 1882 with Samuel Garwood as president and four Bodines as other officers, but none named Sharp is listed. The canning company continues to this day, with new management, ownership and name.

At a peak in its progress—1883—the Williamstown Glass Company did a quarter-million dollars worth of business annually. To achieve this the firm bought 5,000 tons of coal, 2,800 tons of sand, 1,000 tons of soda-ash, 4,000 tons of cordwood, 23,000 bushels of lime, and 1,500,000 feet of box-boards a year.

Still on 6 acres as in 1835, the Williamstown works by 1883 now covered this land

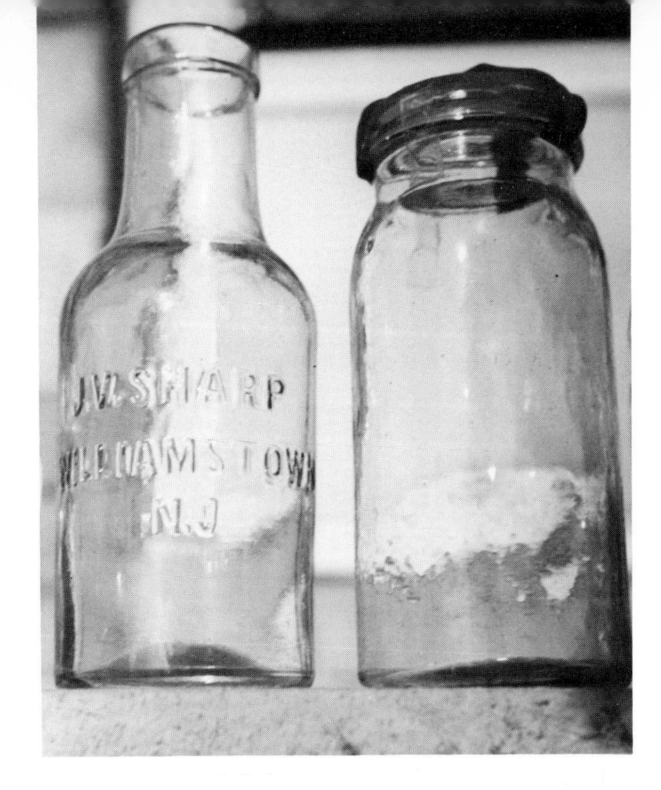

Fig. 110 WILLIAMSTOWN'S OWN. Both the bottle and the former contents were produced in Williamstown. J. V. Sharp was a major canner of tomatoes. RIGHT: Williamstown fruit jar.

with three large furnaces, lehrs, a 2-story pothouse 20 by 80 feet with a 20 by 40 foot wing, a packing house, five large storage sheds, a steam sawmill and gristmill combined, blacksmith and machine-shops, offices and a large general store, and 50 houses for glassmakers. Thirty other workers owned their own homes on surrounding small farms.

Some 375 people were employed—blowers, shearers, machinists, tending-boys, packers. The Bodines were proud to announce that a railroad switch ran through the glassworks, that telephone wires linked all parts, that the office had Western Union connections with Philadelphia. The Bodines also owned neighboring tracts of timber and farms, whose products they sold, making for quite a self-sufficient settlement.

By the early 1880s Williamstown was blowing precision glass for apothecary use, in sizes from ½-ounce to two gallons, patent-medicine bottles to order, fruit jars, pickle bottles, and "German flint" ware for mustard and catsup bottles.

An 1886 price list tells that Williamstown was blowing not only the above-named glass and three of their 1835 specials—Godfrey's Cordial, Turlington's Balsam and Opodeldoc—but also the following bottles and jars:

Swiss Cologne
Aqua de Florida
Wines
Schnapps
Porter, lager and Weiss beer
Soda and mineral water
Club sauce
Carboys, 1 qt., ½ gal.
Demijohns, 1 gal. to 16 gal.
Bateman's Drops
Mrs. Winslow's

Flasks, plain and union
Picnic flasks
Yeast powder
Ox Marrow
Inks, including cone
Cone mucilage
Snuffs
Sponge varnish
Cod liver oil
Steer's
Prescription bottles: paneled, flat, oval, *et al.*

In wide demand for its good workmanship, the staple ware was being shipped to all parts of the United States and Canada but, surprisingly, especially to such glassmaking regions as New England, Pennsylvania and New York. Large shipments were also sent to California and southern states.

All this large and varied array from a glass center almost unknown to collectors today!

The Huguenot Bodines whose enterprise had established several major glassworks in Jersey were drifting away from the Williamstown factory. John F. Bodine who had once been a practicing glassblower entered public life in 1864 with his election to the New Jersey legislature. In 1873 he was appointed a Gloucester County judge, a post he held for five years, and then was elected to the State Senate.

In the first 17 years of the 20th century the Williamstown works changed from a family-run factory to corporate business specializing in handmade mold-blown bottles, several carloads of which were shipped out daily from the rail siding which still bounds the property.

By 1915 the firm, owned chiefly by the Garwoods, was producing liquor and beer bottles almost exclusively. And then the unthinkable happened: in World War I the federal Prohibition Act, outlawing alcoholic beverages, was passed. The Williamstown Glass Manufacturing Company had put all its glass in one basket, out of which the bottom suddenly fell. With its market abruptly wiped out, the company closed its doors in November of 1917 and went into bankruptcy, thus ending 82 years of expert glassmaking at Williamstown.

Retired glassmen in the area still recall that the plant had six furnaces, among them, one each for amber, blue and emerald glass, and one for clear flint. With such an array of colorful and highly malleable metal to challenge them the gaffers of Williamstown must have indulged their creative talents to the full. At least one such artistic object had the spotlight of a Parke-Bernet auction focused on it in a major sale of early American blown glass in 1940, the Grace S. Fish collection. This was a clear and opaque white vase blown in 1850 by Henry Beebe of Williamstown. The catalog describes his creation, No. 355, as a trumpet-shaped vase with gauffered rim and a heavy baluster stem above a wide flat circular foot. Even in a year that still had overtones of the 1930s Depression, Gaffer Beebe's vase sold for a then substantial sum of $65.

Although its furnaces and lehrs have vanished, numerous buildings of the Williamstown Glass Company remain on the site, in the heart of town, a triangle bounded by Main and Chestnut streets and Blue Bell road. A present-day tavern there was once a boarding house for single glassmen. Factory warehouses still stand, behind hardware and lumber stores. Many of the look-alike 2-story houses with steeply pitched roofs were tenant houses for glassworkers' families. As was the custom at early iron furnaces, the homes of the "bosses" were also close by the factory, the better to keep an eye on the work. The Washington Hotel at 334 Main Street is the same one, though changed in appearance, that was advertising as a stagecoach inn during the year the Freewill Glass Manufactory opened. And if you chance to chat with an oldtime glassman he may refer to Hamtown, another name that Williamstown acquired, because at one time the workers received part of their pay in hams.

The Richards at Jackson, Atco and Lebanon

JACKSON GLASS WORKS and Atco Glass Manufacturing Company were in two adjoining villages in Camden county but had quite different histories and owners though often the same glassblowers or at least the same families of glassmen. Jackson began when the United States was just beginning to feel the pains of the Industrial Revolution, but produced hand-blown glass for half a century. When Jackson's fires were extinguished, Atco went into blast, in a different locale, and continued to the automation of the 20th century.

JACKSON GLASS WORKS 1829-1877

A reporter for *The American Banner*, who in 1853 visited Jackson Glass Works, tucked away amid the sand and pines of southeastern Camden county, was astonished at what he found. In the April 30 issue he wrote:

> "*Jersey Glass*—We were shown a beautiful specimen of blue glass . . . made at Jackson Works, by *Americans.* Our informant states that our own countrymen have proved more successful in this department of labor than the best *imported* hands."

All buildings of the former village of Jackson have vanished and much of the site is now a plowed field where blue glass keeps turning up, not broken modern glass but definitely furnace slag. Not only is blue found in abundance but also bright green, amber, deep and light aqua, and "black" glass. The only red glass I have found has been flashed, such as that used for church windows in the 1870s.

The puzzle is that Jackson has the reputation of having been only a window-glass house. From the information above, it is probable that Jackson in its early days was a tableware and bottle glass furnace and then after the Civil War may have specialized in window-glass which then had a large market.

Built in 1827 Jackson Glass Works was named of course after a flamboyant American President and was founded by members of a renowned dynasty of ironmasters: the Richards family who owned hundreds of thousands of forested acres in the environs of Batsto and Atsion, their iron-smelting furnaces and forges.

Jackson Glass Works and its surrounding village were the creation of Thomas Richards, brother of Samuel who was successful as Atsion's ironmaster, a career Thomas had no taste for. His sons, Thomas, Jr., and Samuel, as they reached majority, joined him in managing Jackson works which quickly prospered. In October of 1851 Richards & Brothers won a coveted national first prize for the best surface quality in window-glass, a silver medal from the American Institute of New York. This accolade doubtless gave them the prestigious honor of furnishing 15,000 panes of glass—55,000 square feet—for walls and dome of the Crystal Palace at the New York World's Fair of 1853. The glass was enameled to a frosty translucence by Cooper & Belcher of Camptown, N.J., a post-Revolutionary name for Irvington.

The Richards' glassworks of 1861, according to the *West Jersey Press*, employed about 90 people, besides 60 woodchoppers and teamsters. With no waterways close by, the glass in earlier days had to be transported over stage roads. The 43 families lived in neat 2-story dwellings with small gardens for each. There was the usual company store, blacksmith shop and "the etceteras of a village."

In the fashion of some ironmasters and glassworks proprietors, Thomas, Jr., during the 1850s built a mansion a few miles from the village, on what is probably the only hill in Camden County. Still standing on Atco avenue in the town of Atco, the manor house does not compare with the grander ones at Batsto and Atsion, but John Regn of Atco recalls hearing that the Jackson house cost $12,000, an impressive figure for its time.

That the Jackson Glass Works was successful we know from the affluence it afforded Thomas Richards and his sons. For dynamic Samuel this wealth brought out his talents as a promoter. One of his most noteworthy achievements was his energetic promotion and financing of the Camden and Atlantic Railroad, conceived by Dr. Jonathan Pitney as the first railroad to the Jersey seashore. Laughed off initially as a "railroad going nowhere" to bleak saltmarshes, the first train on July 1, 1854, chugged to a halt at a seaside fishing village which the railroad's designer, Richard B. Osborne, had foresightedly named Atlantic City.

Not surprisingly, the Camden & Atlantic tracks ran right through the outskirts of Jackson, a gladsome fact that offered the Richards glassworks speedy transport to the Philadelphia market, only 18 miles away by rail. In 1862 a spur of a north-south railroad, the Raritan & Delaware Bay, was built and also passed through the edge of Jackson.

The junction of the two rail lines became a terminal and was called, logically, Junction, but Samuel Richards visualized something better. By 1866 he and his brother had planned a 60-acre town around Junction and called it Atco, after a local Indian name, Atco-Atco.

The Richards-planned map of 60 streets soon became a lively progressive community, thanks to advertising as a health resort in the pines, with rail facilities for industry. One of those industries would be a glassworks, not Richards-owned.

After the death of Thomas, Sr., on Oct. 17, 1860, his golden wedding day, the Jackson Glass Works firm name became simply "Samuel Richards." When the paper town of Atco became a living thing, Thomas, Jr., sometimes described as an eccentric, gave that place his undivided paternalistic attention.

The Jackson Glass Works apparently weathered the Civil War with three furnaces still in operation. Then in 1876 the *West Jersey Press* stated that "Mr. Richards has permitted the fire in his glass factory at Jackson to go out, for the purpose of repairs." There was then only one furnace to repair, a sign of impending decline. The following spring another kind of "fire" swept and partially destroyed the Jackson works. In August of 1877 there was an assignment of the few remaining assets of the Jackson Glass Works. This by no means meant insolvency for the Richards family, with their diverse financial holdings. What caused the failure of the once-successful Jackson works? Very likely it was lack of wood for fuel. In any case the glassworkers who were now out of jobs were able to get employment at the steam-powered glass plant which opened in Atco in 1884.

To the end, Thomas Richards, Jr., was loyal to Atco and made weekly visits there from Philadelphia. Jan. 2, 1910, happened to be his scheduled day for this trip to Jersey. He was then 82 and it was an icy day, but he would not be deterred. On the steps of a subway station he slipped and fell—to his death from a fractured skull.

ATCO GLASS MANUFACTURING COMPANY 1884-1908

Atco was a window-light works, but on Wednesday nights during the blowing season you'd never have known it. That was "Girl Night."

After a strenuous day that began at 1 in the afternoon and lasted until nearly 9 p.m., the second-shift men knocked off work and proceeded to blow novelties dear to the hearts of the girl-friends. The latter all came to watch, and they had ringside seats, for a platform had been built along one wall so that visitors could parade along the boardwalk, to see and be seen.

John W. Regn of Atco at the age of 80 and with a good memory recalled those good old days when he was a snapper for Atco. He remembers that the blowers would make almost any glass objects their girls wanted,—pitchers, bowls, vases, hats, canes. A handsome baton made in Atco and now owned by Mr. and Mrs. Albert E. Duble, has spirals of aqua and clear glass, with flowed-in colors of delicate pink and yellow.

The star performer in extra-curricular glasswork proved to be John A. Hoffman who began work as a blower for Atco when it opened in 1884 and before that had been a shearer for the Jackson Works. The year 1879 must have been a momentous one for Hoffman. The local paper announced that on June 9 he was married to Miss Mattie E. Lull of Shamong. Then on Sept. 11 the newspaper told about one of Hoffman's glass creations displayed at the Atco Fair:

> "An exhibit of rare beauty and merit in our late Fair was a tablet of glass, with a beautifully designed Family Record engraved upon it with a diamond. The plate was some two and a half by three feet, and very neatly framed in Walnut. The glass was made by Mr. John A. Hoffman in 1878, and the engraving was done by his friend Joseph Marshall of Bridgeport, Pa. in the same year. The whole work was beautiful in design and most skillfully executed. Crowds of admirers were about the picture almost constantly. The background was black velvet, giving the engraving on the glass a white silvery appearance."

John Regn knew Hoffman's son John, Jr., when he too worked for Atco, but there are no descendants of the family in the Atco locality and efforts to trace the decorative plaque have proved unavailing. Regn stated that Atco made colored window-glass for churches, and also a crackled glass made by sprinkling drops of water on the cylinders while they were warm. Atco's Catholic church originally had windows of this crackled glass.

Mrs. Dolly Wiley, aunt to Mrs. Duble, recollects Atco's Wednesday nights as Family Night, when children came with parents. The furnace, which was an 8-pot one, was raised, Mrs. Wiley distinctly remembers as she had to look up to see the blowers on a high platform. When she was a youngster houses of all glassblowing families had a cane tied with

Fig. 111 MEN OF ATCO. Windowlight blowers, 1899.

a ribbon hanging in the front window, a badge of honor which she envied as her family were not glassworkers. She remembers that the tenant houses at the Jackson Glass Works ran parallel to what is now Jackson Road but were set back about a city block from that road. There were so many of the houses that they gave the appearance of a small factory town.

Atco Glass Manufacturing Company was organized by John T. Wilcox, a local businessman who had just previously owned the Atlantic Comb Company which made tortoise-shell ware in Atco, James Mulligan of Philadelphia, and Edward H. Flood, a glassman. Wilcox as manager brought in a steam plant from his defunct comb works. Blowing started in April 1884. At the height of its operation Atco employed about 50 workmen, some recruited from midwest plants and others who had been employed at Jackson. Wilcox appears to have had problems of attaining a profitable operation, with the result that Flood was made manager. By 1893 financial difficulties had become so acute that the plant was reorganized as a co-operative called the Atco Window Glass Company, with Flood still manager. The stockholders were all glassblowers, except for two farmers. Atco blowers who subscribed were John Hoffman, Caleb and Jesse Githins, George Bates, Harry Cheeseman, Alfred Andrews, William Simpkins, James Parks, Edward Hall and James Champion. Three Winslow blowers, Clarence and James Van Schoick and John Baird, were also stockholders.

The co-operative appeared to be prospering when in March 1899 all but the main building was consumed by flames—flattening house, office, cutting room and warehouse which held some 13,000 boxes of window glass. The loss of about $35,000 was partially insured and so it was decided to rebuild. The plant continued in work until 1908, during which time the American Window Glass Company held a controlling interest.

A photograph made in 1899, evidently before the fire, includes the following workers: George Kelling, George Knoll, Jack O'Neill, John Wynocker, George Bates, Robert King, William L. and James Duble, Henry Brodhead, Charles Regn, Walter Bebe, James Parks, Frank Ware, Horace Watson, George Frankle, Fritz Kohler, George Johnson, Herman Hoffman, Edward McClain, Dan Newman, three members of the Wood family, and loyal gaffer John Hoffman. He is still referred to as an artist in glass.

FISCHER CUT GLASS COMPANY

In 1915 the Fischer Cut Glass Company was operating in Atco and gave employment to 14 people, according to a report at that date from the New Jersey Bureau of Industrial Statistics.

LEBANON GLASS WORKS

At one entrance of New Jersey's Lebanon State Forest, a wooded enclave of 22,200 acres lying mainly in a triangle between highways 70 and 72 is the now leveled site of the Lebanon Glass Furnace, erected in 1851. Here at what was the edge of the Jersey Pine Barrens in the mid-1800s and still is today, Thomas Richards Sr., and his son Samuel built a bottle factory on glass sand that stretched for miles in aptly named Woodland township.

Having had prior success as glasshouse owners at Jackson, the Richards presumably had a profitable venture in Lebanon, for a village of some 60 houses sprang up, with such essentials as a sawmill and a store, and at one period about 150 men were employed, indications of a large volume of glassmaking here in the wilds near Chatsworth. After a short time Lebanon switched to window-lights which it produced until 1866. Ironically, Lebanon's very success conditioned its demise, for the owners, having cut down thousands of trees for miles around, had no alternate cheap fuel. In capsule, Lebanon typified what was happening to Jersey glass works at a time when Pennsylvania and New York had abundance of both wood and coal to stoke their furnaces. As with their iron smelting, the Richards family scourged the land, with no thought to reforestation, and when it had become useless they moved back to Philadelphia.

Was free-blown glass made at Lebanon? Probably. Historians Woodward and Hageman wrote in 1883 that Lebanon enjoyed a reputation for "clear crystal" of superior quality. Such a description then did not necessarily mean lead glass, but considering that the Richards family had received awards for "white glass," it is fair to assume that Lebanon also made a good grade of clear glass.

LIVINGSTON GLASS WORKS

This glassworks, unknown to modern collectors, was operating in 1882 in the piney region of the Lebanon Glass Works, because the post office address was listed as Woodmansie in *The Industries of New Jersey.* Livingston Glass Works, however, was not on the same site as Lebanon Glass Works.

Window-lights at Batsto and New Columbia

Batsto is the only one of New Jersey's many old glassmaking villages to be preserved as part of a State historic site. As late as 1955 Batsto was just another one of New Jersey's forgotten ghost towns but, now undergoing restoration by the State, the village attracts thousands of visitors each year.

Yet Batsto was preserved not because two window-glass furnaces operated here from 1846 to June 6, 1867 but because the hamlet had one of the principal iron furnaces in the colony and the state of New Jersey. Successful almost from its founding in 1766, Batsto Furnace and its adjacent forge became a Pittsburgh of the Revolution. Col. John Cox as ironmaster sent wagon loads of cannonballs and army kettles to the Continentals defending Philadelphia and to Washington and his troops encamped at Valley Forge.

Three years after the war had been won Col. William Richards, a man of "gigantic mold and great physical strength" who had served with Washington at Valley Forge, became owner of Batsto Furnace and amassed a fortune from it, smelting bog-iron.

In the 1840s the discovery in Pennsylvania of hard-rock magnetic ore close to coal and good transportation spelled doom for Batsto iron. The furnace bellows gave its last wheeze in 1848.

But ironmaster Jesse Richards had seen the handwriting on the furnace wall. He knew he was going into glassmaking, from which Samuel Richards at Jackson had profited.

The first window-glass was blown at Batsto on Sept. 6, 1846, from a 4-pot furnace. Demand for its product soon required the building of a second furnace. A curiosity is that blowers' places at the ports were drawn by lot.

A severely critical record was kept of each blower's work, such as "Glafs very stony," "Glafs good," or "Middling." Considering the variation in quality it is not surprising that four grades were established. In 1848 they ranged from Union Extra, Union First, Greenbush Patent and Neponset Patent; later the grade names were Star & Moon, Jesse Richards, Sterling and Washington.

Customer complaints in 1851 were not only that grades were not uniform, glass was often cut short of measure and large sheets were bowed but also that lights sometimes arrived broken, without a particle of packing.

Yet just down the road (at what is now Nesco, three miles west of Batsto) the New Columbia furnace in charge of William Wescoat was awarded the New York Institute's first prize, a silver medal in 1851 for the best color in window glass. And that same year the Institute gave a silver medal to Samuel Richards and his sons at Jackson for the best *surface* in window-glass.

With shipments going to Boston, New York and Philadelphia by schooner, Batsto Glass Works nevertheless did a large volume of business, not only in window-lights but in panes for street lamps. Total expenses for a season's "fire" in 1851 were $67,375. No mention is made of profits.

In 1850 the owners paid $6,996 in blowers' wages and $1,769 to flatteners and $1,796 to cutters. The old house produced 8,889 boxes (of 100 feet of glass) and the new house made 8,982½ boxes at an average cost of $1.10 and $1.17½, respectively.

Charles and John Getsinger are among the most noted of the glassblowers listed. In 1865 blowers at a new 4-pot furnace were Joseph Murphy, John Sylvester, John Garrett and John Hankins, with John Leeds as batchmaker.

On May 27, 1866, Batsto Glass Works burned to the ground, thus ending a century of manufacturing in the village. That year appears to have been the only one in which this furnace operated. After Richards' death in 1854 only a single 4-pot furnace was fired per season. Following the 1866 conflagration a furnace was rebuilt for the autumn blast but on Feb. 12 a new crisis broke: the workmen, unsuccessful in their demands for cash instead of company scrip, went on strike. Within a fortnight they had been persuaded to return to blowing. Hard pressed themselves for cash, the Richards closed down Batsto Glass Works once and for all on June 6, 1867. By 1868 Batsto properties were in receivership.

After several previous summers of archeological excavations at the glasshouse site, by 1970 locations of the following structures had been uncovered: a flattening oven, two melting furnaces, a pothouse, a lime shed, the cutting house, wood-storage arches and an annealing oven. Tentative plans are to reconstruct a furnace and the flattening house. As window-light blowing is a craft now extinct in the United States, only a diorama can show the full process.

Opposite "glasshouse square" are a group of 2-story cedar-boarded dwellings, formerly the "pigeon houses" lived in by glass workers. On weekends one or two of the houses are open to the public.

The second floor of Batsto's original general store has an instructive display of historical flasks, fruit jars made in New Jersey, bottles, whimsies and other articles blown in nearby glasshouses of the past, as well as an exhibit of a gaffer's chair and tools. Some descendants of blowers who lived in Batsto village recall that witchballs and walking sticks were made here in pale aqua glass.

NEW COLUMBIA GLASS WORKS (Nesco)

This window-glass house, which was located just south of route 542 in the hamlet of New Columbia, now called Nesco, was producing glass in 1845, a full year before Batsto did, according to a ledger now at Batsto. Jesse Richards and his partner James M. Brookdale owned New Columbia works but it seems likely that the man who built the furnace, William Wescoat, was responsible for the superior glass which won him a silver medal in 1851 from the American Institute of the City of New York. In 1848 Richards and Brookdale had already dissolved their partnership, and Wescoat carried on alone until at least 1858. Petit & Company of 163 Front Street, Philadelphia, had been the agents.

In the glass exhibit at Batsto is William Wescoat's silver medal, also a metal stencil for stamping window-glass packing boxes.

Fig. 112 VASELINE GREEN footed sugar bowl (TOP) has vertical ribs, pattern molded. Bell-shaped cover with bird finial is set in galleried rim. An impressive piece, 9¼ inches high. Aquamarine sugar bowl with domed, knopped cover set in flaring galleried rim. H. 5¾ inches. Compote, light green, on bell-shaped foot with folded edge, is attributed to New York State but is in Jersey tradition. *All from William T. H. Howe sale of 1940. Courtesy Parke-Bernet Galleries, Inc. Photo by Taylor and Dull.*

Fig. 113 NEW YORK STATE lilypad and pitcher in the South Jersey technique, blown from light green glass. Said to be from Saratoga Glass Works (1844-1860), though most of its output was dark green. Pitcher has threaded neck and applied handle. H. 8⅝ inches. Bowl has folded rim. D. 11¾ inches. *The Melvin P. Billups collection, courtesy of the Isaac Delgado Museum of Art. Photo, courtesy of the Corning Museum of Glass.*

Fig. 114 BOLD STROKES of dark amber and milk-white glass swirl over a handsome pitcher set in a pedestaled cup of amber. Although assuredly South Jersey style, in the Victorian period, this masterpiece seems unlikely to have been made by John Getsinger, as he has been credited. He owned a window-glass works at Bridgeton but his descendants say he was a cutter, not a blower. H. 7½ inches. *Corning Museum of Glass.*

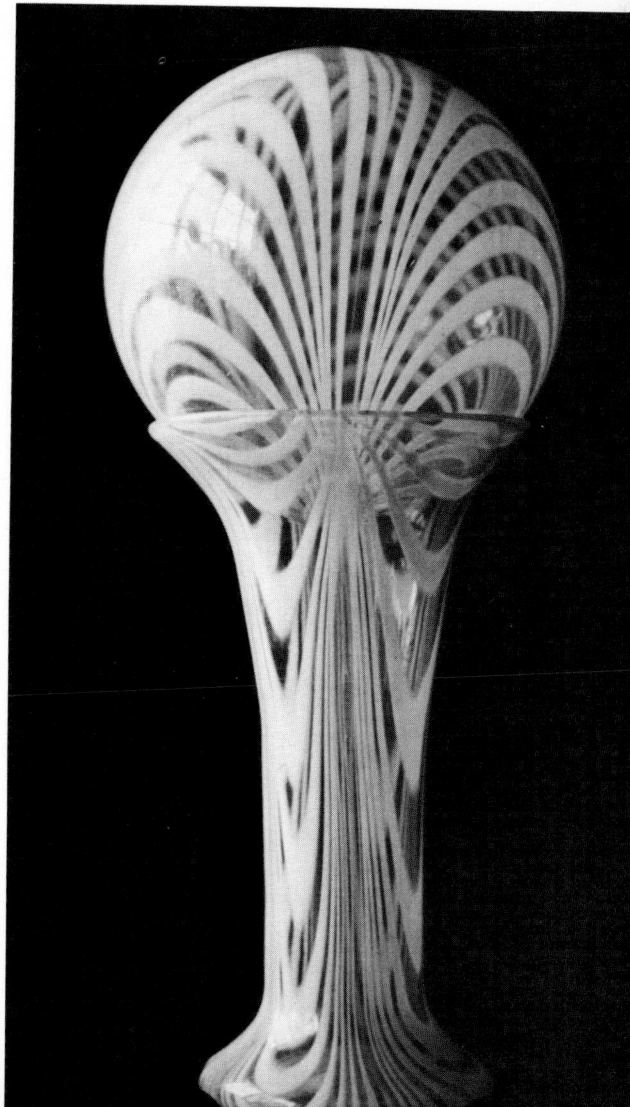

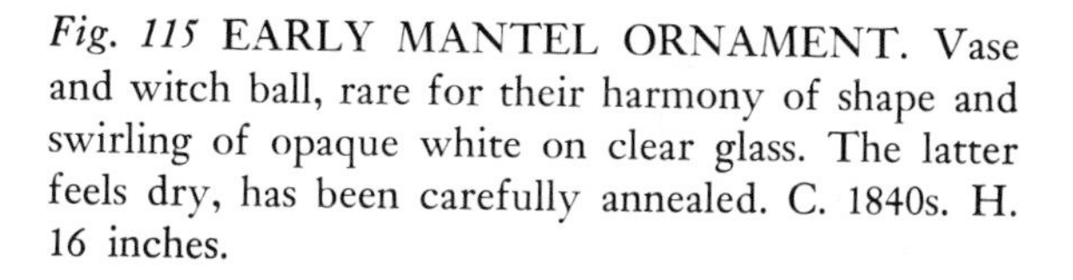

Fig. 115 EARLY MANTEL ORNAMENT. Vase and witch ball, rare for their harmony of shape and swirling of opaque white on clear glass. The latter feels dry, has been carefully annealed. C. 1840s. H. 16 inches.

First Mason Jar: Crowleytown

If you were to picnic on the edge of a creek at Crowley's Landing which fronts the Mullica river in Wharton State Forest and is about a mile east of Batsto on Route 542, you would be at the site where the first Mason fruit jar was blown. The blower of the experimental jar at Crowleytown's Atlantic Glass Works was Clayton Parker, an expert glass man from Bridgeton. Mason's first patent was March 7, 1856.

Numerous myths surround the story of the Mason fruit jar. One is that John Landis Mason himself blew the first screw-top jar. Mason was never a blower but was a Vineland tinsmith who devised the metal seal and rubber gasket that combined to make the best jar seal up to that date.* Another myth is that the commonest patent date on Mason fruit jars —Nov. 30th, 1858—means the date of manufacture. This date is meaningless in estimating the age of a fruit jar and was used on thousands of them, both legally and illegally, up until about 1902. One glass company reports that it receives about 400 letters a year from persons who think they have an antique Mason jar, because of the 1858 date. Another myth is that the first Mason jar was blown at Tansboro. One old time glassworker is reported in print as having seen Leon (sic) Mason blow fruit jars at Tansboro, despite the fact that John Mason did not know how to blow glass. He leased the Tansboro works for a brief period several years after his first jars were developed at Crowleytown.

One of Mason's early jars was found nearly intact at Crowleytown by J. E. Pfeiffer of Pitman. Like many others, this jar is embossed MASON'S / PATENT / NOV. 30TH/ 1858, but unlike others has two dots under "TH." Toulouse reports this jar also has sharp shoulders and markedly square angles at the base, very like Mason's patent drawings.

A one-of-a-kind emerald-green quart jar matching the square shoulders and sharp bottom angle of the above jar, has a unique brass cap, unlined, with the early date of June 2, 1857, below the word MASON'S. In the center of the oval of lettering is the numeral 2. This rarity, owned by a leading New Jersey collector George G. McConnell, has the glass itself embossed on the side with MASON'S / PATENT / NOV. 30TH / 1858.

An 8-pot furnace worked by a dozen blowers, the Atlantic Glass Works is interesting also because its agent and later its manager was glassblower John Huffsey, brother of Samuel Huffsey who owned the Millford Glass Works in the 1850s. In 1852, a year after the Crowleytown furnace was built, the following advertisement for the two houses appeared in "Philadelphia as It Is" by R. A. Smith:

*Homer Brooke testified in a U.S. Circuit Court on Jan. 21, 1920, that his father William Brooke, developed the screw neck to take a threaded closure and that Mason obtained a mold through fraud and had it patented.

DURAND DESSERT GLASS (1924–1931) has rose-pink bowl with white loopings in peacock feather pattern; stem and foot of pale amber. H. 3 7/8 inches. *Courtesy, Corning Museum of Glass.*

PLATE 12

ROYAL PURPLE in color, pattern-molded in the Durand Optic Rib design, the shape is rare for Vineland Flint Glass Company. 16 ribs. H. 9 inches.

BLUE LUSTER Durand lamp with spider-web threading of gold luster. Antiqued bronze fittings designed especially for lamp. H. of glass with base, 14 inches.

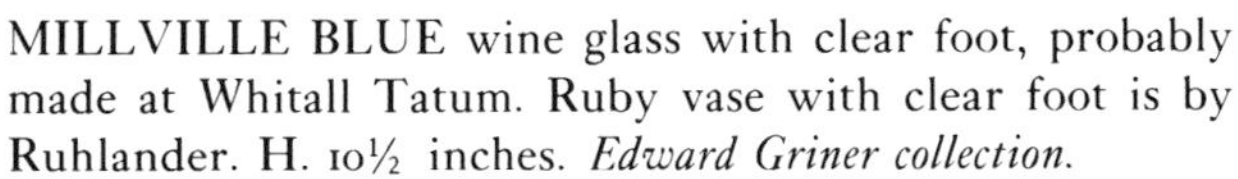

MILLVILLE BLUE wine glass with clear foot, probably made at Whitall Tatum. Ruby vase with clear foot is by Ruhlander. H. 10½ inches. *Edward Griner collection.*

MOORISH CRACKLE Durand lamp in trumpet-flower form with overlay of Etruscan red on pale amber has vertical fissures created by splashing cold water on hot glass. Overall iridescent spray. H. 15½ inches. Original metal base.

PLATE 13

MASSIVE MUG with graceful handle of deep aqua swirled in opaque white. H. 7 inches. Grape-amethyst jelly glass with fold-over rim has 20 ribs. H. 3 inches. Minature cobalt pitcher.

Atlantic and Millford Glass Works
Crowleytown and Millford, Burlington Co., N.J.
Manufacturers and Dealers in Every Description
of Druggist Glassware
J. Huffsey & Co.
Office, No. 50 N. Fourth St., above Arch, Phila.

In 1858 Burling Brothers took over the furnace which is said to have been closed down in 1866 but was still listed in the 1869 census. Furnace slag in strong colors of emerald, violet and amber are a promising sign that attractive household glass may also have been blown here for individual use.

The rich blue-green glass was made into bottles for porter (once a favored South Jersey beer), which have an embossed eagle design and the words CROWLEYTOWN/N.J. A place name does not necessarily indicate place of manufacture, but in this case fragments of the design and lettering in identical glass have been found on the site. The latter now is State property and digging is prohibited.

BULLTOWN

Samuel Crowley, also built the 5-pot Bulltown furnace, 2½ miles east of Crowley's Landing and just north of Route 542. A contemporary map of these two settlements bears the impressive title of Plan of Property belonging to the Burlington, Atlantic, Cape May and Philadelphia Glass Manufacturing Company. Built in 1858, this was a bottle works and it is said that some early Mason jars were blown here after Crowley left the Crowleytown furnace. The site is now on a privately owned cranberry bog and there are no visible remnants of the Bulltown furnace, which operated until about 1870.

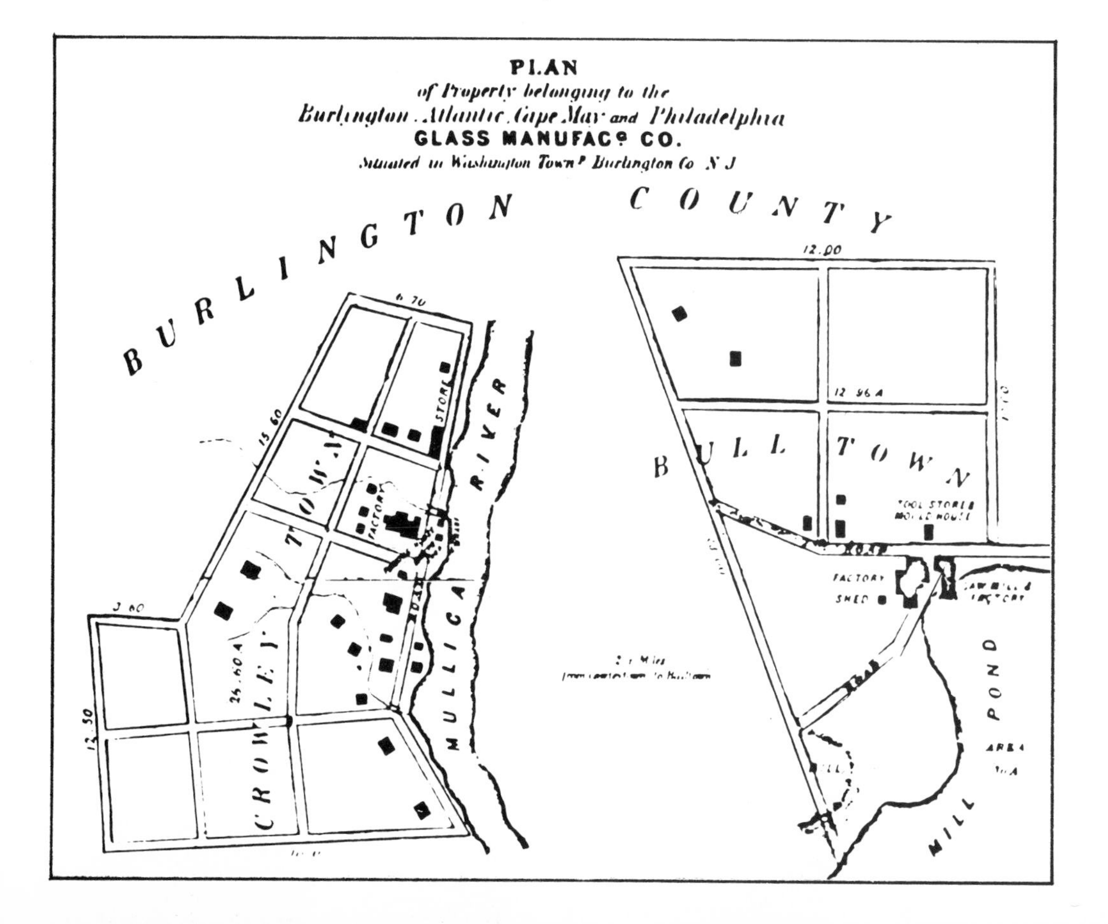

Hermann City

In 1860 two New Yorkers, Scott and Rapp, invested heavily in plans for a model glassmaking community on the outskirts of Green Bank, which they called Hermann City. Significant is the fact that the large furnace was built by a man named Bloomer, said to have been an expert in furnace building. Blumer was the family name of Solomon Stanger's wife, and the early Stangers and their relations were in demand as far away as Pittsburgh and Louisville for their knowledge of furnace architecture.

Charles W. Wapler was superintendent of this woodland furnace which produced not only hollow ware but glass buttons, Christmas tree stars and lights, and glass fruit, such fragile objects that none seems to have survived for identification.

The existence of Hermann City and its glassworks proved to be as ephemeral as the ornaments made there. Within six months John R. Rapp had died and soon the entire project disintegrated, helped along by conditions leading to the financial depression of 1873. Ruins of the furnace lasted until about 1920.

A State ranger in the Wharton State Forest, Rodney Koster, who is a descendant of the Rapps, has found vials and bottles at the Green Bank and Hermann City sites. The story that a schooner laden with glass was scuttled in the Mullica when Hermann City failed is just a tall tale, says Koster, and not worth a scuba dive.

Fig. 117 1885 RUINS of Hermann City Glass Works, a costly venture that lasted only six months when a financial depression developed. Location was just west of Green Bank on the Mullica river.

Camden on the Delaware

EXCELSIOR FLINT GLASS WORKS 1841-1859
CAPEWELL & BROTHER
J. G. CAPEWELL & SONS
KAIGHN'S POINT GLASS WORKS

One of the reasons posterity seems to have forgotten the once esteemed Capewell glassworks is that it had the above diversity of names, to which might be added the initial and short-lived one of James G. Capewell and Bamford Glass Works, a baptism that took place in 1841.

"Rich Cut Glass" was how the firm advertised its ware in its dying year of 1859, when pharmaceutical articles of flint glass were also being made here. Throughout its life under the Capewells, Kaighn's Point Works made blown, cut, engraved and pressed glass of excellent metal. Even after the Capewells failed in 1859, partly as a result of the panic of 1857, a half dozen other companies continued glassmaking here to 1867.

John and James G. Capewell who, with John Bamford, first organized Excelsior were sons of an important glass man, Joseph Capewell of Cambridge, Mass., both successful entrepreneur and skilled gaffer. He was a founder in 1826 of the Union Glass Works of Philadelphia at Kensington, one that competed with the Dummers of Jersey City for awards and the market for table-ware and luxury glass. Edward Austin, brother-in-law of the Capewell sons, was bookkeeper and at various times supervisor of the Capewell enterprise through its lifetime. Edward's father, Charles B. Austin who died the year before Capewells was founded, had also been a founding partner of Union.

From another noted glassmaking family, the Swindell Brothers of Baltimore, the Capewells hired William, renowned for his expertise in blowing flint glass. Edward Swindell who had been an experienced cutter at Union also went to work for Excelsior.

With so much talent going for it, Excelsior nevertheless started off in a modest way: a small furnace, nine accomplished blowers, and the requisite number of cutters and engravers. Demand for the Kaighn's Point ware apparently was immediate, for the firm soon became the leading industry of Camden, the prosperity abundant enough for the owners so that they became known as community improvers and benefactors.

In a decade and a half of glassmaking by proficient blowers and cutters and knowing managers who concentrated on high grade objects, some beautiful glass must have been turned out. The paradox is that collectors can scarcely name one item made at Capewells. Luckily, an unusual cruet (Plate I) and a fine goblet are owned by a descendant, E. Ralph Capewell. The late Mr. and Mrs. Leon Carigan of Medford showed me an identical goblet (Fig. 118) and identified it as Capewell, at a time when we had not even been discussing Camden glass. An inverted cone with a knopped and ringed stem, the glass has six hand-cut arched panels, a refreshing change from the usual cup-shaped drinking vessel.

From Walter B. Swindell, in the mid-1920s the senior member of Swindell Brothers Glass Works, Mrs. Knittle learned that the family owned three beautifully cut decanters which were blown by William Swindell at Excelsior.

In 1843 Capewell & Brother exhibited at the Franklin Institute's fair "a cut glass decanter with nine compartments that was much admired," but other than this citation it won no award. Then in 1846 Capewell & Bros. exhibited here again, this time glass "chiefly intended for chemical purposes," and called "very creditable to the manufacturers."

With such close personal affiliations with the Union Glass Works of Kensington, Excelsior's style almost had to be derivative, so we may well look to Union's awards from the Franklin Institute. As early as 1831 Charles B. Austin (Edward's father) was exhibiting a clear cut-glass bowl and stand, salad and fruit bowls and a decanter. By 1842 Union Works was taking a silver medal—in national competition—for colored glass. In 1846 the judges seem to have been bowled over by Union's creativity: "Cologne and toilet bottles, opal, turquoise, enameled, green, chameleon, &c were made in an open or hollow ware furnace, of bottle glass. Many of the tints are as rich as would be expected in flint glass while the invoice price of the ware is so low that it must secure a constant demand. The hock, cologne, and toilet bottles of colored opaque body are considered deserving a First Premium." This might be the time to point out that many a Jersey gaffer worked for Union of Kensington. If they made "chameleon" glass and exactly what it was we'll probably never know.

Although various Capewells were owners of the Excelsior Glass Works from 1841 to 1859, the firm acquired its alternate name of Kaighn's Point Works because that was its location on the Delaware, a full block bounded by Kaighn Avenue, Sycamore, Second and

Fig. 118 GRACE in design, proportion and simple arched cutting is exemplified in this handsome flint goblet from the Capewell or Excelsior Glass Works established in Camden in 1841. Knop and ringed stem with circular applied foot. *Courtesy of E. Ralph Capewell.*

Locust streets. The property, sold by heirs of John Kaighn, enabled the Capewells to have their own wharf at Kaighn's Point and they maintained another at the foot of Chestnut Street in Philadelphia, as well as their own boats plying between the two cities, an advantage most of their competitors did not have. The Philadelphia offices at 11 Minor Street were just opposite those of Charles B. Austin & Company.

At the end of the first decade, John Capewell became the sole owner but in 1854 a stock company was organized with John as manager, and his brother James, Edward Austin, Hewling Haines and James Tuthill as directors. The capitalization was not to exceed $150,000, and the real estate investment no more than $50,000, but the total was evidently too much for the times, for in 1857 the company failed.

James B. Capewell and his sons John B. and Joseph M. took over. Bravely, they continued advertising cut glass and druggists' ware in the Camden *Democrat* of 1859, yet in that very year the works was sold at sheriff's auction for $2,700.

From 1859 to 1864 the following five firms tried their hands at running Kaighn's Point but each lasted only a few months: Union Glass ManufacturingCompany, Cochran & Company (George Cochran, son-in-law of Andrew K. Hay?), Bowman and Chisholm, Thomas Burns, and U.S. Glass Works. The sixth firm, Duffield & Company, whose officers were Thomas J. Duffield, Calvin H. Test and John B. Powell, appeared to meet the challenge, for by 1865 they were melting some 14 tons of glass a week and employed 80 persons. With Thomas Creech as superintendent the firm was making and marketing a well diversified line of flint glass such as table-ware, lamp shades, and drug, confectionery and perfume bottles. As the future looked rosy a $15,000 expansion was planned that included another furnace.

Then suddenly in 1867 the company failed and the furnaces went out of blast, never to be fired again. Did the glass on hand stay in Camden?

Today all trace is gone of Excelsior and its fine glass is most likely attributed to the New England Glass Company or to Sandwich, catch-alls for so many hasty attributions.

WESTVILLE FLINT GLASS WORKS

J. B. Capewell & Company had a rebirth in 1865 as the Westville Flint Glass Works, managed by James G. Capewell. Doing well with a 5-pot furnace and planning an 8-pot one, according to the *West Jersey Press* of Dec. 27, 1865, the firm had been in operation for seven months at a 5-acre location fronting on Big Timber Creek and the Camden & Atlantic Railroad. Claiming 40 years of glassmaking experience, the owners offered to produce any kind of fine ware but in that year were specializing in lamp chimneys. Young J. B. Capewell, but recently returned from service "in the darkest hours of the rebellion," had received a patent in 1864 for glass castors. They were so highly regarded that a set of four were encased in silver for the bed in which President Andrew Johnson slept.

CRYSTAL GLASS MANUFACTURING COMPANY

This Camden firm, the Crystal Glass Manufacturing Company, seemed to spring up full-blown, larger than life, when it was incorporated in April, 1886, the only glassworks then in the city.

A newspaper report of a fire which destroyed the factory on Mar. 29, 1889 shows surprisingly that Crystal was then owned by Whitney Brothers. The news article states that the plant would be rebuilt but that meantime 200 men were out of jobs.

No ramshackle operation this, for there were six buildings, two of iron and four of frame, "lately fitted up with all the latest machinery," according to Prowell. Probabilities are that the business had been in full production some time before incorporation.

The main factory was 78 by 88 feet and 40 feet high with a large central stack and 12 smaller ones. Here were facilities for 100 glassworkers, and there was also a pot-making room, which would indicate a busy operation.

Although the firm's name might suggest a flint glassworks like that of the Capewells, the Crystal company focused entirely on bottles: wine, beer, Weiss beer, porter and mineral bottles, flasks, demijohns, pickle jars, and other kinds of green and amber bottles.

The founders had evidently selected their market with good business acumen, for they announced that they were also making private mold bottles for the trade in New England and adjacent states. J. R. Runge was president and P. Strang, treasurer. A. C. Lamar, secretary, was thoroughly seasoned in glassmaking for he already had two factories employing 150 workmen in Woodbury, with a capacity for 1600 boxes of window-glass a week.

The business office was at 9½ Market Street, Camden, and the factory was located on Front Street below Kaighn avenue. Some Camden directories list Joseph Wharton as an owner of the Crystal Glass Manufacturing Company about this time.

CAMDEN GLASS WORKS

Owner of this virtually unknown glasshouse was Joseph Wharton, an American pioneer in the manufacture of nickel and once owner of most of the 100,000 acres now comprising Jersey's Wharton State Forest enclosing Batsto Village. Howe's Camden Directory for 1883 through 1885-6 lists the Camden Glass Works as located at Tenth and State Street but Prowell's history of Camden gives the starting date as "several years" earlier and the close as 1884.

Fig. 119 COBALT FLINT MUG Jersey style with applied handle and foot. H. 4 inches. Amethyst decanter flask with optical effect created by inverted ribbing. Sheared neck. H. 8½ inches. Sapphire blue bowl of soda glass slightly swirled. D. 4½ inches. Early Clevenger.

Medford: 90 Years of Glassmaking

In Medford today at Main and Trimble streets, there is a row of white houses somewhat like those in subdivisions where one drives round and round searching for an exit. One difference is that these houses were built in the 19th century just for Medford glassworkers. Nearly all alike, the dwellings were then called tenements, but nowadays, neatly kept up and sometimes enclosed by picket fences, the houses are not unattractive.

In the previous century the tenants were served by three outdoor hand-pumps. All water had to be carried from the wells, until a case of typhoid developed and then the town piped in water. Formerly the houses were heated only by corner fireplaces. Dominating the scene was the glass furnace, right at hand, where sparks and soot fell upon wash hung out to dry, and later the steam engine drowned out all conversation. The tall, brick chimney-stack was still standing until the late 1940s when one windy day it toppled with an earth-quaking roar. The furnace had gone out of blast for the last time in 1923, at this, the Star Glass Works which opened under that name in 1894.

During that interval the factory went through several hands. The last owner was John B. Mingin, who had long been a prominent citizen of Medford. Assisting him in the management were Samuel Garwood and Frank Reily who had charge of the sales office at 226 North Fourth Street, Philadelphia.

Yet the Star Glass Works was but the last phase in what now appears to be a 90-year history of glassmaking at Medford. Such quantities of glass were produced here that slag is so solidly packed it cannot be bulldozed out.

Printed sources on Medford glass, such as McKearin, Knittle and Van Rensselaer, trace their information to Charles S. Boyer, a former president of the Camden County Historical Society, who made invaluable contributions to New Jersey's history. He gave 1850 as an initial date, when William Porter owned a glass furnace in Medford.

From firsthand local research, however, I find plentiful evidence that there was a well-established window-glass furnace in Medford at least by 1836 and probably earlier. Some of this background follows.

Mr. and Mrs. Clifford Prickitt, who lived in Medford all of their lives but traveled widely, came from what was once called "moneyed circles." Mrs. Prickitt is the daughter of John Mingin. Mr. Prickitt's mother used to associate with the "railroad Goulds," and she saw the golden spike driven in for the railroad west, in 1859, as her father was a founder of the Southern Pacific Railroad.

A 25-room pillared house on Main Street, Medford, was a Prickitt family home from 1855 to 1950. It had been built in 1836 by a man who earlier had established the first glass furnace in Medford, a successful window-light works. The original owner of the mansion had been awaiting a shipload of glassmaking chemicals, evidently with the idea of producing fine colored glassware, but the vessel sank in the Atlantic passage. As a result the owner of the mansion failed, and sold it to the Prickitts, in 1855. Dormer windows in the house have the small panes made at this hitherto unreported glassworks.

Supporting this information, the late William Simkins, at age 82 and like many gaffers looking about 20 years younger, showed me an antique cabin in Medford that has early handblown windowpanes. As a blower for Star, he recognized the "stones" and cords as typical of much early window glass.

Boyer reported that William Porter was running a glassworks in Medford by 1850, but it seems unlikely that the early window-light furnace was on the same site. It is worth noting, however, that two early ink-sanders of bubbly aqua glass have been found intact on the main Medford site.

The Woodbury *Constitution* in 1854 reported that "A barn attached to the Glass Works of Wm. Porter, Esq. at Medford was burned down." He was the son of Joseph Porter, a principal owner of the Waterford Glass Works, and after his father's death in 1862 took charge of that factory. He had evidently left Medford some time earlier for in 1860 the works was known as Cochran's Glass Factory. Small clear bottles have been found locally, embossed as C Co.

Although printed sources say that about the 1860s Medford was making pressed glass, there is no evidence to support this statement. Pressing, in fact, is entirely against the tradition of mold-blowing which persisted at Medford into the 1920s, one of the last in Jersey to produce handmade bottles.

Boyer *et al.* stated that in 1863 Yarnell & Samuels of Philadelphia bought the Medford

Fig. 120 IMPRESSIVE ARCHITECTURE distinguishes the Medford Glass Works of 1873, built of brick and neatly shingled. Note three boxes of cullet in foreground. Yarnell & Trimble were probable operators at this date. *Rare photo from collection of Everett F. Mickle, Medford. Copy and print by Tom Barnett.*

MEDFORD GLASS WORKS,
MEDFORD, BURLINGTON COUNTY, N. J.
Demijohns, Wines, Porters, Minerals.
PICKLE JARS, FLASKS, ETC.
Mason's Porcelain Lined Fruit Jars.
PARTICULAR ATTENTION PAID TO PRIVATE MOULDS.
Yarnall & Trimble,
147 SOUTH FRONT STREET,
New York Store, 58 Murray St. PHILADELPHIA.

Fig. 121 YARNELL & TRIMBLE were still operating Medford Glass in 1875, although previous reports say the firm bought the factory in 1875, improved it, then had no funds to operate. Advertisment from *Crockery Journal,* July 8, 1875, one of many that year. Note wide range of articles.

works, then spent so much money improving the place that they had no funds for operation. This may well have been true for that date but later, as can be seen from Fig. 121, Yarnell was actively producing glass here in 1875.

As can be seen from the Yarnell & Trimble advertisement, which appeared frequently in the *Crockery Journal* for 1875, an impressive variety of glass was being blown. Some of the ware, such as demijohns and wine and porter bottles would quite likely have been made in dark green and amber.

The C. B. Tice Company, of which Clayton B. Tice was the head, was making hollow ware at Medford in 1864, according to an apprentice's indenture for one Jos. Broom, which the late Miss Mary Hudson of Millville showed me. Joseph Ayres was a succeeding owner and he in turn was followed by Louis Arland. Some time after the Civil War the factory is said to have been making fancy table ware, but no examples have come to light. Medford still has some elderly glassworkers and their families but those I have interviewed have no knowledge of table ware made here.

Mrs. Knittle wrote that in the earlier days of the Medford works it was known to have produced handsome colored glass that might have been attributed to Stiegel or Wistarberg but she cites no evidence. As Waterford Glass Works made colored ware, it is possible that William Porter continued the practice when he owned Medford furnace but as that was some 75 years after Stiegel's heyday, it seems unlikely that blown glass from these two sources would be confused.

A copy of a handbill received through the kindness of Mr. and Mrs. Everett F. Mickle reveals that on Nov. 2, 1887, the glassworks was up for public sale, lock, stock and barrel:

PUBLIC SALE
MEDFORD GLASSWORKS

A lot of ground 5 acres, on which is erected a Glass House with Pot Oven attached, Pot House, Mill House, Engine House with engine (8 horse) and pumping engine, Smith Shop, Packing House, Warehouse, Store and Office and all other necessary buildings.

At the same time will be sold 22 tenement houses either single or in blocks as desired. Also barn with stabling for 9 horses, some dwelling houses and lots and several vacant lots of ground in and near Medford, also a parcel of land two miles distant containing 28 acres.

Francis B. Reeves, Trustee
20 S. Front, Philadelphia

Information is lacking as to the names of the previous owner. The buyers are believed to have been a group of 12 glassblowers. As the advertisement tells, the Medford Glass Works functioned with a pot oven. For this, one large batch of metal was melted and everyone worked until it was used up, regardless of the hours. Much later a tank furnace, which furnished a constant supply of molten glass, was installed, and the men were able to work in regular shifts. At one time the men on the 5 p.m. to 2 a.m. shift became noted for their group singing while they worked. On a balmy evening the townspeople would drop in and listen to glassworks harmony.

Star Glass Works had a bottle plant making varieties quite similar to those mold-blown at the Cape May Court House factories, and in sizes from ¼ ounce to 32 ounces. The emphasis at Star seems to have been on fast efficient production, leaving little time for offhand blowing, except for whimsies such as buttonhooks, chains and rolling pins. At its peak of prosperity the Star Glass Works employed about 250 persons.

The Star company did not issue tokens or scrip but did have merchandise books in denominations of $1, $2, $5 and $10. A worker would pay cash for a $10 book and then could buy goods at the store. This arrangement especially suited the wives as it meant that the glassmen wouldn't "blow" $10 on a Saturday night.

Edward Wills is now the grocer in the same store, at 138 S. Main Street, that served Star, and his father Edward, Sr., was foreman of the factory. He himself was a carry-in boy at Star when 12 years old but also managed to go to school. The late E. T. Carigan whom I interviewed some years ago, was storekeeper for the factory, and Mrs. Carigan operated the packing house.

Because he was a nephew of John B. Mingin, Edward Johnson who is now a Medford merchant, was allowed to start blowing early at Star and became a proficient gaffer, in a plant that had many expert blowers. "Remember the bent-neck nursing bottles?" he asks. "Well, another fellow and I got so we could make 330 *dozen* of those in a day. Some of the bottles were shaped like a duck. We got $7 a day at that time. Five-year apprentices got half pay."

In those days Star Glass had 10 shops with five men to each shop. Brick tunnels carried steam, water and other utilities underground from one building to another. After the factory closed children took over the tunnels as playgrounds, would go racing through them, then pop up from underground like jack rabbits, to the astonishment of passersby.

Fig. 122 MEDFORD SHOPS in full blast 1905. FROM RIGHT TO LEFT, scene shows some progressive stages of glassmaking: AT RIGHT, marvering the gather on a marble slab; blowing into an iron mold as the mold-boy (in striped sweater, with derby hat beside him) prepares to close the mold; LEFT OF POST, the gaffer in his chair finishes a glass article; FAR LEFT, a carry-in boy prepares to take a finished bottle to lehr. *Photo, courtesy of Everett F. Mickle. Copy and print by Tom Barnett.*

Fig. 123 STAR GLASS FACTORY, 1894-1923, at Medford was last of a series starting with a windowglass plant in 1830s. Star furnace was steam-powered.

For the Campbell Soup Company Star Glass devised the first lock-top catsup bottles, difficult to blow as they had precision-grooved necks to fit metal caps.* Flat paneled bottles for vanilla, conical ones for Gouttman's drops, blob-top sodas and minerals, and miniature champagnes and cordials were among the numerous mold-blown containers. A popular sample bottle to hold liquor, shaped like a nail, and aptly called a "spike," was blown for local hotels for the year-end holidays. A clear clam bottle with metal top was another of these miniatures. Large quantities of handblown rum bottles were packed in salt hay, then a Jersey crop from its seaside marshes, and shipped to Puerto Rico and Central America.

Star Glass had its own brand-marked liquor flasks in several sizes, flat bottles impressed with a star and the words WARRANTED (star) FLASK/ 7 OUNCES / UNION MADE. Examining the loving care that Star blowers put into these and other throwaway bottles, it is saddening to think that such talent was not applied to containers of handsome design like the 19th century ones of Whitall Tatum or to table ware like that of the Jersey City Dummers.

* A perfect example, with paper label intact, is on exhibit along with some other Jersey glass collected by Charles S. Boyer, at Pomona Hall (1726), Euclid and Park Blvd., headquarters of the Camden County Historical Society.

Fig. 124 "STAR" BOTTLES. FAR LEFT, soda bottle; CENTER, ink sander in bubbly aqua, one of two found on site, may have been made by earliest glassworks at Medford. Conical bottle for Gouttman's drops; RIGHT, two liquor flasks marked WARRANTED/FLASK/UNION MADE.

Fig. 125 Glass turtle.

Fig. 126 MEDFORD COMPANY STORE about 1895. Arms akimbo and standing on steps is John Mingin, owner of the Star Glass Works, Medford, at that date and into the 1920s. *Collection of Everett F. Mickle. Copy and print by Tom Burnett.*

Tansboro—
A Multi-Colored Works

Like numerous Jersey furnaces with considerable longevity the Tansboro Glass Works functioned under various managements with brief intervals of quiet in between. This 8-pot furnace started about 1848 and did not go out of blast for the last time until July 1885. Tansboro Works was known principally as a Norcross family enterprise, with Bodines active in the late years.

Leaders in the initial venture, known as S. Norcross & Company, were Samuel Norcross and Joseph Heritage who were the managers. Among other important stockholders were William Peacock, Benjamin Thackara, Lester Gager and Matthias Simmerman. The latter married Rebecca Norcross and the two families were closely associated in the glassmaking. After a few years the stock company was dissolved but Samuel and Uriah Norcross soon resumed the business of bottle-blowing.

Alonzo Norcross, a great-grand-nephew of Samuel Norcross, was so kind as to let me see a Norcross ledger of the period 1853 leading into 1856. Contents of the ledger will be discussed later in connection with archeological findings at the site of the Tansboro furnace.

The Norcross brothers continued to operate the glassworks for a time, then leased it to John L. Mason, of Vineland, inventor of the famous Mason fruit jar. As Mason was not a glassblower but a tinsmith, it is likely that the Mason connection was a sublease from Joel Bodine and Charles Adams who leased the plant from Norcrosses from 1862 to 1872.

It is not true that the first Mason jar was blown at Tansboro, as Prowell erroneously wrote and some other authors copied. The prototype for Mason's best known patent of Nov. 30, 1858, one of his many "improved" jars, was blown at Crowleytown, now a picnic spot along the Mullica River in Wharton State Forest, and Clayton Parker, an expert glass man of Bridgeton, blew the jar in 1856, then made variations according to Mason's suggestions.

In the winter of 1858, Mason was neither at Crowleytown or Tansboro but had set up a shop at 257 Pearl Street, New York, to make caps for his jars—the latter were to be blown to fit the caps. By 1863 Mason was no longer listed in New York directories but was supervising blowing of jars for quantity production at Tansboro. This further improved jar was an immediate success. By 1865 Mason had returned to New York. In 1874 he sold his patent rights to the Consolidated Fruit Jar Company of New Brunswick.

Bodine and Adams were still preparing for the autumn fire of 1872, as witness this letter of October 16 to James Norcross:

Bodine & Adams
Hollow Green Glassware Manufacturers
Tansboro, N.J.

Dear Sir:

If at the 1st of November we should want a boy to tend in the factory may we depend on yours, at the wages paid last year? If so please let us know and oblige

Yours
Bodine & Adams

Frank Bodine was the last known operator of the Tansboro works which at its peak employed about 150 people. Only hollow ware was ever made here.

In the 1853-56 ledger, entries were often made by Samuel Norcross himself and also by Trial Westcott, evidently his clerk. Simmermans were still active in the firm according to the 1855 records and on November 13 of that year Matthias R. Simmerman was paid $10 for expenses to New York. One of the blowers was Abraham Burdsall who during the month of May in 1854 was blowing liniments, oval prescription bottles and pint flasks. Among the articles blown in large amounts were Dr. Berry bottles, 555 dozen in a single listing. Panel bottles, thin flat ones for prescriptions and patent medicines, and castor oil bottles were also being blown. The hollow ware most often listed, however, were flasks, such entries as 11½ doz. pt. flasks and 15½ doz. flasks.

Fig. 128 AUTHENTIC TANSBORO GIMMAL bottle, one of a kind, is rare for its applied leaf decoration. Clear glass ornamented on curved sides with narrow bands of rigaree. Bottle has been in the Gager family, co-founders of the Tansboro Glass Works, until 1970; now owned by the Corning Museum of Glass. H. 8 inches.

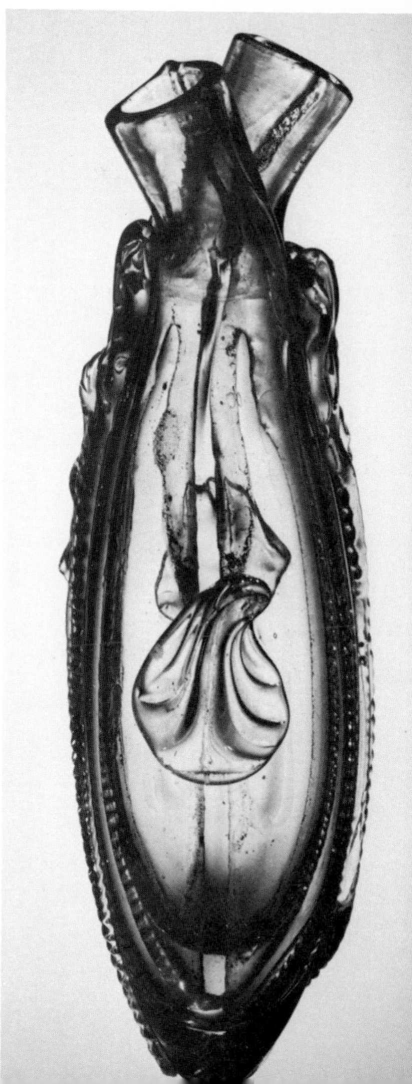

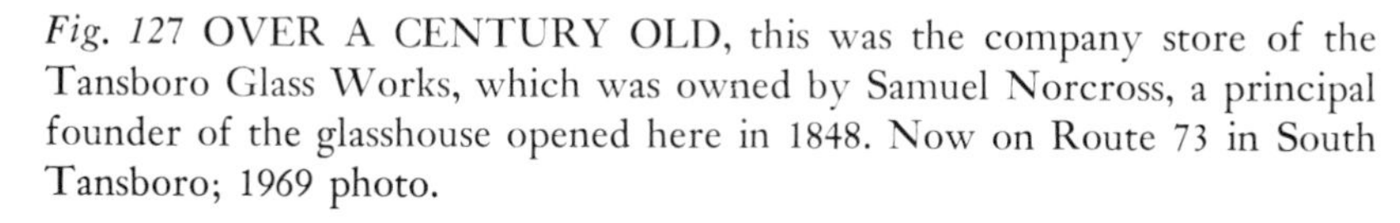

Fig. 127 OVER A CENTURY OLD, this was the company store of the Tansboro Glass Works, which was owned by Samuel Norcross, a principal founder of the glasshouse opened here in 1848. Now on Route 73 in South Tansboro; 1969 photo.

The mystery of the kinds of flasks made is partly solved by our archeological check at the Tansboro site where we found a pit of glass artifacts so varied as to seem almost a catalog of colors and shapes. The colors were so vivid and distinctive that we could match slag to finished bottle necks, and thus know that this was no mere cullet dump.

Recovered intact was an aqua pint flask, one with a ½-inch ribbon seam down the sides. Large fragments of the same type of flask, pints and quarts, were found in reddish amber, grass green and bright olive.

The variety of attractive, lively ambers and greens was remarkable, as if the formula-maker had tried to give customers a brand color. Blue glass was produced at Tansboro, Mr. Norcross said, but we did not find any at this particular site.

Necks of bottles show a varied range also and embossed lettering was precise. Among other fragments found were:

Necks of large blob-top bottles in blue-green emerald, grass green, light honey amber, and reddish amber. Similar colors were found in bottles that had single- and double-collared necks. Some sheared lips.
A front panel of a large red-amber oblong bottle embossed as REED'S GILT EDGE 1878 TONIC.
A bottle embossed SODA WATER / HENRY REHM / HOBOKEN, N.J.
Three-inch necks only ¾ inch in diameter, aqua.
Flat-topped flanged collars on high-shouldered round aqua bottles. Two cone ink bottles. Thin aqua bases similar to those of fruit jars.
Portions of square gin bottles in "black" glass (dark olive green), with walls ¼ inch thick.
Aqua bottle neck with a diamond pattern below ring at base.
Other evidence of pattern molding: portions of a bulbous bottle in thin grass-green glass which has ¾-inch fluted panels.

The Norcross family showed me a light blue, swirled, two-handled vase with indented waist, which they said was blown at Tansboro, surely by an apprentice, because of the lopsided shape. The vase proved to be a less full-blown copy of identical blue and amber ones I have, and of which I have seen two others in New Jersey. The distinctive swirl indicates that a dip mold was probably used, and the vases may have been for a customer order rather than spare-time blowing. The unusual bright colors at Tansboro, however, must have tempted the skilled gaffers at this furnace into creating some exceptional take-home glass. From clear glass one blower fashioned a gimmal bottle that was handed down in the Gager family until 1970 and is now in the Corning Musuem of Glass.

Site of the glassworks is on Route 73, near South Tansboro elementary school, the furnace gone and replaced by residences. Opposite is a weathered unpainted dwelling that once was the company store owned by Samuel Norcross. Close by are three tenant houses, now modernized. At one time Samuel and his brother Uriah owned a stage line that ran through Long-a-Coming, now Berlin, and down this Blue Anchor road to Absecon on the shore. One of the Norcross stages is now owned by historic Batsto Village and is used to take visitors on a gay ride to the street where glassmakers and iron-workers once lived.

CRIMPED AND CRACKED vase in cornflower blue, blown by August Hofbauer in his Vineland art glass plant. Red pitcher with clear applied handle is also by Hofbauer. *Barbetti collection.*

DEVIL'S FIRE mantel ornaments. Pine-tree shapes of clear flint glass have flame-like core splashing with red, yellow, blue and green glass. Precision baluster stem like those used for Whitall Tatum pharmaceutical jars indicates Millville origin, Applied circular foot. H. 11 inches.

PLATE 14

VIOLET PITCHER blown by August Hofbauer with inverted thumbprint is unusual, also, for 2-quart size and contrasting handle of peacock blue-green. *Barbetti collection.*

"SHEAF OF RYE" CALABASH is virtually identical in shape and ribbing with the Fislerville Jenny Lind calabash. Laurel branches are inverted above a sheaf of grain superimposed on a rake and a pitchfork. Reverse has an 8-rayed daisy or star. A similar bottle by Sheets & Duffy of Philadelphia has their name embossed above the star. Quart, in typical South Jersey aqua. *George G. McConnell collection.*

LIFELIKE FISH. A difficult feat achieved by Angelo Ponzetto of Vineland, who applied fins and eyes after shaping three colors of glass into naturalistic forms. Blue-back fish required greater dexterity as it is cased over yellow-orange end-of-day glass. Fish rest on applied clear base. H. 11½ inches. C. 1920s.

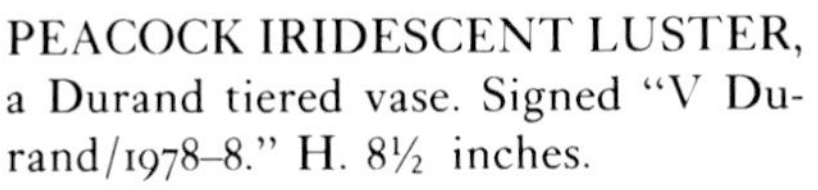

PEACOCK IRIDESCENT LUSTER, a Durand tiered vase. Signed "V Durand/1978–8." H. 8½ inches.

The Quintonites

IN SALEM COUNTY on Alloway creek, about six miles downstream from the site of 18th century Wistarberg, is another glassmaking village where cylinder glass was blown from 1863 until about 1908. Unlike Wistarberg this village still has numerous tenant houses built for glassmakers and the original company store.

Surprising, considering the high mortality of New Jersey glass firms when hand-blown ware became too costly, the Quinton Glass Works became ever more prosperous. Now under the name of Hires Turner Glass Company of Wilmington, Del., with descendants of the founders active in its management, the firm has become one of the nation's leading distributors of architectural glass.

The company store, now the office of Smick Lumber, started Quinton's window-light works on its way. As early as 1850 George Hires, a Salem county boy of 18, decided that farming was not the life for him so he took a job in the Quinton store. Within a year the owner decided the store should be called Smith & Hires. In 1862 Hires' younger brother Charles bought out Smith's interest.

Noting the growing demand for high grade window-glass of large size for commercial buildings, the three men in 1863 joined with John Lambert to organize the Quinton Glass Works in which each invested $8,000. Blowing began Oct. 24.

Within a year Smith retired from the company and in 1866 Charles Hires returned to farming and sold his share to George R. Morrison. In the next year Lambert withdrew, and when Morrison left in 1870 George Hires was sole owner for two years. Then Charles Hires returned. Shortly thereafter the Hires brothers took in three New Yorkers as members, the name becoming Hires, Halthaus, Prentice and Ward. An energetic teenager of 19, William Plummer, a brother-in-law of George Hires, joined the company and over a two year period made such important contributions that he was admitted as a partner in the firm which had become Hires & Company.

A quaint illustration from the *New Historical Atlas of Salem and Gloucester Counties* indicates that by 1876 the Quinton Glass Company had become a thriving community. The atlas reported in that year:

> "The Quinton Glass Works, with the dwelling houses for their employees, cover an area of about seven acres. They are conveniently situated on the south bank of Alloways Creek, thus enjoying unsurpassed facilities for the transportation of their products and materials. The Company owns and runs a steamer between Philadelphia, New York, and Baltimore.
>
> "The works have an annual capacity for three million feet of glass. They have, as one of the most prominent features of their establishment, a Belgium oven, the entire castings of which were imported from Europe. This oven turns out a superior quality of glass, nearly equal to the French plate, and certainly superior to any manufacturer elsewhere in the United States. The Works are admirably arranged, and under the superintendence of the Hires Brothers, who are well versed in the intricate and multiform processes entailed in the manufacture of glass.

The products of the Quinton Glass Works find a ready market in nearly every state of the Union, the California trade being particularly extensive. They have furnished as much, if not more, glass to the Centennial Buildings [in Philadelphia] than any other firm, and it is needless to add that it gave entire satisfaction. They employ about one hundred and fifty workmen, most of whom live in the neat cottages belonging to the Works. In addition to the Works proper, the Company have a very extensive general store, steam grist-mill, and other convenient auxiliaries to their immense business."

Among the buildings used in manufacturing were two melting furnaces, flattening and cutting houses, a pot room, a box factory and an engine house to operate the bellows for draft. The large rectangular furnaces had swing-pits seven feet deep on each side. Above the pits, at about floor level, were platforms, each of which led to a melting pot. The blowers stood on the platforms as they elongated the hot ball of glass to about five feet, and 11 inches in diameter. Many kinds of specialty glass were produced, such as silvered—for mirrors —plate and enameled.

To speed deliveries the firm in 1878 opened a Philadelphia office and warehouse on Filbert Street between Seventh and Eighth streets. That was the year in which the present Hires Turner Glass Company was organized. John Turner had come from Land's End, England, as a lad of 17 and worked in the glass division of John Lucas & Company, Philadelphia. Having become acquainted with the Quintonites he was invited to head the Philadelphia office. In 1911 Turner followed George Hires as president. Samuel Gilmore was president from 1926 until his death in 1936 when William Plummer, Jr., held the office until 1963. John A. Hires is president of this largely family-owned company now in its second century. Among noteworthy modern installations of glass by the firm have been the State Department Building and the British Embassy in Washington and glass curtain walls like those of Wyeth Laboratories, Philadelphia.

Fig. 129 PROUD WIELDERS OF THE BLOWPIPE are these windowglass workers assembled about 1900 at the Quinton glasshouse. Firm is now the Hires Turner Glass Company of Wilmington, Del. *Courtesy of William Plummer, Jr.*

The Fislers, The Moores and Jenny Lind

FISLERVILLE GLASS WORKS

JENNY LIND, "the Swedish nightingale," proved herself as much of a showman as her impresario, P.T. Barnum. Before she would even embark for the United States she insisted on a guarantee of $187,500. When she finally arrived at New York's Castle Garden on Sept. 4, 1850, there had been such prolonged publicity that three New Jersey glasshouses—Fislerville, the Whitneys and Samuel Huffsey—were ready for her with the now famous Jenny Lind calabash bottle with her portrait blown in the glass. Which factory had the first bottle? Probably Whitneys because they spelled her name JENY. The other two houses had time to correct this mistake.

The Fislerville Glass Works had special reason to honor the American debut of Jenny Lind in 1850, for this furnace was making its own debut in the autumn of that year. No wonder that the owners presented a Jenny Lind calabash with a portrait of their glasshouse on the obverse and above it a banner proclaiming FISLERVILLE GLASS WORKS.

A Fisler of Fislertown founded the Fislerville Glass Works ! His name was Jacob P. Fisler, Jr., a descendant of an industrious family who had emigrated to South Jersey in the mid-1700s. The location of the new furnace was 75 wooded acres on the east side of the Glassboro-Malaga turnpike on what is now Delsea Drive in Clayton. The name Fislerville was changed to Clayton in 1867.

Benjamin Beckett was Fisler's first partner but withdrew by 1851 and Edward Bacon bought Beckett's shares. As Fisler and Bacon they made glass until 1856 when Bacon was killed in a train accident. Fisler then went out of glassmaking but rented the furnace to John M. Moore who soon bought the entire compound.

MOORE BROTHERS

From then on a new industrial era was ushered in to Clayton. By 1859 new members of the firm of John M. Moore & Company were George C. Hewitt and Jeremiah D. Hogate. D. Wilson Moore, brother of John, bought Hewitt's shares in 1863, resulting in Moore Brothers & Company. The outfit was also known as the Clayton Glass Works but business stationery indicated a preference for Moore Brothers. In 1880 Charles Fisler, Harry Steelman and Francis M. Pierce became board members, but for all time the firm remained Moore Brothers.

Fislerville had five dwellings in 1850 but by the 1875 census the population numbered 1500, not great in size still, but for the glass business from then on until about 1912,

Fig. 130 FISLERVILLE JENNY LIND calabash probably blown in 1850 when Fislerville Glass Works was founded in the village known since 1867 as Clayton. Clevenger reproductions show much less detail in the portrait and are blown in vivid colors. Aqua quart. McK. GI-101. Glass factory on reverse of GI-101 is only 1½ stories as compared with 2-story structure on Huffsey bottles. Fislerville calabash has scalloped neck line.

everything was zoom. From a hamlet operation Moore Brothers had quickly advanced into modern industry.

By 1880 the Clayton Glass Works covered 20 acres on which were four large glasshouses, five huge warehouses, a large general store, a spur to the West Jersey Railroad, a carpenter shop, large elevated coal bins, and a steam plant which powered a sawmill, a gristmill, and a machine shop and served to create a tremendous draft for the furnaces.

The annual value of products sold by the firm was quoted as half a million dollars. Some 600 tons of glassware were made each year. This required 4,000 tons of sand; 1,200 of soda; 2,400 of lime. Some 7,500 tons of coal and 3,600 cords of wood were needed for fuel.

The company owned 100 tenant houses which were described in 1875 as being roomy and substantial and of far better grade than usual in company villages. About 100 additional houses had been sold to longtime employees.

In the 1880s Moore Brothers employed about 400 persons. Among glassmen who became well known in the 20th century were the three Clevenger brothers and their father, Otis Coleman and Paul E. Winner. The latter, when I talked with him in 1960, was then in charge of the 3 to 11 p.m. shift at Clevenger Brothers who were then blowing reproductions of the Fislerville Jenny Lind calabash, in blue, grape, emerald, amber and amberina. The original Jenny Lind bottle of a century earlier has been found chiefly in aqua but also in amber and various shades of green.

Recalling his former days at Moore Brothers, Mr. Winner said the workmen had special names for the four factories: the Big House, the Little House, the Dinky and the

Wild Cat Furnace. He remembered blowing mostly amber beer and soda bottles. Noted for well-made glass, Moore Brothers also produced large quantities of pharmaceutical bottles, their own patented Mason fruit jars and Carter's ink bottles.

In 1970 one of the most desirable of the Moore fruit jars, with yoke and thumb-screw and the name embossed in script—John M. Moore & Co/ Manufacturers/ Fislerville, N.J.—sold in South Jersey for $125. The buyer had the jar packed elsewhere and shipped to the west coast, where it arrived broken. John M. Moore would have been incredulous at such prices for his fruit jars.

Lewis De Eugenio of Glassboro is the proud owner of a Moore Brothers quart Mason jar in a rich cobalt, one of four known to exist.

FISLER & MORGAN . . . F. M. PIERCE COMPANY

In 1880, the very year when Dr. Charles F. Fisler joined Moore Brothers, he withdrew to organize a new glassworks, Fisler & Morgan, at the north end of Clayton. With him were Albert S. Fisler and Henry and Walter Morgan. Starting off with an investment of $20,000 they erected on a 10-acre tract a large factory with a steam mill, a machine shop, a packing house, an office and a large store. Walter Morgan withdrew from the firm sometime before 1883 at which time the business seemed to be prospering and employed about 100 workers. A few years after its founding the new glassworks was sold to Franklin M. Pierce and operated under the name F. M. Pierce Company.

Fig. 131 RARE BEEHIVE SALT of cobalt non-lead glass with 8 hand-tooled rings. Found in private home in Clayton and tentatively attributed to Fislerville Glass Works, 1850s. H. 3¼ inches. *Ex-McKearin collection. Courtesy, Corning Museum of Glass.*

The Clevenger Brothers of Clayton

The Sesquicentennial Exposition held in Philadelphia in 1926 had an unexpected and certainly not generally known effect on Jersey glassmaking.

The story was told to me by Ernest C. Stanmire, antiques expert and South Jerseyan who had long known the three glassblowing Clevenger brothers of Clayton.

"We heard there was glass on exhibit at the Sesqui," he said, "so the Clevengers and I went over to take a look. There we saw one of the original log cabin Booz bottles made by Whitneys at Glassboro, with a valuation tag on it of $160. Later, Allie Clevenger said, 'Why we could make those easy enough if we had a mold.'

"That started me looking for old Whitney molds—after all, the original Booz bottles were blown only three miles from Clayton. But I couldn't find a trace locally. Then I went to see an oldtime pattern maker I knew in North Philadelphia. I combed through his castoff stock and suddenly came across half of an original pattern—not a mold—for a Booz bottle. Later I went back and searching every inch of the warehouse I at last found the matching half. From that we had a metal mold cut in Millville, and we were in business."

The Stanmires were already in business as the Clayton Antiques Company and they were prepared to buy glass which might be blown by the Clevengers. Not only that, Ernest Stanmire loaned Allie Clevenger the money for materials to build a simple one-pot furnace. The lender was surprised and touched when, with the furnace built and ready for blowing in 1927, Allie returned $7 he did not need.

From that time forth, most Clevenger glass has been hand blown by oldtime gaffers in the early South Jersey manner, although Allie, the last of the Clevenger brothers, died June 22, 1960.

Just who *were* the Clevengers?

The family came from Batsto where the father William worked in the window-glass furnace in operation there between 1846 and 1866. When hard times fell upon Batsto he moved to Clayton to take a job as shearer or furnace tender for Moore Brothers. In the custom of the day he soon had his sons at work there too. The youngest, Allie, was a carry-in boy at 11, as was a child who became his life-long friend, the late Otis Coleman. One of the other boys was helping at Moores' as early as 7 years. The brothers, in order of decreasing age, were Thomas, Lorenzo and William Elbert, but known everywhere as Tommy, Reno and Allie. The latter was the only master blower, though all three spent most of their lives glassmaking.

When Moore Brothers closed just before World War I the Clevengers were at loose ends, doing odd jobs, making rugs, as glassblowers were a glut on the market, for whom there was no job insurance, no pension, no Social Security.

The Booz bottle brought luck to all. It caught on, and Stanmire, *au courant* for the

Fig. 132 WILLIAM (ALLIE) CLEVENGER blowing glass at Clayton, 1930s. *Photo by the late Samuel M. Langston; courtesy of Frederick Jackson.*

small collector who wanted pressed milkglass chickens, as well as the more advanced collector who desired free-blown pitchers but couldn't afford early Jersey ones, helped the Clevengers to select glass that was in demand. Low prices of that day can make even a collector of reproductions quail: handblown Jersey pitchers to 12 inches were only $1; Booz bottles in amber, $2; handblown hats, 50¢.The times were rising to a fall, the financial crash of 1929. Because the real crash in South Jersey had been the death of glass factories, the disaster was just one from bad to worse. The Clevengers kept on making glass. The story, unverified, is that they filled a 3-story house with blown glass, unsold at the time. The report sounds true because some attractive lilypads have appeared in recent times.

But in the mid-1930s Ruth Webb Lee, best known as a writer on pressed glass, was after the Clevengers with a Carrie Nation umbrella, although she never mentioned them by name, only illustrated their glass. The Clevengers probably never heard of her, but among collectors her name is not revered in South Jersey.

Writing a column in the now defunct *American Collector,* she railed against this un-named enemy, although she is considered the spokesman for the most flagrant copyist of all: pressed glass, a copy industry that threw hundreds of craftsmen out of work.

"The latest from that unregenerate territory," she wrote of South Jersey, was lilypad bowls (copied by the Clevengers, but all freeblown, not stamped out by press) and that "Color range is astonishing, emerald green, cobalt blue, violent purple." Emerald and cobalt were early South Jersey colors; purple, violent or peaceful, was rare. "Old pieces would be lighter in weight." Quite. "The lilypad is thicker than it should be." Indeed. "Old pieces would be lighter in weight. . . . surface in old seems softer, less harsh and brilliant . . ." Assuredly Mrs. Lee pointed out three obvious differences, which should have made it clear that the Clevengers were not faking anything. All of their advertising and that of Stanmire's clearly stated in large type: "Finest Reproductions of Pressed and Blown Glass," at scarcely survival prices, while copyist pressed glass was still in good demand. Mrs. Lee said soft wear was a point of test, one I can't fully agree with after seeing how often glass blown by a member of a family was so highly prized that it was placed on a shelf for show and never used.

Collectible Clevenger glass was that which was freeblown rather than mold-blown, for a brief time about 1930, and which emulated household ware made in the first half of the 19th century in South Jersey. The following are some of the general types:

Lilypad vases, pitchers and bowls
Uncovered sugar bowls and creamers with crimped feet
3½-inch pitchers with plain feet and intense colors of emerald, violet and sapphire
Footed serving bowls with folded rims
Finger bowls
Flat pans with slanting straight sides

About the time that Emil J. Larson's glass from his Vineland home furnace was becoming known in 1934, Ernest Stanmire switched from the Clevengers who were well under way by this time, and Philip Glick of Clayton took a hand in advising them.

Fig. 133 PURPOSELY PRIMITIVE are the grape-colored jelly glass and sapphire mug made at Clevengers' about 1930; H. 5 inches. Expanded diamond flask is still being blown at Clevengers'; amethyst; H. 5¾ inches.

Fig. 134 CLEVENGER reproduction of an early violin flask.

Fig. 135 3-MOLD AMETHYST DECANTER in sunburst and diamond pattern (McK. GIII-9) was made by Clevengers' in 1930s and 1940s. H. 10½ inches.

Fig. 136 EMERALD SUGAR BOWL in South Jersey style, blown by Otis Coleman at Clevengers'. Applied handle and crimped foot. H. 4 inches. Flip glass in Millville blue. H. 8 inches.

Fig. 137 GEN. DOUGLAS MACARTHUR flask originated at Clevengers' in World War II. Obverse is embossed GENERAL/MACARTHUR in arch over portrait and below it: KEEP THEM FLYING. Reverse has large letter V flanked by two American flags and topped by the date 1942. At bottom of V are three dots and a dash, signifying the radio code for V. Overall in script is the motto "God Bless America." Base initialed CB. Amber ½ pint.

In 1950 Allie Clevenger married Myrtle Whilden, widow of Rodney Whilden, who brought a remarkable dowry: molds made from fine specimens of 3-mold glass in the sunburst pattern (G III-9 of McKearin). Whilden had four pieces of this glass which he sold to a collector for $4,800, but before doing so he had had remarkably precise molds made of a decanter and a pitcher in the set. These became part of the Clevenger catalog line, under the name Stoddard pitcher, decanter, vase and jug. The latter two were adapted by hand-finishing of the first two. When blown by gaffers like Otis Coleman, the decanter and the pitcher were phenomenal reproductions, sharp and clear. Even the experts were sometimes confused. Mrs. Myrtle Clevenger Bowers recalls that one of the items was on exhibit in a museum and labeled "made in Sandwich, Mass." She called the curator to inform him of the error, but he insisted he was right. Thereupon she asked him to open the case for examination of the glass and was able to prove the expert wrong.

The Booz bottle is another amazingly accurate reproduction. In the original Whitney bottle the roof-top corners were found to break, so these were slanted. The Clevengers had the same experience. The original bottle had a faint period after the word "Whiskey" on one side. This is missing in the copy, about the only way of distinguishing a Clevenger from a Whitney. Despite the date 1840 on the roof, these bottles were made in the 1860s for E. G. Booz of Philadelphia. The 1840 log cabin souvenirs of various kinds were made to honor Presidential candidate William Henry Harrison, but this bottle is not truly a log cabin, as the McKearins pointed out. Rather, it represents one of the "pigeon houses" such as South Jersey glassblowers lived in, a fact no one seems to have noticed. Still today the name Booz is common in the Salem area (the word "booze" for liquor was in use at least a century before the Whitney bottle appeared). At least one famous collector was so enchanted with the Clevenger Booz bottle that he bought 150 of them.

The Clevengers reproduced the Jenny Lind calabash bottle which was introduced in 1850 by the Fislerville Glass Works, named for the town which in 1867 became Clayton. Although a popular bottle it is by no means a faithful reproduction; for one thing, the portrait of the famous singer was rather carelessly drawn. The McKearins wrote that the "Counterfeit of Fislerville type" holds exactly one quart; I find that the Clevenger Jenny Lind holds 30 ounces. Besides the aqua and green of the Fislerville original, the Clevenger calabash was made in a rather intense shade of fuchsia.

Clevenger glass, when the furnace was owned by the Clevengers, came in a rainbow of vivid colors which helped to make it popular from coast to coast. Deep aquamarine was used, of course, in making some of the freeblown ware in the early South Jersey tradition. Other colors were amethyst, grape or fuchsia, purple, light gray-blue, turquoise, cornflower, cobalt, vaseline, light green, grass green, emerald, golden amber, medium amber, amberina and red. The Stanmires assure me that the Clevengers never used combinations of colors such as amber pitchers with clear handles. The one-ton tank furnace was usually filled daily with just enough metal of one color to be worked from 6:30 a.m. to 3 p.m.

For one week the Clevengers concentrated on making clear glass in the early South Jersey style for Frederick Jackson, this Malaga dealer reports. The only such article I have seen is a bowl which has a faint and attractive golden hue, though made from milk-bottle cullet.

Fig. 138 SAPPHIRE LILYPAD pitcher has two tones of blue created by varying thickness of glass. Entire body above "waves" is skillfully threaded. Pleasing proportions and good workmanship marked this pitcher blown by Otis Coleman at Clevengers' in the 1930s. H. 7 inches.

Besides the articles previously described, the following glassware was made in large quantities for the standard repertoire, was photographed in a brochure, and much of it is still being blown today. Objects that proved difficult to blow, such as the square candy-jar pitcher, were withdrawn from time to time. The following list is not meant to be comprehensive but to suggest by the descriptive names the forms and patterns.

FLASKS AND BOTTLES

- Eagle and grape
- My Country—flag
- Washington-Taylor
  (above, modeled after
  Coffin & Hay flasks)
- Albany Glass Works—sailboat
- Diamond
- Quilted diamond
- Sunflower (copy of Whitall-Tatum)
- Success to the Railroad
- General MacArthur
- Scroll
- Banjo
- Crown
- Elephant
- Violin, 10" and 7½"
- Washington figural, 10" and 8½"
- Daisy and button

No flasks or bottles have been made from original antique molds, except as described for the Booz log-cabin. Some flasks were embossed CB on the bottom.

Fig. 139 GAFFER'S SKILL in blowing is shown by matched pair of lilypad vases which in turn match freeblown glass of the early 1800s. Well-formed emerald vases blown in the 1930s by Otis Coleman at Clevengers'. H. 8 inches.

Fig. 140 CLEVENGER (1930s) of attractive design and color in early Jersey style. Emerald pitcher with sheared lip, applied handle and crimped foot; H. 4¾ inches. CENTER, sugar bowl blown in melon-shaped dip mold; slightly bubbled cobalt; H. 3 inches. Aqua sugar bowl by Otis Coleman, which is often confused with authentic early Jersey; applied handles and crimped foot; H. 4 inches.

PITCHERS	JUGS
Stoddard sunburst	Stoddard sunburst
Quilted diamond	Rose-in-snow
Square candy jar	Jenny Lind
Melon	Doughnut
Star and shield	Onion
Hobnail	Camphor
Moon and star	Sunflower

Among other items were miniature boots and hats, mottled end-of-day lilies, hobnail tumblers, star-and-dewdrop plates and salts, paneled grape goblets, book-end vases. The large pitchers, about 2-quart size, were made by Tommy Clevenger.

During the 1930s a type of folk-art glass was freeblown in limited amounts. Among these were heavy mugs with broad applied handles, blown in cobalt, sapphire, emerald, amber and red. Although engagingly primitive in shape they are virtually free of bubbles and would never be confused with frothy Mexican glass. Tumblers in the same style, and now likely to be called jelly glasses, were also free blown. Tall, conical beverage glasses, footed, were blown in a swirled dip mold.

Ernest C. Stanmire reports that the pressed glass which Clevengers sold, such as paneled grape goblets, hobnail tumblers, star-and-dewdrop plates and salts, was made by August Hofbauer at his Vineland shop. The Clevengers made only handblown glass.

In 1964 Allie Clevenger's widow married William S. Bowers who had had long experience in the production of glass though not as a glassblower. As experienced glassblowers became more and more scarce and their best gaffers died or retired, Mr. and Mrs. Bowers decided to close the furnace. But then at the eleventh hour, Mr. and Mrs. James Travis arranged to take over. Still under the name of Clevengers they operate the furnace as before and now and then add a new item to the Clevenger line. At the time of the furnace sale, Mrs. Bowers also sold to dealers numerous early freeblown articles—lilypads, bowls, pitchers, vases—now appearing on the market.

Among well-known blowers who have worked at the Clevenger furnace are Otis Coleman, August Hofbauer, Vermont Frie, Harold Robb, Paul E. Winner, and Charles Westcott.

Woodbury's "Green Era"

To own a coach and four seems to be a dream for many a man, especially when sudden wealth accrues.

There was "Baron" von Stiegel who, when his 18th century glassworks at Manheim, Pa., made him rich for a time, used to come roaring up to his manor house amid a great fanfare of trumpets in a coach and four. About that same period in New Jersey, ironmaster Peter Hasenclever, who also took unto himself the courtesy title of "Baron," rode around to the Ringwood mines in the Ramapo mountains in a coach drawn by four horses. Today there is the Duke of Bedford helping to keep his English estate solvent with a revival of an ancestral custom by charging American tourists for rides in a coach and four, with an accompanying ta-ra-ta-ra of trumpets.

But in staid Jersey of the 1880s who would dream of being a party to such nonsense? No less than Col. George G. Green of Woodbury, the patent medicine king.

There are still people alive today who recall Col. Green's coach, "The Tally-ho," drawn by four matched horses flicked on by a liveried driver. A footman, who tootled a brass horn to warn Woodbury pedestrians, helped ladies with ruffled parasols to alight at Gray Towers, the chateau which Col. Green had commissioned to be built in 1878 on Cooper Street.

For Col. Green, whose wealth was rooted and flourished in just three medicinals—August Flower Syrup, Boschee's German Syrup, and Ague Conqueror—his coach and four and his castle were only embellishments on a way of life that bouleversed Woodbury, then a quiet Quaker village first settled in 1683, today the seat of Gloucester County.

Unlike many a man of wealth remembered only for profligate eccentricities or penny-pinching exploitation, Green was an innovator who transformed and benefited communities and industries that came within his orbit.

Born in 1842 in Woodbury (Clarksboro), George Green was a hometown boy who not only made good there but was a prophet as well, one whose activities presaged, in fact demonstrated, a much-needed era of manufacturing efficiency and consideration for employees.

His father, Lewis M. Green, who later became mayor of Woodbury, started in a small way making August Flower Syrup and German Syrup, with enough success to send his son to the University of Pennsylvania medical school. After two years, in 1864 the son volunteered for the Union Army where he was made assistant surgeon of the 142nd Regiment of the Illinois Volunteers and attained his rank of colonel. Unlike the devious "Dr." Thomas W. Dyott of Philadelphia, Col. Green never used the title of "doctor" to sell his proprietary formulas.

Fig. 141 PALACE AT WOODBURY, N. J.—The Victorian mansion and gardens of Col. G. G. Green whose medicinal syrups created a fortune for him, two glassworks, and affluence for Woodbury.

After the war Green began manufacturing the syrups in Athens, Ohio, but soon moved operations to Woodbury where success was so rapid that he bought out his father's share and was soon able to pay him $40,000 yearly royalties.

A new phenomenon of heavy advertising promotion in which he was a pioneer was partly responsible for Green's stupendous sales which must have reached into the billions of bottles, so large that the colonel went into the glassmaking business. By 1883 Green's Laboratory was mailing out 5,000,000 free almanacs for distribution on two continents: many were translated into Spanish, French and German. Covers of some depicted a sort of Norman Rockwell homefolks comic scene (see illustrations), sure-fire appeal. The calen-

Fig. 142 CARTOONS, SOFT SELL in free almanacs distributed in editions of 5,000,000 in 1883 spread the virtues of Green's August Flower and German Syrups. Calendars were translated into Spanish, French and German. *Courtesy, Gloucester County Historical Society.*

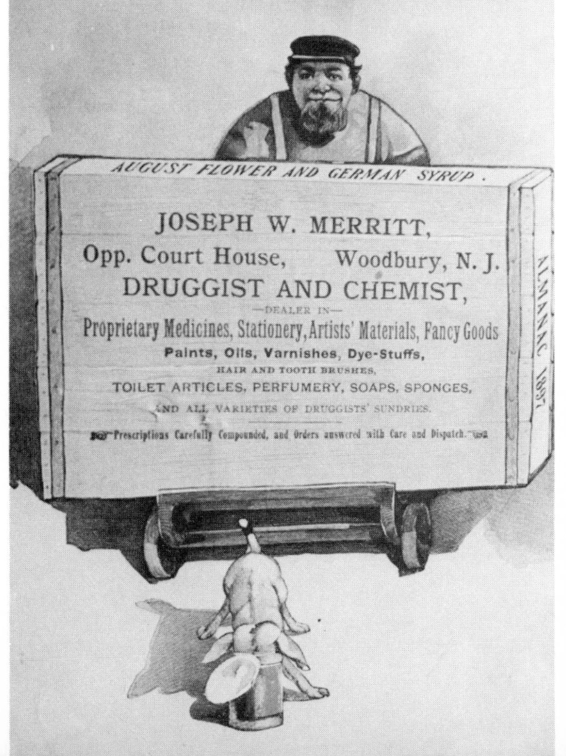

dars had maps of each of the United States where they would circulate and a list of thousands of dealers. Nine presses were kept constantly running to print almanacs, labels, cartons, package inserts, posters and signs for Green's medicaments. The blizzard of white paper sent out in the mails alone was so huge that Woodbury had the seventh highest post office revenue in the state.

Hitherto unheard of sanitary care in preparing patent medicines was undoubtedly another factor in making best-sellers of August Flower and German Syrups. At a time when the newly discovered antibacterial principles demonstrated by Pasteur were only beginning to filter down, Col. Green was heating his syrups in tanks fired by steam, probably assuring a sterile product that did not deteriorate in tropical countries or on long ocean voyages. Green's new laboratory, as described by G. E. Pierson in 1883, must have been nearly a half century ahead of its time when bitters and tonics were often "whipped up" in some vermin-infested warehouse:

> In the bottling room "twenty-eight young ladies are engaged in filling the bottles with medicine. The facilities here are first-class. Rubber hose, fitted with nickel-plated faucets and connected with the reservoirs or tanks of medicine in the room above, runs to the centre and sides of the room, where are constructed stands or tables . . . Rows of bottles are ranged on these tables, and the process of filling them becomes simple, complete, rapid, and cleanly, the end of the faucets being inserted in the neck of the bottle . . ."

Although the village of Woodbury then had no water works, Green's Laboratory had its own water plant, at Roe's Hill two miles south of town, with a capacity of 20,000 gallons an hour, a further aid to cleanliness and sanitation.

Like most patent medicine bottles, Green's were the boringly plain flat, paneled ones, but unlike the usual containers of dark brown glass which hid the often-muddy liquid, the Woodbury bottles are a medium aqua; as of 1970 a pair of unopened bottles showed the contents to be pale amber and in suspension. A corkscrew came packed in each carton.

Fig. 143 MODEL FACTORIES FOR MEDICINALS, good working conditions for employees, and good works for Woodbury made Col. G. G. Green not only rich but popular. Note his chateau in the left background.

Unlike so many kinds of bitters and other 19th century nostrums, Green's medicines were not mainly alcohol. At $1 for a bottle containing only about a half pint of liquid, these syrups would have been a very costly way to buy alcohol. In view of the widespread sale of Green's products, especially in foreign countries, where there was no temperance movement, they probably contained some efficacious pharmaceuticals. Green's Ague Conqueror, for instance, may have included some substance like Peruvian cinchona bark, a centuries-old folk-remedy for malaria (ague), from which 19th century chemists extracted quinine, virtually a specific for the disease. Green insisted that his product did not contain actual quinine.

Green's formula room was always kept locked, even from the earliest days of the establishment. The name August Flower Syrup suggests that it might be compounded of goldenrod, asters and Queen Anne's lace. By odd coincidence during the research for this book, a glass worker named August Flower was found listed among employees at a plant not in the Woodbury area. A large question mark hangs in the air.

THE WOODBURY GLASS-WORKS COMPANY

So great was the thirst on two continents for Green's syrups that the patent owner decided it would be more efficient to make his own containers, and so with George G. Green as president the Woodbury Glass-Works Company was incorporated in 1881.

Probably for the first time in the history of glassblowing, here was a factory that had an architect, Paschal Madara, who drew up some "well-executed designs."

A life-long manufacturer of glass, Christian A. Madden of Clayton was picked as superintendent. He in turn chose none but sober and industrious personnel, and the record after two years' blowing was that not a single day had been lost through drunkenness and "not a more quiet and orderly set of men can be found; instead of profanity, which is too often the case in factories, there is singing of hymns and innocent songs, with merry laughter, making it a pleasure to associate with or live near them."

Superintendent Madden, though, was having an experience to try the patience of Job. Well in advance of the "time" for such, a tank furnace built from the Foster patent had been installed, ran well for a season, then succumbed to a plague of accidents. Having faith in the new invention, the board of managers got another continuous tank built but it too collapsed. "This second failure so discouraged Mr. Madden that he resigned his position and resumed his former occupation as a glassblower."

To fill the breach, Jacob Pease, originally a blower from Glassboro, but for the previous 13 years the superintendent for Hagerty Bros., makers of druggists' ware in Brooklyn, N.Y., was enticed to come to Woodbury for a similar job. Deciding that for blowing "a general line of glassware," the old system of pots had it all over tanks, Pease on Jan. 20, 1883, ordered the tank razed to its foundation. Within 13 days a pot furnace of improved design was built, the pots were sheared, and blowing had started, a record "never before equaled" and accomplished through the "gratuitous skilled labor" of a few of the blowers. By chasing The Machine back into the shadows the glassworks soon redeemed the early losses and became so successful as to need a second factory in the summer of 1883,

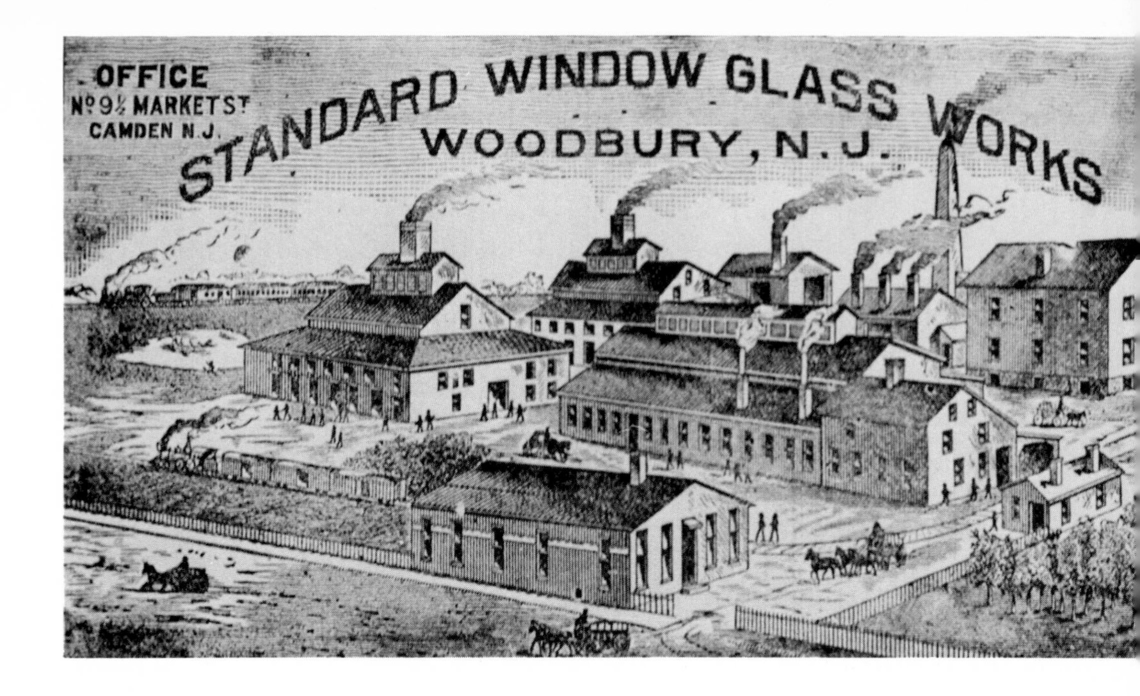

one with four sets of annealing ovens. The stresses had been too severe for secretary-treasurer Israel C. Voorhies, however, who died an untimely death.

Most of the blowers were from Glassboro, Clayton and Salem, many of them stockholders. Among the prominent names were John Runge, William Connally, Aaron, Joseph and Charles Andorfer, William Dilks, Jonathan Parker, Daniel Parker, William Stratton, William Griscom, William Keebler, Peter Mossbrooks, Daniel Lutz, Barber Crist, Thomas C. Pennington, Augustus Schulz, William Riley, John McClellan, Jonathan Newhern, James Parks.

Although most of the bottles made went to Col. Green's Laboratory, other orders were also filled. In the glass collection of the Gloucester County Historical Society, 58 N. Broad Street, one discovers from Green's syrup bottles, glasshouse slag, and free-blown ware such as a calabash decanter that the glass was a rich aquamarine. Probability that any color was added seems unlikely, but considering the craftsmanship of the gaffers, chances are that excellent ware was made for home use, pieces that perhaps now are attributed to a much earlier day.

WOODBURY STANDARD WINDOW GLASS WORKS

For his many construction ventures Col. Green had need of window-glass in huge quantities. As a result he organized in 1882 Standard Window Glass Works with himself as chairman and these other principal stockholders: general manager, John Iszard Estell of the Estellville family of glassmakers, Benjamin C. Brown, S. Paul and Henry C. Loudenslager. By 1883 a second furnace had to be built to satisfy demands, the whole at a cost of nearly $40,000. In that year the two furnaces employed 60 men and had a capacity of 50,000 boxes of glass annually, sizes not stated. Situated in North Woodbury, this subsidiary was in the first ward on land later occupied by the Woodbury Coal Company.

These two glassworks and Col. Green's Laboratory in 1882 gave employment to as many as 600 persons. The volume of business in that year exceeded half a million dollars, a stunning, announced fact that must have made some glassworks owners wonder if they shouldn't be *filling* their bottles.

A pioneer in personnel relations, the colonel used to hold annual conferences for his 19 salesmen. On the last night of the sessions the drummers were entertained by Col. and Mrs. Green at a formal dinner at Gray Towers. Most of Woodbury turned out to see the guests arrive in swallowtail suits and high silk hats which were *de rigueur* for the party. For other entertaining the Greens had three steam yachts, one of them the *Lottie Green*, anchored on Woodbury Creek, and a summer place at Lake Hopatcong. For the amusement of the populace Col. Green had set out a half-mile trotting track on one of his 42 farms around Woodbury.

What Woodbury citizens were probably most proud of was the Green Block, financed by syrups, a square at Center and Broad streets. In the heart of this large edifice was an "elegant" opera house seating a thousand people who were regaled with operettas, concerts, lectures. In 1916 a fairy operetta called "A Day in the Woods," was playing here for children, admission 15 cents. The Green Block became Woodbury's civic and social center; it also housed Common Council chambers, four large stores, many offices and "a spacious armory and military parlor."

The colonel meantime had established Canadian syrup centers, presumably supplied from Woodbury. Seeking alternate investments, Col. Green, who is recalled as a man of decision, proved to be equally successful in real estate ventures as in bottled goods.

As far back as 1887 he created Altadena, California, and today the main street is still named for him. In Pasadena he built Green's Hotel which in 1900 was the largest and most luxurious on the West Coast.

With such pleasant accommodations available, the Greens began spending all their winters in California, and they traveled there in style, aboard a private railroad coach which to Woodbury was known as the "Palace Car." It became an annual custom for Col. Green and his family to have Thanksgiving dinner in the Palace Car before their departure for the west. Each November, too, Woodbury citizens had the privilege of trooping through the Palace Car—fingering the claret velvet curtains, marveling at a train that was a home in itself: parlor, bedroom, bath, kitchen and—a word not then coined—dinette.

Green's Laboratories did not cease production until shortly after World War I. The colonel lived to be 84, in 1925. He is still recalled as a silver-haired gentleman who himself brought out apples for children skating on nearby ponds.

Rarely have patent medicines had such a tonic effect on a whole town, indeed, an entire county, without the need to imbibe a single spoonful of the elixirs. To paraphrase Salvador Dali writing at a later date: Green was the color of those years!

Whimsies and Miniatures

Witch Balls, Symbols of Magic

Spherical little bottles with short necks appeared in 17th century England in response to requests from devout householders for containers of holy water. Word spread that the families owning such bottles were protected against evil spirits, especially witches, and so the demand increased. As decades rolled by, the bottles became balls of colored glass, and with no water, holy or otherwise, but still often hung at a window, just to be on the safe side.

By the 1820s when the Nailsea glassworks was making thousands of pastel frivolities in glass, witch balls had become ornaments, but still with overtones of "Don't walk under a ladder." Less credulous persons found witch balls useful as covers for pitchers, which accounts for the increase in size.

With the strong influence of Nailsea glass that descended on South Jersey, many such local witch balls were blown, especially since even an apprentice could easily make one. Those of aqua glass, misnamed "Jersey green," were matched with pitchers of the same metal and served as a foil against insects. Ornamental witch balls were often made in amber, sapphire blue, grass green and amethyst. Among the most attractive are those of swirled opaque white and transparent aqua, some a foot in diameter.

Cobalt blue and red globes are sometimes found at sales, which the novice may mistake for witch balls. Usually these were light globes, some even 20th century, and too slick and mechanical to evoke early English or Jersey witch balls.

In 1970 the Japanese were still making small fragile globes of colored glass, about three inches in diameter, for fishnet floats, some of which are often bought in American shops as witch balls. Current reasonable price for these is about $1 for buyers who recognize them as floats, whereas some of the large Jersey tri-colored globes may sell for around $30.

In New Jersey the witch ball had its finest hour about the 1850s when it came back to the hearth as a mantel ornament. These were almost always in pairs, a trumpet vase upholding a sphere, both of them swirled. A triumph of the Jersey glassmaker's art is shown on page 163, in which the globe seems to flow in perfect rhythm from the vase.

English glass centers radiating from Stourbridge, which exhibited great ingenuity in attracting public demand, began making witch balls with transfer prints inside. Duplicates have never been reported for the United States, but I have seen similar ones with paper paste-ins such as were used for sugar Easter eggs and early valentines. Some of these were made by Anthony Lehberger of the Salem area, whose granddaughter has examples. Lehberger was a Jersey glass virtuoso blowing at the famed Gillinder Glass Factory created especially for the Philadelphia Centennial in 1876.

Fig. 145 ROLLING-PIN of amber glass.

It is cozy to think that the early Jersey glassblowers who made witch balls were above believing this glass had power against witches. But be it remembered that in the 18th century a witch was hanged in Salem. Massachusetts? No, in New Jersey.

Myths, though, can be distorted after some 300 years. In 1968 when a Jersey glass gaffer of 70 years experience was asked to blow a witch ball to match a pitcher, he backed off saying, "Good luck don't happen to them who make witches' balls."

And Magic Inside Rolling Pins

New Jersey housewives whose menfolks brought home blown rolling pins didn't pay much respect to the article, though they found them useful for shaping pie dough. Glass rolling pins, nevertheless, have an awesome history going back to about 1790 in England when the first "Bristol rollers," appeared, according to G. Bernard Hughes.

Like witch balls, rollers were credited with magic, but for quite different reasons. In England, Hughes has determined, these rollers were blown especially to be salt containers, which evolved out of necessity.

From the beginning, salt has been the very stuff of life, a need satisfied instinctively by animals as well as man. When civilizations developed, men hoarded salt as a precious commodity, and by the Middle Ages householders in Europe and Britain often had their salt supply consecrated by the church, to protect against evil.

Governments were quick to recognize the taxable worth of a substance then more essential than silver and gold. From 1694 to 1829 the English Crown made it illegal to sell salt except by weight and taxed it heavily. Like a man putting his 12-year-old scotch under lock and key, housewives no longer kept salt loose in a box, but in wide-mouthed corked bottles.

By the time of the Napoleonic wars, salt was being taxed 30 times its retail price, a fact that made the proverbial "pinch" minute indeed. About 1790 the first salt rollers appeared in the Bristol glassmaking region, writes Hughes.

These earliest rollers were open at one end to admit a ground-glass stopper which kept out dampness and filching fingers. Of "black" glass that was dark olive-green in the light, the rollers tapered toward the knobbed ends which made useful handles for hanging the containers at the hearth. Reverence for the salt rollers was such that they were cleaned daily, to bring good luck and good health.

But as the years went by non-believers began using the rollers to shape pastry, and to accommodate the need glassblowers made the sides parallel. A novelty and souvenir craze began when a few blowers turned out rollers in Bristol blue (cobalt), some with multi-color raindrop splashes or swirled with opaque white. The next elaboration was painting with enamels or inscribing with good luck mottoes such as "To wish ye well."

Then someone conceived the idea of blowing rollers to hold exactly a pound of tea, at a time when it cost a guinea a pound. These became an immediate success as wedding gifts. Some were filled with candies as gifts for sweethearts who used them for luck in making wedding pastries. Many were decorated with appropriate nautical mottoes as "sailors' charms," for bon voyage gifts. If the roller was broken during the voyage this was regarded as a warning of misfortune ahead.

So popular were the rollers that every major glass center in England was blowing them. In Scotland the Allowa Glass Works specialized in transfer-decorated ones. As late as 1865 they were still being made at Nailsea. According to Hughes, since 1910 English reproductions have been made in the thousands, many lavishly gilded.

The New Jersey and other American rollers can usually be differentiated from the English counterparts. The latter tend to taper toward the ends, one of which is usually open to admit a stopper. Jersey rollers which look like, and were generally made to be, utilitarian rolling pins were blown in such standard colors as aqua, amber and blue and were never ornamented with gilt inscriptions or decalcomanias. A Bristol-blue roller with sea-chanteys written in gold script or an opaque white one with transfer prints of pastoral scenes is almost certain to have been made in the British Isles.

Lilies of the Furnace

Glass lilies can be easily made by anyone with a modicum of experience, which probably accounts for the quantity of remarkably crude and ugly ones, usually in heavy glass and splotchy opaque colors, being sold as souvenirs today.

In earlier times when a blower had only standard clear or aqua glass for lunch-hour creations he seemed to concentrate on graceful design. Some fine clear lilies, the flower eight inches in width, were fashioned at Gayner Glass Works of Salem, N.J. (Fig. 150)

In the late 19th century, says a native of Bridgeton, glass flowers were blown for use on coffins at winter funerals here, but no examples appear to be extant today.

Window Greeting Cards

Around the nub of the 20th century Millville householders had a Christmas decoration that may well be unique. These were oblong glass "cards," about 4x6 inches, etched with holiday greetings, to hang in a parlor window. Some also were made for Easter, but cards for other occasions are not known. Merchants seeing these hanging signs must surely have copied the idea for business window cards of etched glass. Perhaps some examples will still come to light from local attics.

Hats, Flip-flops and Chains

No matter how stingy the boss about glass for spare-time fancies or how inept the glassman there always seemed time and metal enough to squeeze out a mini-hat. And some not so mini. One about nine inches in breadth, sold at auction in 1969 for about $30.

As most of the glass hats were copies of stove-pipe hats or beaver hats with a round precise crown, some patent-medicine-bottle molds seemed ideal for blowing the crown of the hat. What matter if part of the glass read "TONIC" or "DR. ZILCH'S" as long as it was just for the kids. While these medicine hats are collectible items, the more decorative are those of pleasing shapes and colors running the gamut of glasshouse formulas. Be it noted, though, that opaque pink and yellow are almost unknown. Amber, blue, green, amethyst, in all their variations, and some of red are the usual ones. Real rarities in shape are those with low round crowns and wide brims curled up at the sides, like those worn by Jersey's raftsmen on the Delaware.

A toy, the flip-flop was somewhat of a cross between a hookah pipe and a hand-held oil can. If one blew down the hollow tube of glass the beeping sound delighted children such as carry-in boys.

Linked chains of glass are among the least appreciated whimseys. As Gaffer Otis Coleman, then in his eighties, said, "The trick is to prevent one link from sticking fast to another. 'Tain't easy." By no means, and if the glassworker adds crimping or color, the difficulties are compounded. Blowers who were forming a chain for a sweetheart, usually added a glass heart at the center of the links which were intended not for a necklace—lengths were about two inches for each link—but for wall decoration.

With the magazine-era of interior decoration in the Twenties, which certainly quelled some atrocities, housewives began to relegate the glass chains to the bottom bureau drawer, then finally to the trash can. And so today the glass chains rank with some other lost folk-art, like strawflower doves of Mexico.

Canes, Walking Sticks and Batons

A principle of glassblowing is that if you start with a gather of variegated color at the end of the blowpipe, when you stretch out the taffylike mass you prolong the original pattern. From this concept, made use of by the early Venetians who expanded and extended millefiori designs, have come the highly decorative walking sticks or striped and spiraled glass made in New Jersey. Like witch balls and rolling pins, these canes originated

in England's Stourbridge region where many elaborate ones were produced to be sold as souvenirs. The New Jersey ones, in contrast, were spare-time creations, often one of a kind, and depended for variation on the small amounts of bright colors that a glassman could scrounge.

One Jersey cane, as an instance, is basic aqua with multiple stripes of amber, blue and opaque white; another is red, white and blue; another is cranberry faintly striped in white. When a blower had only "green glass" to work with he might twist the cane for variety. Handles were usually knobs or shepherd's crooks. Lengths varied from three to five feet; if shorter, it usually means that the cane has been broken off.

A sophisticated style of baton is attributed to Durand's factory. Cased over a gilt core, this glass is diagonally striped in yellow, maroon and white, allowing the gold to show through as a fourth stripe. Fitted with a metal-tipped cork, the baton may have held candies or even liquor.

Miniatures

In glass not everything small is a miniature. Salt dips and salt dishes are not miniatures of anything. The Jersey beehive salts and others were made small because their contents were used sparingly.

Jersey miniatures in general are tiny versions, doll-size, of pitchers, sugar bowls, milk bowls and other useful objects. Very definitely, miniatures are not the minuscule objects made by lampworkers, who are not described as glassblowers. Rather, miniatures are such objects as pitchers about two inches high and clearly made with the blowpipe, rather than shaped over a Bunsen burner flame.

Small cordial glasses, of which many were made in early Jersey times when liqueurs were precious, should not be considered miniatures. Some of these are the same height as mini-pitchers, but are by no means small versions of anything, even though they resemble English wine goblets.

Small cobalt or clear glasses with hexagonal panels are not the miniature tumblers they seem to be but instead are "shot" glasses holding an ounce of distilled liquor. Usually of heavy pressed glass and made in abundance in other states, few are found here as pressed glass was not the style in this state where artisans prided themselves on the intricate art of blowing.

Fig. 147 WHIMSEY PIPE from Millville has leaf prunts like those applied to *wald* or "forest glass" made in Germany of the 1700s. Clear, 15 inches long.

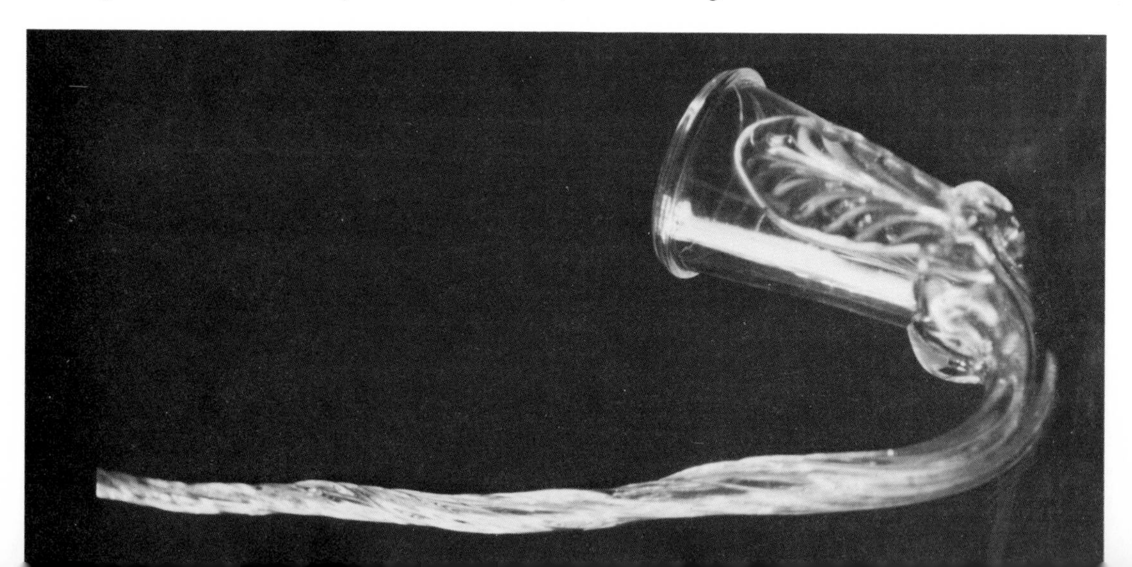

Salem: Sachem Bitters, Electric Jars and Souvenirs

Goggle-eyed visitors at the United States Centennial exposition held in Philadelphia in 1876 could take home such wondrous glass souvenirs as these, and, even better, watch them made:

> Gorgeous Birds of Paradise, with spun glass plumage hundreds of miles in length, Turkish Smoking Pipes, full rigged Ships, Cupid's Chariots drawn by Swans, Love Scales, Cinderella Slippers, elegant busts and medallions of Washington, Lincoln, Grant, Franklin and Goshorn; Deer, Dogs, Fishes, Birds, Bonnets and Curls, Sparking Candles, Baskets, Crosses, Bottle Imps, Candelabras, Goblets, Vases, Cups, Philosophers' Water Hammers, Pulse Glasses, Baskets of Flowers, Cigar Holders, Fancy Decanters with figures inside, Individual Salts, Alphabetic Plates, Liberty Bell Mugs, Pneumatic Balloons, Payton's celebrated Marking Pens, and hundreds of other useful and ornamental specimens of Fancy Glass Work.

Among the latter were Temperance Glasses with which you could "treat a hundred of your friends, and still have enough left for as many more," just how was not explained in the advertisement.

The Philadelphia Centennial concerns the subject of Jersey glass not only because novelties similar to the above were being made in the state but also because at least one master of the blowpipe in the Centennial glassworks show was a Jerseyan, Tony Lehberger, and chances are there were others. Tony was a blower for the Gayner Glass Works of Salem, N.J., and as a virtuoso in glassmaking was on loan to the Centennial for feats that would amaze visitors.

A never-failing magnet for crowds, the glassblowing exhibit was housed in its own special building "on Fountain Avenue between the Catholic Total Abstinence Union Fountain and the Fifty-Second Street entrance to the Centennial Grounds," which were in Fairmount Park. Designed in the best tradition of suburban-railroad-station architecture, the glass factory which cost $15,000 was sponsored by Gillinder & Sons, owners of the Franklin Flint Glass Works in Philadelphia. A much-publicized structure, 109 by 60 feet, of glass and wood, the building also had an annex 36 feet square with a furnace having a capacity to melt three tons of glass every 48 hours. Employing 85 people, this was a large and complete glassworks with a pot-arch, a glory hole and an annealing oven 50 feet long. John K. Martin was superintendent of the works and Thomas W. Mellor was supervisor of the engraving department.

A curious fact of many a Jersey glassblower's life is exemplified by Tony Lehberger, for although Salem's glassworks made only bottles, not art glass, somehow the real gaffers acquired the knack of blowing charming novelties like many named in the Gillinder advertisement.

A well-known museum has an example of Jersey glass which was ascribed by a long-gone curator as "probably Salem County circa 1840." The fact is that after Wistarberg which flourished in the 18th century this county had no other glassworks until about 1862.

HALL, PANCOAST & CRAVEN
SALEM GLASS WORKS

The pioneer in the town of Salem was Hall, Pancoast & Craven. Through the kindness of A. H. Smith I have had the privilege of seeing some pages of the company's mold book, the earliest date shown being 1865. One of the revelations is that the company was lending its molds to various glassmakers, not only to the Bodines at nearby Williamstown but even as far afield as Brooklyn, N.Y., to Hagerty Bros., a major competitor of Whitall Tatum & Company. Philip Doflein of Philadelphia who had made molds for T. W. Dyott was now making some for Hall, Pancoast & Craven, among them, 2-oz. cone inks and a "Cocaine Mould Flint."

Among the molds listed is "Sachem bitters," an item prized by bottle collectors, a 9½-inch barrel shape with horizontal ribbing or hoops and a plain center embossed OLD SACHEM /BITTERS /AND/ WIGWAM TONIC.

Other molds owned by the firm are described by the record keeper as follows:

Hex. Pickle jar	wine demijohn	Mucilage
½ gal pickle jar	wine, Boston style	Horse liniment
British oil	Schnapps	Bateman
Citrate mag.	port bottles	Pedler's
Barrel mustard	porter—Vincent Hathaway	Lemon syrup
Pie fruit jars	Mineral oil	Lyon's (tooth) powder
Arnica (salve)	cod liver oil	Pepper sauce
Turlington's (Balsam)	Brandy peach jars	Horseradish
Opodeldoc*	seltzers	½ pt jelly cups
Genuine Essence	P. Davis pain killer	

Names at the back of the book may be those of blowers, such as Westcott and Ayers. The recorder kept a curious one-word weather-table, such as Calm, Rainy, Snowing, Sick.

Starting in 1862 as a 4-pot furnace owned by Henry D. Hall, Joseph Pancoast and John V. Craven, the glassworks in 1870 became Craven Brothers, and so continued at Fourth and Broadway until 1895, when a general store owned by the Cravens was also listed in Boyd's Directory for that year.

The firm incorporated in 1895 as Salem Glass Works which greatly expanded, becoming one of the leading industries of Salem county. John L. Dilworth, of a family long associated with the ownership, writes me that in the days of hand-made bottles the colors were light and emerald green, amber and blue.

*What did Opodeldoc have that made it an all-American favorite remedy throughout the 19th century? O. Henry, who had known the inside of prison before he became a writer, tells in his short story, *One Touch of Nature,* about a second-story man who commands his sleeping victim to hold up his hands. When the burglar discovers that the solid citizen is quite ready to yield the cash but cannot raise his hands because of stiff joints, the thief sits at the foot of the bed and chummily tells of wonders he discovered in Opodeldoc for rheumatism. A story with a happy ending . . . Every Jersey glass collection needs one Opodeldoc.

Salem Glass Works was sold to Anchor Cap and Closure Company in 1934, which merged in 1938 with the Hocking Glass Corporation. Now the Anchor Hocking Corporation, a fully automated plant but still on the shores of the Delaware, the firm today is one of New Jersey's major industries.

HOLZ, CLARK & TAYLOR

The advent of Salem's first railroad, in 1863 connecting with Camden, induced still another glassmaking company—Holz, Clark & Taylor—to locate here in the early 1860s, also on Broadway, at Front Street. Continuing until 1879 in 1874 the owners leased the property to John Gayner who eventually bought the factory and in 1898 incorporated as the Gayner Glass Works.

Holz, Clark & Taylor are known for three fruit jars, one of which is marked HOLZ CLARK & TAYLOR set in an arc with SALEM N J beneath and 'PAT' APPLIED FOR on the bottom. A variation of this is embossed on the back THE /SALEM/JAR.

CLARK'S / PEERLESS, marked SALEM on the bottom, is also attributed to Holz, Clark & Taylor although the jar was produced during Gayner's management. This is known because the jar's Lightning closure was not invented until 1882.

Holz, Clark & Taylor are also said to have made a variation of the Hunter-Fisherman calabash, a bottle that was one of Jersey's earliest pictorial decanters, made previously by several glass works.

GAYNER GLASS WORKS

Even as late as 1963 the office of Gayner Glass Works has been in a house of great historic interest, with a date of 1691 at the peak of the gabled roof and a fireplace in every room. At 32 West Broadway, near Front Street the 2-story brick building was often called the Governors' House, as royal governors, among them Lord Cornbury, frequently occupied the house in Colonial times, and the provincial congress of West Jersey also met here on occasion. Since 1964 every vestige of this ancient building, one of the most historic in New Jersey, has been destroyed, replaced by corrugated metal structures.

The oldest settlement in western Jersey, Salem has numerous historic sites, among them, the centuries-old Salem Oak, and many of the citizens are lineal descendants of 17th century families.

John Gayner, however, arrived here in 1874, from Waterford Works where he had been producing colored lamp shades and glass stained by a new technic. Leasing the plant owned by Holz, Clark & Taylor, then eventually buying it, Gayner developed a prosperous business which was inherited by his descendants who sold their interests in 1956 to Universal Glass Products. Some of the following information was supplied to me in 1961 by Robert Kerr, sales manager for the firm then planning to move to Philadelphia, and a long-time Gayner employee.

The top floor of the office once had a sample of all major Gayner glass but during the consolidation many articles were discarded. Among those remaining, one of the most

Fig. 148 POST-CIVIL WAR TIMES at Gayner Glass Works, Salem, N.J.

Fig. 149 HISTORIC BRADWAY HOUSE, 1691, Salem home of Colonial Governors, and for the office of Gayner Glass Works, was destroyed in the mid-1930s to make room for a corrugated metal building.

Fig. 150 SALEM LILY made at Gayner Glass Works in clear glass has a naturalistic look; 12 inches long.

unusual is a 2-quart bottle with an inside thread and a matching glass stopper, a combination proving so difficult and costly that the bottles were soon discontinued. Squat demijohns of 5-gallon size were made for Welch's Grape Juice. Some of the early 15-gallon demijohns had "laid-on" necks. Large square battery jars in aqua and even some experimental round ones also were salvaged. A bottle for holy water was among the many special orders blown at Gayner. Described as a tincture style etched with the words "Holy Water," the container had a ground-glass stopper to which was applied a glass rod with a sponge attached. The "crow's-foot" bottle was for cordials and had a long-stemmed neck at the base of which was a bird's claw spreading over the round bottle.

THE / GAYNER / GLASS-TOP is a moldblown fruit jar which precedes the machine article of this name as mentioned by Toulouse. The reverse of the blown jar reads Mfd by Gayner Glass Works / Salem N J.

Another Gayner jar dating from about 1890 shows a symbol of the world globe surrounded by ELECTRIC FRUIT JAR. Another hand-made, marked LEOTRIC in an oval panel, bears the same mark on the bottom as does the Electric: Reg. T. M. No. 43,288.

A fine specimen of the skill of some unknown Gayner gaffer is the clear lily above, 12 inches long, which shows a feeling for the natural flower's contours.

Salem's glassmakers in the 1890s had plentiful outlets for their wares right at home for the town had three canning factories and the Mason Pickling Company. Henry Acton's Bottling Establishment advertised as Always on Hand: Germania Steamed Champagne, Champagne and Plain Beers, Porter, Ale, Soda, Sarsaparilla, Ginger Ale, Pear Cider, Raspberry, Orange Champagne.

Among glassblowers listed in Salem in 1895 were Frederick C. Gayner, Charles Goslin, John W. Gayner, John A. Getz, Harry Rain, John S. Eva, Frank W. Reinfried, Thomas Crean.

In its Alexander Grant House built in 1721, the Salem County Historical Society has an intriguing collection of Jersey handblown glass, much of it in aqua. Years ago much of it was claimed to be from Alloway, but nowadays with the re-assessment of what might have been made there, no one, not even a visitor, wants to state what is Wistarberg and what is post-Civil-War.

ALVA GLASS MANUFACTURING COMPANY

When times were depressed in glassmaking, blowers unable to obtain jobs close to home sometimes organized co-operatives. That is how the Alva glassworks started. As the *South Jerseyman* of June 3, 1890, phrased it, a syndicate of Salem glass blowers incorporated in that year as the Alva Glass Manufacturing Company. Nathaniel S. Fox, formerly of the Wilmington Glass Works in Delaware, apparently was the organizer and was named secretary-treasurer but Robert Torrens was president. Other organizers were blowers Whitall Mingin and David McGuillen, and John Fox, a packer. Superintendent was Joseph R. Westcott. Of the 28 employees, 11 were blowers. Although having relatively few employees, Alva must have had high productivity as it had four shops, two glory holes and three ovens. The tank had a capacity of 4½ tons. Located near Major's Wharf, the factory's main building was 106 by 48 feet.

The fact that the company made 14-ounce, flat panel bottles, difficult to blow, indicates proficient blowers. Other commercial bottles among those blown were for Bixby's Shoe Dressing and Ammonia "ovals."

On June 16, 1891, the stock company bought out Nathaniel and John Fox and continued in business for most of the decade. As the new century approached, Alva glassworks ran into difficulties and on June 14, 1899, the building was leased by the Philadelphia Pickling Company. A hopeful note for the blowers was that Salem's other glassworks had grown to considerable size, and perhaps there was employment for all.

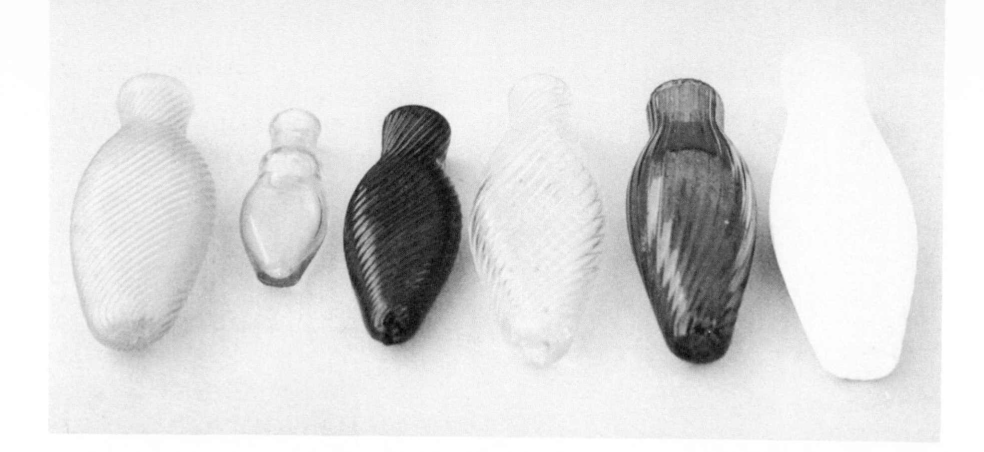

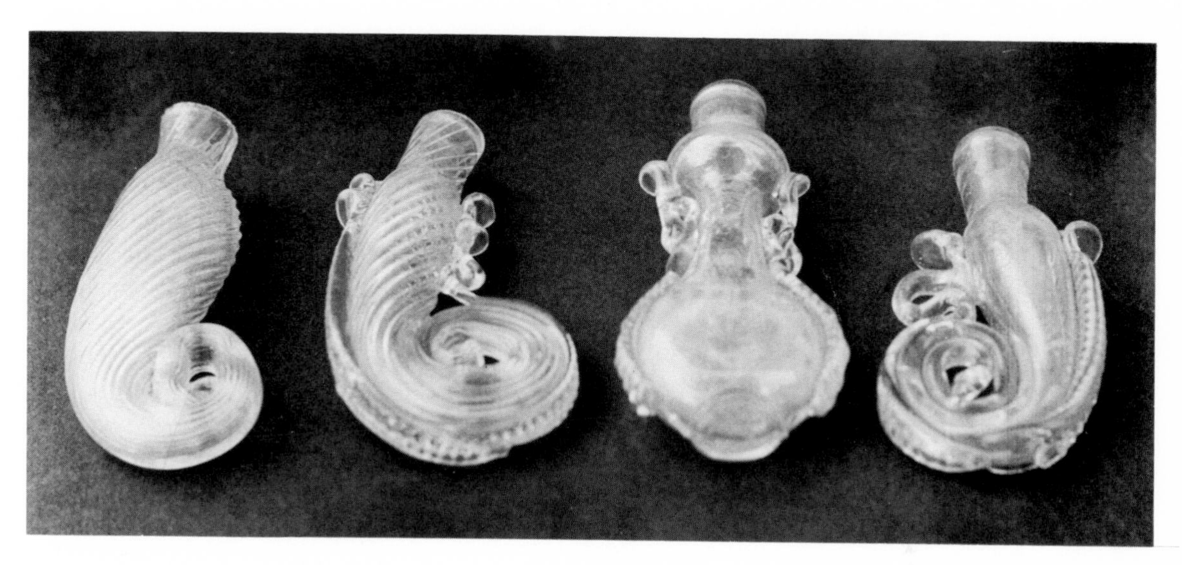

Fig. 151 "SMELLING BOTTLES." Usually these charming miniatures did not hold perfume but aromatic crystals of ammonia, scented with lavender or attar of rose, to revive fainting ladies, and were made small and flattened to be tucked into a glove, a purse, or a bodice. None is made to stand alone and most are 2½ to 3 inches long. Smelling bottles are recorded in account books of Stiegel's Manheim glass works. As many bottles like those shown here were found in New Jersey's Salem county, which had no glasshouses between Wistarberg and the 1860s, Jersey for once gets credit for having made such 18th century bottles. Their bright colors of emerald and cobalt and amethyst, amusing seahorse shapes, and lacy quilling must have been highly appealing to belles in Philadelphia's high society before the Revolution.

THE TOP ROW: pattern molded in cobalt, emerald and aqua, the ribbing swirled to the right. The tiny bottle second from left is freeblown. IN THE CENTER ROW, seahorse bottles, aqua and clear, had the ribbing blown in a mold but the tall spirals are free formed as is the rigaree. Seahorse bottles in the bottom row are prized as they are freeblown and spiraled in stripes of opaque white and light blue over clear or aqua glass. *Yoerger collection.*

Bridgeton—
Town of Twenty Glassworks

Bridgeton is often referred to by collectors and authors of glass books as if it had had in its history only one glass company, the Bridgeton Glass Works. That name was used only as an alternate for a brief time during ownership by Potter & Bodine, yet "Bridgeton Glass Works" is as carelessly bandied about as the category "Millville" is for 19th century Jersey ware. Far from having been a one-glassworks town, Bridgeton in and about 1889 had 20 such factories.

Although so close to that great center of Jersey glassmaking, Millville, which had its first furnace in 1806 by virtue of the enterprise of James Lee, a Philadelphian by way of Ireland, Bridgeton did not have glassworks until 1836 when Nathaniel L. Stratton and John P. Buck set up a furnace here at the convenient head-of-navigation of the Cohansey river. Some of the most charming and collectible half-pint historical flasks were blown here and probably would never have been credited to New Jersey except that they were boldly embossed BRIDGETOWN NEW JERSEY or BRIDGETON NEW JERSEY. George Washington/Jackson flasks and the sailboat half pint are still not credited to Stratton Buck & Company.

It's a fairly sound speculation that Messrs. Stratton and Buck were needled into making historical flasks when they saw from consistent advertisements in the *Bridgeton Observer* that an outlander, "Dr." Dyott of Philadelphia, must have been coining money from empty bottles. Dyott's advertisement of Feb. 12, 1826, which ran often in the *Bridgeton Observer* advertised, besides druggists' ware, these flasks: Washington and Eagle, LaFayette and Eagle, Dyott and Franklin, the ship Franklin & Agriculture, assorted Eagles, Cornucopia and Eagle, and ribbed flasks (Pitkin type—see Clementon), all enough to make today's collectors deliriously happy.

Stratton, Buck and Company, if they had wished, could have made copies of the Dyott flasks. They chose not to do so. Instead, they came up with a bewigged Washington and another popular hero, Andrew Jackson, both so labeled on ½-pint flasks. They also produced that perennial symbol of the Jersey Shore, a sloop, on three different ½ pints, two with large single stars on the reverse and one embossed BRIDGETOWN NEW JERSEY, the early name for the community. Still another sailboat flask, a pint, is, fortunately for identification, embossed BRIDGETON NEW JERSEY on the obverse in an oval enclosing a portrait of a man with bushy Van Dyke beard, whom the McKearins called Kossuth. If the person is indeed Kossuth then the flask must have been made about 1851, a year when Joel Bodine & Sons had taken over the Stratton-Buck glassworks. Why the McKearins stated the glasshouse making this flask is unknown is mystifying.

A ½-pint flask with an unidentified portrait on each side, in classical Roman style, is described in *American Glass* as of unknown provenance. However, the flask is so astonishingly similar in style and metal to other Bridgeton ½ pints that prospects are it was made there. It is sometimes called the Scott-Byron flask (McK GI-114).

One Washington pint flask bears a likeness of Gen. Zachary Taylor on the reverse, which is encircled by the words BRIDGETON NEW JERSEY. A quart Washington flask with both sides embossed BRIDGETOWN NEW JERSEY shows a portrait which the McKearins pointed out is a good likeness of Henry Clay. New Jerseyans were in a dither when it was announced that "the Great Compromiser" would vacation in 1847 at one of the state's famous seaside resorts, Cape May. Joel Bodine & Sons undoubtedly would have rushed the blowing of flasks honoring the eloquent and good-looking Kentucky Congressman. Arrived at Cape May he was mobbed by admirers every time he tried to take a stroll on the beach. Some of the bolder bathing beauties came armed with scissors and tried to snatch locks of his hair. Far from being pleased by such adulation, Henry Clay was irked by it and cut short his visit.

STRATTON, BUCK & COMPANY

Because Stratton, Buck & Company made flasks impressed BRIDGETOWN NEW JERSEY or BRIDGETON NEW JERSEY such bottles have sometimes been attributed to a mythical factory called the Bridgeton Glass Works. At the time Washington, Jackson, Clay, Taylor and sailboat flasks were being blown in Bridgeton the one glassworks there then went under the names of the principal owners at specific periods, though all, leading up to the Cohansey Glass Works of the 20th century, were on the same site at the foot of Pearl Street on the Cohansey river. For accuracy therefore it would be well to drop the name Bridgeton Glass Works and to ascribe articles according to the following firms and periods.

Glass Ware.

To Druggists, China, Merchants, Country Store keepers, and Dealers in Glass Ware.

20,000 groce of Apothecaries Vials.
15,000 do Patent Medicine do
1000 do Cologne water do
2000 do Mustard and Cayenne do
7000 dozen Quart Bottles
3000 :: half gallon do
3000 :: Washington & Eagle pint flasks
3000 :: La Fayette & Eagle do
3000 :: Dyott & Franklin do
2000 :: ship Franklin & Agricul. do
5000 :: assorted, Eagles, &c do
1000 :: common ribbed do
4000 :: Eagle, Cornucopia, &c half pts
4500 :: Jars, assorted, all sizes [bottles
5000 :: Dreggists & Confectioners show
5000 :: do packing Bottles, assorted
2000 :: Acid Bottles gro. stopps. [sizes
3000 :: Tincture bottles, assorted sizes
3000 :: Mineral water bottles
6000 :: Snuff bottles
5000 Demijons, different sizes.

With a variety of other Glassware, all of which is manufactured at the Philadelphia and Kensington Factories, and in quality and workmanship is considered equal and in many of the articles superior to English manufacture. For sale by

T. W. DYOTT,
Corner of 2d and Race St. Phila.

Fig. 152 Feb. 12, 1826 issue of the Bridgeton *Observer.*

Nathaniel L. Stratton and John P. Buck built the initial furnace in 1836 and small bottles were the first articles blown, according to I. T. Nichols writing in 1889. Owning great tracts of land and conducting a well-patronized general store besides the glassworks, for a time Stratton Buck & Company had the largest business in Cumberland county. But after a destructive fire in 1841 and the death of John Buck in 1842, Stratton gave up the making of glass. Rebuilding the plant, John G. Rosenbaum then operated it until 1846 when he sold out to Joel Bodine & Sons who had successfully put the Williamstown works in continuous operation after others had failed.

JOEL BODINE & SONS

The Bodines in 1855 sold the factory to a firm known as Maul, Hebrew & Company who, as the phrase then was, "made a failure," in the same year. At a sheriff's sale the plant was bid in by Gen. David Potter of Bridgeton and Francis I. Bodine of Philadelphia. As Potter & Bodine they considerably expanded the works, running it under this name until 1863, during which period it was sometimes called the Bridgeton Glass Works.

Potter & Bodine rushed into the Battle of the Fruit Jars, against such major competition as Whitall Tatum and several houses making Mason's Improved Jar. After April 13, 1858, when Mason patented his new jar, the Bridgeton firm on Oct. 19 patented and embossed their jar Potter & Bodine/ Air Tight/ Fruit Jar/ Phila. This jar was one of the old-fashioned wax sealers.

On June 5, 1852, Potter & Bodine were featuring in advertisements repeated frequently in the Bridgeton *Chronicle* "Baker's Patent Fruit Jar," a clamp-top jar.

COHANSEY GLASS MANUFACTURING COMPANY

In 1863 Potter sold his shares in the Potter & Bodine firm to J. Nixon Bodine and Francis L. Bodine, sons of Samuel Bodine. By 1870 these aggressive glass entrepreneurs incorporated as the Cohansey Glass Manufacturing Company; as late as 1899 Francis and J. Nixon were president and vice president, respectively, with W. G. Millikin as secretary and W. M. Bodine as treasurer. Cohansey was far and away the most successful of the Bridgeton manufacturers producing hand-made glass.

The Cohansey fruit jar, embossed as "Pat'd. July 16, 1872" was one of the most successful of the home-canning containers. Advertisements running often in the *Crockery Journal* of 1874 and 1875 show the "New Cohansey" to have been an all-glass top with a single wire bail. For customers who preferred metal tops Cohansey advertised jars with anti-rust liners under the name "Protector," a predecessor. Cumberland County Historical Society in Greenwich has on display ½-gallon Cohansey jars in attractive amber. H. Millard Chew of South Jersey remembers that his family opened 25-year-old jars of brandied peaches from such containers and found the contents not only non-lethal but delicious.

By 1899 Cohansey had two hollow ware and three window-glass plants on six Bridgeton acres with a West Jersey Railroad extension along Glass Street. At peak operation the factories employed 500 men and boys. In 1899 the payroll was $10,000 a month for 400

Fig. 153 July 8, 1875, *The Crockery Journal.*

persons. Property and stock valued at $250,000 were making glass assessed at over $300,000 a year. Furnace intake each year was 4,000 tons of white sand, 800 tons of lime, 800 tons of soda, 8,000 tons of coal, 1,200 tons of coke, and about 2,000 cords of wood, as well as lumber, hay, and straw for packing.

Besides the Cohansey fruit jar which was still giving the Mason jar strong competition in 1899, the Bridgeton firm made druggists' bottles, and vials, beer and wine bottles, carboys, bottles and jars for acid. Private molds, their advertising said, were a specialty, one of which was described as "a handsome syrup bottle for an Eastern firm," name not stated. Scott P. Tyson writes me that he has a letter showing that Charles Yockel who had been in business in Philadelphia since 1855 was making molds in 1879 for Cohansey.

Cohansey had a huge store dealing in dry goods and provisions, of which George Ireland was manager. Once again the Bodines had demonstrated their skill as entrepreneurs in glass.

The Franklin Institute in its 1874 awards failed to pick history's winner in the Battle of the Fruit Jars. The judges termed John L. Mason's patented jar as merely "creditable," a kiss of death as compared with Cohansey's third place of honorable mention for its display of fruit jars: "The most of the jars are filled with fruit, and they seem to be successful in preserving the contents from the action of the air." That year Cohansey also presented green and brown glass bottles, very large cylinders, flasks and electrical insulators.

Glass Only in Contact With Fruit.
No Separate Parts to be Mislaid---Cover in One Piece.
No Wrench Required to Open or Close.

—o—

New Cohansey Fruit Jars.

Glass Cover in One Piece. Anti-Rust Lined Metal Top.

Elastic Pressure by Spring Clamps on Shoulder Joint.

The Clamp can be turned back after fruit is cool, and PROVE the Air-tight Joint Perfect.

Every Jar being inspected, there is no trouble in using.

Inquire of nearest Wholesale Dealer or write for samples and prices.

—o—

Our PROTECTOR JARS, with Anti-Rust Lined Metal Tops, long and favorably known, have the same principles and advantages and are cheaper in price.

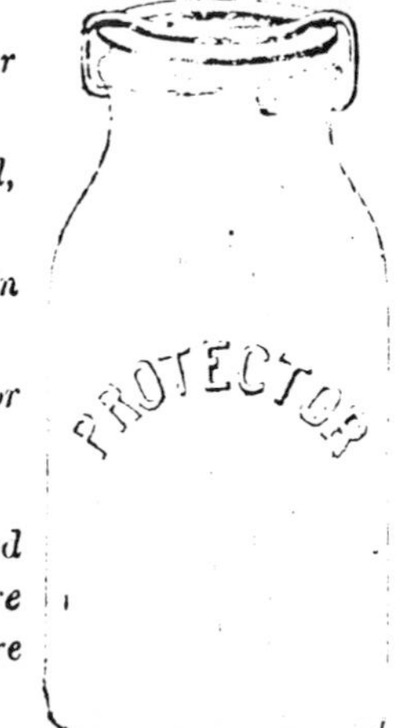

Cohansey Glass Manufacturing Comp'ny,
Manufacturers of Window Glass, Bottles & Fruit Jars,
N. W. Cor. Third & Arch streets, PHILADELPHIA

Worth noting also for the year of 1874 was that the Franklin Institute awarded second prize, a bronze medal, to the Dempsey Wicker-Covered Glassware Company of Philadelphia, which encapsulated many a Jersey carboy and demijohn.

Cohansey, said the *Crockery & Glass Journal* of June 17, 1875, had a large order of window-glass for the upcoming 1876 Centennial Exposition at Philadelphia. The highest commendation perhaps was that Cohansey's excellent window-glass had an important market in California because the product had proved its "ability to better stand the passage around Cape Horn," thereby largely displacing French glass.

GETSINGER & SON

With its 20 glass factories in 1889, few in Bridgeton transacted so large a business as that of John E. Getsinger & Son, wrote contemporary historian I. T. Nichols at that time.

As Getsinger & Allen (William H.) the firm opened in 1879 with one window-light furnace on South Laurel Street near Steamboat Landing on ground leased from the estate of John Buck, and then built a second factory in 1881. By 1882 John E. Getsinger, a native of Port Elizabeth, had taken his son John Baptist (he later became a well-known tank architect) into the firm and bought new property on Grove Street, South Bridgeton, overlooking the Cohansey, and erected still another factory. In 1883, the same year when Allen left the firm, one more plant was established.

Within 10 years from their start in 1879 the Getsingers had one hollow ware factory and three window-glass plants doing an annual business of $200,000 from an invested capital of $75,000. By water and rail—they owned a branch to the main line of the West Jersey Railroad—they shipped most of their glass outside the state, to New York, Philadelphia, and southern and western states. A specialty for which they developed a reputation was "Newton" brand window-glass, high quality and double thick.

Besides making bottles of almost every sort, the Getsingers contributed to the Battle of the Fruit Jars. Getsingers' workmen blew Mason jars, in competition with Potter & Bodine's Baker jar of the 1850s and the Bridgeton Cohansey, still popular as late as 1875.

Two hundred men and boys earning a total of $7,000 a month carried on Getsingers' work, from blowing, to making the firm's own pots, to packing. For each seasonal fire the Getsinger furnaces swallowed up 600 tons of lime, 600 tons of soda, 2,500 tons of white sand—superheated by 6,000 tons of coal, 1,000 tons of coke and 1,000 cords of wood.

An advertisement for Getsinger & Son (John E. and J. Baptist) in Boyd's Cumberland County Directory for 1889-90 solicited private-mold business and featured "Bottles, all styles and colors." Druggists' ware, demijohns and fruit jars were described as a specialty. The directory of the same year listed Harry G. Getsinger as a glass cutter and Robert G. as a glassworker. The Getsingers were still in business in Bridgeton as late as 1895.

"Jackie Getzinger" Pitchers

Justly publicized, this pair of 7½-inch pitchers in dark amber with opaque white whorls have a strident vigor that delights moderns. Originally owned by the McKearins, the pitchers according to their information were made by a South Jerseyan named Jackie Getzinger. As a German-speaking family of Getsingers operated the Eagle Glass Works at Port Elizabeth in the 1830s and a later family owned Getsinger & Son at Bridgeton in the 1880s, the McKearins are of the opinion that the pitchers could have been made in either place. However, I have talked with Bridgeton Getsingers (all spelling their names with an "s") who state that John E. Getsinger and his son John Baptist were cutters, not blowers, and none has heard of a Jackie Getzinger. I have been unable to find descendants of Port Elizabeth Getzingers.(See Fig. 114.)

CUMBERLAND GLASS MANUFACTURING COMPANY
CLARK WINDOW GLASS COMPANY

In everything but money value of glass blown, these jointly owned firms were on a larger scale than the Getsingers. In 1889 when the federal income tax collector was not even a nightmare on the horizon, such a moderate claim as an annual business of $200,000 against a high payroll of $95,000 for 300 men and boys at the Cumberland company seems surprising.

Their glass plant would have been today's collectors' dream as there were four hollow ware factories making "almost every variety of bottle in colored and green glass." Like other hollow ware makers in Bridgeton, the glass here was soda-lime, for which the annual raw materials were 1,400 tons of soda, 48,000 bushels of lime, 3,000 tons of sand, melted by 6,000 tons of coal. The 1,400,000 feet of lumber used in 1889 indicate outside shipments of the wares.

From 1890 until 1908 all the Bromo-Seltzer bottles were handblown here, and presumably some other cobalt glass as well. In the 1890s the firm made opal ware.

Operating first in 1880 on Water Street, then moving soon to North Laurel Street so as to be near the West Jersey Railroad, the firm was headed by R. E. Shoemaker, with S. M. Bassett as secretary and superintendent; and C. W. Shoemaker, treasurer.

The Joseph A. Clark Window Glass Company, established December 1882, had a related management: C.H. Shoemaker, president; W.C. Mulford, treasurer; and S. M. Bassett again as secretary. The 50 hands, drawing about $2,500 in monthly pay, produced plate glass, still experimental in 1882, with an annual value of $60,000, from an invested capital of $25,000. Daily ingredients for the batch included two tons of soda, four tons of sand and two tons of lime.

By 1899 Cumberland had three continuous tanks, one of them a split tank operating with two different colors. This furnace was equipped with hand presses and hand-blowing shops. As the 20th century opened Cumberland Glass had bought out More, Jonas and More, also Bridgeton, which utilized one continuous tank and hand-blowing shops. A decade or so later Cumberland became the dominant industry with seven continuous tanks and some 1,200 workers, one of the largest glass factories in the nation. By 1920 Cumberland itself was purchased by the Illinois Glass Company and thereupon began its complete transfer to automation.

MORE, JONAS & MORE GLASS WORKS

Collectors' hearts may quicken a bit when they learn that More, Jonas & More made green and amber hollow-ware and had fully as skilled gaffers and nearly as large a trade as did the Getsingers and Cumberland Glass.

Making "every description of bottles, principally druggists'-ware," and consequently having a wide range of molds and blocks, the factory's conditions were right for offhand blowing on lunch hours. Some of the emerald and amber pitchers that have brought substantial prices at Manhattan auctions undoubtedly have come from such forgotten glassworks as this major one established in 1882 at North Bridgeton along the West Jersey Railroad near Banks Street.

Owners were Robert More, Jr., George Jonas and Richard More. Some time prior to 1889 Robert More, Sr. and William H. Allen, late of the Getsingers, organized a window-light company known as More, Jonas, More & Co.

The joint firms employed 175 men and boys, at monthly wages of $6,000, whose blown glass was valued at $125,000 a year, on an invested capital of about $50,000. The furnaces consumed daily three tons of soda, three tons of lime, eight tons of sand and 15 tons of coal. Like the Getsingers, the firm used German clay, regarded as preferable, as well as American for pots. A drawing made about 1889 shows sizeable modern buildings; these were along sidings of the West Jersey Railroad and the Jersey Central Railroad, an indication of shipments to metropolitan areas.

In 1889 Cumberland Glass Company purchased More, Jonas & More which then had one continuous tank and handblowing shops. This became Cumberland's "B" Factory, which in 1920 was one of several acquisitions by the Illinois Glass Company in their automation program.

Some decorative lilies, in amber as well as clear glass, were made here from 1910 to 1920, recalls H. Millard Chew whose family is related to Clarks and Shoemakers.

In 1920 the Illinois Glass Company purchased the combined factories of Cumberland and More, Jonas and More and converted them to automatic glassmaking. As 95 per cent of the buildings were then of wood construction, a complete change-over to fire-proof structures was put into effect. Today as a division of Owens-Illinois, the complex is one of the most modern of New Jersey's major glass plants.

EAST LAKE GLASS WORKS, HOLLOW-WARE

A glasshouse all but unknown today, that of Kirby & McBride, also called the East Lake Glass Works, might well have been the source of collectors' glass, for the major output was wine and beer bottles, shapes that lend themselves to more fanciful items. Though established only in 1885, by 1889 the firm employed 80 men and boys turning out glass valued at $75,000 annually, a then substantial sum for utilitarian bottles. David McBride was superintendent of the plant that paid out $3,500 a month in wages.

Handily located in East Bridgeton on the Cumberland-Maurice River branch of the Jersey Central Railroad, the factory in 1889 was using annually 465 tons of soda, 840 tons of sand, 12,000 bushels of lime, 400 bushels of salt; 1,600 tons of coal and 315 cords of wood for fuel; and 350,000 feet of lumber for packing bottles.

Fig. 154 FERROLINE BLACK GLASS plates were pressed in the 1880s at Benjamin Lupton's glassworks, in a joint venture with inventor, Enrico Rosenzi. Bird plate, 13½ inches. *Henry Lupton collection.*

PARKER BROTHERS GLASS FACTORY

No less than Clayton Parker was president of Parker Brothers Glass Factory established in 1885 at West Bridgeton, foot of West Commerce Street. It was Clayton Parker who at Crowleytown in 1856 was blowing screw-top fruit jars under the critical eye of John L. Mason of Vineland, for which he later obtained several patents.

In 1899 the five Parker brothers were making the fruit jar lids and were just then filling an order for 50,000 gross for the Mason *Improved* Jar, which was patented in 1858. From a 3-pot furnace the brothers were also making some pressed ware, a specialty called the Ointment Jar with a nickel-plated screw top, in sizes of ¼ to 16 ounces. As of 1890 the Parkers were also filling orders for 40 private molds.

Besides the Parker brothers, 15 people were employed at an average of $10 a week. Eight tons of soda, 30 tons of sand, and 40 tons of coal were used monthly, small potatoes by the standards of some other Bridgeton works. But the Parkers had prestige and having begun business in 1885 they were still blowing glass in 1901.

WEST SIDE GLASS MANUFACTURING CO., LTD.

Benjamin Lupton set up this furnace in 1879, about a mile below Bridgeton as it was then, on the west bank of the Cohansey. Other members of the firm were Samuel L. Harris, president, Robert Herritz, Abraham Clive, Charles Mullen, Hiram Duffield, Robert Brokel, George C. Lupton and Charles G. Hampton, most of them practical glassmakers. Besides blowing Mason jars, ink bottles and other hand-made containers, this factory employing about 25 men and boys, made considerable amounts of black pressed glass trademarked as "Ferroline." Its inventor, Enrico Rosenzi, born in Palermo, Italy, and later a citizen in Bridgeton, became associated with Lupton in putting the patent of July 21, 1881, into effect. The inventor made the exaggerated claim that Ferroline ware was as indestructible as iron (hence the name), but it proved to be as mortal as other glass.

The Ferroline trademark is a spread eagle on a pine branch, and a paperweight replica in this truly black glass is still owned by Lupton's descendants who also have plates, a doorknob, and a lamp base. Ernest C. Stanmire reports that in the 1920s he bought from the Luptons bowls, cups and saucers, plates and vases. A favorite pattern was a border of ivy leaves, with a large rose in the center of plates, or sometimes a spray of lilies of the valley. Another central motif is a flight of birds over a nest in a tree-top. (See below). The

glass bears the name Ferroline, the trademark symbol registered June 26, 1883, as well as the patent date and a code number.

The factory burned to the ground about 1885 and was not rebuilt.

PERFECTION FUNNEL WORKS

Said to have been in 1890 the only establishment in the world devoted to making funnels, Augustus Gersdorff's company turned out each year a million of these objects so essential for filling the multi-millions of Jersey glass bottles, from medicaments such as laudanum to milder anesthetics like applejack.

The "Perfection Funnel" was made of tin, copper and glass and when the metals had been polished they shone "like beaten gold." Nelson Bavier was superintendent of the plant which was located near East Lake Glass Works, but oddly the main office was in Washington, D.C. An indispensable operation for the late 19th century bottle-boom in southern New Jersey, sparked by too-long-delayed railroad service.

GLASS-BOTTLE-MOLD FACTORY

Bridgeton in 1889 had a bottle-mold plant so excellent that it was supplying iron molds not only for numerous South Jersey glasshouses but also filling orders from Canada and southern states.

Owners Richard Trenchard and Charles D. Crickler started in a small room on Broad Street "with the help of a small boy in addition to their own [boys?]." By 1889 the partners had one of the largest mold factories in the nation, a 3-story plant on Atlantic Street, near Commerce.

Junior partner Crickler was a practical mold-maker who said the firm could turn out any design for any glass article, not just bottles. Interviewed in 1889 he said that besides their $12,000-a-year mold work they had just made a press for Col. G.G. Green, the patent medicine man of Woodbury, which "manufactures the most perfect glass sign ever invented." If Madison Avenue or Main Street could only find one!

Chilled iron patterns for mold-blowing were produced by 12 to 15 skilled mechanics. The payroll was $600 a month in 1899 and Messrs. Trenchard and Crickler had a $15,000 investment in the factory where lathes, drill presses and planers were run by steam.

Fig. 155 ALSO-RANS ONCE, GOOD AS MASON'S NOW. Fruit jars from the era when competition was desperate for food preservation. LEFT: Whitall Tatum of Millville; RIGHT: Bridgeton's Cohansey jar, both collectible today.

DANIEL LODER

Boyd's Cumberland County Directory for 1889-90 lists a glass manufacturer of this name as being near the Cumberland Glass Works but no other details are known.

Some Bridgetown-Salem Gaffers of 1877

When glasshouse managers needed journeymen blowers they could call on men like these who were listed in the 1877 edition of Boyd's Business Directory for Bridgeton and Salem:

> Joseph L. Carney, Joseph Ferrell, Joseph Finch, Addison Flack, William F. Fulmer, P. B. Headley, Frank M. Hill, Andrew, Casper and George C. Hoffman, William Launder, Adam H. Knight, Peter Lutz, Archibald and Stiles McHenry, John T. McKensey, Charles F. Marshall, Benjamin F. Parker, William Penton, Frederick Smith, Charles and George Souders, Theodore F. Strong, L. F. Thompson, Robert Torrens, George Wise, Edward Welser, Benjamin B. Westcott, William Wildermuth, Anthony and William Van Hook, and Andrew Vanderslice.

Fig. 156 Bridgeton wharf on the Cohansey river.

Fig. 157 MOLD-BLOWN SODA BOTTLE with blob top and metal bailer was made for a Fairton bottler. Turtle-back inkwell, also known as humpbacked or igloo, was mold-blown at many Jersey glassworks from the 1860s on. *Boeckle collection.*

Fig. 158 MILLVILLE ATMOSPHERIC FRUIT JAR has laid-on ring and glass lid held by thumbscrew metal clamp. Although back of jar and top of lid are embossed WHITALL'S PATENT/ JUNE 18th, 1861, this is the patent date for quite a different jar. The actual patent date for the Millville Atmospheric is Nov. 4, 1862. John M. Moore & Company, Clayton, had already patented a jar with a yoke and thumbscrew seal on Dec. 3, 1861.

Fig. 159 GREEN SPELLS WOODBURY, this time the father of G. G. Green who made a fortune from these paneled bottles and their contents. LEFT: two typical early drug vials; CENTER: the distinctive shape of Turlington's Balsam such as was made at Squankum (Williamstown).

Fig. 160 PRIZE BOTTLE, LEFT, marked Gloucester Co., with the S printed backwards; CENTER: an F. A. Schuster bottle from Woodbury; RIGHT: a soda from Berlin Bottling Co., a place once called Long-a-Coming. Blob-tops, all. *Boeckle collection.*

Fig. 161 CLAYTON WAS FISLERVILLE and here the twain have met; Brewster bottle was a private mold. *Boeckle collection.*

Fig. 162 THREE WHITNEY MASON JARS, all highly collectible. Made at Glassboro. *Boeckle collection.*

Millville and Whitall Tatum

"Down in southern New Jersey, they make glass. By day and by night, the fires burn on in Millville and bid the sand let in the light.

"Millville by night would have delighted Whistler, who loved gloom and mist and wild shadows. Great rafts of wood and big, brick hulks, dotted with a myriad of lights, glowing and twinkling every shade of red. Big, black fumes, shooting out smoke and sparks, bottles, bottles, bottles, of every tint and hue, from a brilliant crimson to the dull green that marks the death of sand and birth of glass.

"From each fire, the white heat radiates on the 'blowers,' the 'gaffers,' and the 'carryin'-in boys.' The latter are from nine to eighteen years of age, averaging about fourteen, and they outnumber the adult workers. A man with nothing hailing from nowhere, can get an easy job at fair pay, if he has boys who are able to carry bottles—many men in Millville need no suggestion from Roosevelt—boys can carry bottles and girls can work in the cotton-mills near by.

"The glass-blowers union is one of the most perfect organizations in the country. The daily wage runs from five dollars to twenty dollars, and from four to eight hours is a day's work. But the 'carryin'-in' boys work nine and ten hours and get two dollars and a half and three dollars a week. Passing back and forth in the pale weird light, these creatures are imps in both the modern and oldtime sense of the word. They are grimy, wiry, scrawny, stunted specimens, and in cuss words and salacious talk, they know all that grown men know. In the use of the ever surviving if not ever fitting, superlative, 'damndest,' they are past masters all.

"Their education has consisted mainly of the thoughts, emotions and experiences that resulted from contact with 'blowers' and 'gaffers,' besides views of a big barn-like space lit up by white hot sand. This has been their universe at those times of day when they were most alive, most wide-awake, most sensitive to impressions. The manufacturers have endowed a night-school, but (the teacher told me) the boys cannot keep their heads up and their eyes open during the sessions, therefore their brains don't make much headway—God help them!"

Entitled "Millville," the above is the opening excerpt from a piece by a student at Knox College, written at a time—the first three years of the 20th century—when he was touring the nation, which in his case often meant "riding the rods" of freight cars. The author, described by fellow students as the "terrible Swede," signed himself Charles August Sandburg, known today as Carl Sandburg.*

Sandburg proved himself, even at that unripened age, a good observer and journalist in what he wrote of Millville, even discovering that the pine belt there had in past millennia been a sea bottom. And who has better epitomized the miracle of glass: "and bid the sand let in the light."

The fires Sandburg wrote about could have flared day and night only at Whitall Tatum & Company, for although Millville has had many glassworks, only they then dominated the scene.

*From "In Reckless Ecstasy," Sandburg's first printed work, published by a fellow member of the Galesburg Poor Writers Club, Philip Green Wright, in 1904 when he owned Asgaard Press at Galesburg, Ill.

From 1806 down to the present moment Millville has had a continuous history of free-blown and mold-blown glass. To anyone who knows the background of Millville glassmaking it is shocking to observe the indefinite attribution of "Millville," a sort of never-never land, made by many collectors who have never set foot in South Jersey. It is hoped that the following pages will shed new light on Millville's 165 years of glassmaking so that collectors will look for documentation of the name of the glassworks where an object was made and perhaps even of the name of the gaffer and the decade in which he created what he wished might be a masterpiece.

THE GLASSTOWN FACTORY

Ever since 1806 Millville has had one or more glassworks in operation. The first one was built by James Lee and others (who had formed the third New Jersey glassworks, at Port Elizabeth) on the banks of the Maurice River. The location, on Buck Street where the American Legion building now stands, became known over the years as Glasstown and was the main Whitall Tatum plant until 1854 when the firm bought the Schetterville or South Millville works.

By 1814 Gideon Scull had become the owner of Lee's furnace and ran it as a window-glass works. Later Nathaniel Solomon was manager for a company of blowers but the venture was not successful for long.

As of 1827 Glasstown, then owned by Dr. George Burgin, Richard L. Wood and Joel Bodine, had become firmly established though there were to be several changes of ownership; Burgin and Wood in 1829, and Burgin, Wood and Pearsall in 1833. About 1828 William Coffin, Jr. of Hammonton went to Millville to operate a furnace known as Coffin, Pearsall & Company but he soon returned to Winslow; the 1833 firm name may be a merger of two separate furnaces.

Scattergood, Booth & Company owned Glasstown in 1836. Then came a change that eventually would affect all of Millville and even recast the glass business: In the words of Capt. John M. Whitall: "At New Year's 1838 G. M. Haverstick and William Scattergood, the former having married my sister Sarah, invited me to join them in the manufacture of glass vials, bottles &c. They had been in the business a couple of years . . ."

Fig. 163 PHOENIX GLASS WORKS is revealed in this $5 "shinplaster" as the alternate name for Scattergood & Whitall, c. 1838, At Millville, Whitall Tatum & Company, successors, later owned a vessel called *The Phoenix. Courtesy of George M. Scattergood.*

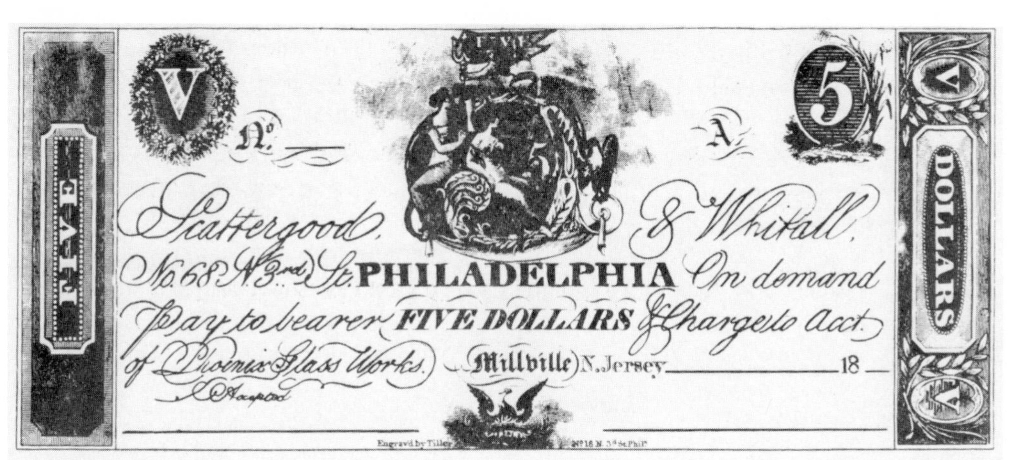

Fig. 164 GLASSTOWN, upper Millville plant of Whitall Tatum & Company, in 1890. Makers of fine pharmaceutical ware, the firm was at the head of tidewater in the Maurice river. Glassworks faced Buck Street, where the American Legion building stands. *Photo courtesy of Jesse Ford.*

From then until 1939 Glasstown was in the firm hands of Quakers. Totally inexperienced in glassmaking John M. Whitall had been a sea captain whose ship the *New Jersey* had been sold because the owner died. Having saved $4,000 at sea the captain put $3,000 into a dry goods business on May 12, 1829 and then asked Mary Tatum of Park Plain, near Woodbury, to be his wife. Both their families belonged to the Society of Friends. So faithful were the Tatums that when they were not at home, the story goes, their horses trotted alone to the meeting house, which is still in Woodbury.

Capt. Whitall didn't do well as a dry goods merchant so he tried wholesaling but when the "Crisis of 1837" was upon the nation, he owed creditors $105,000 and went into bankruptcy. As he had assets in merchandise and good debts, his creditors agreed to settle for 75¢ on the dollar.

William Scattergood, living at Millville, appeared to have considerable knowledge of the glass business, for the firm, then known as the Phoenix Glass Works, did well even after the financial panic. G. M. Haverstick soon retired and the name was shortened to Scattergood & Whitall. Capt. John continued living in Philadelphia, as he did until his death, although later prosperity from glass afforded the family summer homes at Atlantic City and Haddonfield.

Then in 1845 Scattergood retired. Meanwhile Capt. Whitall and his wife, residing in Philadelphia, were not active at Millville. Instead, they were busy with the "contrabands from the South." These were Negroes seeking haven in the north. The Whitalls were running an "underground railroad"—Capt. Whitall had established the St. Mary Street Adult Mission for Negroes and for nearly 15 years was its superintendent.

Fortunately for the Millville glass business, Franklin Whitall who, his brother John said, had a good business education, joined the firm and was manager for three critical years of 1845 to 1848. Moving to Millville he stayed with the organization until 1857. Standards of excellence initiated by him appear to have continued with Edward Tatum who became a member in 1848, when the name was changed to Whitall, Brother & Company and a Philadelphia office and store was opened at 410 Race Street which was occupied until 1930. A New York office opened in 1852 at 96 Beekman Street, continuing until 1868. When C.A. Tatum entered the firm in 1875 he took charge of the New York office at 46 Barclay Street a year later. After I. Franklin Whitall withdrew in 1857 the firm name changed to Whitall Tatum & Company; then on incorporation in 1901 the name became Whitall Tatum Company. Even before incorporation the glass company had become a giant, usually called Whitall Tatum and famed for the extraordinary high quality of its moldblown ware.

Fig. 165 BOTTLETOWN. The huge Whitall Tatum glassworks at South Millville, formerly Schetterville, about 1898 when smoke was a symbol of prosperity. Maurice river in background. *Courtesy of Kerr Glass Mfg. Co.*

SCHETTERVILLE: THE SOUTH MILLVILLE PLANT

Eventually this tail wagged the dog: Glasstown disappeared entirely and Schetterville or South Millville became synonymous with Whitall Tatum. But it was far from so in the beginning.

Schetterville was a hamlet originating in 1832 when two brothers, Frederick and Phillip Schetter, came from Baltimore to set up a window-light furnace a third of a mile south of Millville. Collectors of historic flasks may be interested in knowing that Frederick, a nephew of John F. Friese, an owner of the Baltimore Glass Works, which made some notable flasks, was permitted to buy Friese's share at "fair value" after his death, but instead chose to settle at Millville. However, he kept in close touch with Baltimore where he traded until 1838 as Tufts & Schetter, glass manufacturers at 46 South Gay Street.

The Schetters were bought out in 1844 at sheriff's auction by Lewis Mulford, leading Millville banker, and William Coffin, Jr., and Andrew K. Hay of Winslow. After one season they commenced making green bottles and vials. Deciding about 1853 that the glass business didn't pay, Mulford planned to sell Schetterville to Whitall Tatum, but they would have none of it. In retaliation, Mulford cornered all the wood for miles around. In a counter-move Whitall Tatum began buying wood from Virginia and shipping it by boat. With this slow and unreliable transport they found themselves frequently running out of fuel. In the end they had no choice but to capitulate and buy Schetterville.

Revolution in the 1860s

Whitall Tatum should have been grateful to Mulford for forcing them into a plant with generous room for expansion: great times were ahead for glassmakers with funds and foresight to utilize technological advances. Despite the Civil War, for Whitall Tatum there would be new transport, new metal, new fuel, new molds, new ware, still hand-blown.

Whitall Tatum had been shipping its glass, packed in salt hay, to Philadelphia and Baltimore via their sloops *Ann* and *Franklin* and to New York via their schooners *Caroline* and *Mary* and the steamboat *Millville.* Then at last in 1863 the railroad came to Millville.

Earliest molds for Millville bottles had been made of clay. In 1839 the company hired Thomas Campbell to make metal molds, and in 1840 he produced the first brass one, sculptured entirely by hand. More molds were made of iron, and crude machinery was devised for making molds. About 1862 a mold-factoring department was created at Schetterville. In 1867 wooden molds were introduced, a vast improvement in the blowing of flint glass which could now be fashioned without the ugly seam lines caused by iron molds.

The first chemical laboratory in the glass industry was set up by Whitall Tatum in 1865 and from then until 1890 was in charge of Richard Atwater. Since then analytical control of formulas for batch mixes has become indispensable to glass manufacture.

In 1863 when Whitall Tatum had two green-glass factories at Schetterville they began making flint glass there, with only limited success. The following year John H. Sixsmith built a new flint glasshouse at South Millville, the same time when William Leighton's formula for lime glass was made known to the industry. This striking improvement over

Fig. 166 COBALT, AMBER, GRAPE. LEFT: cobalt footed bowl with applied stem and fold-under foot. H. 4 inches. CENTER: dark amber, swirled dessert dish with drawn circular foot; attributed to Schetterville. H. 3½ inches. RIGHT: grape-colored goblet is rare in that its lovely shape was produced by drawing and tooling, with only the foot applied. H. 7 inches.

ordinary flint glass began to be used commercially for table ware but Whitall Tatum, making their own variation, found the formula economical enough to use for their best grade of pharmaceutical bottles. By 1883 the firm had 10 flint glass furnaces producing about 12 million pounds of lime glass a year. The new glass demanded new fuels and after various experiments with furnaces and producer gas, Whitall Tatum in 1897 became the first company to make flint glass in both the day tank and the continuous tank.

The new formula glass emerged from the annealing ovens clear and brilliant, but best of all it was easily controlled in the blowing. These advantages set off a wave of spare-time blowing which produced some famous gaffers and paperweight makers like Ralph Barber, John Ruhlander, and John Fath, whose art glass is discussed on other pages.

Miscellaneous ledger pages dated 1889, possibly a foreman's daily record, show how large Whitall Tatum was compared with other glassworks of that year, for a total of 1,512

Fig. 167 WHITALL TATUM'S SOUTH MILLVILLE PLANT. Rare photo of 1890 shows setting where famous gaffers like Ralph Barber, John Ruhlander and others made paperweights and unique freeblown glass in spare time. *Photo courtesy of Jesse Ford.*

people were employed at the two locations. In 1844 the 26 glassworks in the state employed only about 1,500. In 1899 at Glasstown 460 persons were working, 139 of them blowers, more than the total number of many glasshouses at that date. In South Millville the work force numbered 1,052, with the astounding number of 211 blowers, including a few pressers. Lamp workers alone numbered 36. Then there was a group of 708 which included packers and boys and evidently others who had not attained the skill of journeymen blowers. Besides clerks and other office workers, the remaining group included a large number of letterers, engravers, cutters and decorators. In a company that had about 350 well-qualified blowers, Ralph Barber and Emil Stanger had to be near-geniuses to stand out. Whitall Tatum of that day was a college for glassblowers.

Plant building was then expanding rapidly. On March 17, 1890, newspapers reported a "terrible fire" as due to a saltpeter explosion but there were no fatalities. In that year two new furnaces and a batch house were built, and a steam piping plant was installed. Some pressed ware was being made, particularly finials of wide-mouth show jars. In 1891 a new 3-pot color furnace was built that included opal, for which production costs were high, the journal noted.

Whitall Tatum Container Design and Its Influence

Whitall Tatum and its immediate predecessors had always made large quantities of patent medicine ware, but from the mid-1860s an incredible variety of well-designed bottles for druggists, physicians, perfumers and food purveyors was introduced. These articles will be discussed in some detail not only because they are of interest to bottle collectors but also because the forms have decided influence in the appearance of offhand glass made by Millville gaffers. The balustered pedestals and the covered compotes which appear often in 19th century Jersey glass are direct reflections of the styles of druggists' show globes made by Whitall Tatum.

As early as 1868 Whitall Tatum began making lettered plate ware and apothecary shop "furniture," which meant chiefly decorative containers for medicinals. In 1876 an amazing variety of druggists' sundries were introduced; chemical ware and perfume bottles were an innovation of 1878. Apparently the first catalog was printed in 1876.

For the subsequent decade or so some of the finest designs ever made to that date for American containers were blown at Whitall Tatum. Some of the articles anticipate Bauhaus Modern design of the 1920s. Others, in their combination of functional line and decoration would hold their own today in exhibits of excellent design such as those of the New York Museum of Modern Art.

A frequent misconception is that Whitall Tatum made paperweights and art glass for commercial sale. All such articles were made by blowers during their lunch hour.

Colors

The 1876 catalog advertised the following kinds of glass: Flint, Green, Amber, Blue and Opal. To this group Dark Green was added some time later, for it appears in the 1888 catalog. A mere recital of the colors, however, is totally inadequate to describe their characteristics, for they were far superior to those of other bottle works of the time and even to that of many firms making table ware and art glass.

The dark green glass was unlike any used elsewhere in 19th century American glassworks. Used most often for small toilet bottles and pomade jars, the color had the blue-green cast of Colombian emeralds. Admitting little light, still, it was never the black or olive green of early wine bottles but instead a jewel-like color. Nor is it the "poison green" often found in some English pharmaceutical jars. Another use was for "acid bottles."

Two kinds of blue were formulated, one, the cold dark cobalt of Bromo-Seltzer bottles, akin to Prussian blue. The other might be described as light-transmitting cerulean or a Maxfield Parrish blue. Softer and lighter than cobalt, this blue has been noted in auction catalogs such as that of the Grace S. Fish collection of American glass, but no source has been attributed. In one Jersey household I have seen a tincture bottle blown from this metal and near it a thin-walled finger bowl that could well have been made from the same gather. The color should not be confused with the grayed or sapphire blue, also attractive, which is likewise found in Jersey pitchers.

Whitall Tatum ambers are not easy to identify unless compared with trademarked items but perhaps are slightly more orange than the Whitney golden amber of the 1850s.

The opal glass is never a flat white but a warm one that even after nearly a century has a polish like white jade. Though not fiery the opalescence is visible on the edges of strong block lettering and the handles of some pitchers. This opal and the dark green

Fig. 168 "ROBINSON'S MIGNONETTE PERFUME," a private label, copperwheel engraved, that is redolent of 19th century gardens. A Whitall Tatum design with hand-facetted, ground-glass stopper. Matching bottle is labeled "Robinson's Ess. Bouquet Cologne." H. 9½ inches. RIGHT: covered compote of clear flint glass, one of matched pair, Millville c. 1860. Inset cover; applied finial has teardrop and sheared top. Applied baluster stem. H. 13½ inches.

emphasize how decorative simple bottles can be when the form and the substance are well met.

The flint glass was of extraordinary clarity and brightness, especially considering its intended use for fairly expendable bottles. The best grade was reserved, of course, for cut and engraved show globes, vases and perfume bottles.

The 1888 catalog noted that on quantity orders "any other colors" could be obtained for certain small objects such as cold cream jars and lip-salve boxes. Noon-time blowers, of course, drew on these extra colors for their palettes, but by the time the true gaffers had discovered how excellent was the flint metal for their own creations, they often had kits in their lockers of unusual supplementary colors.

Sand for the flint glass was brought in by rail from Ohio where washing was done on a large scale and more economically than Whitall Tatum could have done at the time. For most colored ware and green-glass, Jersey sand was used, as impurities were less likely to be visible in colored metal.

Entering into the laboratory ware field about 1886, Whitall Tatum for a very short time produced some of the articles from borosilicate glass. George M. Scattergood reports that chemical flasks and hydrometer jars blown from this metal are as bright today as when they were made; they are scarce and bear no identifying marks.

Black glass that was completely lightproof was being blown in 1902 for one type of prescription bottle in sizes from ½ to 4 ounces.

There surely was no medicine-bottle maker who went to so much trouble to give customers the utmost choice and special service from a large standard line or from custom molds. Finding that some customers could not afford an individual mold cut for about $400, Whitall Tatum devised an inset lettered plate that cost only about $2 to $10. For any unusual shapes a wooden mold was recommended. In 1876 two large shops were busy making molds.

By far the most decorative and appealing of Whitall Tatum items still available are bottles made for the physician's or the druggist's stock of medicines: the tincture bottle and the saltmouth, both made as early as 1876, at least, with raised glass labels hand-lettered and decorated in combinations of goldleaf, white, black and scarlet. The tincture bottle was a cylinder with round shoulders and a precise, mushroom-style, ground-glass stopper. The saltmouth was square with rounded corners and had a wide circular mouth, also with a flat-topped stopper.

"Shop Furniture"

This was the name given to tincture and saltmouth bottles mentioned above, the containers with Latin labels that looked so professional on druggists' shelves or in doctors' offices, and also included neatly styled ointment jars and tablet containers. Shop furniture was blown both in green-glass and in flint, the latter being the most expensive. The buyer could have his choice of these four grades of green glass:

X WARE.	Blown in an iron mold, made with special care and nicety. Smooth bottoms.
XX WARE.	Superior surface and free from mold mark. Smooth bottoms.
XXX WARE.	Superior surface; no mold marks. Punted. Hollow flat cut stoppers.
XXX WARE.	Same as XXX but with "Stoppers Richly Cut."

Fig. 169 1880 APOTHECARY SHOPS carried this fine glassware of Whitall Tatum. Ointment jar, LEFT, in amber has inset cover with acorn finial, etched label; H. 6¾ inches. Pure gold leaf label on tincture bottle in amber, H. 5½ inches. Saltmouth jar, RIGHT, has costly recessed label hand-painted in red, gold and black on white. H. 9½ inches.

Blue and amber bottles were obtainable in XX quality. Flint-ware tincture bottles and saltmouths were usually blown from clear glass but could also be had in blue, now rare.

Recessed Ware

The most decorative of the medicine containers was the recessed ware which was designed for tincture bottles and saltmouths. Although impressed as Patented April 2, 1889, the bottles were fully described in the 1888 catalog. Before that time the beautifully lettered glass labels edged in gold were subject to chipping because they were raised above the body of the jars; few perfect labels are found today.

With the new method, a process at one time directed by Nelson Ward, a rectangular recess providing space for a glass label was cut into the bottle mold. A thin piece of glass, label-size, was then bent into a metal mold to fit the depression and annealed. Next, the pharmaceutical name such as PIMENTA was lettered backwards on the glass, which was edged in goldleaf. With resin and beeswax the label was then affixed to the recess, and thus the bottle had a smooth flush surface. The effect of a mass of these bottles lined up on shelves in a neat apothecary shop was enormously decorative, and no doubt confidence-inspiring to patients. In 1902 the recessed ware was also being blown in blue glass.

Made by a time-consuming hand process which was too costly when machine-blowing became established, recessed ware ceased to be. Then, in the 1930s when George M. Scattergood joined Whitall Tatum he revived this ware when he discovered in Lancaster, Pa., a letterer worthy of past efforts. The pharmaceutical bottles became such a success once more that the letterer soon had a staff of some 40 workers. The major customer was the U.S. Navy which used the bottles for sickbays on its ships. What could be more confidence-inspiring than labels like B. JUNIPER or BALM GILEAD?

Then one day during World War II a Japanese shell in the South Pacific shook up a sick-bay. Some of the wounds were caused by shattering Whitall Tatum recessed bottles. Without much more ado they were declared missile hazards. In Lancaster, Pa., a prospering industry and many hopes were shattered too. George Scattergood says ruefully that remaining recessed jars were sold by some department stores as antiques. Whether or not, they still are desirable bottles.

Prescription Bottles

Over a score of styles for prescription bottles were illustrated in catalogs of the 1880s, mostly flat paneled or oval and not out of the ordinary except in the quality of their making. All were available for custom embossing. Illustrations of some lettered plates showed customers as far afield as Canada, England and Germany.

Fig. 170 LEEDS DEVIL cologne bottle named for an old Jersey "ha'nt" of the bogs. Jersey Devil here has a leonine head, wings and a sea serpent's tail. Opalescent glass, a Whitall Tatum special for E.S. REED'S/ SONS/ APOTHECARY/ ATLANTIC CITY/ N.J. embossed on face. Heart-shaped glass stopper has cork liner. H. 6 inches. OINTMENT JAR of opal glass has raised letters in black.

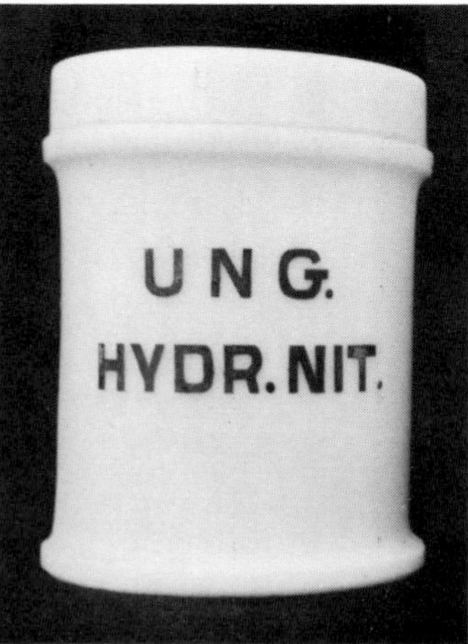

Show Globes and Jars

Under this prosaic label some gracefully shaped and exquisitely cut, engraved or hand-decorated jars, urns and hanging "lights" for apothecary windows were made at Whitall Tatum from at least the 1870s well into the 20th century.

Some of the show globes that were not cut or engraved are being reproduced today, by machine, but the hand-cut ones will never come again. Where most of the originals are is hard to say, as few museums collected them and antiques shops seldom display them.

When Caesar was conquering Britain his ship became lost one night off the coast of Wales, according to a tale by George M. Scattergood. When the vessel was about to be dashed against a reef, the captain spied a red binnacle light and thus succeeded in piloting the boat safely to land. There it was discovered that the guiding light came from an apothecary shop. In gratitude for the rescue Caesar decreed that thenceforth apothecary shops should show a colored light to guide the distressed.

Whatever the legend for the origin of drugstore lights (before neon, that is) the facts are that Whitall Tatum & Company did most, through their impressive show jars and handsome bottles for medicines, to give American pharmacies a professional look. The show jars and pedestals were offered at low cost, and once a druggist had bought some of these impressive pieces he was inclined to spruce up his entire shop. Dispensing physicians also bought the ware.

One series of these urns could well have graced a sideboard of the times. Named in the catalog of 1888 as Grecian Vases or Pineapple Urns, they consisted of two or three pear- or pineapple-shaped vases, the bottom one on a pedestal, the upper and smaller ones set like stoppers into the others. The early "pineapples" were undecorated lime glass, intended to hold vari-colored water. With increasing demand the urns were engraved with floral sprays. Maximum price for a 3-piece engraved decanter set was $4 in 1888.

Some of the Grecian vases, 32 inches tall and holding about two gallons, had an overall hexagonal cutting and were priced at $16. Others had an overall thumbprint faceting. Still others were cut in the Strawberry-Diamond pattern which some collectors seem to think was exclusive with Bakewell of Pittsburgh. Clarence S. Reeves, an engraver of laboratory equipment from 1906 to 1956 at Whitall Tatum, says his father Charles Reeves, Jr., for many years was a cutter and stone-engraver of these show globes and vases. A pair of beautiful pitchers in ruby over clear flint glass were blown by Ralph Barber and delicately cut by Charles Reeves (see Plate 1).

Whitall Tatum also made Decorated Vases which were not transparent but had an overall background simulating green or Tennessee marble, with thick bases and finials of black and gold, the height, 26 inches. A gilded medallion, hand-decorated, read PURE DRUGS or TOILET ARTICLES. Pedestals 13 inches high and given a realistic marble finish were supplied to support these urns.

A Combination Show Jar had a lid and a base decorated in plain black and gold bands; the globe between, holding two gallons, was clear. Supplied also was a pedestal, marbleized

Fig. 171 BAUHAUS MODERN? No, Whitall Tatum's fine pharmaceutical ware of the late 19th century. "Unknown designer of this functionally handsome glass was half a century ahead of his time. Ointment jar, left, of opal quality glass; base impressed WHITALL TATUM & CO./PHILA. & N.Y. H. 5 inches. Unbroken verticals in flint glass for apothecary jar. Ground-glass cover has ice-like oblong for handle. H. 9 inches.

Fig. 172 GRECIAN VASE SHOW BOTTLES. Hand-blown in three pieces, all hand-cut and engraved. 1886 Whitall Tatum.

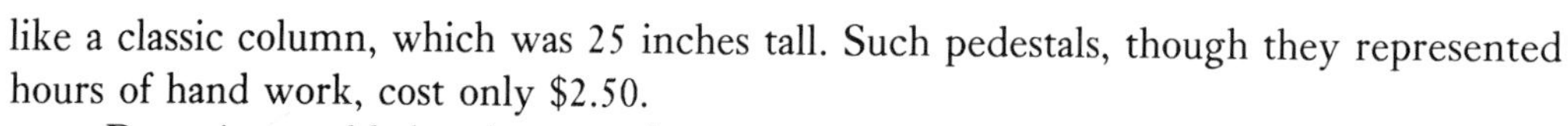

like a classic column, which was 25 inches tall. Such pedestals, though they represented hours of hand work, cost only $2.50.

Druggists could also choose a glass mortar, a foot high and covered in gold and the words PURE DRUGS inscribed across the middle. Transparent glass graduates, two feet high with a gilded top edge and a red ribbon lettered PURE DRUGS & CHEMICALS, were another badge of the profession.

Ten gallon Decorated Show Jars with bulbous gilded caps were quite stunning when decorated with a coat of arms in gold, green and scarlet. For the $15 cost, the words PURE DRUGS would be lettered on and the coat of arms changed as desired.

One of the most splendid of these jars turned up a few years back with the national emblem of Costa Rica emblazoned on a gold medallion. The occasion was the sale of about 2,000 museum jars (often similar to show jars) by former Clayton dealer, Frank Gilbert, who purchased the collection from the Philadelphia Commercial Museum which since the 1890s had housed it to exhibit exotic seeds, grains, and even fruits from all over the world. One such jar still has pawpaws well preserved in an unknown liquid. To see so historical a collection dispersed was distressing but apparently no New Jersey museum was interested in bidding on the lot or even a portion of it. Among the many attractive containers were columnar ones about 20 inches high, on a stemmed inverted foot, with whirled stopper and neck in a torch-like design.

Usually thought of as utilitarian jugs for shipping liquids, carboys at Whitall Tatum were offered, at least in 1888, in flint glass beautifully cut in the strawberry-diamond pattern, making them look like 2-gallon decanters, today either unobtainable or possibly attributed to Pittsburgh and New England glassworks.

By 1905 the show globes, if the catalog be a guide, had succeeded to excess. The attractive earlier vases had been retained but in addition there were large amphoras and ewers, well designed in themselves but "trimmed" with bronzed metal fittings in unsuitable lacy patterns. Some of the tall ewers were set on curlicued metal tripods that look like Victorian wicker tables. Large numbers of this product are said to have been junked in the 1933 Depression.

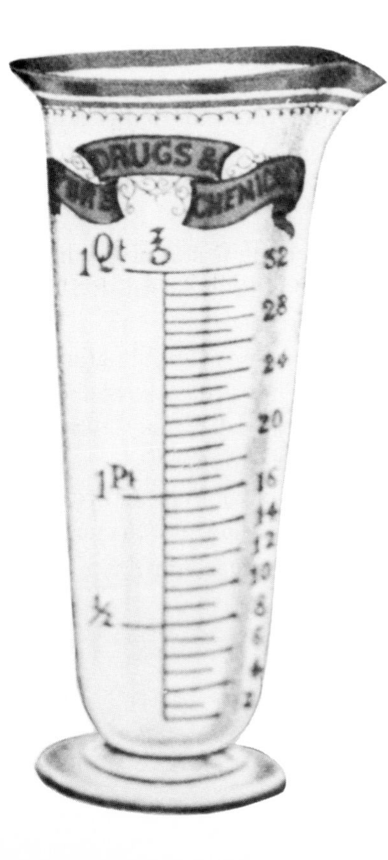

Fig. 173 Clear or frosted 24-inch graduate hand-painted in red, black and gold; 10 gallon show jar with gilt cap and elaborate coat of arms in red, green and gold sold in 1888 for $15.

Fig. 174 FLINT GLASS CARBOY cut like fine tableware in Strawberry-Diamond and Fan pattern at Whitall Tatum; two-gallon size cost $10 in 1888.

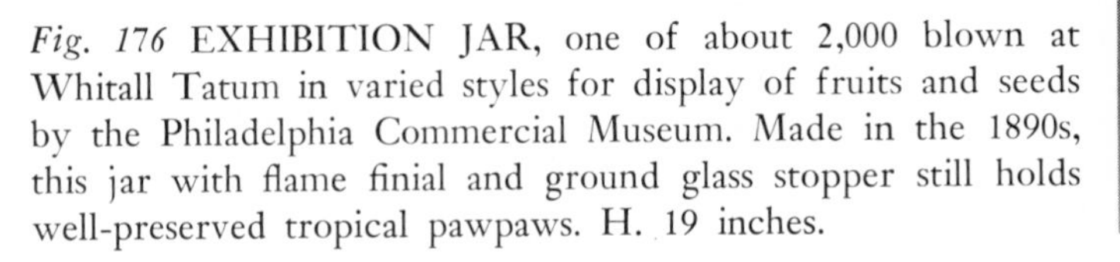

Fig. 175 12-inch gilded mortar with 16-inch pestle; show globe pedestal, 13 inches, decorated in green marbleized effect.

Fig. 176 EXHIBITION JAR, one of about 2,000 blown at Whitall Tatum in varied styles for display of fruits and seeds by the Philadelphia Commercial Museum. Made in the 1890s, this jar with flame finial and ground glass stopper still holds well-preserved tropical pawpaws. H. 19 inches.

Perfumers' Wares

The year of 1888 was very great for perfume, if one judges by Whitall Tatum catalogs. The 1876 catalog had three pages of perfume bottle listings, but in 1888 there were nine pages listing some 360 different shapes and sizes of perfume and cologne containers. By 1902 the list was down to four pages.

Not only were these bottles hand-blown flint glass, they often had special non-bottle shapes such as Heart and Clock and were frequently "richly cut and engraved." The best rivaled fancy glass from Bakewell or other well-publicized glass factories of the north. As so few of these perfumes appear now in South Jersey one wonders if they are not usually attributed elsewhere. For example, the bottle engraved with the word "Perfume," on page 231 matches the drawing of a cologne bottle from a Whitall Tatum catalog, opposite, yet this is one of a pair found in Maine. All of the toilet articles were not only blown with fine precision but also usually had an elegance not common at a time when good design was in a state of decline.

The Caswell Cologne was a staple named for the firm of Caswell-Massey Company, still lively in Manhattan today, who were perfumers to George Washington.

Especially fascinating is the last page of the 1888 catalog, one devoted to "Stoppered Pungents," (see page 240) with strong modern shapes. The final footnotes to perfume are the "Ottar of Rose Bottles—Richly Cut and Gilded," about four inches long, at $2.25 a dozen. Where have all the Ottars of Rose gone?

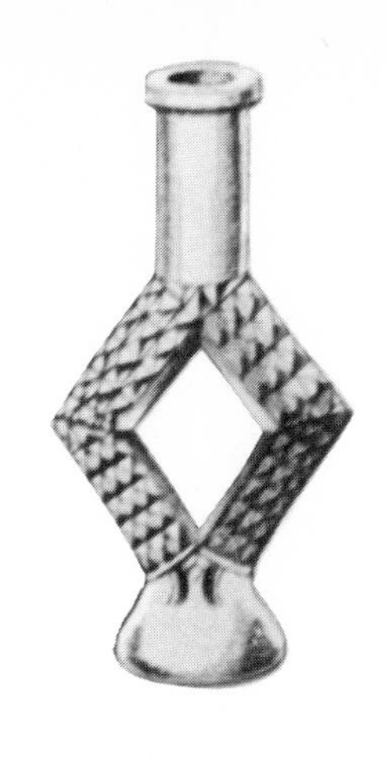

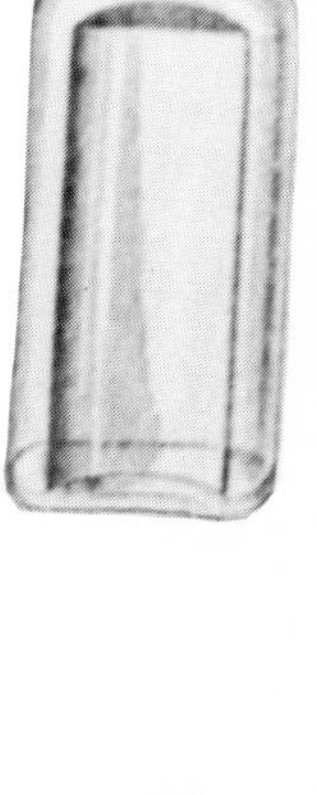

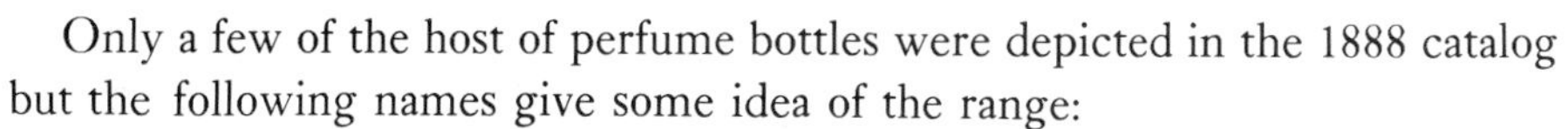

Only a few of the host of perfume bottles were depicted in the 1888 catalog but the following names give some idea of the range:

Bellows
Open Book
Greek Cross
Panel Whisk
Hour Glass
Square Fiddle
Satchel

Snail
Shell (scallop)
Fish
Bear
Elephant
Horseshoe
Clock

Jug Handle (small pitcher with ovoid stopper)
Night-blooming Cereus
Grape Decanter (pebbled finish)

Barrel
Tassel
Acorn
Rose
Flower
Daisy
Hand

Pineapple
Diamonds, raised
Gothic Panel
Mirror Cologne
Long Champagne
Slipper
Wheat Sheaf

Chinese Fan (decorated with heron, pines and crescent moon)
Fancy Rhombus, with hobnails
Egg (split in half horizontally)

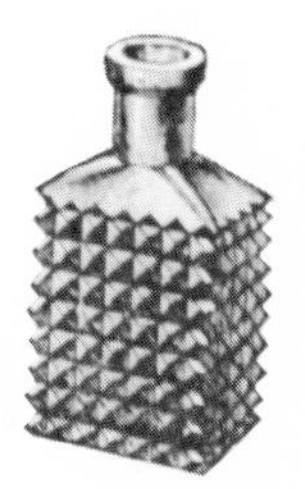

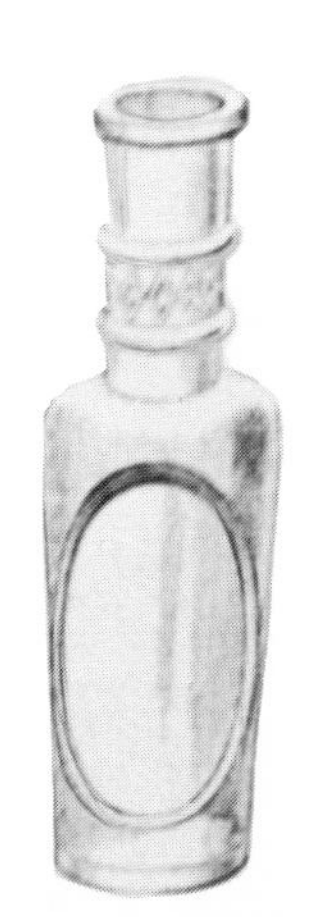

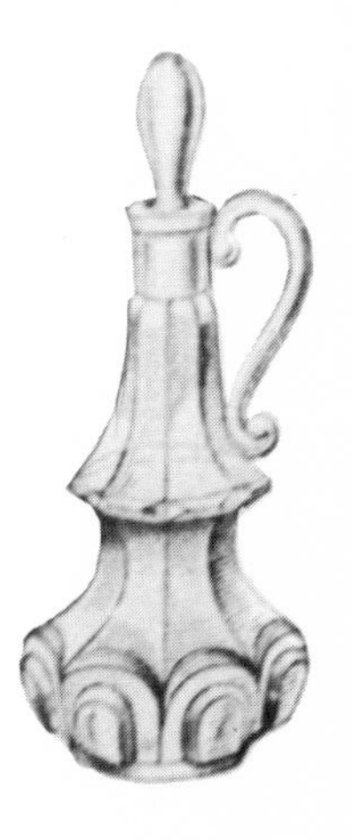

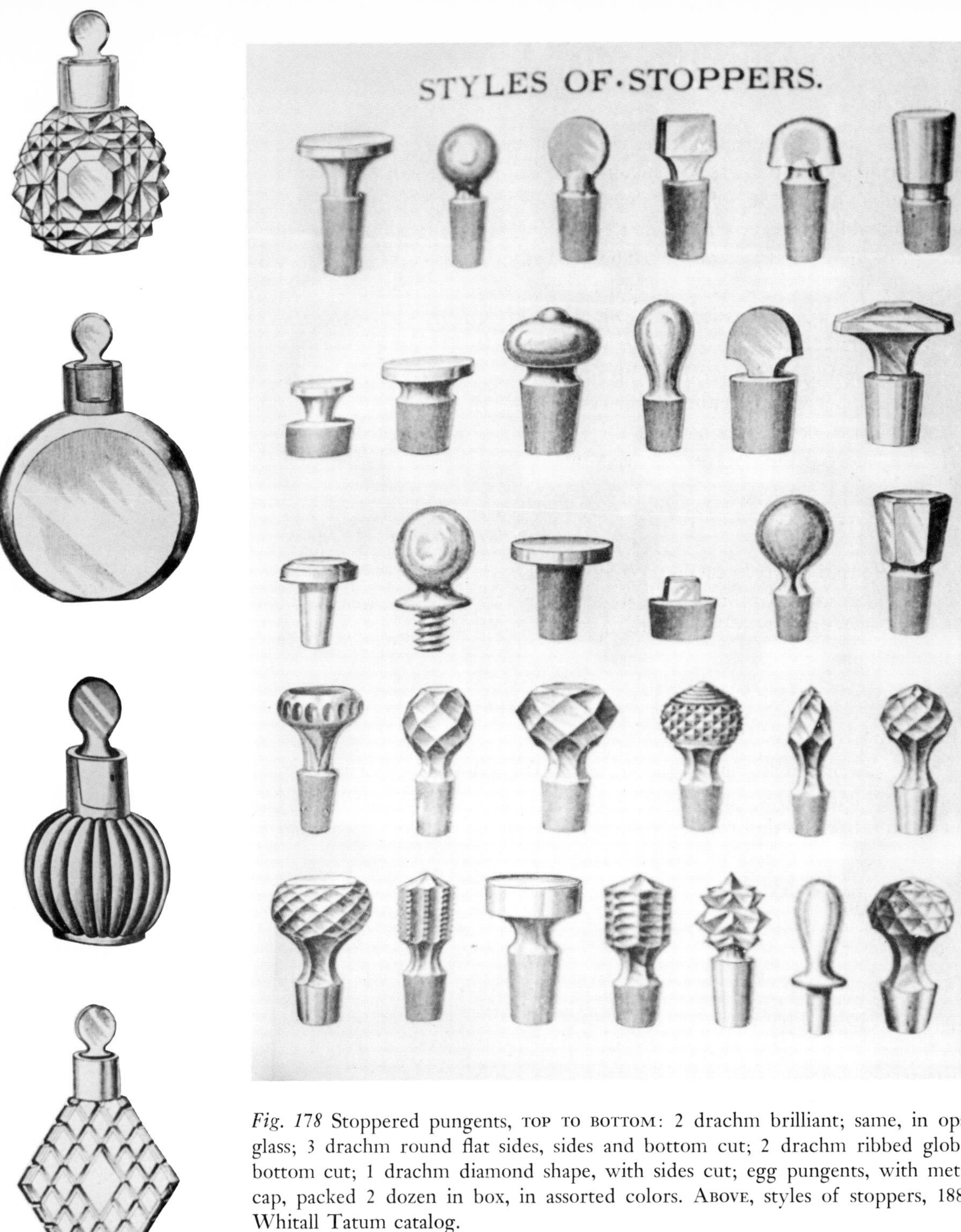

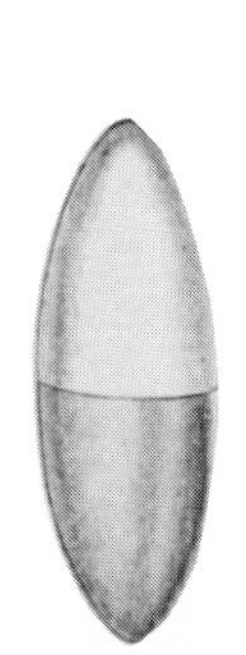

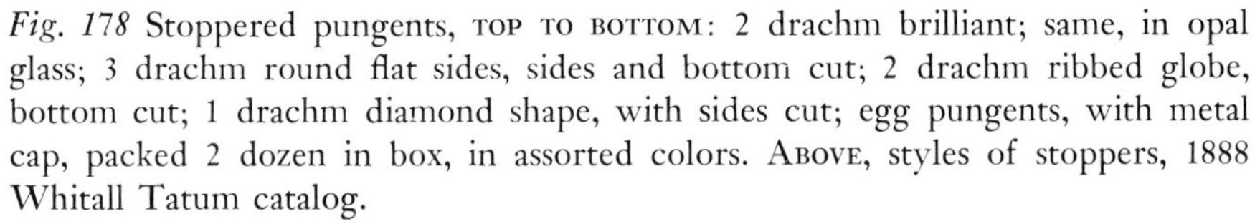

Fig. 178 Stoppered pungents, TOP TO BOTTOM: 2 drachm brilliant; same, in opal glass; 3 drachm round flat sides, sides and bottom cut; 2 drachm ribbed globe, bottom cut; 1 drachm diamond shape, with sides cut; egg pungents, with metal cap, packed 2 dozen in box, in assorted colors. ABOVE, styles of stoppers, 1888 Whitall Tatum catalog.

Poison Bottles

Most "Poison Bottles" are likely to be rather late products because the movement for public health and safety was late in coming to fruition. Possibly ahead of the times, Whitall Tatum announced in the 1876 catalog: "a new line of bottles, of a deep cobalt color," the surface of which was "covered with sharp diamond-shaped points, tastefully arranged," in sizes from ½ ounce to 16 ounces. These warning containers, said the catalog, would be especially useful for "Liniments, and for the various poisonous articles, as Laudanum, Corrosive Sublimate, Oxalic Acid, Oil of Vitriol, &c., which are likely to be kept in the family medicine closet."

By 1888 Whitall Tatum had virtually improved itself out of a market by inventing a warning stopper which, with variable corks, could fit any bottle. Having sharp diamond-points and saw-tooth edges of glass, this stopper impressed with the word POISON was indeed a "stopper" in darkness or daylight.

Hyacinth Glasses

An item in the 1876 catalog of special interest to collectors is the listing of Hyacinth Glasses, because they soon disappeared. As the illustration below shows, each glass had room for one bulb and ample space for upright roots. The holders were made in white, blue, amber and purple.

Spirits Bottles

Although the 1876 catalog pictures Dark Wine Bottles in amber (cylindrical with long necks) and listed "green and black" schnapps and sarsaparilla bottles, Whitall Tatum did not go into beer bottle production until about 1927 or make hard liquor containers until

Fig. 179 ORANGE-AMBER PAN, an 18th century shape; diameter 6 inches. Red hat-shaped toothpick holder, made from a bottle mold; late 19th century. Hyacinth bulb-holder in soft blue; Whitall Tatum. H. 8 inches.

Fig. 180 LARGEST BOTTLE EVER MADE, a product of two shops at Whitall Tatum about 1902. Exhibited at St. Louis Exposition 1904 but never returned to Millville. Principle makers, LEFT TO RIGHT: Emil Stanger, Tony Stanger, John Fath and Marcus Kuntz. *Courtesy of Kerr Glass Mfg. Co.*

after Prohibition, about 1936-37. One of the quart whiskies, made for "Golden Wedding" brand, is probably unique for it is amber with an iridescent finish. Invented by one of the employees, James Gagin, the color was produced with an acid spray applied while the bottles were hot, just prior to annealing. Sample bottles were embossed Pat Applied for/WT/Other pats pending. Some quarts of Canada Dry sparkling water in lime glass were also given this iridescence and may still be found.

"Coca Wines," mallet-shaped bottles, were listed, in sizes from 4 and 8 ounces to pints and quarts. Were these for early cola drinks?

Barber Bottles

In 1888 and into the 20th century Whitall Tatum made four styles of barber bottles in clear lime and opaque white glass: a 16-ounce champagne, a 16-ounce hock bottle, a 10-ounce bell bottle and a pint with a wide circular base tapering to a narrow neck. Several types of labels were supplied at 15 cents each, but no illustrations are shown for such descriptions as Keystone, Oriental design or Keystone Chromo Head.

Largest Bottle Ever Blown

Two Whitall Tatum gaffers, Emil Stanger and Marcus Kuntz, best known today for their paperweights, collaborated in making a 108-gallon bottle, man-high, said to have been the largest bottle ever blown. With co-operation of the management, these two men helped by Tony Stanger and John Fath were the principals who made the bottle for display at the St. Louis Exposition of 1904. The bottle was not blown by lung power but by compressed air. Because of the huge size, a special square block had to be built for the bottle, as well as its own pit, pot and oven. A hit at the fair, the gigantic bottle never returned to Millville, and the only visible image now is the adjacent photo. According to the Bridgeton *News* of March 18, 1957, the bottle was said to have been broken in St. Louis or en route back.

In 1904 the same crew, having the needed special equipment on hand, made "the second largest bottle,"—67 gallons. This one survived 53 years, until it was shipped in 1957 to be a show-piece at the convention of the Glass Bottle Blowers Association, also held in St. Louis. Packed in a special case with steel straps and shipped by air freight, the bottle

Fig. 181 "SECOND LARGEST BOTTLE," 65 gallons each, made by the same shops at Whitall Tatum as the 18-gallon container. Man at the right is believed to be Marcus Kuntz; identity of the other is not known. *Courtesy of Kerr Glass Mfg. Co.*

arrived with one end of the crate stove in. When the crate was opened "the second largest bottle" was just a lot of cullet.

Glass bearing the impress of WHITALL TATUM & CO. or abbreviations of this name were made some time before 1901. In that year the firm was incorporated and the trademark became simply the initials W/T set in an inverted triangle. Thousands of objects made before 1901 of course had no identifying marks. Among the first were bottles with rough pontils, for at a very early date the firm expunged pontil scars by polishing. Still later were the plain bases without pontil marks, and then the bases impressed with various trademarks. In the 20th century, two numerals on the base indicate a year: as 30 for 1930. Mold numbers are also shown.

Early in its history the firm developed a reputation for high quality which it always maintained. In 1854, then known as Whitall, Brother & Company, in their exhibit of green-glass at the Franklin Institute fair the articles were described as "of excellent quality." Some years later when the firm had become Whitall, Tatum & Company the Franklin Institute awarded it second prize, a bronze medal, for "a large number of very good specimens of Druggists' and Chemists' Glasswares, Bottles, both in white and colored glass and samples of white and green glass fruit jars, vials, &c." At the National Centennial Exhibition held in Philadelphia in 1876 the company had a large display of chemists', druggists', and perfumers' wares in lime and green-glass. The exhibit was commended for the good quality of the glass and "for useful productions in great variety."

Food Containers

The re-usable glass container might be said to have originated at Whitall Tatum. Their good-looking catsup bottle shown in the 1876 catalog was calabash shaped; indeed, was called a flask and could have served as a table decanter. The fluted pepper sauce holders would be an ornament today, if one could find such. The Fancy French Brandy Fruits, curved cylindricals with two wide-spaced applied rings, were delectable filled and decorative empty. Mustard jars were barrel shaped; chow chow bottles with broad round shoulders could serve again for home-canning. Pickle jars were blown in at least three attractive styles—square paneled, square gothic, and hexagonal—and came in sizes up to a gallon. Then there were jelly and honey jars, "rounded-square" maple syrup bottles, tall thin club sauce containers, milk jars (so labeled), and lemon syrup bottles.

So multifarious were the glass objects blown at Whitall Tatum that space here allows for further mention only of some of the oddities or the especially well designed.

Nursing bottles by themselves would make a quaint collection. Some were regionally named. A baby could sup from The Baltimore, called a nursing flask and so shaped, or from The Millville, violin-shaped. One called The Bronx was graduated and had the name impressed diagonally across the measuring scale. Then there were The Empire, the Three Star, The Home, The Acme, The Normandie, and the "shoe-shaped." The Handy was patented Feb. 24, 1891, for an improved pattern having no inside corners. Most had the names embossed in large letters, a baby's ABCs.

Three styles of aquaria were hand blown. One which came in sizes up to 20 gallons was cylindrical with a slight flare at the top and a foldover edge, with today's functional-modern look. Another was a swinging sphere with chains for hanging. A third was a globe set on a high inverted-cone base, a concept that many a gaffer found admirable for a compote, a vase or a pitcher,—which often appeared at major auctions of American glass.

Snapped up at an early date because of their usefulness were the Confectionery Ring Jars, advertised in the 1876 catalog, in sizes of ½ pint to 2 gallons. Cylindrical with rounded lids, they have three rings of glass applied at harmonious intervals, some of these rings in cobalt. Tablet jars, holding as much as four pounds, were soon discovered to be useful in kitchen and bath, and so have been reproduced by machine. But the ground-glass stoppers, the terraced lines of the tops, and the good quality of the metal make the copies seem worthless. These tablet jars appeared relatively late, are not in the 1888 catalog.

Counter urns are a direct throw-back to Jersey's late 18th century sugar bowls and jampots. Like the latter, the urns are footed and have a teardrop shape which flows into a high conical cover. The latter is inset and has a sliced-off knob. Although these look like candy jars they were in use as early as 1876 by druggists and dispensing physicians.

Even the several toothpowder bottles had style, with a domed cover and a finial. Whitall Tatum cold cream jars in opal glass set a pattern now used by most manufacturers, but the look is not the same when the lid is metal instead of glass and the label is paper.

Small ink bottles were of a kind found at many glassworks: the round cone, the turtleback and the fluted pyramid. Fluted cone mucilage bottles resemble inks. The large square carmine ink bottle was a masterpiece of geometric design.

Even the bell jars for laboratory use were pleasing objects: the tall knobbed one, a bulbous one, a short one like a food cover, and a cork-top jar. Battery jars were round, unlike the usual oblong ones.

Much favored today by decorators, 10- and 12-gallon carboys were long a Whitall Tatum staple, supplied either "naked" or boxed, in salt hay. Besides the plain collared neck, some had screw tops or ground-glass stoppers. In contrast, maximum size of the demijohns

Fig. 182 TWINE HOLDER and pitcher in clear glass edged in blue, a favored technique at Whitall Tatum in the 19th century. Twine holder, H. 4 inches. Pitcher with applied curl handle, 3½ inches.

was five gallons and these were advertised as covered, that is, with woven wicker. Reports persist that large numbers of Whitall Tatum demijohns were shipped "naked" as containers for Welch's grape juice, a non-fermenting product originated by a Vineland dentist, Dr. Thomas B. Welch, in 1869.

Among off-beat items were cupping glasses for blood-letting, bird bottles and baths, and gallipots. The latter were small jars for resins, and the name was antique slang for apothecaries.

Although catering mainly to druggists and physicians rather than to patent-medicine makers, Whitall Tatum as late as 1902 was offering bottles for that ancient nostrum Turlington's Balsam, and two other standbys, Opodeldoc and Bear's Oil. For home use there was a neat medicine chest of cherry wood containing 12 bottles, and one in mahogany with 18 case bottles and jars for which labels would be furnished—sets that are probably mistaken today for ship-captain's cases.

When druggists began adding soda fountains, Whitall Tatum was ready to help as early as 1888. They made recessed bottles for ice cream syrups, tumblers for sodas, cut-glass spoon holders, cut-glass bowls for crushed fruit, and a colorful glass banner advertising soda flavors from Blackberry to Vanilla.

A fateful year for Jersey glassblowers was 1899 when the Whitall Tatum giant employed a mechanical engineer, A. S. Granger, to design means for making machine-formed bottles. The following year an experimental plant was set up at South Millville, in charge of Benjamin T. Headley and Mervin C. Bard. From then on automation steadily increased, producing an entirely new line of expendable containers in wide variety. Surprisingly, some mold-blowing shops were still maintained.

By 1938 Whitall Tatum was reaching the end of its story. In that year George S. Bacon who had been manager of the company for 46 years retired and a glassmaker, Samuel Berry, had completed 76 years of service with the firm.

In 1939 Whitall Tatum was bought by the Armstrong Cork Company and soon became a fully automated glass manufactury, producing billions of machine-made containers. In 1969 the Millville glass division of Armstrong was bought by the Kerr Glass Manufacturing Company, a pioneer in making glass containers, with numerous national branches.

James Lee would have been astonished at the force he had set in motion.

Fig. 183 VESSEL *PHOENIX* on the Maurice river in the 1870s transported Whitall Tatum glass to Baltimore and New York.

Wheaton of Millville

ALTHOUGH NOT FOUNDED until 1888 Wheaton Glass Company of Millville is, with its allied industries, the second largest employer in South Jersey.

The founder, Dr. Theodore Corson Wheaton, was born at Tuckahoe on Aug. 24, 1852, the son of Amos and Harriet (Hann) Wheaton. At age 19 Theodore Wheaton had visions of a maritime life and he shipped before the mast on a coastal freighter, but *mal de mer* abruptly cut short that career. The young ex-sailor then apprenticed himself to a Dr. Way, a pharmacist and physician in South Seaville.

In 1872 Theodore Wheaton enrolled at the Philadelphia College of Pharmacy and Science where he received a Ph.G. degree in 1876. He at once enrolled in the medical college of the University of Pennsylvania and although he worked his way through college he obtained his M. D. degree in 1879. The following year he married Bathsheba Brooks Lancaster and they returned to South Seaville where their first son was born in 1881.

Country practice offered little for an ambitious young doctor and so in 1883 the family moved to Millville, then a thriving town of about 9,000, mostly Whitall Tatum glassworkers and textile mill employees. Dr. Wheaton opened a drug store and an adjoining general store. He also practiced medicine but the daily visible success of Whitall Tatum & Company in blowing bottles for druggists and doctors soon induced the young physician to switch careers again.

Five years after arriving in Millville Dr. Wheaton went into the bottle-making business, one that third and fourth generation Wheatons are continuing. Starting in a small way with a 6-pot furnace operated by a dozen men and twice as many boys, Dr. Wheaton soon found a ready market for bottles and glass tubing, still among the firm's specialties. Records of the early glass made are scarce but the main kinds are said to have been clear flint and amber. At one time a considerable amount of cutting was done.

The firm name was T. C. Wheaton & Company until 1901 when it was incorporated as T. C. Wheaton Company. By 1926 the firm was able to buy out one of its competitors, the Millville Bottle Works, established in 1903, after the death of the founders. (The physician's desk set of five amber and five cobalt bottles above has embossed on the base: M. B. W./ MILLVILLE.) In 1966 the firm name became the Wheaton Glass Company.

The first automatic machinery was not installed until 1938, but today glass production is a very model of automation. In one assembly no hand touches the container from raw batch to a finished cologne bottle decorated in two colors, a distance of 300 feet.

Oldtime blowers of the Glass Bottle Blowers Association, most of them now long gone, who fought hard to keep the hand craft alive would be gratified to learn that Wheaton

Fig. 184 AMBER AND COBALT DRUG SET for doctor's desk. Ten blown bottles, one impressed on base with M B W / MILLVILLE (for Millville Bottle Works). Ground glass stoppers, copper holder. Bottles 3¾ inches high.

has recently established a handblowing shop which shares a building with an industrial electronics firm, so that the two may work together.

The odd fact, only newly appreciated, is that electronics has need for special precise and clear glass that Man makes better than The Machine.

The new shop is run by about 45 employees working according to the old German system of reheating glass in the glory hole. The modern notes are the four new 1500-pound tanks and two 5,000-pound tanks. Besides blowers and gaffers the hand shop has blockers —using old style cups of cherry wood—mold boys, warming-in boys, and carrying-in boys, none of them children any more.

An expert from the Netherlands is instructing in the fine points of blowing cathode tubes and other electronics glassware. In much glass for hospital, laboratory and other scientific use, exact strength and uniform thickness of the walls is vital, an essential which The Machine can afford to be careless about when producing throwaway bottles. Jersey blowers, from the 1850s until about World War I acquired great skill in precision blowing and this art is now being taught to young recruits.

Fig. 185 COIN BANKS in contrasting South Jersey styles. Bowl-shaped clear bank has loops ending in crimped leaves. H. 6 inches. Tall bank with green and clear crown undoubtedly was made by same blower as one on *Plate 4*. H. 9½ inches. *Courtesy Wheaton Glass Museum.*

Although the real business of Wheaton's hand shop is to make electronics and laboratory ware, there have been some interesting decorative by-products. Among these were 550 bottles of black glass given an iridescent spray, which were blown for the 1969 convention of the International Carnival Glass Association. Because members met in St. Louis, one side of the bottle is embossed with the Gateway Arch and the other with the "Spirit of St. Louis." An amusing anomaly is that the original carnival glass was machine made but that the reproduction is handblown in a mold, a difficult job because of the narrow neck and wide body.

Some of the new crop of gaffers at Wheaton can expect to participate in a new type of glassmaking before long. In a plan conceived by Frank Hayes Wheaton, Jr., to honor his grandfather, a Victorian village is now in process of construction at Millville. Focus of the village will be a replica of the T. C. Wheaton 1880's furnace in blast, with real live glassblowers at work.

Wheaton Village is already well underway on a tract along route 55 near Whitaker Avenue where a lake has been created. The present Wheaton Glass Museum was moved to the village in 1970.

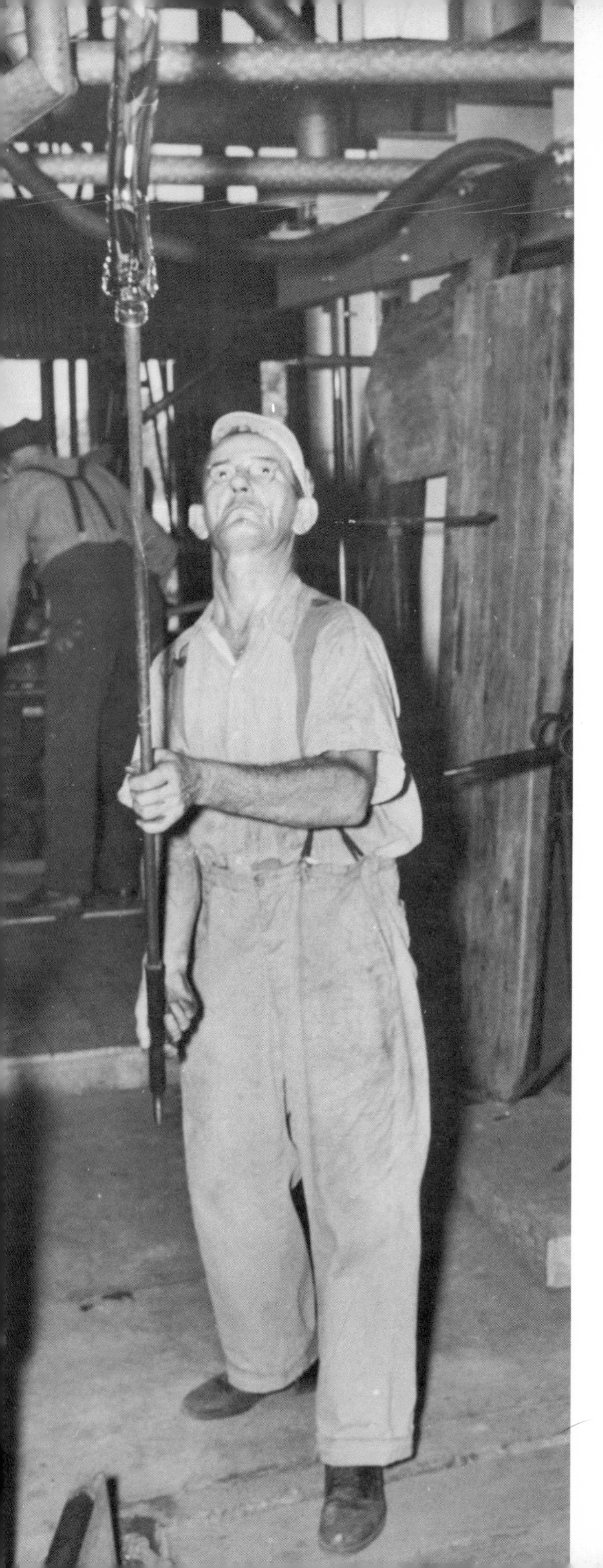

Fig. 186 BLOWER ELONGATES A GATHERING by centrifugal force, in preparing to fashion a cylinder of glass.

Fig. 187 RED-HOT GATHER of glass just taken from furnace in background is held by SECOND MAN FROM LEFT. IN EXACT CENTER, marver where gather is rolled into a small cylinder before blower starts blowing. Man with blowpipe, RIGHT, expands a parison of glass into a mold as mold-boy in pit, FOREGROUND, readies for proper instant to snap mold shut.

Scenes illustrate basic operations for nearly all glass hollow ware made in New Jersey from 1739 at Wistarberg through the first decade of the 20th century:

1) gathering molten glass from the furnace, on the end of a blowpipe; 2) marvering or rolling the gather on a flat marble or metal surface called the marver; 3) expanding the parison into the desired shape by free-blowing or by blowing into a mold (this is *not* pressing); 4) final shaping, finishing and decorating the object with liquid glass, at the gaffer's chair. Depending on the complexity of the article blown several trips for reheating at the "glory hole" may be needed to keep the glass malleable. Final step is annealing, a slow cooling in an oven or lehr.

Fig. 188 GAFFER TWIRLS with left hand a nearly finished glass graduate and shapes foot with pucellas held in his right hand. *Photos, courtesy of Wheaton Glass Company.*

The Jersey Roses and Other Paperweights

The most beautiful, poetic and original American paperweight ever created, out of the blue, was the Ralph Barber rose, usually called, unfairly, the Millville rose.

This upright lifelike rose encased in a sphere of crystal was originated by one man while working as a blower for Whitall Tatum around the turn of the century.

So all-pervasive is the legend of New England as leader in glassmaking that one rumor has it that Ralph Barber got the idea for a rose weight from a Sandwich worker. No one to date has ever produced such a prototype or even the name of the maker.

As for that Sandwich rumor, Ralph's brother Harry told me, "We had roses in our garden in Millville and Ralph studied and studied them until he came up with an iron crimp with petals that looked like a real rose. Alex Quernes, head of the lamp works at Whitall Tatum, made the leaves."

Barber roses rarely appear on the market, but an auction price a decade or more ago was $2,400. Ruefully, Harry said, "We used to sell them to gift shops and drug stores in Jersey for $1.50 apiece. Most times, Ralph would give them to people he liked." Ralph's daughter remembered that when she was a child her parents used to trade visits with an out-of-town family. As a hostess-present Ralph would take along a rose. These visits were frequent enough so that the other family was acquiring a fine collection of the weights. Realizing that the roses were increasing in demand, Mrs. Barber remonstrated with her husband, but to no effect. Today his daughter has none of the roses, a fact that hurts. But what really annoys Barber's daughter is that the family who received a collection of roses as a gift, later sent out feelers to see if they could buy some weights from her.

Many things conspired to make Ralph Barber just one of the crowd but he simply did not fit a mold. His life style was as original as the Barber rose.

He was born into a glassmaking milieu, Manchester, England, in 1869. When he was about 12, his father, a glassblower, brought his wife and their children to the United States where he found a job at Dorflinger's in White Mills, Pa. The eldest son George, already a blower, soon went to Toledo to blow those incredible inventions of Thomas A. Edison: light bulbs. Though young, Ralph went along, for coaching from George. After a time, the men took jobs at Honesdale, Pa., and then were soon ready to meet the test at Dorflinger's —blowing thin crystal for formal dinner tables.

It was about 1889 that the family of 10 Larsons arrived at Dorflinger's from Sweden and they and the Barbers became longtime friends. Never during the stay in White Mills did either Ralph Barber or Emil Larson even think about making any rose weights, contrary to a published report.

Then came word for Ralph's father of a job open at Whitall Tatum, whereupon he settled his large family in Millville, and Ralph also soon had a job at the Schetterville factory. George seems to have returned to Ohio; at least he later sent Ralph some ruby cullet from the west. Schetterville or South Millville was the Whitall Tatum plant which had the best local metal and many skilled gaffers. Young as he was, Ralph soon surpassed most of them.

Two articles, one by Ruth Webb Lee and the other by Edward W. Minns, which appeared in the now defunct *American Collector* of 1938 are full of errors about the Millville rose, yet so firmly believed that even reliable museums are perpetuating the serious mistakes in their exhibit cards. It is time that these errors be refuted once and for all.

Minns states that paperweight making began at Millville in 1867 when the Whitall Tatum Company opened its wooden mold department. What in the world does a wooden mold for shaping bottles have to do with flat or spherical paperweights? They could not possibly be made in such a wooden mold or any wooden mold. What was significant about the late 1860s was that Whitall Tatum then introduced its lime glass, a high grade metal that was more malleable than previous formulas. Minns says that paperweight making began almost as soon as the wooden mold department opened. It is doubtful that weights were even the first articles blown with the new glass; useful articles like pitchers were more likely to have had priority. Minns' own description of how rose weights were made shows that no wooden molds were used.

In another flagrant error Minns says that 1880 was the period when John Ruhlander (whose name he misspelled as have nearly all writers on Jersey Glass) and Ralph Barber began making offhand ware at Whitall Tatum. In 1880 Barber was 11 years old and had not yet seen Jersey, while Ruhlander had never set foot in the United States!

Mrs. Lee did not repeat the above errors but added some of her own. One of the most absurd was that the best Barber roses were made while he worked for Durand Flint Glass. Quite the opposite is true. Barber's finest roses were made at Whitall Tatum where he had the most compatible combinations of clear and colored glass. Mrs. Lee stated that Durand's factory was in Millville, instead of Vineland. The noted firm of Hagerty Brothers of Brooklyn, N.Y., she located in Millville and dated it from 1802 instead of the late 1850s.

Mrs. Lee showed an illustration of "Glass Parts Used by the Barbers." The articles

Fig. 189 A BARBER OPEN ROSE shaped and colored to resemble the wild variety, of an intense pink. Although the flower has 15 petals the shape differs radically from those made with the crimp shown in *Fig. 199* for the hybrid variety of rose. Magnum size but not footed as were most of Barber's paperweights. Three leaves. *Yoerger collection.*

Fig. 190 RALPH BARBER, SECOND FROM RIGHT, described in his lifetime as "the greatest glassblower in the U.S.A." Shop scene at Whitall Tatum, Millville. Others not identified. *Photo courtesy of Harry Barber, D.D.S.*

include lampwork leaves which of course were needed for the roses, but most of the display is of colored cane slices and small flowers, none of which was used by Barber. These slices of candy-like cane were used for millefiori weights, never made by the Barbers and even unknown as a Jersey product.

The three Barber brothers were not of a close age, as Mrs. Lee claimed. Harry was 18 years younger than Ralph.

A red, white and blue weight inscribed with the name Kizzie Pepper was not made by Barber, as Mrs. Lee stated. Instead, the weight was made by the late Charles Pepper for his wife, I am informed by his son G. Vernon Pepper whose mother had the Biblical name of Keziah and the nickname of Kizzie.

The Lee article gives the impression that Ralph and his two brothers would work for an entire afternoon making paperweights. Whitall Tatum & Company were generous to blowers in the use of glass, but spare-time blowing was strictly a lunch-hour product, not even end-of-day. In later years when the privilege of free metal began to be abused, the practice was stopped entirely.

After many experiments in shaping metal crimps at home that would make realistic roses, Ralph achieved what he thought was a passable flower, and from about 1904 to 1912, when he left Whitall Tatum, he made some of his most beautiful roses, according to Harry. The latter was in a position to know as he was Ralph's assistant in those years, and at home, for part of that time, they shared the same room.

One day Ralph said, "Brother, it's time we talked about your education." It *was* time, for Harry was about 12 then. By unhappy coincidence that was just the time when their father lost his job in a Baltimore glassworks, not for incompetence but because 50 years was the cutoff age.

"There wasn't any choice," Harry told me. "My father wasn't able to get a job, so I got one as carrying-in boy. I used to wear out a pair of shoes a week sliding to the ovens. We had to work that way. My mother collected the $2.50 a week as she needed it, so my total pay for a week's work was 12 cents." Tears came to his eyes as he thought of the high school education he had missed.

There were happier times, though, when Harry had become proficient as a helper. Ralph came bounding in one night, "Brother! We've got a challenge!" something he loved. "You know our glass fish? Well, we've got to make one with *scales.* The one you and I worked on I took to the Elks' Club and they thought it was great. But some bloke said, 'But why doesn't it have scales?' I said, 'That's easy. I'll bet I can put scales on one or I'll stand drinks all around.' "

"So we had to produce, and did," said Harry. As he described it the process seemed like one used later in the 1920s in making the Moorish Crackle finish at Durand: cold water was dribbled on hot glass causing it to fissure. To make these fissures in the shape of scales must have required fast reflexes.

The Barber Rose was the cause of some ruptured friendships. Harry recalled that in the years when a Barber pink rose had become financially desirable a guest in his home surreptitiously pocketed one. When challenged the guest produced the weight and said he had taken it only as a practical joke. But Harry Barber didn't see the point of the joke, only the end of a friendship.

Even while Ralph was perfecting his skill in making the rose, he would not allow co-workers to see the petal crimp. This led to attempts to snitch it from his locker, so Harry often was put on guard duty.

The most serious event of this nature occurred about two years before Ralph died in 1936. The incident related by Harry was that their old friend Emil Larson sent a mutual friend to borrow one of the weights to show off at a party, to which Ralph readily consented. Days went by and the rose was not returned. Finally, after two weeks of wonder and worry, the Barbers demanded return of the weight, which was done promptly. But that very year Larson came out with his first magnum rose, a good facsimile of a Barber, and immediately was in the business of selling more. The Barbers never forgot or forgave.

No one knows how many roses Ralph made as the family did not keep records of them. Larson estimated that about 100 of his survived breakage in annealing. His roses have four leaves, in translucent emerald green, while Barber's had three, reported Harry and others, in opaque malachite green. As Barber did more experimenting than Larson it is difficult to place fixed limits on what he made. He told Harry that his weights were always footed, with a collar between the foot and the rose. His rarest and most beautiful roses were those with a bud and set on a balustered pedestal. Ernest C. Stanmire, among the first dealers to sell the Barber rose, remembers the colors as pale pink, rose pink, white, yellow, and deep ruby, but definitely no orange. After many unsatisfactory trials of gold ruby for the blossom, Barber at last was successful in obtaining one with a lime base that matched Whitall Tatum's clear lime and so helped to prevent breakage in annealing. Minns learned that the D. P. Gleason Company of Brooklyn, N.Y., shipped Barber 150 pounds of this ruby glass, 15 pounds of green and two pounds of straw opalescence. This order of glass may account for the fact that Barber succeeded in producing many weights whereas talented men like Ruhlander and Stanger evidently did not even though they used similar crimps.

In Barber's lifetime there were few imitators of his rose. Although many of his co-workers wanted to know the secret, as there was no high price on the rose at that time, the incentive was lacking. But in the last decade or so there has been a fever of rose-making or at least of crimp-making in the Millville-Bridgeton area. Some of the atrocious copies are being offered and bought as Barber's. Among the faults are a very greenish globe instead of clear, an intense orange color unlike any rose, unrealistic leaves or none at all, lack of a foot, striae and ripples in the crystal, rough marks of wear or damage. White roses have always had a lower value. A Chinese rose weight was made supposedly as a copy of the Barber; if so, it must have been made by hearsay. One paperweight expert described it as poor in color. I would say that in form it resembles a stepped-on dahlia and bears no relation to the wineglass shape of a hybrid rose.

In the summer of 1901 strollers on the boardwalk of Atlantic City were astonished to find that a fiery furnace had been set up to blow glass, so that tourists could take home mementoes of their visit. This was no lamp works for making small animals or paperweights inscribed "Home, Sweet Home," but an orthodox hot-glass furnace.

The organizer was the late Arthur Saunders of Millville and the gaffers were no less than Whitall Tatum experts: Emil Stanger, Marcus Kuntz, John Ruhlander and Ralph Barber. The group was known as the Bohemian Glass Company. Among the extraordinarily handsome pieces blown were pink-and-white pears and opaque pink cups and saucers and pitchers. These are almost indistinguishable in color from the Wild Rose glass made at the Mt. Washington Glass Company of New Bedford, Mass., operated by Saunders' father.

The experiment in new colors and shapes was cut short when fire consumed the small furnace, but the project no doubt was a spur to the making of art glass, particularly cased ware, in Millville. The rose crimp in Fig. 199 was given to Ruhlander at this time, from which all of his roses were made, and it is said that the other three men received identical

Note.—During the Depression of the 1930s the federal Works Progress Administration with the co-operation of Armstrong Cork Company which had recently purchased Whitall Tatum, set up a glassmaking project for unemployed workers in Millville. The men not only made freeblown ware but some also tried their hands at rose paperweights. Supplied with perfected crimps and a deep red glass for the flower, a few workers turned out some lovely rose weights. Once again there was the exasperating problem of matching glass: every single rose weight cracked. The result—a curiosity instead of a collector's paperweight.

Fig. 191 MODEL used by Ralph Barber in making a paperweight crimp.

crimps. Barber, however, had been producing rose paperweights before this, from a variety of crimps which he designed himself or had made. I have not had the good fortune to see any rose weights documented as made by Stanger, Kuntz or Ruhlander. Michael Kane did not make rose weights, I have been told by his grandson.

When Ralph Barber moved to Durand's Flint Glass Works in 1912 as superintendent he no longer had opportunity or metal to make roses and art glass as he was busy supervising the exacting chore of blowing linings of vacuum bottles. Even when Durand opened its art glass shop in 1924 it was not Barber who was chosen to head it but Emil Larson, although occasionally Barber designed some glass such as the Venetian Lace pattern. In 1931 when all of Durand was absorbed by the Kimble Glass Company of Vineland, Barber became superintendent there, over the most nerve-wracking kind of blowing: x-ray tubes. A tube inspector of that time said recently that even the check-out job was exhausting as not one "seed" was permitted because of danger of explosion when the tubes were in use.

It was at this time that a publication of the American Institute of Glass described Ralph Barber as "The greatest glassblower in the United States," an accolade awarded chiefly for his skill in blowing x-ray tubes.

When Barber died at the age of 67 his obituary read that he "was the first man to blow a thermos bottle in this section of the country." Not one word about the Barber roses or art glass, for those were then regarded as toss-off novelties.

This splendid gaffer may well have rejoiced that he had met all his challenges, but to outsiders the tragedy is that so great an artist in glass had so fleeting a time in which to practice that art.

Fig. 192 NATURALISTIC ROSE crimp of brass, one of many shaped by Ralph Barber seeking to create the most lifelike glass rose. With 12 petals, one now missing, the curled edges of this paperweight crimp contrast markedly with the smooth formal petals of the Ruhlander crimp, *Fig. 199*, said also to have been used by Barber.

THE MODERN MILLVILLE ROSE

The Millville rose blooms again, thanks to two young men working in partnership: John Allen Choko, Jr., and Albert Morgan Lewis, Jr., both employed at the Wheaton Glass Company of Millville.

Having worked in spare time as a team for only a little more than a year the men have already achieved some exquisite miniature rose weights in the style first developed by Charles Kaziun and also made by Francis Whittemore. Such miniature roses are lampwork, shaped with a gas flame or Bunsen-burner type of heat. The Barber and Ruhlander roses, in contrast, are usually magnum in size and were made at the conventional glass furnace. Like Ralph Barber, these men have several disparate talents, traits revealed even in boyhood.

Born in Millville on July 4, 1935, Jack Choko, the first of the partners to attempt a rose weight, as a boy was capable of building anything he could imagine and could do it in a fraction of the time it would take anyone else, says his friend from grammar-school days, Berwyn C. Kirby. He writes, "Jack built a scale model of an Atlas rocket for a contest in such fine detail that the company refused to give him the prize without an affidavit confirming him as the builder. Jack has been amazing his friends for quite a few years." He is now a glass designer and model maker for Wheaton.

Jack Choko is one of four family generations involved in the glass industry of Millville. His father managed Shull Bros. Glass Company, owned by his grandfather. His great-grandfather William Shull was founder and co-owner of the Shull-Goodwin Glass Works which in 1888 was sold to Dr. T. C. Wheaton.

Albert (Pete) Morgan Lewis, Jr., was born in Camden on Sept. 14, 1937, and moved to Millville at the age of three months, thereby doubtless changing the history of fine paperweight-making. As a boy, Pete's delight was anything mechanical, a talent that has culminated in his skill as a mold-maker for the Wheaton Glass Company.

Growing up in a town historically noted for paperweights, as youths these men became interested in collecting such weights. Jack Choko was the first of the two to make a rose crimp as he had a small machine shop at home. The partnership was born, reports Berwyn Kirby, when "Pete stopped by Jack's one day while Jack was struggling with his new challenge, the rose paperweight. That's all it took to unite these ambitious men . . . In Jack's small machine shop they are able to manufacture rose and tulip crimps and most of the other tools necessary in their work. Jack and Pete rank the rose as one of the most difficult to perfect. At the present time they have focused their attention on set up flower

Fig. 193 DEEP PINK weight of rare beauty, fashioned from gold-ruby and opaque white glass by John Choko, Jr., of Millville, bears his initials in a cane on the base. Deep green leaves and faceted sides. D. 2¼ inches.

Fig. 194 COBALT BLUE MINIATURE ROSE, white-tipped, reveals the skill in paperweight-making of Albert M. (Pete) Lewis, Jr., working at Millville in 1971. Base has a cane with the maker's initials, P.L. D. 2¼ inches.

weights . . . Jack and Pete identify their weights with a small cane they made with red JC or PL initials enclosed in a white background."

The high degree of perfection attained by these modern paperweight makers of Millville is apparent in the adjoining illustration, even though the lovely colors are not revealed.

Origins of Gold-Ruby Glass

A. Woodruff Harris tells me that Ruhlander and a number of other Whitall Tatum gaffers who made objects containing gold ruby glass bought their gold from Gillinder Glass Company of Philadelphia. The gold was supplied in round bars about 6 by 2½ inches, which were heated prior to glassmaking and snipped off into desired lengths. As Harris points out, metals used in glassmaking must be in the form of oxides or have some dispersal agent so that the metal will go into solution with the batch and give it color; otherwise the gold, for example, sinks to the bottom of the pot. An oldtime dispersal agent for gold is aqua regia, a mixture of nitric and hydrochloric acids.

In the British Isles and the United States a long-standing legend, no longer credited, is that a gold coin dropped into clear molten glass will transmute it to the glowing color of a ruby touched with magenta. Ronald Gordon Newton of the British Glass Industry Research Association in 1967 raised the question of historic evidence for such use of metallic gold. His query to the Newsletter of Committee B of the International Commission on Glass brought replies in the issue of August 1969, which indicated firm disbelief in the superstition. However, when a laboratory test was conducted with metallic gold at BGIRA, the molten metal sank to the bottom, as expected, but was surrounded by a layer of reddish glass about 4 mm. thick. More details of the enchanting legend appear in an article by Newton in the *Journal of Glass Studies* for 1970. It is worth noting that to bring good fortune a New Jersey ironmaster, James P. Allaire, is on record as having tossed a gold "double eagle" into an iron furnace for its first blast.

Other Flowers

One of the loveliest of the upright flowers, which originated in Jersey, is a pale pink water lily, probably a Barber because of its fine workmanship and its three leaves. A companion in the Sinclair collection is a pink and white lily, slender-throated with large broad leaves. Probably one of a kind is a light red tulip, its saw-toothed petals edged in white. Some very attractive crocuses have been made, usually without leaves, in yellow or mauve-pink streaked in white.

The Umbrella or Mushroom or Fountain

Nomenclature is needed for some Jersey paperweights, especially those that look as if a white umbrella had been sprinkled with confetti that "ran" in the rain. Formerly called lily weights, this was a name too easily confused with real flower forms. The central mushroom shape in white or cream colored glass is pulled down in points and is sprinkled with colored glass before being covered with clear metal. These kinds of glass did not present the problems of annealing caused by combining ruby and clear of two different metals, as for flowers. The mushrooms range from bad to fine, the best being those precisely fashioned into inkwells. Gaffers best known for making these were Emil Stanger, Marcus Kuntz, John Ruhlander and Horace Rhubarth. Ruhlander mushroom weights have no added color, except when enlarged into inkwells. The handsomest inkwells are those with striped patterns, attributed to Emil Stanger (see Plate 17).

Pictorial Weights

A common variety of South Jersey weights, made in the 1860s to the 1920s, are pictorials with sure-fire mottoes such as "Home Sweet Home" over a scene of a cabin and a well, picked out in color against a white ground. Hundreds of such county-fair souvenirs were made, which exhibit about as much talent as painting in oil by numbers. The weights were built up from ready-made steel plates with the pattern intaglio-cut, into which the maker dropped powdered colored glass, then covered with clear metal.

Superior weights on this principle are those in which the scene such as a ship, a hunter and his dog, Rock of Ages and others are upright, then covered with powdered white and colored glass. The best of these are attributed to Michael Kane who came from Ireland to work for Whitall Tatum. He died in the 1920s. Some of his weights were domed and faceted. An unusual weight in this style is a gray horse standing against a light blue background.

Devil's Fire

The cedar swamps of early South Jersey often showed moving bluish lights after dark that sent chills through lonely riders and even frightened horses. Devil's Fire or Fox Fire, the natives called these awesome lights, now known to be caused by a phosphorescence in rotting wood, a light similar to that of fireflies. How glassmakers tried to capture this fire is shown in an imaginative paperweight, an inkwell, and mantel ornaments (Plates 14, 16) probably all made at Whitall Tatum in the late 19th century.

INCOMPARABLE pink rose by Ralph Barber is set on handsomely tooled pedestal. First decade, 19th century.

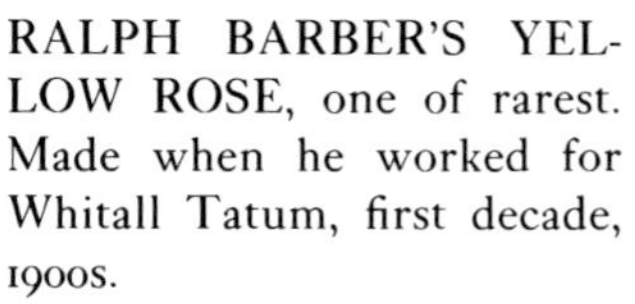

RALPH BARBER'S YELLOW ROSE, one of rarest. Made when he worked for Whitall Tatum, first decade, 1900s.

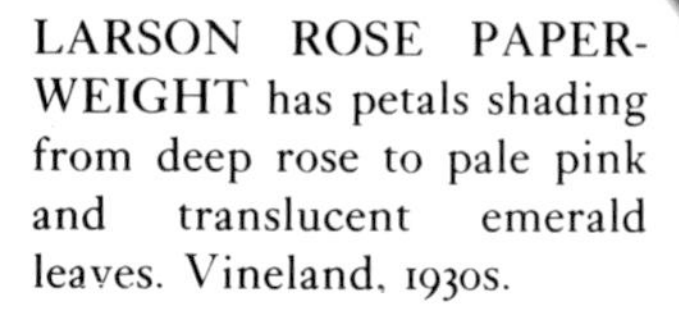

LARSON ROSE PAPERWEIGHT has petals shading from deep rose to pale pink and translucent emerald leaves. Vineland, 1930s.

DEVIL'S FIRE paperweight (left) and ink bottle, circa 1875, were made in Millville, probably at Whitall Tatum. Devil's Fire paperweights may have been an attempt to simulate "fox fire," a nocturnal phosphorescent glow from rotting wood in South Jersey pine forests. *All photos, courtesy of the John Nelson Bergstrom Art Center and Museum.*

PLATE 17

WITCH BALL of ruby and opaque white probably made at Whitall Tatum. Lilypad pitcher with threaded neck and crimped applied foot exhibits pleasing contrasts of swirls and curves. H. 8 inches. *Edward Griner collection.*

MATCHING UMBRELLA INKWELLS, unusual for their striped pattern, attributed to Emil Stanger working at Whitall Tatum in early 1900s. *H.M. Smith collection.*

ROSE-PINK RUHLANDER. Swirled in clear, rose, and opaque white, pitcher is notable for handsome design of its strong but graceful handle and sweep of the sheared mouth; base is formed in a wooden mold. C. 1898. H. 10 inches. A NATAL-DAY GIFT from John Ruhlander to one of his daughters, the mauve-pink cup with scalloped rim and applied circular foot could be mistaken for one a half century earlier. H. 3½ inches. *Owned by Ruhlander descendants.*

John Ruhlander

"This is the prettiest piece of glass I ever made."

John Ruhlander of Millville reached for the inside pocket of his jacket and pulled out an exquisite little basket of rose and blue glass with lacy ruffles, and held it out for his family to admire.

Then as he set the basket on a table in the chill room, he was horrified to see the fragile glass break in half. His children, not appreciating the virtuosity that had gone into the making of the delicate basket took the disaster fairly calmly, for they had often seen their father bring home fantasies in glass.

"If we had realized what skill went into the blowing of that basket he was so proud of we would have at least tried to patch it together, but it was thrown out as junk," says one of Ruhlander's daughters.

The reason the basket broke points up two of the many heartaches in glassmaking: one, a sudden change in temperature from warm to cold can cause glass to break if it has not been thoroughly annealed; and two, glass combining two or more colors used to be more likely to break.

Up to now there has been no attempt to record the fantasies in glass for which John Ruhlander had a natural talent. When each of his children was born he usually brought home a specially designed cup or glass for the newborn. For his wife he made elaborately beautiful fruit compotes, three tiers high. Other fanciful objects or pitchers were given to friends.

Today's collectors, major and minor, few of whom have seen an authenticated example of this gaffer's work think of Ruhlander as the South Jersey man who made "umbrella" paperweights and inkwells. When descendants of Ruhlander told me that "he could make anything in glass," a frequent and deserved description of Ralph Barber, the phrase in this instance seemed at first to be based on family loyalty. After seeing widely isolated examples, well authenticated, one must agree that Ruhlander was a major talent in Jersey glassblowing.

As Ralph Barber and Ruhlander were among the leading makers of free-time glass at Whitall Tatum and were contemporaries there in the first decade of this century, it is worthwhile to consider the contrasting school from which Ruhlander derived.

Where the Barbers stemmed from the English tradition of glassmaking in the Manchester region, John Ruhlander, who was born in or near Hamburg, Germany, in 1860, appears to have become a journeyman after serving his apprenticeship there. He then began following the glass trade in Alsace-Lorraine, Coblenz, Cologne, and other cities along the Rhine, with some time spent also in Switzerland. Later he and a covey of young men went to Cuba—probably Havana as the only urban center—to do glassblowing.

Fig. 195 GAFFER JOHN RUHLANDER and friend at Millville homestead, early 1900s. Blower of fine pharmaceutical ware for Whitall Tatum, in his free time Ruhlander created ruby pitchers and cups, fine paperweights and inkwells, and a unique 16-part decanter.

From Cuba Ruhlander came by ship to Philadelphia (all dates and periods he stayed in various localities are uncertain to descendants). It was but logical progress to move from Philadelphia to the Glass State, Jersey, and a stint with the Whitney Glass Works in Glassboro.

Even before arrival at this point, Ruhlander was undoubtedly a gaffer with background in sophisticated form and decoration, from the Flemish and German to the Venetian and Spanish.

From the Whitneys, Ruhlander traveled the few miles to Millville where he arrived, still unmarried, but not for long. He married a Philadelphia girl, raised a family, and lived in Millville until he was 75 when he died on Feb. 6, 1935. Although he was only nine years older than Ralph Barber, who died the following year, somehow Barber seems much the younger and livelier. Both were men who should have been devoting their full energies to art glass instead of workaday pharmaceutical bottles.

Besides paperweights and inkwells made by Ruhlander (and to be described below) I have had opportunity to examine, photograph and check the background of 12 other glass creations of his. All were either owned by his descendants or had been owned by glassblowers who assisted him in his "shop." In no case was there an intermediate dealer.

A unique object is the 16-part decanter, pictured on the opposite page, which was made with the assistance of A. Woodruff Harris to whom the bottle was later given by Ruhlander as a token of longtime friendship.

In one collection which includes four Ruhlander pitchers which were bought from Charles Pepper (no relation to the author) who also worked with the gaffer, three of them, all about 10 inches high, are similar to Fig. 197 with diagonal stripings of white, ruby or blue on clear glass. The fourth and most beautiful of the pitchers is opaque rose-pink glass with a clear handle and in color is a duplicate of that known as New England Peachblow. More accurately descriptive was its predecessor: Wild Rose. (See Plate 2.) As noted in the preceding chapter on Ralph Barber, Ruhlander was one of four gaffers who amazed the public and made exquisite glass at a furnace on Atlantic City's Boardwalk in the summer

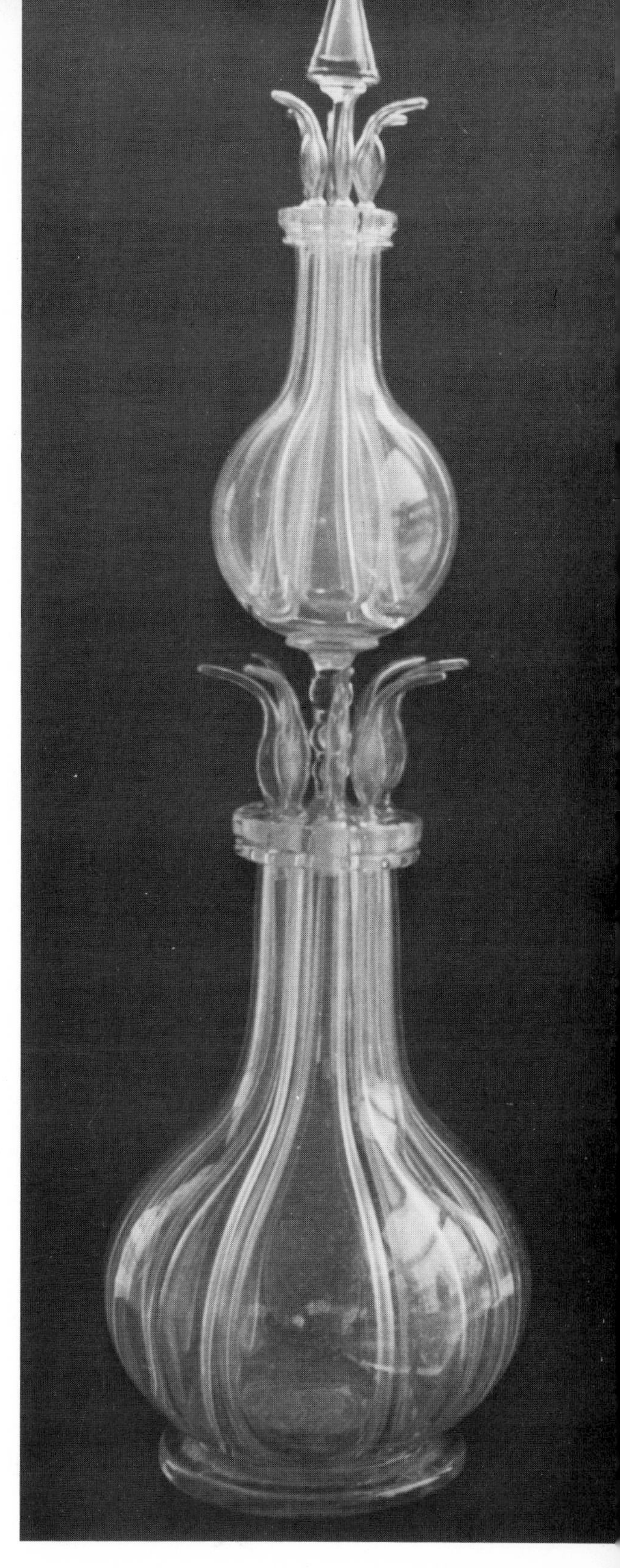

Fig. 196 16-COMPARTMENT DECANTER ... IT POURS. Whoever invented the multi-section liqueur bottle is dead but the man who helped Gaffer John Ruhlander form this 16-compartment decanter standing 28 inches high is vitally alive today at 83. As a reward for long years as his assistant at Whitall Tatum & Company, John Ruhlander gave this decanter to A. Woodruff Harris. The bottle was made in 1907.

To appreciate the difficulty of making this double-tiered, 16-part bottle one must understand that each of the grapefruit-like sections had to be a separate gather, a separate blow. The miracle is that the sections of each tier are uniform as if mold-blown, which they definitely were not. To blow the second tier in a proportion that flows gracefully upward from the base is another difficult feat. To create the whole required phenomenal control, teamwork and rapid action, comparable, say, to a fast game of jai alai.

Ruhlander conceived the design, did the blowing and finishing, while Harris acted as gatherer and made the neck rims and the applied circular foot. The spouts, which pour and are removable, were made in the Whitall Tatum lamp room. The top decanter can be detached from the lower one which is 9 inches in diameter.

A rare combination of precise workmanship and balanced design, the handsome decanter is made of clear flint glass. Describing the "elastic" flint glass used at Whitall Tatum, Harris says, "You could work glass down there before it froze."

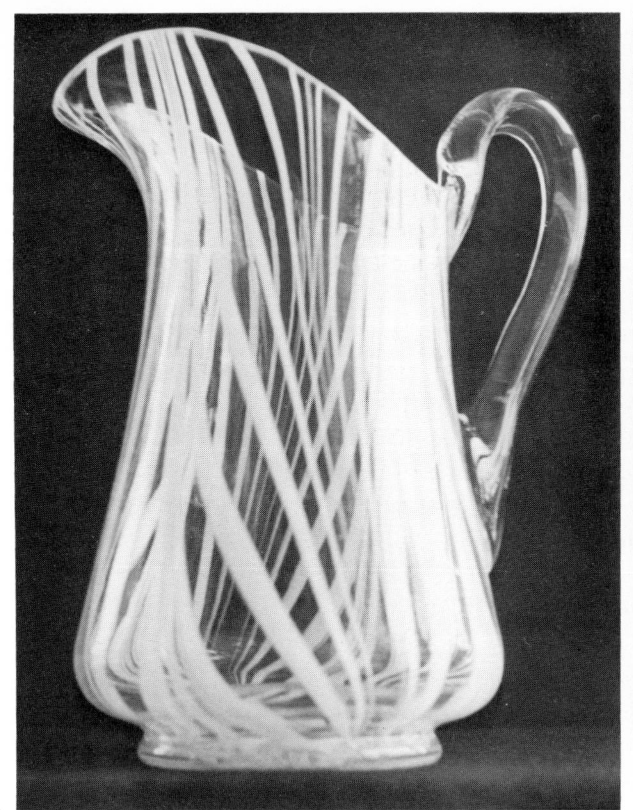

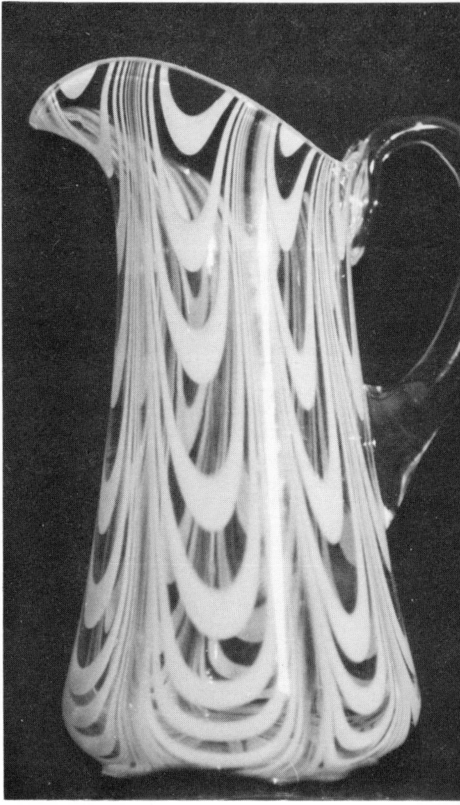

Fig. 197 JOHN RUHLANDER PITCHER with stripes of opaque white and clear, made at Whitall Tatum. Note contrast of straight lines with wave-like treatment of maker's contemporary, Ralph Barber. H. 10½ inches.

Fig. 198 RALPH BARBER PITCHER. A masterpiece of line, functional shape and imaginative decoration. Few other gaffers had the skill to control the opaque white in scallops. Clear lead glass, sheared mouth, applied handle. C. 1905. H. 9½ inches.

of 1901, a project organized by the late Arthur E. Saunders of Millville. The significant fact for the moment is that in the 1880s Saunders' father was in charge of the Mt. Washington Glass Company, New Bedford, Mass., where Peachblow glass originated.

A Ruhlander punch cup in the same lovely rose-pink but from another collection is definitely known to have been made at Atlantic City, as was a pink and white pear. Many of the pears were blown in that summer and were sold, it is said, to the Libbey Glass Company. It's a safe bet that all knowledgeable collectors would attribute the pears to the Mt. Washington Glass Company. The Atlantic City glassmaking was so little known that I have been unable to find any oldtime glassmakers who have heard of it.

The charming pink glass cup with crimped edge (Plate 17) was a christening present to one of Ruhlander's daughters. Showing a Venetian influence, the cup is not the same kind of cased pink glass as that described above.

Among Ruhlander glass I have not seen but which has been described to me by his descendants was a pear-shaped money bank in clear flint with white loopings and elaborately twisted handles. Most collectors seeing such a bank and not knowing its history would call it early 19th century Jersey. Also once owned by the Ruhlander family was a 3-tiered fruit bowl of ruby glass which was topped by a trumpet-shaped vase, also ruby.

Ruhlander descendants tell of but have not seen a glass baseball and bat that Gaffer John blew for the evangelist Billy Sunday. Since evangelism was much in demand for glassmakers' towns and baseball was popular, this seems a probability. The ball and bat are said to have been deposited in a midwest museum but my search has failed to locate it.

A metal crimp used by John Ruhlander in making magnum rose paperweights is shown below, and according to descendants and a co-worker this was the only one he used. As the petals are all regular and formally set this would indicate a somewhat late mold, made after the trial-and-error research of Ralph Barber, the innovator. Members of the family state that Ruhlander's roses were all the usual rose color.

Ruhlander made many of the "mushroom" or "umbrella" weights and inkwells, as did Marcus Kuntz and Emil Stanger. Crude ones were made by workmen less skilled, as these weights were far easier to form than natural-looking roses and the colors did not pose the almost insoluble problem of differing coefficients of expansion.

The umbrella weights do not look at all like flowers, unless possibly a white morning glory. The central object is a mushroom-colored or white umbrella with the points drawn down. The top of the umbrella is often sprinkled with multi-colored glass like confetti but the most interesting ones are inkwells with the panels of the umbrella in alternating stripes of color. Ruhlander umbrella paperweights were always white glass encased in flint and had no added color. The inkwells, however, showed color both in the base and the stopper, an effect that is surprisingly modern and colorful.

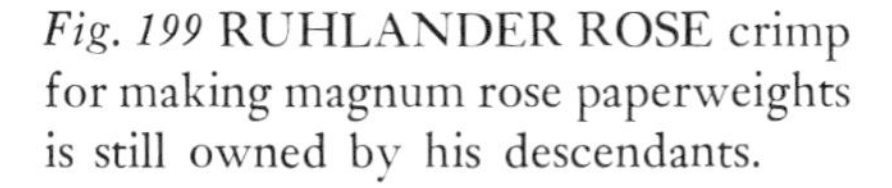
Fig. 199 RUHLANDER ROSE crimp for making magnum rose paperweights is still owned by his descendants.

Fig. 200 RUHLANDER-HARRIS TOOLS. LEFT TO RIGHT: the *crutch*, a type of wooden block used for preliminary shape of a parison of glass. Inside of cup has ball-bearings. *Shears* for cutting away excess glass; steel *tooling rod* for shaping; *calipers* with a hook, used by John Ruhlander for pulling down points of his famous umbrella paperweights.

The mushroom weights, however, do not compare in rarity and beauty with the fine magnum roses. As with the latter, the price commanded should depend on skill of workmanship and good color and design.

Some over-elaborate "what-nots" which have been called flower holders, though no one would dare tamper with their laciness by adding flowers and water, have been attributed to Ruhlander. Many of these were made at Stourbridge, England, from about 1865 to 1895, a region Ruhlander had no contact with. A number of these with three trumpet-shaped vases set in small metal rings sometimes are seen today in New Jersey but are unlikely to be Jersey-blown. (See Wakefield for illustrations.)

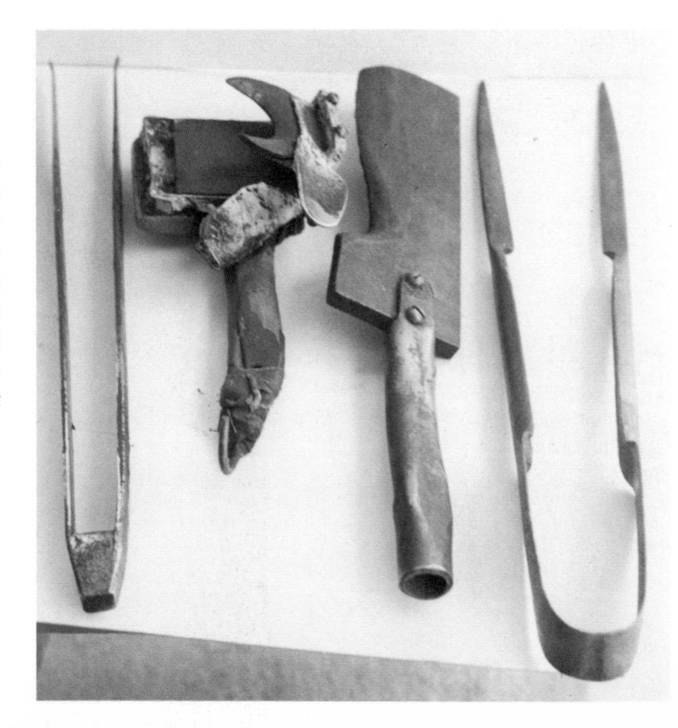

Fig. 201 LEFT TO RIGHT: metal *spring tool* or *tongs*, often a carrying tool; *clapper*, top layer of which was raised to help in inserting and shaping a foot; *pallet*, in early times called a battledore, for shaping footed glass; *pucellas* or jack, the modern term, probably the most useful of the glassblower's shaping tools.

Fig. 202 DOCUMENTED WHITNEY PITCHER, ovoid in shape, remained in one glassblower's family for over half a century. A sunlit and slightly bubbled amber, with a distinctive handle and applied foot. Rough pontil. H. 7inches.

Fig. 203 UMBRELLA PAPERWEIGHT attributed to Emil Stanger. *H. M. Smith collection.*

Fig. 204 DECORATIVE FLASKS. LEFT: rose and opaque white swirls, collared lip. RIGHT: clear and opaque white, sheared lip. H. 8 inches.

Charles Pepper, a Millville Gaffer

A BLOWER and a gaffer and a paperweight maker at Whitall Tatum, Charles Pepper who lived to be 92 and at 80 was still fashioning glass for Wheaton's was born in 1868 at Buckshutem. At the age of 9 he went to work as a tending boy, walking the distance of 4 miles twice a day to Whitall Tatum at Millville.

G. Vernon Pepper's recollections of his life in Millville not only reveal much about the impressive creations of his father but also about the way of life of Millville's best gaffers, of which Charles was one.

Economically speaking, the glassblowers were the elite of Millville. They were being paid $60 a week at a time when unskilled labor was paid a dollar a day. Vernon Pepper relates that journeymen had to rise by steps from the ranks, much in the fashion of officers in a corporation. Charles Pepper, for instance, moved up to servitor in one of the Whitall Tatum shops, in which servitor was ranked as the second man among three blowers, each of whom had a tending boy. Pepper later progressed to blower and then to gaffer. The Big Shop at Whitall Tatum was once comprised of Marcus Kuntz, John Fath and Emil Stanger. At a later date Charlie Pepper moved up to the Big Shop, starting again as servitor, then being promoted to blower and finally to gaffer.

Some fine offhand pieces made by Charles Pepper have doubtless been attributed to Ruhlander whose name is far better known, outside of Millville, as a glassmaker and to whom Pepper for a time was assistant. One creation is described by Vernon Pepper as a large and beautiful pitcher of gold-ruby glass with six matching goblets, all of which were given by Charles' wife to a guest who admired the set. Charles also made the kind of striated pitchers blown by Barber and Ruhlander. A unique object was a 12-foot chain with movable links, centered with an anchor of glass about a foot high. This article was sold to a dealer for a couple of dollars.

When the Barber family came to Millville they moved next door to the Peppers. The first time he learned about rose paperweights, says Vernon Pepper, was about 65 years ago and these were the ones made by Ralph Barber. No others were mentioned. Vernon Pepper knew Emil Stanger well but does not think he made roses.

About 150 paperweights made by Charles were collected by his son. The weights were stored in his father's room and in his last illness he began giving them away to his many visitors. When the family discovered the giveaway, the collection was down to about a dozen of the less desirable items. Apparently no magnum roses were made by Pepper but an interesting crocus remains. A sample of excellent workmanship is a magnum bubble weight of emerald green encased in clear flint.

Fig. 205 CROCUS PAPERWEIGHT, magnum size, has striated rose and white blossom. Probably made at Whitall Tatum.

Fig. 206 GAFFER FINISHING CARBOY at Wheaton Glass Company is Charles Pepper who also made paperweights and artistic freeblown glass. *Photo, courtesy of the Wheaton Glass Company.*

Minotola Glass Company
George Jonas Glass Company

The life of the Minotola Glass Company was one long labor dispute producing the bitterest strife in the entire history of the glass bottle blowers union of New Jersey, a record going back to 1846.

This glassworks started placidly enough, during the early 1890s, in the traditional manner of South Jersey furnaces as far back as 1812 and William Coffin's day at Hammonton. George Jonas of Bridgeton began buying land about 1893 in an unsettled piney region about five miles northeast of Vineland. Today the small community of Minotola is just west of Route 54, the main road between Hammonton and Vineland.

Traditionally, too, George Jonas first built a sawmill, then cut lumber, then built tenant houses, even before he set up a glassworks. He also built a company store which was to become a sore point in the labor warfare. Today the old store and office are owned by Albert Costa for the sale of farm baskets and crates for fruits and vegetables, which create one of New Jersey's major industries, after the leading one of tourism.

A forgotten business custom comes to light from records of the Minotola Glass Company, which is wonderfully revelatory of its history. Penny postcards were the sole means of placing important orders for glass bottles. Carbon copies seem not to have been invented, and wet and dry copiers were as unimaginable as men walking on the moon.

One of these penny postcards shows that not only was the George Jonas Glass Company of Minotola well established by October 23, 1896, but that Hagerty Bros. & Co. of Brooklyn, major competitors of the other leading pharmaceutical glassmakers of the day, Whitall Tatum of Millville, were exchanging molds with Minotola. This custom of exchanging bottle molds, not recorded in books on glass hitherto, is documented also in the chapter on Salem, and of course opens an entire new question of provenance. Hagerty Bros. & Co. wrote to Minotola:

> "Kindly send us 8 oz. florida [water] or castor oil mould that was shipped to you from here on Aug. 4, 1896."

In 1889 Moore Brothers of Clayton was writing to Minotola to say they didn't know about the molds the Jonas company inquired about.

Astonishing also is the postcard revelation of the wide range of attractive and interesting bottles that were being handblown at Minotola even while machine bottles were turned out. A pineapple bottle was a standard item at Minotola at least as late as 1898; when the Philadelphia Pickling Company said:

> Please ship at once ten trays of ½ pint pineapple Bottles; 10 trays of 16 oz. Chow Chow Bottles, long necks; 5 trays of ½ Pt. Oils and 5 trays of 16 oz. Chow Chow Bottles, short necks, original mould, all light green, and oblige . . .

A startling product for which the George Jonas company received an inquiry on price was for Hirsch's Sweet Violet Perfumed Ammonia for the Toilet and Bath. The label was printed in violet ink and the picture of the bottle also looked to be of violet glass. Is there one such extant today? The same Manhattan firm requested a car load of pint catsup bottles.

Orders were coming thick and fast, on penny postcards:

Otis Clapp & Son, Boston, Jan. 5, 1897.
Please send us 50 gross of our 12-oz. green amber Blakes.

Phoenix Plumbago Mining Co., Phila. July 26, 1901. Please ship us at once 20 gross Dressing bottles. P.S. The bottoms of the dressing bottles are *very weak* & a great many break. Please look into this matter carefully.

Baker Bros. & Co., Baltimore, Glass Mfrs. June 17, 1897. We want 10 to 15 gr 8 oz. Sodas light green glass . . . Party do not want deep green glass.

Greenwich Packing Co., 462 Greenwich St., N.Y. Please send two boxes 7 oz. Honey bottles *flint glass.* J. J. Quinn.

H. F. Voss, Grocers' Sundries, Brooklyn, Oct. 18, 1898. Please send (10) ten cases Imposted ½ pts. Oils.
A while later the same firm wanted Sweet Oil Bottles and Screw top Catsups, for which they recorded an office at 63 Wilkinson avenue, Jersey City.

Alart & McGuire of 66 Madison street, New York, who advertised as importers and manufacturers of Pickles, Cauliflower, Sauerkraut, Vinegar, Catsup, Olives, Sauces, Etc., wrote George Jonas they would favor him with bottle orders as fast as needed.

C.C. Stutts Glass Co., 145 Chambers St. (N.Y.) Bottle Warehouse. July 19, 1898. If we return the ½ Pt Syrup mould to you will you make Ten Cases L.G. (light green) promptly. If so call Land. (A New York phone number was listed, still a rarity at that date.)

The letterhead of the George Jonas Glass Company in 1907 warned that "All orders are accepted subject to delays by reason of strikes, the action of the elements, or other cases beyond our control." A postcard of 1901 from the T.C. Wheaton glassworks in Millville bore a similar notice, for with the success of the first bottle-making machine, members of the Glass Bottle Blowers Association became frantic with rage and anxiety at the prospect of losing their jobs. At Minotola the threat was all too real, for one furnace had already been converted to producing machine-made bottles. Furnace No. 1, when Jonas owned the plant, continued to make handblown flint ware. One shop in this furnace blew wine and whisky bottles exclusively with John Husted and Jesse Comer as blowers. Olive and cherry bottles were blown by Glen Layton, William Sheets and gaffer Charles Rose; catsup bottles by William Moore, Chester Tharp and gaffer Garrison. The Ernest brothers blew flat panel bottles and the gaffer was their father. Furnace No. 3, a smaller one known as the dinky, was used alternately for blue glass in making Stafford inks and Bromo-Seltzer bottles and for amber glass required in snuff and other jars and tonic bottles.

Realizing that bottle-making machines were rapidly improving in efficiency and that the clock could not be turned back, officers of the GBBA recommended co-operation so that blowers would have other employment in plants setting up machines. But the glassmen were aghast at this waste of their talents. They promptly struck the Jonas plant. Nor were they alone. In the year 1903 some 500 glassmakers were on strike in South Jersey.

The George Jonas Company quickly brought in strike-breakers from "the West." All of the newcomers were young and the local people were frightened of the "scabs."

Then one night a member of the Glass Bottle Blowers Association was shot and killed. The union's president, Denis A. Hayes, flatly accused the company's strike-breakers of the murder. Twice during its stormy history the plant suffered fires, once being entirely burned.

Rather than yield to union demands, George Jonas sold the Minotola works to the Shoemakers who owned the Cumberland Glass Company of Bridgeton. They changed the name to the Minotola Glass Company and the plant was finally unionized on July 25, 1908. Subsequently the Illinois Glass Company bought both the Bridgeton and the Minotola works and then merged with the Owens glass company to become Owens-Illinois of Bridgeton, now a fully automated factory and one of New Jersey's major corporations. It is said that Owens-Illinois had planned to move the factory to Minotola but that feelings were still so bitter there that it was decided to close that plant. Minotola was phased out as a glass factory in March 1921.

L. G. Taylor who had been manager at the George Jonas Glass Company began organizing the first glass works at Cape May Court House in 1901. Then in 1906 he sold his share to George Jonas who gave the works the name of Cape May Glass Company.

It is not known if interesting offhand glass was blown at Minotola, but certainly the furnaces used metal of excellent color and quality, and blowers who could fashion the complicated bottles mold-blown there must have been equally adept at freeblown ware.

Fig. 207 PINKISH AMETHYST VASE with clear-cut lines is attributed to New Jersey, c. 1855, though in the style of English Bristol of that time. Applied foot is deftly tooled. H. 7¾ inches. *George Horace Lorimer collection. Philadelphia Museum of Art. Photo by A. J. Wyatt, Staff Photographer.*

The Upper and the Lower Factory at Cape May Court House

Late bloomers, these two glass works ran separately, not at a court building as a stranger might assume, but in an historic town still called Cape May Court House, the county seat of Cape May County since 1745.

Each factory had formal names, though seldom used by the local people. The Upper Factory was called the Cape May Glass Company, though at first it went under the name of Taylor and Stites who founded it. The Lower Factory was initially named the Hereford Glass Company, for nearby Hereford Inlet on the Atlantic Ocean.

The arrival of the Cape May Glass Company in town was awaited almost breathlessly, for the community was apparently undergoing a depression. The following excerpts from *The Gazette* tell the story:

> Nov. 22, 1901: "Vacant houses are filling up fast with families moving into town by reason of the Glass industry, and tenements will be in great demand."
> Nov. 29, 1901: "The new glass company has fires under its tank and is pushing the repairs as fast as possible in the hope of beginning active operations in a week or ten days."
> Dec. 6, 1901: "The first bottles were made at the glass factory here yesterday . . ."

On Jan. 10, 1902, the paper ran a plea entitled "Sustain our Glass Factory," which declared that a forthcoming report of the New Jersey Bureau of Labor and Statistics would show that in the glass business 74.1% of the industry product went to the employees' wages, in iron and steel 69%, and in brewing only 5¼ %. The editorial, plus the energies and ingenuities of the workers and the owners, must have been effective for the Cape May Glass Company enjoyed a thriving business until it closed in December 1924, by which time machine-made bottles were taking over the field.

The Upper Factory was located at the junction of School House Lane and the Reading Railroad, and some of the barn-red buildings were still standing there at the Samuel Croiter Feed and Coal Company until April of 1968 when they were burned in the riots ensuing after the assassination of Dr. Martin Luther King. The Lower Factory was located about a half mile south of the Upper Factory on the west side of the Reading Railroad at Hereford Avenue, almost in Mayville.

This Lower Factory or Hereford works was formed about 1908 by L. G. Taylor, Dr. Julius Way, Charles Vanaman, W. J. Taylor, and numerous glassblowers who took stock in the company, among them Claude Young and Charles Taylor. Although Hereford appears to have been a success from its inception, the stockholders met on Oct. 22, 1909, and voted unanimously to liquidate. This paved the way for a take-over by the Cape May Glass Company.

Fig. 208 CAPE MAY LIGHTHOUSE BOTTLE, blown at Cape May Court House glassworks, is embossed with the name SEAWORTH BITTERS CO./CAPE MAY NEW JERSEY U.S.A. *Couresy Cape May County Historical Society*. ABOVE: glass hat.

Harry Stites and L. G. Taylor, who had formerly been manager of the Minotola Glass Company before it was closed by a bitter strike, were the first owners of the Upper Factory, but in 1906 Taylor sold his share to George Jonas who had been owner at Minotola during the strike of the Glass Bottle Blowers Association. When Jonas bought into the firm he changed the name to the Cape May Glass Company and that of the company store to the Cape May Supply Company and brought in some employees from Bridgeton's Cumberland Glass Works, of which he was a principal owner.

From the quality of commercial ware blown and the variety and good design of the creative free-blown glass made in spare time we know that both the Upper and the Lower Factory had some exceedingly talented gaffers. The shop teamwork too was such that production was amazingly high. A record still cited by old-timers was this output of three blowers, William John Bethel, George Garretson, and Martin Spalding, in one 8-hour day:

755 dozen 14-ounce cologne bottles
650 dozen vanilla bottles (paneled and difficult to blow)
250 dozen quart bottles

That fixed The Machine, for a while at least. Why, it took Leroy May and his brother Howard one entire day just to pack that glass.

Mainstay of both plants was bottles, some of the most unusual, attractive, and collectible, yet not widely known to today's collectors of mold-blown containers. The glass ranged from the typical containers for sodas, beer and whisky to bottles for cologne, perfume, bitters, vanilla extract, Bromo-Seltzer, citrate of magnesia, and catsup, as well as for medicines sold by druggists and dispensing physicians. Regularly every year came an order from a southern company for 20 gross of bottles in which to put their Snake Oil, for sore muscles and possibly arthritis.

Unlike the Williamstown glass works which went to the wall when the Prohibition amendment became law, the Cape May Glass Company had other than liquor bottles to soften the blow. Among these was the bent-neck nursing bottle, "The Baby's Companion," and the glassman's salvation. Great quantities of mold-blown bottles were made for leading pharmaceutical manufacturers such as Parke-Davis and Sharp and Dohme, as well as for the Coca Cola Company.

One of the most attractive historical bottles is a replica of Cape May Lighthouse, built in 1859 at Jersey's southernmost point. In amber glass with clear stoppers these are embossed SEAWORTH/BITTERS/CO/ CAPE MAY/NEW JERSEY/U S A. Two sizes, one 11½ inches high and the other 6½ inches, are on exhibit at the museum of the Cape May County Historical Society in the old court house building, open Saturdays in July and August. Though not large, the display is worthwhile also because there is other glass which likely was blown at Cape May Court House, including several cologne bottles. An aqua flower pot was blown at Whitall Tatum. Here too is a snuff bottle owned by Dr. Randolph Marshall, a grandson of the original Randall Marshall who founded Marshallville Glass Works with Frederick Stanger.

Harry W. Stites was mold-maker for the factories, who had associated with him George Hewitt and George Albus, the latter in mold repair. With sand coming from Millville, Williamstown, and Vineland, the glass was of high quality. At a late period the silica came from Pennsylvania, the place not known.

Flint glass as well as lime was made, and besides clear glass there was a wide color range: aqua, amber, green, cobalt, sapphire. Given the above conditions and the presence of many skilled gaffers, one might expect interesting extra-curricular creations. From ware surviving in some families, we know this to be true. Besides spiraled canes, lilies, chains and other novelties there are some well-formed and imaginative vases, decanters, cruets, pitchers and paperweights. The best of the latter, indeed, are as good as many from Whitall Tatum blowers but quite different in concept. Judging from colors added, it seems probable that some of the weight makers had small stocks of yellow, orange and red coloring for their own use.

In June, 1968 I had the pleasure of meeting with two seasoned gaffers, retired from the Cape May Glass Company: Claude Young, then 93, and Jack Bethel, then 80, who were longtime friends.

Karl Dickinson, a Cape May County historian, had told me that Claude Young had made at least 20 fine paperweights and given them all away. With Claude Young's help I finally tracked down one of the weights and found it to be a handsome magnum size, with gloxinia-shaped upright flowers worked in yellow, opaque white, orange, green and black. Fully the equal of the best similar ones made by the St. Clairs of Elwood, Indiana, Young's weights were fashioned well before the Hoosier "lilies" became publicized. A pale amethyst vase with strong widely spaced ribs is evidence of Young's skill too in free-blown glass.

"Everything made at Cape May Court House was hand blown," said Claude Young, "even Coca Cola bottles." He blew Cape May Lighthouse bottles and his specialty was jars and large bottles. Young noted that the larger items took longer to blow and as all payment was on a piece-work system, the small flat paneled bottles paid the best provided a blower had the knack for making them as Young's friend Jack Bethel had had, and also Owen Tozour, another skilled gaffer.

Born in Glassboro, Young started out at Clayton as an 8-year-old tending boy at Moore Brothers for Henry Clevenger who was batch formulator there and who later became master shearer at Cape May Court House. Having become a journeyman glass-blower, Young subsequently worked at factories in Bridgeton, Montreal and Point Marion, West Virginia. Already working at Cape May Glass when the Hereford plant opened, Young recalls these two as having the best shops, with good pay and working conditions, and pleasant managers.

Jack Bethel had come to Jersey as an expert glassblower from Pittsburgh, a reversal of a mid-19th century migration of Jersey gaffers to Pittsburgh. After what might be termed a postgraduate course at Whitall Tatum in Millville he came to Cape May Court House and quickly earned a reputation as a master blower, in special demand for producing the paneled vanilla bottles. His shop, one of nine, consisted of three blowers, a mold boy and a carrying boy, all of them fast and efficient workers, he said.

Like his friend Claude Young, Jack Bethel made fine paperweights but in a quite different style. One which he displayed is a bubble weight having an interior core of sapphire blue covered with clear flint, a type often ascribed to Pairpoint. Another specialty of Bethel's were well-shaped clear-glass lilies splashed with orange, yellow and blue, and resting on a curled stem.

Besides the individuals named above, some of the other skilled blowers in these two factories where precision workmanship was demanded were George Charlesworth, George Bonn, Harry Curless, William Stites, Louis Amrose, Winfield Jones, Harry Spalding, George Tozour, Howard Charlesworth, Sr., Chester Comer, Sr., Louis Bakley, Charles Brown, Elwood Smith, George Simpkins, Sr., Harry Law, Herbert Wells, George Wright, Charles Peterson, Sr., Edward Stone, William Wright, Samuel Leuallen, Alfred and William Scull, Benjamin Taylor, Robert Mossbrooks, Benjamin Tozour, Jr., Charles Roorbach, Rem and Pat Taylor, Somers Norton, Joseph Amrose, John Babbitt, and J. Wesley Dilks.

Blowers were paid by the gross of acceptable bottles blown, according to a price list agreed upon by the owners and the Glass Bottle Blowers Association. In the early 1900s the rate paid here for every 144 of the vanilla bottles was $1.22; for the 7-ounce nursing bottles, 97 cents; for small prescription bottles, 57 cents; and for 1-ounce perfume bottles, 55 cents. Employees could draw only "market money" each week, as the final payment was not given until the end of the season, an arrangement that kept workers on the job and helped curb profligate spending. If the wages seem pitifully small, it might be noted that in 1910 sirloin steak was selling for 16 cents a pound here. In 1908 when Clarence McGraw came from Bridgeton to be manager of the company store at the Cape May Glass Company, the owner of the Bellevue Hotel asked him if $6.00 a week would be too high for room and board. For each meal, including breakfast, the hotel offered three kinds of meat—glassmen ate hearty—and the price of a dinner was 50 cents.

TOPAZ AND RUBY CANDLESTICKS designed at Durand to match a gold-ruby compote, ruby plates and footed, ruby dessert dishes (see example below), all with ribs edged in white. Teardrop pedestal is ribbed, as is foot with folded edge.

GOLD LUSTER DURAND vase with iridescent mauve spider-web threading. H. 11½ inches.

PLATE 18

SUBTLE COLOR reveals Hofbauer's skill in compounding formulas. Pitcher, a true violet, has claw handle of deep turquoise. Clean-lined vase is also turquoise. Both objects have a frosty, bubbled look, interspersed with confetti-like color. *Barbetti collection.*

PLATE 19

DURAND RUBY BOWL hand cut to clear in rose pattern has amber foot and base of bowl swirled in white feather design, a difficult combination resulting in an object of rare beauty. *H.M. Smith collection.*

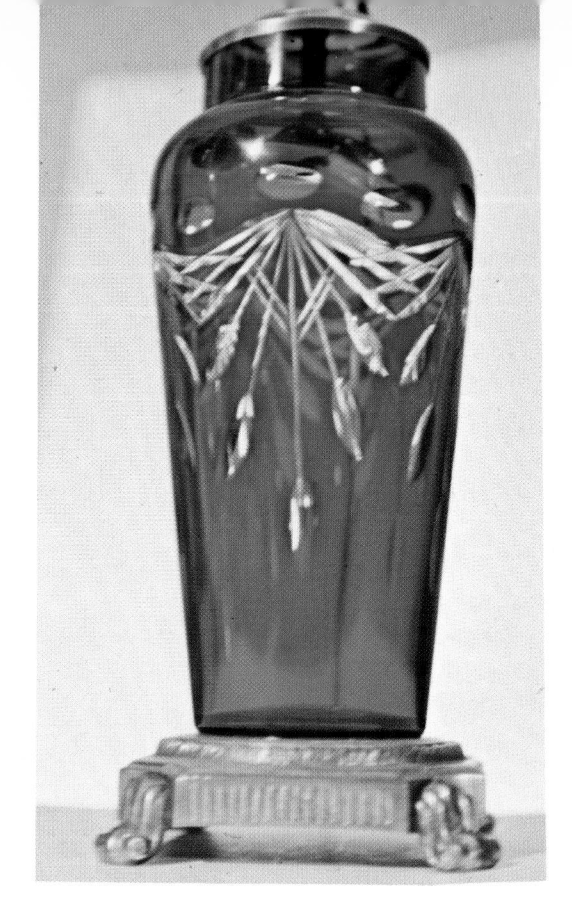

LAMP OF COBALT OVERLAY cut to crystal in pattern designed by Charles Link, head of cutting shop at Vineland Flint Glass Works. H. of glass, 9 inches.

EXPANDED-DIAMOND pitcher made by Emil J. Larson at Vineland in 1930s. Early Jersey style is expressed in double strap handle, fold-over rim and circular applied foot. H. 9½ inches.

ORANGE AND CHARTREUSE LUSTER Durand vase swirled with silver luster in King Tut pattern. Deep orange lining. Signed "V Durand/1710–8." H. 8 inches.

The Durand "Fancy Shop" in Vineland

WITH THE UTMOST rue, an auctioneer at a 1969 sale in New Jersey said through the microphone, "Well, I never thought I'd see a piece of real Stiegel sell for less than Durand."

The Stiegel glass he held up was a beautiful cobalt expanded-diamond pitcher which had once been in his father's collection. It sold that day for $125. Yet at that very sale signed Durand art glass owned by the same collector sold for as high as $300 for a vase. A few weeks earlier at another Jersey sale Durand reached even higher peaks of $450 for a King Tut vase.

Avid collectors of Durand art glass seem undeterred by current prices, but they may feel they were born too late; for in the depths of the 1930s depression, when Durand's Vineland Flint Glass Company went out of business, King Tut vases and the firm's whole range of decorative glass were offered at the factory for $5 an item. People with spare cash and an appreciation for beautiful glass loaded their cars with these $5 articles. Over the years if the owners needed funds they would sell Durand glass at a profit of $25 to $35.

Then in the 1950s Walter P. Chrysler, Jr. began collecting Durand and other art glass on a large scale for the Chrysler Art Museum of Provincetown which he established on Cape Cod. As he paid premium prices to get objects he especially wanted, all Durand glass increased in price. This in turn stimulated private collectors to buy, partly in hopes of further appreciation, which did occur, a spiral that is still continuing. As a result, most Jersey museums failed to acquire representative collections of Durand.

The prices quoted above are for iridescent or "gold" opaque glass such as was pictured in the Durand catalog. For one-of-a-kind objects the price soared. In 1942, for instance, the owner of an 18-inch vase with a scroll-like pattern called the Green Leaf design (not the usual Durand leaf or vine pattern) refused an offer of $5,000. Once there was a 24-inch punch bowl, a tray, and 18 or 24 cups in this pattern, which were shown at buyers' conventions held at places like Chicago's Palmer House, but they have disappeared, probably into private collections.

Who? What? When? Where? Why? was "Durand"? It is surprising how few collectors of American blown glass even recognize Durand glass, much less know its story. In the past few years Mr. and Mrs. Ted Lagerberg, Mr. and Mrs. Ray Grover, and Albert Revi in their books with handsome illustrations have done much to show why Durand glass is collectible. Sam Farber and Philip Glick, South Jersey antiques dealers, were among the first dealers to recognize that Durand glass, so popular before the 1929 stock market crash, would again have a future.

Durand art glass was the last in time of a style brought to fruition by Tiffany, was co-existent with the Steuben Glass Company founded by Frederick Carder, and followed the end of Quezal glass. Being last, Durand had the opportunity of correcting the mistakes of its predecessors. Durand glass had the advantage of being produced by a "shop" or team who had blown glass together before, at Quezal, and who performed as smoothly as a chamber music ensemble.

The Durand "fancy shop" as it was known in Vineland was a fortuitous union of a half dozen persons whose life, in retrospect, seems to have been geared for just that purpose.

The original inspiration was that of Victor Durand, Jr., who had been born in 1870 at Baccarat, France, where his father and grandfather had been blowers at Cristalleries de Baccarat, long noted for exquisite glass. As a boy Victor Durand worked briefly there but at the age of 14 came to New Jersey to join his father who had been employed for about a year at Whitall Tatum in Millville. After a few years the younger Victor went to work for the Wheaton Glass Company, also in Millville.

Teenager Victor must have had a yen to see more of his new homeland, for during the next eight or nine years he worked at glasshouses in West Virginia, Ohio, Pennsylvania, even Canada, meanwhile acquiring a broad knowledge of glassmaking.

On returning to New Jersey in 1897 he and his father organized the Vineland Flint Glass Works and leased a former green glass furnace, that of the Vineland Glass Manufacturing Company which had been founded in 1892. The Durands converted the furnace to one for flintware and began producing lamp chimneys and bottles, then gradually expanding into precision ware such as laboratory glass and tubing. About 1915 the firm began making towel rods and other bathroom fixtures from colored opaque and opal glass. From this metal some rather attractive vases were made in spare-time blowing and the green was used by Ralph Barber for leaves on a few of his rose paperweights. A specialty of the house had become the inner cores of vacuum bottles, and Barber, whose true forte was the creation of art glass, was confined to being superintendent of "vacuum blowing."

So expert were Durand's blowers that by 1920 the factory, of which the younger Victor was then the sole proprietor, had become the largest individually owned glassworks making tubing in the nation. Durand had had ample occasion to learn about Tiffany's burnished gold table ware, the success of Frederick Carder with the infinite variety of colored glass at his Steuben works, and the exotic formulas of Martin Bach, Sr., who founded the Quezal Art Glass & Decorating Company in 1900 and was also creator of some of the magnificent Tiffany iridescents. Then in 1921 Martin Bach, Sr., a Frenchman from Alsace-Lorraine, died. His son Martin Jr., privy to all his father's secret formulas, carried on as president until 1924 but felt unable to continue, and the company ceased to be.

Thrown out of work by this decision were a quartet who had made much beautiful glass for Quezal, named for the flamboyant quetzal bird of Guatemala. Having to search for new jobs were Emil J. Larson, long a gaffer for Dorflinger's, Harry and Percy Britton, skilled glassmakers from Corona, L.I., and William Wedenbine, formerly with Steuben, at Corning, N.Y.

Much of my information about Durand glass and the chance to examine many examples of it came from Mr. and Mrs. Larson and Mrs. Martin A. Bach, Jr. As early as Oct. 15, 1921, Martin Bach had received a letter from Victor Durand inviting him to discuss plans for an art glassworks at Vineland. Bach was eager but there were problems in the way. Larson had given up glassblowing and settled his family at Hammondsport, N.Y., on

Fig. 209 PEACOCK PATTERN VASE, LEFT, gold-ruby with feather loops in white. Brilliant lead glass. Vineland Flint Glass Works. Durand. H. 9½ inches. *Fig. 210* LIGHTNING zigzags over silver-blue luster make a striking vase, the core of which is red. Though not signed, the base is unmistakably Durand. H. 9 inches.

a chicken farm. Then early in 1924 on a business trip to Ohio Mr. and Mrs. Bach discovered the other three men working together again as a shop. They too were enthusiastic about making fine glass for Durand. Larson agreed to join all again, and with incredible speed, the Durand "fancy shop" was blowing its first glass Dec. 1, 1924. Mrs. Bach still has a pair of experimental candlesticks, ruby with the peacock feather design.

Within two years Durand art glass had reached the pinnacle: first prize, a gold medal at the Philadelphia Sesquicentennial International Exposition of 1926, for a representative collection of gold ruby and iridescent glass. From then on, enthusiasm and creation were boundless. As Sam Farber, personal friend of Victor Durand, has said, the group never stopped experimenting until the doors closed in 1931.

In that short span essentially the same team originated and hand-fashioned thousands of intricately decorated and colored objects. Martin Bach was superintendent, formula-maker and designer. Larson was gaffer or head of shop and designer of prototypes, while Harry Britton, an equally fine blower, was chief decorator doing the threading and whorled designs. His brother Percy was gatherer and Wedenbine was servitor. At one time Joseph Hofbauer also was an assistant. Having made the art glass project his hobby Durand continually offered suggestions for new forms, decorations, and colors.

The Vineland Flint Glass Company and the Kimble Glass Company of Vineland had been competitors who joined forces in 1911, then separated in 1918. Again in 1931 plans had been made for a second merger of the two firms, but in that year Victor Durand met an untimely death when the car he was driving struck an abutment.

Evan Kimble bought out the Vineland Flint Glass Works and many of the workmen in the laboratory glass division found employment with his firm. But members of the art glass shop soon learned that the end had come for it as surely as for its originator, Victor Durand.

Two principal types of glass were made in the Durand "fancy shop": opaque and transparent. By skillful use of colors and basic types of decoration an astonishingly wide range of vivid effects was achieved.

Opaque glass was usually reserved for vases, rose bowls, perfume atomizers, and lamp bases and shades. All were more expensive to produce because they required several stages of decoration. A vase might have an allover metallic iridescence, a lining in a contrasting iridescence, a vine and leaf decoration in still another color, and the whole encircled with criss-crossed threads called Spider Webbing. Much of the opaque glass was either iridescent with a brilliant metallic luster or was crackled by a process exclusive to Durand and said to have been created by Emil Larson and Martin Bach to simulate ancient Mediterranean glass; hence the names of Egyptian Crackle and Moorish Crackle. The best pieces have a strong primitive texture and shape; others, needing interior lighting, made attractive lamp bases, while some remained dull. Because of the frequent breakage in making not much crackle ware has survived. Thick bands of red or green or cobalt glass were swirled around a basic parison such as light amber or opaque white. Sometimes a third layer was added, in opaque white. The hot parison was then dipped in water, which caused the outer layer to crack into irregular rivulets. The blower then reheated the parison and expanded it to the desired shape. Expansion caused encrustations and revealed the transparent color beneath. A subdued metallic spray usually was the final finish. The Lava decoration, produced with a silver luster, is a most apt term for the appearance.

Among the rarest Durand glass are the acid cut-back and the Cameo vases, in which a raised design was produced on cased or layered glass of contrasting colors by acid etching. In the Cameo glass copperwheel engraving was also employed. The most unusual vases are flattened spheres with floral or geometric designs etched in the glass which was likely to be in two subtle shades of one color. A splendid example of these cameo-cut globes is in two tones of amethyst and is in the collection of the New Jersey State Museum at Trenton. See Plate 1 for a rare cameo vase from the Chrysler Art Museum.

Durand transparent glass was reserved mostly for tableware, in such variety that entire dinner sets could be assembled, all handblown of course, for a price. Even in the Twenties the overlay cut glass plates retailed for $110 a dozen. All of this transparent glass has a peculiar ring not heard in usual lead glass, a metallic sound as if one were striking a bronze bell. The difference in sound is a way of distinguishing transparent Steuben and Val St. Lambert glass from Durand. Table ware made by the Vineland Flint Glass Company in the 1920s still retains a sparkle and brilliance remarkable for its age. Some of this glass was treated with an oil bath and steam treatment which gave it the name of Oil Luster glass, a name which seems undesirable to retain today because it is confused with the metallic lusters of Durand opaque glass. The oiled glass, which was pale yellow, known both as Ambergris and Spanish Yellow, besides being used for some dinner ware was also the core for most opaque glass.

The lists below show the possibilities for ringing numerous changes from basic colors and types of decorations.

Durand Opaque Glass

COLORS	TYPES OF DECORATION
Gold luster	Spider Webbing
Silver luster	Peacock feather; a feather-like design often on iridescent glass
Orange luster	Heart and Clinging Vine: leaf and vine pattern often in contrasting luster
Midnight blue luster	King Tut, a "pulled" decoration in allover pattern with whorls
Peacock blue luster	Hard Optic Rib, a paneled pattern with widest ribs about 2 inches apart. Optical effect evident only in transparent glass
Ambergris luster: pale amber with slight golden luster	Crackle or Lava decoration
Scarlet	Acid Cutback
Lady Gay Rose: soft rose pink	Cameo
Parakeet green	
Chartreuse	
Opal: ivory white, not a true opal or opaque white	

Durand Transparent Glass

Gold ruby: deep rose pink often edged in white	Peacock feather
Emerald	Cutting
Sapphire	Engraving
Spanish Yellow: pale topaz edged in green or cobalt	White Linings
Grape purple, rare	Venetian Lace: pale topaz with fine threads of opaque white blown as part of the glass. Often edged in cobalt
Red, rare	Optic Rib; hard rib has sharp edges; soft rib gives appearance of undulations
Gold ruby and clear overlay	Colors often combined: topaz for stems of glasses with cups in green, ruby or blue
Sapphire and clear overlay	
Emerald and clear overlay	

Fig. 211 CRANBERRY-PINK PIPE edged in white, identical colors used at Durand for dessert sets in 1920s. L. 17 inches.

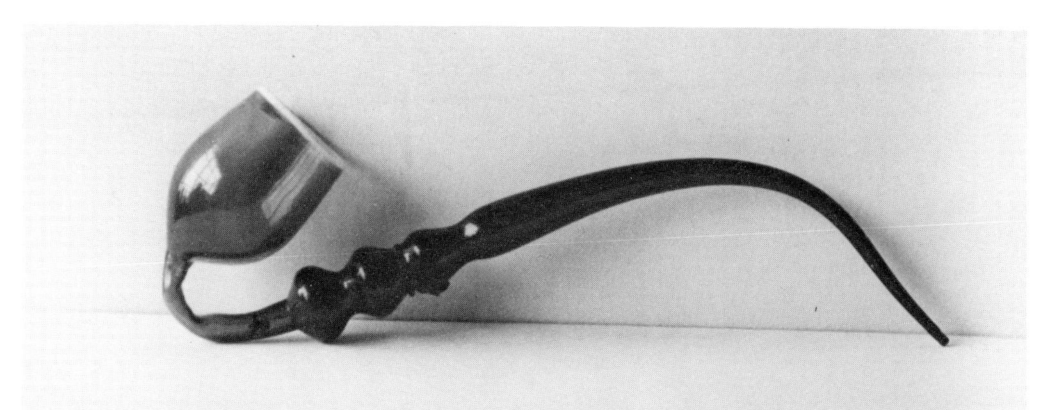

Signatures

Earliest Durand glass was not signed. Only when it became evident to Martin Bach and the Durands that their art glass was in demand at buyers' conventions did signing start, and not always then. Some glass was signed simply "Durand" written in script by whoever had time. The more frequent signature is a large V with the word "Durand" inscribed horizontally across the V. Numbers such as 1970-12 indicated, first, the shape number from catalogs and then the height. Signatures were made with a dental drill. Today signatures are being faked not only on Durand glass but also Tiffany, Steuben and Quezal, with the result that signed pieces do not carry the higher price tag they once commanded. Mrs. Bach says that she has even seen Durand glass signed "Vic"! Original signatures were not filled in with an aluminum pencil as has been suggested, but to reveal the method would only encourage more fakery.

Durand Lamps

Contrary to widespread opinion, Durand lamps are rarely vases which owners have had drilled and adapted for lamps. The Vineland Flint Glass Company marketed a large variety of art glass lamps, from tall end-table styles to bedside lamps and wrought-iron torchères with Moorish Crackle up-turned shades. At first, though, Durand lamps were only a sideline for Ernest Dorrell of Alloway and Martin Bach, Jr., who formed the L. & S. Shade Company in that tiny village to utilize an excess supply of Quezal glass shades. To this line they added lamps which they made from seconds of Durand vases. As the orders increased, the partners began to sell their lamps through Durand's sales representative in New York City, Emil S. Larsen. Learning of the success of this venture, Victor Durand about 1928 decided to produce complete lamps with harmonizing hand-painted parchment shades and antiqued metal bases for the art glass. Few of the shades, which were decorated by Dorrell, Mr. and Mrs. E. C. Reed of Atlantic City, and various individuals in Vineland, have survived. Lamps which are converted vases or rose bowls are likely to have shiny gilded stands, whereas the custom-designed Durand lamp bases have a bronze look in neoclassic style (Plate 12). Some lamps had the glass lighted from within. See the Moorish Crackle lamp in Plate 13.

Globes which look like bubble paperweights were made in Durand's "fancy shop" as night lights, complete with stands that had an inner light to refract the bubbles. Sometimes faceted (opposite), these bubbled lights, made in clear, amber and sapphire, have a small foot, unlike the broad base of paperweights. Globes of similar size for decorative lights were made of overlay glass—emerald, sapphire and ruby cut to crystal.

A catalog page illustrating some Durand glass in color is imprinted with the name of Emil S. Larsen & Co., 225 Fifth Ave., New York City. This was the main showroom for Durand glass. The name of the sales representative is often confused with that of Emil J. Larson who did much of the blowing for the "fancy shop." Emil S. Larsen who spelled his name with an "e" was a Dane and was not a glassmaker, whereas Emil Larson who was Swedish had spent most of his working life as a glassblower. The catalog sheet, for the trade, shows prices such as $12 for a peacock feather vase and $38 for a compote set. The agent received a 10 per cent markup.

Fig. 212 NIGHT LIGHT, LEFT, bubbled and faceted, was designed at Durand, to be placed on electrified stand. H. 4½ inches. *Fig. 213* SELENIUM RED glass, a kind used in the Durand "fancy shop," fashions this candy dish with pleated edge, ornamentation favored by Hofbauer. D. 8 inches.

In New York Durand glass was sold in quantity by B. Altman, Macy's and Gimbel's. Shows for buyers were held at the Hotel New Yorker and in Chicago, at the Palmer House. Durand glass was very popular in the Chicago area, where Marshall Field's was a leading outlet. In the South, Neiman-Marcus was a principal distributor, while close to Vineland in Philadelphia all the important jewelry stores and department stores, from Bailey, Banks & Biddle to Wanamaker's, sold Durand art glass.

LINK'S CUTTING SHOP AT DURAND

Some of the loveliest glass to come from Durand was created by Charles D. Link of Bridgeton, a cutter, not a blower. His finest cutting was done on cased lead glass—cobalt or emerald or ruby, sometimes amber, over clear.

As master cutter for Durand's "fancy shop," Charles Link exhibited a restraint that was not known in the Brilliant period of glass cutting, which had a coarseness that caused it to lose favor. Still in private Jersey families are complete dinner sets—serving plates, salad plates, goblets, wines, footed desserts and matching plates—cut by Link and other New Jersey artisans.

Years before Victor Durand had set up his art glass department Charles Link was famous in his own right for a glass-cutting plant which he and his brother George owned, a building still standing in Bridgeton at the northwest corner of Broad and Atlantic streets. The cut glass was so superb that Philadelphia merchants beat a path to their door.

"Even in 1915 when money was tight," says Arthur Link, son of Charles, "Link glass was bringing high prices, $25 to $40 for pitchers, fruit bowls, salad bowls, vases, creamers and sugar bowls."

Fig. 214 BRILLIANT CUTTING AT BRIDGETON by Charles Link's Aetna Glass Shop at Broad Street and Atlantic Avenue. *Fruit bowl owned by Link's descendants.*

Fig. 215 MATCHED PAIR OF CRYSTAL VASES from Aetna Cut Glass in Bridgeton. Charles Link, owner of the factory in the early 1900s, later became head of the Durand cutting shop, Vineland. *Link collection.*

This was the Aetna Cut Glass Company and it was here that Charles Link evolved what he named the Bridgeton Rose, a restrained pattern that later became almost a signature of Durand cutting. A handsome cobalt-and-clear cased lamp base in the rose design is shown on Plate 19. A matched pair of heavy lead glass vases and a fruit bowl in the Bridgeton Rose pattern cut at Aetna appears on opposite page.

Among the rarities in Durand glass are vases and bowls in which the upper third are transparent ruby, emerald or cobalt cut to clear in a flower spray while the major part of the object has a peacock feather design created in the blowing, not the cutting.

Some very contemporary-looking drinking glasses—waisted highball glasses, wines and short tumblers, as well as decanters—were created from the 2-toned cased glass by cutting down to the clear in a band of thumbprint faceting. Another modern design was a large daisy or sun with irregular petals or rays, often used on vases.

KIMBLE ART GLASS

Evan E. Kimble had little interest in art glass nor did the public have much money for it in the depressed 1930s. Hence Durand glass was disposed of locally at low prices and the balance sold for $1 an item to a Philadelphia department store. Against his better judgment Col. Kimble was persuaded to try out one new design. This was a raindrop-splashed opaque glass, pleasing in pastel shades of blue, yellow, mauve and green. Mostly vases in simple classic shapes, the glass is clearly an imitation of Steuben's Cluthra, so named by British-born Frederick Carder who adapted it from marked Cluthra glass designed by Christopher Dresser in the 1880s for James Cooper & Sons, Glasgow. The glass was marked with serial number, year and a K. In better times, Kimble glass might have sold but after a two-year trial it faded away as did Durand art ware, to find a new public in the 1960s.

Fig. 216 KIMBLE VASE mingles yellow, white and orange in cloudlike pattern. Blown at Col. Ewan E. Kimble's flint glass works in Vineland, c. 1932. Signed in silver script: 1812 7K Dec. 31. (latter indicates color of decoration, not date). H. 6½ inches. *Courtesy of the Chrysler Art Museum of Provincetown.* LEFT: typical Durand signature.

Larson Glass

Emil J. Larson can best be described as a glassblower's glassblower. The late John Liljequist, an expert cutter and engraver for Dorflinger Glass Works at White Mills, Pa., told me that when Emil Larson put a fine, even red or green or cobalt edge on crystal, other glassmakers at Dorflinger's gathered round to watch this feat.

After Durand's art glass works closed in Vineland in 1931, Larson who had been head of the shop was at one period blowing glass for the Wheatons of Millville. Mrs. Frank H. Wheaton told me that, as a wedding present for her and her husband, Larson blew a 50-piece cobalt glass dinner set, complete with cups and saucers, in a space of *four days*, and working only in his *spare time.* The Wheatons have from time to time had this dinner set on exhibit in the Wheaton Museum.

One of a family of ten children, Emil Larson was born Sept. 25, 1879, in Sweden where his father Axel was an expert blower at the noted Kosta works. Axel Larson and two fellow workers were induced to move to Birmingham, England, to blow blanks for Bacchus & Son. For reasons unknown the project was not a success and within months the Swedish workers were discharged without payment for return passage.

Two of the blowers left for the United States and soon obtained jobs at Dorflinger's, which was then one of the largest American works engaged in blowing and cutting fine crystal. Hearing of the plight of the stranded Larsons, Christian Dorflinger paid the passage for the entire family. While awaiting a train to White Mills, Emil, then nine years old, and his little sister strayed away. The train was called and the Larsons had no choice but to board it without the missing two children. Emil Larson never forgot the kindness of Americans who looked after him and his sister in a strange land, until Christian Dorflinger located them.

Nearly all the family worked at Dorflinger's in one way or another but Emil became a master blower in this factory noted for expert craftsmen. He stayed with the firm until it closed during World War I. Subsequently he became a gaffer for the Pairpoint Company of New Bedford, Mass., when they were producing colorful art glass. As described in the previous chapter he was the gaffer for a noted "shop" making art glass for Quezal and for Durand. During his long years as a blower and finisher he created thousands of pieces of some of the most beautiful glass made in the United States.

A little known aspect of his work is what he preferred to call Larson Glass which he produced during the Depression of the 1930s, in a one-pot furnace at his home in Vineland. It was here that he made all of his rose paperweights. Contrary to a recently published report, Larson not only never made any rose weights at Dorflinger's, he had never heard of any such at that time. Two other types of glass made by Larson at home are intriguing to collectors because they were in the style of rare Stiegel glass and rare early South Jersey lilypad objects. As none was marked, the problem of identification is often difficult.

In color and form, Larson reproductions of Stiegel flasks, small pitchers, toilet bottles, salts, and diamond-patterned sugar and cream sets are sometimes so like the originals as to pass for such if collectors are not aware of the difference in metal and particular detail. Expanded-diamond pocket bottles and the ribbed pitchers made by Larson have the jewel tones of blue-green, amethyst and sapphire found in 18th century Stiegel but the latter glass is thin walled, lighter in weight and, except for the bottles, is likely to be lead glass. In contrast, Larson rarely used flint glass during the hard times of the 1930s.

Philip Glick, a Clayton dealer who for over four decades has been an admirer of Larson' phenomenal dexterity in glassmaking, was first to suggest that he test his skill with

Fig. 217 DEEP VIOLET PITCHER which Emil Larson documented as having made at his home furnace reveals his skill in harmonious shaping and threading, though working non-lead glass, without a helper. Blown in an 18-rib dip mold. Crimped foot and fine strap handle. H. 6 inches.

Fig. 218 LARSON COMPOTE in a blue lighter than cobalt matches an 11-inch plate. Probably made while this master craftsman worked for Wheaton, after Durand closed. Non-lead glass. H. 7 inches.

Stiegel reproductions. When the tests proved successful, Mr. Glick became the sole agent for this glass in South Jersey.

Mr. Glick allowed Larson to borrow some of his choicest Stiegel, such as a diamond-daisy flask, in order to make mold copies. Some of the molds were simply plaster-of-Paris ones which permitted about 10 to 15 copies to be made. Larson already had a swirl mold and he obtained an inverted diamond mold from a closed Brooklyn factory. Some other molds he had made or even carved himself from fruitwood.

The Larson-Glick collaboration was not done with intent to deceive. As evidence of this, the late George McKearin asked the Glicks to send him samples of all reproductions made by Larson, which they did. Then a major collector of Stiegel as well as other blown glass, McKearin would often travel by bus from upstate New York to Clayton and would present the contents of two large suitcases of glass for identification, Mr. and Mrs. Glick recall.

Today, with a whole new generation of collectors on the scene, novices who are not watchful may pay Stiegel prices for Larson reproductions. It is important to note that half-pint ribbed flasks similar to Stiegel have been made in many countries at various times because this was a convenient, non-slip pocket bottle. For example, the clear flask in Fig. 59, which was also made in cobalt, was blown at the Holmegaard Works in Denmark about 1825. A Larson amethyst, diamond-patterned flask is shown on Plate 10.

Besides such ribbed or swirled flasks and diamond "quilted" ones (as well as miniatures), Larson is known to have blown toilet bottles in cobalt and deep grape-color, like the one on Plate 9. Footed Stiegel-type salts he made are not flint as were those from Manheim. Footed sugar bowls with domed, knopped covers which Larson made with a diamond pattern are blown from cobalt and a rich wine-colored metal. Low bowls formed in the diamond mold are sometimes mistaken for midwestern articles of the 19th century.

As for glass in the antique Jersey style which Larson produced, these were nearly all free-blown and hence were not literal copies but were adaptations done in the Jersey-German tradition. An example of this is the dark amber pitcher (Fig. 29) with unusual star-pointed foot and precise swag ornamentation. Other pitchers and bowls have lilypad

Fig. 219 EMIL J. LARSON in 1963.

decoration and carefully applied threading. As with Stiegel copies, the colors of this Larson glass were rich and unusual, such as a true violet. Some of these colors were supplied by Larson's brother John who was then working with stained-glass pigments for a Swedenborgian church near Philadelphia.

Larson glass in the Jersey style was not sold direct to the public but through dealers of whom the principal South Jersey ones were Ernest C. Stanmire from the Pitman area and Harold J. Wells of Merchantville, as well as Philip Glick.

As an example of Larson's phenomenal versatility he also made ash trays and small bowls in the Swedish modern style of the 1940s.

Most of the objects made were relatively small as Larson had no helper at his backyard furnace. His incredible skill in working alone is revealed in some clear flint wine glasses, a gift to Mr. and Mrs. Glick. The elaborate and tall balustered stems are the kind usually made with the help of a foot-man, yet Larson shaped six of these wines in a solo operation.

The first magnum rose paperweight that Larson ever made was in response to a challenge by Ernest C. Stanmire who said he would pay $25 for the first one. In 1934, long after Ralph Barber stopped making the rose weights he originated, Larson achieved that first rose. Mr. Stanmire recalls that Larson roses he bought were yellow, white, rose, pink and orange, with one in blue. Larson said he made only three of the latter. His roses usually have four translucent green leaves and 11 or 15 petals fairly evenly spaced. The rough pontils on some look like 4-leaf clovers. Like the Barber roses, Larson's, or at least the best of them, are footed. Of about 150 roses Larson made, he estimated that not more than 100 survived the annealing oven.

When Emil Larson was in his 84th year I spent many hours with him and his wife, examining glass which he had made at various periods in his career. At that time he looked a good 20 years younger than his chronological age and was as erect as royalty.

He was quick to remember articles he had blown, even where he had made them, and as quick to deny objects he had not blown. A grape-colored scent bottle (Plate 9) in Stiegel style he readily selected as one he had made, and added that any similar cruets with handles were not his. He smiled with pleasure when he recognized the exquisitely made violet pitcher (Fig. 217) which had been in the McKearin collection.

He seemed horrified when shown a cobalt swirled flask with a seam. He said he had never made fancy glass blown into a mold with pressure. Larson glass has no seams, he emphasized.

The Larsons showed me a miniature rose paperweight which was one of Charles Kaziun's firsts. While he was employed as a lamp-worker at the University of Pennsylvania during a 5-year period he was a frequent weekend visitor at the Larsons' home and from the master learned how to make rose weights for which he is now famous, though he had never made any magnum paperweights, according to Larson. In Larson's words, Kaziun never did make any weights with hot glass but has always been a lamp-worker, though one of the best.

Larson's phenomenal ability to duplicate any form of glass, from a Chinese rose jar to Venetian *latticinio* as well as to create new forms, either in an ancient tradition or ultra-modern style, makes him a nonpareil among gaffers. If only someone had preserved a sample of all his finest creations!

August V. Hofbauer, Gaffer

SEVENTY-FOUR of his 86 years August V. Hofbauer of Vineland spent as a glassworker. Shortly before he died in June of 1968, "Pop" Hofbauer, as he was known to all, was delighted to be doing exhibition blowing at a glassworks near Hammonton.

In his lifetime he had been not only a facile blower but also a formula man admired for the subtle and varied colors he culled from his brain on a moment's notice, and for three decades was the owner of an art glass house in Vineland.

Born in Vsetin, Austria, on Feb. 18, 1882, "Pop" Hofbauer began his lifetime in glass on the usual bottom rung, as a carrying-in boy at the age of 11. At the Vsetin glassworks he became a master blower, working in the Bohemian tradition of glowing colors and in styles similar to those of European glassmen who at one time were employed by the Boston & Sandwich works.

At the age of 31 Hofbauer came to the United States and while adding to his experience managed to see a good bit of the country at such glass centers as Morgantown, West Virginia, the A. H. Heisey Company of Newark, Ohio, and Chicago. He then put in a stint at the Millville International works but by 1921 was blowing chemical and laboratory ware for the Durand Flint Glass Company of Vineland, where he and his family decided to make their home. Like Ralph Barber and some other expert gaffers, Hofbauer because of his proficiency and accuracy in blowing was confined to monotonous scientific ware which consistently had to be blown to micrometer measurements. All the while Emil Larson and Harry Britton, working under the same roof, were making art glass for Durand's "fancy shop," where Hofbauer's son Joseph was an assistant.

Like yeasty dough overflowing a bowl, the need to create artistic glass could not always be contained. Barber had a relentless drive to perfect his rose paperweights while blowing x-ray tubes for a living, Ruhlander made Venetian style banks and epergnes in spare time, and Emil Stanger formed his unusual mushroom inkwells. Hofbauer's chance for taking up creative glassmaking again came soon after 1931 when the Durand works was absorbed by Kimble Glass Company.

In 1932 when the Depression of the 1930s was about at its nadir, Hofbauer courageously organized his own firm, the Vineland Glass Works, Inc., where, though he began by making laboratory ware, he soon introduced art glass that sold nationwide. That his formulas were not only for colored glass is shown by the fact that he was among the first to make heatproof percolators. The factory still stands at 549 East Avenue; at the height of activity about 100 persons were employed. The art glass was sold through Gimbel's and other department stores and gift shops.

Fig. 220 GLASSBLOWER'S WEDDING DAY in Usetim, Austria. From the age of 14 a glassworker, August Hofbauer came to the United States in 1913, became renowned in the art of glass formulas as well as blowing. Much of the product of his Vineland works is mistaken for Victorian Sandwich glass.

Almost consistently Hofbauer's glass of this period is mistaken for late 19th century articles made at Hobbs, Brockunier & Company of Wheeling or the Boston & Sandwich works or the New England Glass Company. Many of the pieces are large vases or pitchers with fluted or ruffled necks. Among other objects verified are bud vases, handled baskets, low bowls or candy dishes with crimped edges, and ash trays.

With this glass Hofbauer had a free hand to demonstrate his special knowledge of formulas. He attempted on a commercial scale what few glassmen would try even for a few samples: the combination of two kinds of colored glass, for objects as utilitarian as pitchers, a feat fraught with the danger of breakage. The deep amethyst pitcher (Plate 14) with a ribbed, claw handle in blue-green exemplifies the combination of exotic colors. These 2-quart pitchers with inverted thumbprints presented still another difficulty: size. Only a few glassblowers are able to control shape, design and decoration in pitchers this large. As the Hofbauer family says, anyone can make a small pitcher.

The inverted thumbprints also created a special problem. They were made by blowing a parison into a small wooden block and the soft glass was then put into a 2-part paste mold (made up the night before from a special glue sprinkled with a fine powder) having an inverted thumbprint. Then the pitcher was inserted into the glory-hole for reheating and next was coated with a glaze of the same color and expanded. The result was a smooth, fire-polished exterior and a thumbprint that created fascinating optical lights and shadows. The Hofbauers and other glassworkers trained on the Continent speak of this method of using paste molds and fire-polishing as the German or European system. Most of the European workers of Hofbauer's time were distressed by what they called the American system: iron molds and an absence of fire-polishing. The latter process indubitably creates a brilliance and sparkle.

Hofbauer's glassworkers also created under his supervision 2-quart thumbprint pitchers of fire red with a crimped mouth and a clear, claw handle. Even the red glass brought additional problems, for if left too long in the glory hole, the red turns amber. Such amberina glass, though popular, is known as a glassmaker's mistake. The desideratum for Hofbauer was a true red pitcher, which he produced in numbers. Hofbauer's daughter states that his Vineland factory also made cased glass.

When his Vineland plant closed down Hofbauer had planned for retirement but in 1960 after his wife and second son died, he accepted an invitation from the Colombian government to build a glassworks in Bogota and to teach glassmaking there. On his return to the States he went to work for the Kessler Glass Works at Bethpage, L.I., where he devised special formulas for lamp bases.

In the last two years before he died Hofbauer, assisted by William Valla of Vineland, who 36 years earlier had been an apprentice in Hofbauer's plant, was making pitchers of opaque white and colored glass swirled in the early South Jersey style. Though the metal at the South Jersey Bog Glass Works was more difficult to work than that which Hofbauer had been accustomed to using, the two men usually completed a pitcher in the amazing time of 10 minutes. The formulas were of Hofbauer's devising also and he produced some unique ones, such as a butterscotch or *café au lait* opaque. For the blowing here he carved his own block-molds of cherry wood.

Where many glassworkers were careless of their health, Hofbauer for years had had his self-imposed physical fitness program. He was a great walker; besides putting in a strenuous day as a blower he would often walk 10 miles. He used to spend considerable sums for medicinal herbs, some of which came from as far away as Czechoslovakia, said his daughter. Most of these packets he gave away to friends with good wishes for their health. To see him as he manipulated fiery glass at the age of 86 one almost had to believe in his medicaments.

Fig. 221 LILYPAD (1968) pitcher and swirled pitcher by Adolph Macho. Both of seagreen bubbly glass, applied handles. White swirls in pitcher at LEFT; maroon threading on pitcher with lilypad swags. Thick walls and leaden weight easily differentiate these from early South Jersey pitchers. Max. H. 8½ inches.

Fig. 224 HOFBAUER'S VIN LAND plant in operation for years. August Hofbauer hims SECOND FROM RIGHT; TO HIS RIG Adolph Macho, Sr., a Czech blow now living in Vineland.

Rubi glass	P.
Sand	1000.
Read Led	100
Pottashe	200
Soda	180
Lime	100
Phocpee Saacee Rolk	10
Klimslein	10.
Berat	10
Kupfer oxidul	10
Zinoxidul	06
	626

Fig. 222 RUBY GLASS, since Syrian times a difficult formula, this one from the intimate notes of August Hofbauer, a true Jersey glass gaffer, whose competitors and friends alike described him as phenomenally expert in glass formulas. He had no need to write them down, and seldom did.

Fig. 223 MADE IN 1967. Creamer and sugar blown in old style at Hammonton but not likely to be confused with rare early ware. Modern white lies on surface like paint; glass seems to sweat, is improperly annealed, cracks easily. Pitcher, 4 inches high.

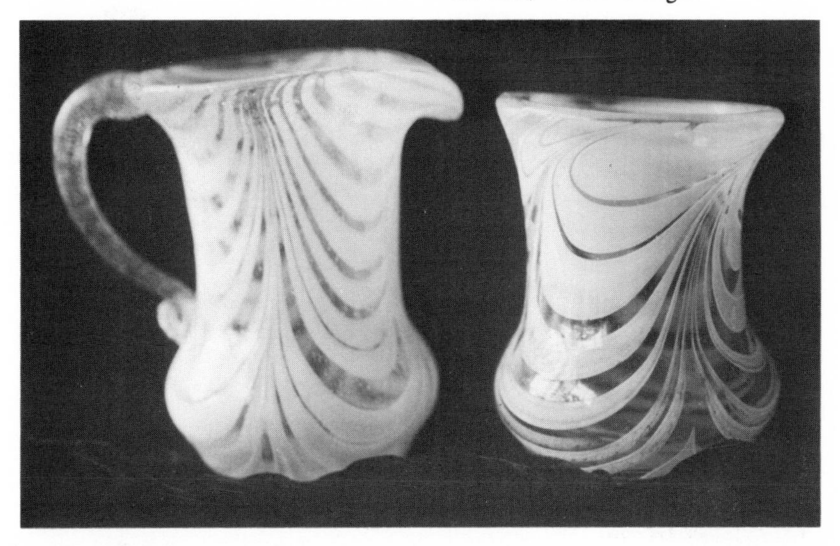

Doerr Glass Company, Inc. *Vineland, 1916 –*

In 1916 when The Machine had already put scores of unmechanized glassworks out of business, Herman Doerr had the courage to incorporate a firm in Vineland which produced handblown ware for use in research laboratories. Since then the automated factories in "the glass triangle"—Vineland, Millville and Bridgeton—have become giants of immense stature, yet Doerr handblown scientific glass continues in steady demand because the blowers are deft in shaping glass to an even thinness, so essential for accurate measure.

Over a 15-year period the plant added its own engraving and grinding shops, which are still maintained. In 1930 Herman Doerr died and was succeeded as president by his son Albert J. Doerr. Then in 1932 a brother, Paul, became chief executive officer.

With the financial pressures of the 1930s depression, the Doerrs tried importing blanks from abroad but found them unreliable. It was then decided to build a modernized furnace for handblowing, with all operations under one roof. Private-mold work was accepted and handblown glass tubing was also made. In 1936 Francis O. Doerr became head of the firm, and a few years later the officers were Francis O. Doerr, Francis J. Doerr and Leo D. Doerr, a father and two sons.

Doerr has a history of employing noted gaffers who have demonstrated their proficiency in creating art glass. For example, Emil J. Larson who had been chief blower and finisher for the Durand fancy shop was foreman at Doerr. The late Angelo Ponzetto who made the fish in opposite and Plate 15 was a blower here. Woodruff Harris who assisted John Ruhlander in making the 16-part liqueur bottle in Fig. 196 is now employed making his specialty, pedestals and feet, for glass graduates and other ware. William Valla, a young man compared with veterans like Woody Harris and Ponzetto, is rated as one of the best of today's blowers and was assisting August Hofbauer at the Jersey Bog Glass Works in 1967. James Vetter, superintendent of the Doerr Glass Company, who has been with the firm for 35 years, enjoys the satisfaction that the oldtime blowers derive from renewing their skills. Among those now deceased, three Swedish blowers, Gus Olson, George Johnson and Ernest Lofgren, are recalled by Vetter as outstanding.

During World War II when metal was unobtainable for luxury use, Doerr designed lamp fonts and bases of glass to supplant brass and other metal. Pencil sketches for molds show the fonts to be mainly pear-shaped and acorn designs, with some amphoras, others with baluster stems. Most of the fonts were sold to New York firms such as the Elite Glass Company, Cut-Rite, Coletta, and the Enterprise Company, who then cut the glass and assembled the lamps.

A Vineland dealer, Evelyn Procaccino, bought pear-shaped fonts in quantity, had them ruby-flashed and then hand cut with grape or rose patterns. The resulting assembled lamps must have been easily mistaken for products of the Sandwich factory.

Fig. 225 JERSEY FISH by gaffer Angelo Ponzetto, Vineland, is clear glass with red air bubbles. About 1920 Ponzetto came from the glass-blowing center on the island of Murano, Italy. H. 6¼ inches.

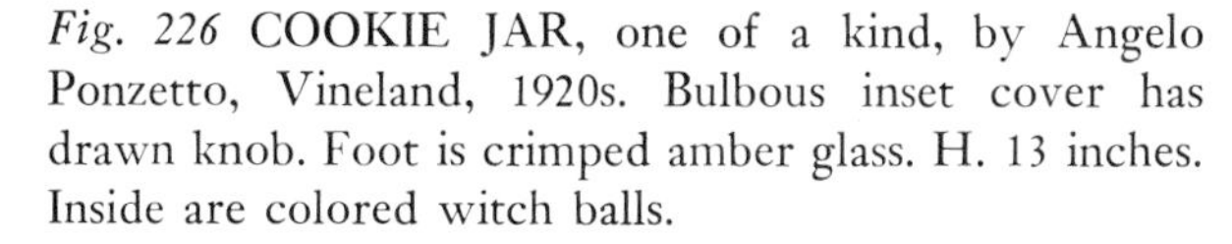

Fig. 226 COOKIE JAR, one of a kind, by Angelo Ponzetto, Vineland, 1920s. Bulbous inset cover has drawn knob. Foot is crimped amber glass. H. 13 inches. Inside are colored witch balls.

A dramatic phase of glassmaking that no one appears to have recorded on film was fairly routine at Doerr Glass, as it was at the Kimble Glass Company, among others. This was the making of narrow-gauge glass tubing. A sample still on hand is a tube only ½ inch in diameter with lengthwise vertical ridges.

The method, as described by James Vetter, was this. A gatherer blew the glass into an iron mold from which the molten glass was extruded in the proper diameter. An assistant then quickly attached the end of the short glass tube to a punty iron (a 4-inch disk with a handle). Then in a sort of fast Peabody one-step the man ran backwards for about 75 feet, all the while stretching out the tube of hot glass so skilfully that it never lost diameter or shape, or even ridges. A helper ran alongside with a fan to cool the glass. When the odd race was run the glass rope was laid on a wooden ladder extending the full distance.

The procedure was considered so hazardous that if a bystander even pretended to trip the racer, it was regarded as just cause for firing the practical-joker.

Epilogue.—As the Doerr furnaces cooled in the warm months of 1970, a message was written in letters of fire: there would not be enough proficient blowers to carry on for the autumn blast. Doerr Glass will maintain its 55-year-old tradition for handmade laboratory ware but these precision beakers, flasks, graduates and pipettes will no longer be blown at the Vineland plant.

Aventurine at Janvier

WHEN FRED OLSON was 12 years old his father died, leaving him as eldest of seven other children and his mother living on a farm at Janvier. Today, at 76 and doing vigorous farm work, Fred Olson recalls the Walsh Brothers glassworks at Janvier, a place not listed on modern road maps but still a viable hamlet near Franklinville on route 538.

This Janvier glassworks was exceptional because in 1901 it was producing a type of Aventurine glass for which the Walsh brothers obtained a patent in 1899. A news feature in 1901 *(Industrial Directory of New Jersey)* gives the impression that only Janvier was making this spangled glass. As collectors of art glass are well aware, Aventurine glass originated with the early Venetians who created a glass flecked with gold.

American 19th-century variations of Aventurine have a bronze or copper tone, and copper was the look achieved by the Walsh brothers, with a product called Goldstone. Fostoria Glass Company of Moundsville, West Virginia, and the Tiffany furnaces when in charge of Arthur J. Nash produced art glass of green Aventurine, with an overall metallic sparkle. Union Glass Company of Somerville, Mass., also made a black glass bespangled with metal, in art forms.

Janvier spangled glass differed from all of these in that it was made in thick sheets to resemble onyx, for table tops, lamp bases, jewel boxes, clocks, and jewelry such as brooches and cuff links. All polished fragments I have seen vary. The base is a caramel-colored opaque glass with swirls of copper-colored spangles. Some pieces also have swirls of opaque chartreuse glass. The look is definitely that of a mineral rather than glass.

Fred Olson comes back into the scene at this point. His first job at age 12 was delivering mail for the Walshes, who also managed the Janvier post office. Pay was one cent for delivering first class mail, no cents for delivering any other class. (It must have been then that Fred decided to make farming his life work.)

"Even as a boy," he said, "I wanted a piece of glass that the Walshes made. A bureau top, it was about a yard long and about 18 inches wide, full of gold spangles."

Did Walsh Brothers blowers make art glass shapes from their Aventurine? If so, none has been identified, but the firm was also blowing blue and green hollow ware, as proved by numerous fragments found by later farmers of the land.

Walsh Brothers are believed to have been in business from about 1897 to 1910. When the furnace went out of blast the remaining stock of Aventurine, reports Fred Olson, was bought by a Clayton resident named Laird who made the sparkling slabs into jewelry.

Edward B. Simkins, grandson of Edward Walsh, supplies new information, from diaries of the founder of Janvier Glass Works. The first mention of a functioning glasshouse appears to be a note of Nov. 5, 1890, and on Nov. 19, 1898 Edward Walsh writes of a new factory, indicating a prior one. Although Edward and his half-brother Sidney were widely known for their unusual glass in the intervening years, letters of 1907 show that Edward was then bargaining to sell the works to an Alabama business man, a sale not consummated, for the furnace later was shut down, possibly about 1910.

A significant fact revealed by Mr. Simkins is that Edward Walsh was born in Birmingham, England, and that his father before him was a glassmaker. As the English were among the first, after the Venetians, to make spangled glass, the Walshes' background helps to account for their success in producing Aventurine.

That Edward Walsh and his half-brother Sidney were continually experimenting with their glass is disclosed in the diaries, and Sidney's house, still standing, apparently was used as their research laboratory. One of the "finds" is part of a small clay crucible or "monkey pot," with colored glass adhering to it. Most interesting of all is a tin box containing small rectangular slices, as if cut from a cane of opaque colored glass. The range of colors is remarkable: sky blue, cobalt, ashes of roses, russet, chartreuse, opalescent light green, butterscotch, pale yellow. Mr. Simkins owns a rich-looking slab of Aventurine, about a foot square and an inch thick, which has no extra color added to its warm bronze background but has gold flecks swirled on in a fan-like pattern, a concept that suggests a table-top in a setting by Louis Comfort Tiffany.

That Aventurine was highly regarded in its day seems evident from a verse sent by an admirer to Edward Walsh:

A cluster of stars in a cloister of stone,
A piece of the paving encircling the throne,
It slipped thro' the portals of heaven unseen,
It is by us mortals called Aventurine.

Fig. 227 MAP OF JANVIER *designed by Edward Walsh,* founder of the Janvier Glass Works in what is now a forgotten town. *Courtesy of Edward B. Simkins.*

Hard Times for Elmer

EVEN MOST old-timers in South Jersey seem not to know about glassworks in the little town of Elmer, but there were three different plants, two of which had a succession of owners.

The first, the Elmer Window Light Company, was erected about 1895 at Park Avenue and Center Street, as a co-operative venture: the town of Elmer built the 8-pot furnace for a stock company of blowers, but officials of Bridgeton's Clark Window Glass Company appear to have purchased the output, as if from a subsidiary. Despite this excellent backing, the firm was sold at sheriff's sale in 1898 to Butcher & Waddington who continued as window-light makers until 1893 when the business ended and Butcher removed his share of equipment to run a similar furnace in Malaga.

For a brief time after 1895 the Elmer works became a bottle furnace, owned by an individual named Deijo who soon found it unprofitable. Then Gibson & Elmer started blowing battery jars which also failed to furnish a livelihood.

Some time after 1900 more Bridgetonians took over the Elmer furnace, men from Shoemakers', Jonas and More, and Parker Brothers. Their firm was called the Novelty Glass Company, a name with exciting connotations for collectors, but what those novelties were is a mystery today.

Earlier, about 1896, Elmer's second glassworks was built by Samuel Bassett of the Cumberland Glass Works in Bridgeton. Located on land now in Elmer's community park, this bottle furnace was known as the upper factory and is the one shown in the adjoining illustration.

After about two years Samuel Bassett moved on to the glassworks in Fairton, and his Elmer works was bought by the Gilchrist Jar Company for the purpose of making battery jars, a project that lasted only until about 1901.

The Novelty Glass Company, simultaneously with their ownership of the first Elmer glasshouse, then bought the upper factory, not to make novelty glass but fruit jars. Unfortunately, the officers bought second-hand molds and did not bother to inquire if they were patented. Owners of the original patent learned of the jars being blown at Elmer, brought suit and won with a settlement that put the company out of business. Last of the ill-fated owners was Isaac Townsend who closed the works about 1908 after a year's work.

The third glassworks, a small one, was set up in the early 1920s in a shoe factory on Elmer Street which had once been the town's largest industry but was partially burned out in 1915. Owned by Powell & Volkaier, this venture failed in 1925, the last of glassmaking in Elmer.

Fig. 228 GOLDEN OLIVE-AMBER wine glass has clear applied stem and foot, with teardrop entrapped in knob. Of heavy soda-lime glass shaped with precision. H. 4¼ inches.

Fig. 229 ELMER GLASS WORKS, built about 1896 by Samuel Bassett of Bridgeton, had several owners making mostly bottles and battery jars, closed 1909. Site is present community park of Elmer. *Photo courtesy of Jesse Ford.*

Swedesboro Glass Works on Raccoon Creek

When a group of eleven glassmakers from Royer's Ford, Pa., arrived in Swedesboro in 1896 to blow glass containers they evidently thought the year had historic significance, for they had themselves, many with long beards, photographed in front of the buildings, which were erected by persons now unknown and had been idle for a couple of years.

The hunch of this group of co-operative blowers, each of whom put $1,850 into the one-pot furnace, proved right, for the project continued, with various personnel changes, to World War I. In 1909 the factory employed 215 persons. Though times were occasionally difficult, as for instance about 1900 when the salesman fell ill and a New Yorker named Birdhoff took over that job and closed out some of the blowers, the co-operative obtained many orders in a period when a number of Jersey works were closed by strikes.

Adam Frederick, founder of the co-op, was so incensed by the high prices charged in the company store at Royer's Ford, Pa., that he quit and vowed he would never again be in hock in this manner. It might be assumed that Adam and his brother Anton, a co-founder, were Pennsylvanians but Adam's son Merritt tells me that the family are native Jerseyans, as were others in the group.

Adam learned his trade at the Whitney works in Glassboro, where he and a friend, though continuing to be classed as apprentices, ran away to Philadelphia and found jobs as journeyman blowers. The Whitney works reported the youths to the glassblowers' union and they were returned. But it wasn't long before the boys ran away again and from then on obtained work as the proficient blowers they were.

Among other blowers in the founding co-op were Frederick and Edward Andorfer and their father Charles (not a blower), also Jerseyans; Abraham Fry, Edward and Rick Dilks of Jersey glassblowing families, Louis and Frederick Weber, and Peter Hildebrand, brother-in-law of the Fredericks. Jack Ware was a blower who arrived in 1898. Batchmaker was Adam's father-in-law, bearded John Long who with his family had once lived at the Batsto Glass Works. Grandson Merritt recalls hearing that their Batsto house was so cold one day that a pot of coffee froze on the stove.

Listed in *The Industrial History of New Jersey* of 1909 as the South Jersey Glass Works, the Swedesboro furnaces was located in a triangle bounded by Broad and Glass streets and Raccoon creek, an area now covered by the Del Monte cannery which in its early days utilized some of the glasshouse buildings. Many tenant houses still remain on nearby streets.

Among known containers blown at Swedesboro were soda and beer bottles, pyramid inks, Castoria bottles, Rumford's baking powder holders, and a quart whiskey bottle. A standard article was a bottle with a twisted neck, blown by Adam Frederick. A 52-ounce carboy was so heavy that it had to have air fed into it to keep it from collapsing.

The kind of glass blown at Swedesboro is displayed in a glass chain with links of green, amber, clear and a light sapphire blue. That the co-op owners had time and style for creative blowing is clearly evident from some existing whimsies, such as a splendid cane in deep amber with three narrow spirals of opaque white. Another unusual walking-stick made by the same blower, at the Woodbury Bottle Works, is lobster red with aqua stripes. A miniature derby hat is also among the objects fashioned by this blower. The craftsmanship displayed certainly must have gone into the making of pitchers and vases as well.

Fig. 230 MADE IN NEW JERSEY. Footed bowl of gold-ruby with clear crystal tooled stem; late 19th century; 6½ inches. Light blue pitcher, rough pontil, curled handle, 3¾ inches. Purplish cobalt pitcher, pattern molded, folded rim, crimped handle, soda-lime glass; 4 inches.

Others Known for Good Glassmaking

FAIRTON GLASS WORKS

Some novelties of Fairton Glass Works may bring a twinge of nostalgia to collectors who recall the objects from childhood: replicas of roast turkeys and hams, which held candies. At first glance these might be mistaken for pressed glass, but they are definitely mold-blown, with metal caps added to the threaded necks. A turkey and a ham in clear glass were blown at Fairton in 1893 by the grandfather of Mrs. Kenneth Ayars and given to his wife when he was courting her. Clam-shaped bottles were also mold-blown in South Jersey but it is not known if these too were commercial articles at Fairton.

Rumford baking powder containers in aqua glass were made here as at various other factories. Embossed with the word RUMFORD and only about four inches high, these round bottles were a favorite with housewives who saved them for nursing bottles.

Square amber bottles for snuff were another staple at Fairton as were aqua inks. Bottles for mineral and soda water and for beer were made in quantity; it seems likely that the beer bottle embossed FAIRTON, N.J. and the name C.E.D. SEILER was made in the town, though such impressing is not positive proof.

Known as Willis-More Glass Company, the firm was organized in 1892 by Furman R. Willis and Azariah More, the latter a son of Robert More, a founder of the large and successful glass plant of More, Jonas & More of Bridgeton. Philip Stathem was president and Azariah More was superintendent as well as secretary of the Fairton factory which shipped glass not only to New York and Boston but as far afield as St. Louis and Salt Lake City. It is reasonable to assume that some of the articles blown were similar to the Bridgeton related company. In 1896 the Fairton group was re-organized and incorporated as the Jefferis Glass Works with an office in Philadelphia. Azariah More, who had learned his trade as a practical glassblower in Bridgeton, continued as manager, in association with Samuel D. Beckett. Glassblowing continued until about 1905.

Fig. 231 Fairton Glass Works, late 19th century. *Courtesy of Kenneth Ayars.*

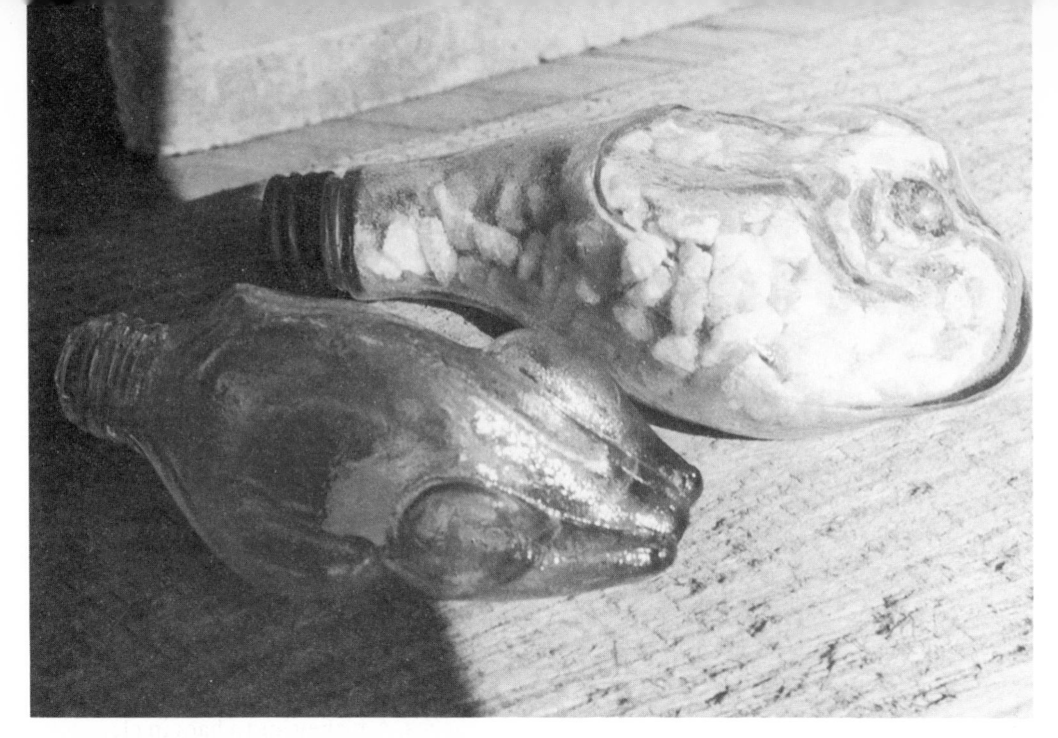

Fig. 232 NOVELTY BOTTLES, BLOWN in a mold at Fairton Glass Works, held penny candies. The roast turkey bottle and the ham were blown in 1893 by the grandfather of Mrs. Kenneth Ayars. Appr. 5 inches long. *Collection of Kenneth Ayars.*

At one period Fairton works had three furnaces, for amber, green and clear glass and kept two shifts of men busy. Locale of the glasshouse is the picturesque town of Fairton along the Cohansey river, about four miles due south of Bridgeton. The actual site is just off Main Street, down Elmer Lane, and is now private property where digging is prohibited.

GLASSMAKING AT BARNEGAT

A reporter for the Mt. Holly *Herald* prophesied in the issue of May 13, 1893: "The glass works at Barnegat will probably be able to declare a dividend now, as it is proposed to manufacture Pocket Bottles for Ocean Grove and other temperance resorts."

No information is available on the dividend or the design of these ½-pint pocket flasks, but the firm evidently was prospering, for on Nov. 15, 1897 it was incorporated with a capital of $50,000 as the Atlantic Coast Glass Company. Incorporators were Thomas E. Ludlam, Nelson G. Douglas and John B. Getsinger, who issued 2,000 shares of preferred stock and 3,000 of common, each with a par value of $10. The building, constructed by Benjamin P. Chadwick, was in those days a pot type factory with fieldstone tunnels under the furnace to provide draft.

That there were three succeeding glassworks at Barnegat is the information supplied by J. Horace Sprague, Jr., who was formerly a gatherer at the last one.

The name became the Barnegat Glass Company on Aug. 12, 1907, when that firm was incorporated and capitalized at $100,000 with shares of $50 par value. The organizers were Edward D. Cronin, Fred Knowlton and Edgar A. Monfort. In *The Industrial History of New Jersey* for 1909 Barnegat Glass Company was listed as making glass vials. One medicine bottle is known to have been embossed E. W. CHEW / BARNEGAT N J.

Some time after 1908 a group of blowers took over the factory, with the new name of the Co-operative Glass Company and continued making anything in the shape of green-glass bottles, from ½-ounce to five-gallon sizes. At this period the furnace was fired by a mixture of compressed air and fuel oil.

In 1908 the Barnegat works had a day and night shift, as witness this lively report from the Tuckerton *Beacon* of Nov. 19, 1908:

> Ed Moore and two similar characters nearly turned the village of Barnegat upside down Thursday night. They took possession of the Barnegat Glass Works and frightened the men on the night shift out of their wits, roused the whole town, and wound up the night in a trip to Toms River where they are safely housed in the county jail. [Ed Moore was described as an umbrella mender.]

The only glass furnace known to have existed in this Atlantic coastal region, close to famed Barnegat lighthouse, Barnegat's works ceased operations in the summer of 1913.

MAGNOLIA GLASS WORKS

All but forgotten, the site of this window-glass house was found through the help of Mayor Hanson of Somerdale and the police department of Magnolia. On the boundary line between these two towns, the furnace was located on Atlantic Avenue where the present pumping station is in Somerdale.During the 1930s local people found large amounts of slag and cullet in the triangle bounded by Atlantic Avenue and Warrick Road, now a nature trail where digging is prohibited. The Magnolia works is believed to have been built in 1899 and was definitely in blast in 1901. After a few years the works burned down and was not rebuilt.

THEODORE R. RAMP

In 1970 Theodore R. Ramp of Egg Harbor City was the last of the independent Jersey blowers who owned a working furnace, at his home on Heidelberg Avenue, as distinguished from individuals who were turning out paperweights and lampwork articles in their homes. Having a full time job as a stationary engineer, Ramp for several years has had a limited output of glass because he confined his blowing to weekends in the cooler months from November to June. Despite the fact that he rarely has had a helper and that he performs all stages himself, from mixing the batch to finishing the article, his glass is well-styled, thin-walled and sparkling. As Ramp had been a blower at August Hofbauer's Vineland plant, his style reflects the pleated edges, the optical effects, and the swirled or fluted molds, all of which he himself carves. Also in his repertoire are some early Jersey style pitchers with curled-up handles. His colors are fresh and vivid blues, pale and golden amber, greens, and amethyst and grape. At the age of 63 in 1970, Ramp is one of the younger active gaffers. Learning his trade as a gathering-boy at the Liberty Cut Glass Works in Egg Harbor, he also was a blower in glass factories in West Virginia.

Some Noted Glass Cutting Centers

GERMAN GLASS CUTTERS AT EGG HARBOR CITY

When those progressive glass entrepreneurs, Andrew K. Hay, Samuel Richards and Joseph Porter who were among the leading promoters of the Camden and Atlantic Railroad, exuberantly rode the first train to Atlantic City on July 4, 1854, among the guests were some leading German citizens of Philadelphia. By pre-arrangement the train paused at a spot in the pines called Cedar Bridge so that the Germans could see for themselves the rich potential for timber and farming but most of all what a haven these uninhabited acres would be for thousands of German immigrants who at that time were being persecuted, along with the Irish, by members of the Know-Nothing faction.

The prospect was so pleasing that by December an association had been formed to buy 40,000 acres. Cedar Bridge was renamed Egg Harbor City, an English translation for the Atlantic estuary which the 17th century Dutch called Eyren Haven, "harbor of eggs," when they beheld the salt marshes massed with nesting waterfowl.

Germans came eagerly to buy lots in the new town with broad streets, all named after noted Germans. Other settlers bought 20-acre tracts outside the village and began clearing them for farming. The 100 per cent German haven had a Moravian church by 1859 and soon became known as the "most German town in the country," where no one spoke English. Toward the end of the 19th century a few Negro families moved in and soon they were speaking German without accent.

Shortly after the Civil War the colonists discovered they had as good a wine-growing climate as that along the banks of the Rhine. The Egg Harbor wines were so excellent that they won a prize at the 1876 Centennial in Philadelphia. The most joyful news came in 1878, however, when Egg Harbor upset tradition by winning an award at a wine fair in, of all places, Paris. At that time Egg Harbor City was surrounded by 700 to 800 acres of vineyards. All of the wine produced therefrom created a demand for demijohns, carboys and bottles, supplied by South Jersey glassworks. An old engraving of an Egg Harbor wine cellar with ceiling-high oak casks shows glass demijohns in the foreground.

In the manner of their forefathers, Egg Harbor Germans held several wine-sampling fairs each year, not only the familiar *Oktoberfest* but also a simple *Weinfest,* a *Winzerfest* and a *Weinlesefest.* All of this *gemütlichkeit* required drinking vessels, which Jersey glasshouses were well equipped to produce in quantity. But who shall say which were the Egg Harbor glasses?

Fig. 233 LIBERTY CUT GLASS WORKS (1903-1931) of Egg Harbor were nationally known for glass in brilliant-cut style.

LIBERTY CUT GLASS WORKS

With the advent of the 20th century some citizens of Egg Harbor went into the glass business, both blowing and cutting. Liberty Cut Glass Works became one of the nation's large cutting firms and from 1903 to 1931 gave employment to hundreds of persons. The company's president, Thomas P. Streitemmeyer, announced in January 1904 that after less than a year's operation $35,000 worth of cut glass had been shipped to customers. The firm then had 32 cutters and polishers. Albert C. Stephany and Robert Ohnmeiss, both local residents were secretary and treasurer, respectively.

Arriving on the scene at the height of the Brilliant Period the company, it is local tradition, favored glass with allover deep cutting, on heavy handblown blanks. Despite the fact that Liberty Cut Glass established a lucrative business with outlets in leading jewelry stores and department stores in most major cities, no catalogs are available, although it is known that a wide variety of tableware and ornamental objects was made. Egg Harbor's centennial booklet of 1955 reports that a large order was placed and shipped for Germany's Kaiser Wilhelm.

At the peak of its operations Liberty Cut Glass employed 250 people in their buildings at Atlantic and Buffalo avenues. A souvenir postcard shows one of the structures to have been a massive box of a building, two stories high. From 1905 to 1917 the firm also had showrooms at various addresses in Brooklyn and Manhattan, the last at 200 Fifth Avenue.

Fig. 234 EGG HARBOR WINERY of 1880s. Note wicker-covered glass demijohns, undoubtedly blown in South Jersey glass works.

Fig. 235 PUNCH BOWL SET intricately cut in the Brilliant Style by Louis Iorio in 1905 for the Empire Cut Glass Company. H. 12 inches. *Courtesy, Iorio Cut Glass Company. Photo, Shepherd Studio.*

THE EMPIRE AND THE IORIO GLASS COMPANIES OF FLEMINGTON

The unflagging energy of some of the master craftsmen is personified by expert glass cutter and engraver, Louis Iorio of Flemington. At age 86 he still puts in an 8- to 10-hour day at the cutting frame and continues to create new designs. Where once he cut massive blown blanks in the Brilliant Style, now he fashions frosted intaglio patterns on thin crystal. He is the first of three generations of Iorios who continue to make glass cutting a successful life work.

The story of Louis Iorio goes back to the beginning of the 20th century and the founding of the Empire Cut Glass Company at Flemington. In the early 1900s Henry Clay

Fry quickly became noted for the high lead content and exquisite clarity of handblown blanks made at his factory in Rochester, Pa. The story is verified that glass bell-ringers of vaudeville used to stop at Rochester to tune up their ware against Fry's "ringing" crystal.

In 1902 Fry was induced to bring an entire cutting and engraving plant to Flemington, along with experienced cutters. The phenomenal quality of Fry crystal and the diamond-like radiance of the Brilliant patterns created a huge demand. At one time the Empire Glass Company employed 178 persons and had some 100 frames in operation. In its last years Empire used pressed blanks, a change encouraged by Col. Fry, and one which ironically contributed to the decline of the firm in 1925. William E. Corcoran had been president throughout the life of the company, and Charles McMullen, formerly with T.G. Hawkes, was vice president.

Shortly after Empire Glass was created, Louis Iorio, born in the Italian province of Salerno in 1884, emigrated with his parents to Flemington. As a youth his first job was handyman at Empire Glass, but not for long. Trying his hand at the cutting frame Louis proved so apt a pupil that he quickly graduated to both cutter and designer. In some of the early Empire catalogs the designs are called simply "Iorio."

When Empire closed Louis Iorio opened his own shop in Flemington. With his son William as business manager, who is also a highly skilled cutter, engraver and designer, they have large displays of their own and imported glass in showrooms and a workshop just west of Flemington circle on Route 202. Here the visitor can watch Louis Iorio perform such amazing feats as free-hand cutting and "picture-engraving" without a pattern. Louis estimates that there are only 150 active glasscutters at work in the United States. His grandson Richard, a University of New Mexico graduate with a major in anthropology, has not only learned the crafts of cutting and engraving but was a practicing glassmaker in the summer of 1969 at the Glassblowing Workshop held in the Hunterdon County Art Center, Clinton.

An excellent museum of glass which covers a span of 3,000 years is another Iorio magnet for collectors. On display are rare Egyptian beads, early Syrian and Roman glass, fine European collectors' items, as well as examples from American glass centers. On exhibit is the massive Empire punch bowl shown in Fig. 235, the brilliance of which has to be seen to be appreciated.

SKINNER CUT GLASS IN HAMMONTON

"My family has a 350-year history as stone-cutters, engravers and glass cutters," Thomas Skinner, Sr., owner of a noted Hammonton glass-cutting firm, told me in 1969.

After he had traced the family peregrinations from Hammonton back to the Dorflinger Glass Works at White Mills, Pa., then to the Pairpoint Manufacturing Company of New Bedford, Mass., and across the Atlantic to the great glass centers around Stourbridge, England, I had to agree that Skinners had been master cutters for a long, long time.

First of the Skinner family to seek his fortune in the United States was William, grandfather of the present head of the firm, known as W. Skinner & Son. William Skinner arrived alone from the Stourbridge region and found himself a job with Pairpoint which was producing art glass of such quality that at the Philadelphia Centennial in 1876 the firm received an award for cut flint tableware and prismatic candelabra. William Skinner quickly adapted to this milieu, soon returned to England to bring his family back with him, and by 1877 had been named a master cutter.

A few years later the family moved to the Pocono mountains where the Dorflingers were producing some of the most delicate cut crystal that had ever been made in the United States. At Dorflingers' the Skinners knew well such other virtuoso glassmen as the Barbers and the Larsons. Thomas Skinner's father used to tell of being toted on the shoulders of Ralph Barber after a heavy snowfall in White Mills, Pa. The Skinner youngster and his brother William grew up to be master cutters also, as the family worked at various shops in Pennsylvania, such as Quaker City and Thylocker's.

By July of 1899 the Skinners had taken the plunge and set up a cutting shop of their own in Hammonton. The year 1899 was also the year in which the present owner, Thomas, Sr., was born, not in Hammonton but in New Bedford. The first building of W. Skinner & Son was opposite the present railroad station on Egg Harbor Road, only three blocks east of the present factory built in 1901 at 317 North Egg Harbor Road.

Entering the field when deep, brilliant cutting was done on crystal sometimes so heavy that a housewife could scarcely lift a pitcher, the Skinners were quickly successful, selling punchbowls, decanters, vases, pitchers, stemware, sugar and cream sets, nappies and tankards to such fashionable Philadelphia retailers as Bailey, Banks & Biddle, Caldwell's, and Strawbridge & Clothier.

A catalog shows the patterns to have been variations of the pinwheel design that characterized a peak of the Brilliant Period of American cut glass. The blanks were extraordinarily clear and heavy, described by Mr. Skinner as "triple-X potash."

Most of the cutters were from the Hammonton area which had plenty of talent to draw on as New Jersey had dozens of good cutting shops in the first two decades of the 20th century, although few of that period have been mentioned in current books. At their height of prosperity the Skinners employed about 150 to 160 workers.

With the advent of World War I, the market for costly cut glass declined and besides there was a shortage of skilled cutters. By 1915 the Skinners, to their chagrin, felt it necessary to produce "figure ware," pressed glass which was sharpened by cutters.

Unhappy over this industry-wide down-grading of hand-cut crystal, the Skinners during the Twenties switched to a new field, designing and making black plate-glass desk sets for fountain pen companies like Schaeffer's and Waterman's. The firm also made cut and mirrored picture frames and table plateaus. This diversification was so satisfactory that ever since the firm has stayed in the business of processing plate-glass bases of many kinds.

Today, after 350 years of glass-decorating tradition there are no young Skinners being apprenticed as cutters.

MISKEY AND REYNOLDS
MISKEY-REYNOLDS-ROTHFUS COMPANY
ROTHFUS-NICOLAI COMPANY
FIGUEROA CUT GLASS COMPANY
ENTERPRISE CUT GLASS COMPANY

From 1901 until 1944 Hammonton had still another major glass-cutting operation besides William Skinner & Son. The latter's competition came from a series of firms evolving from that of Miskey and Reynolds who set up a cutting shop in the old water-powered mill built by William Coffin at the foot of Hammonton lake, opposite the present Kessler Memorial Hospital. Although it is difficult to identify glass cut by Miskey and Reynolds they were known for heavy lead glass in Brilliant patterns.

In 1906 Miskey and Reynolds joined with John F. Rothfus, who had been a cutter for Skinner. Then in 1912 Rothfus went into partnership with Henry Nicolai, an arrangement lasting only two years, for in 1914 Rothfus and Charles H. Struck organized the Figueroa Cut Glass Company. Employing about 100 persons, this became one of the leading glass cutting shops of South Jersey, but the 1920s and the decline in demand for heavy cut glass spelled the end, as for so many other shops. Among their patterns were a naturalistic Rose, the Chair Bottom or Harvard cane pattern, and a medallion like that in the Russian cutting. Too many patterns were often combined in one object, and the more attractive articles were those limited to one motif such as the caning squares.

Rothfus in 1926 bought out a small firm, the Enterprise Cut Glass Company, and in the style of the times changed to light weight blanks with shallow cutting, usually realistic floral designs. The cutting shop ran successfully until 1944 when Rothfus died.

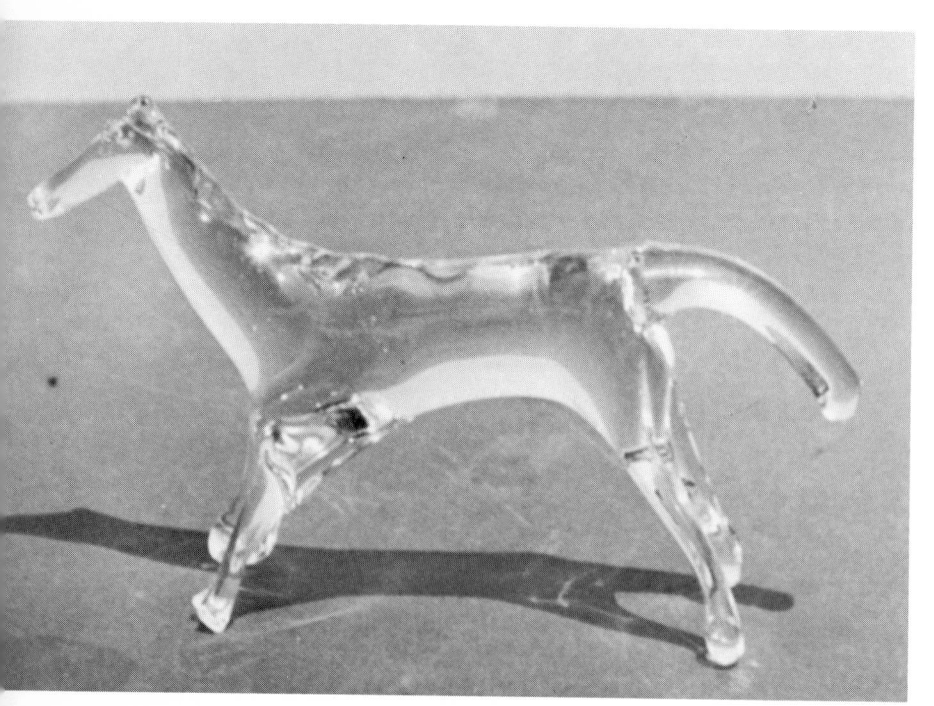

Fig. 236 RACE-HORSE made by Louis Giacomelli.

How to Care for Fine Glass

Calling on a dealer I know I chanced upon an attractive early Jersey glass vase which was marred by a milky deposit inside. "What happened?" The dealer's wife replied, "Oh, I kept flowers in it this summer." Result: a worthless piece, because chemicals in the water had left an irremovable cloud.

Much sadder was the case of a beautiful glass fruit bowl, owned by a collector I know, which had been a presentation piece from royalty to Joseph Pulitzer. The collector's wife put fresh flowers in the bowl and within 12 hours it had split neatly down the middle. A painful lesson: don't put liquids in rare glass.

Some glass is so temperamental that it may crack just in standing too close to another piece. So never stack valuable glass or put pieces touching one another.

Glass may crack merely from being brought quickly from a cold temperature to a warm one, and vice versa. If you have some choice pieces don't let them remain outside in your car on a cold night, then bring them into a heated room or you're likely to find them cracked. Glass needs an even temperature.

Antique glass is in its glory on window shelves. But bearing in mind the hazards of temperature changes, consider also that even sunlight sometimes alters the color of glass. For example, some clear glass may change to pale amethyst. And a window invites damage from wild balls, hailstones, wind and lightning.

Notwithstanding dangers like the above, one of the greatest enemies of glass is dust. Some of the finest collections of glass are owned by men, many of whom dust their own treasures. But some antiques dealers seem to think that the dustier their wares the better the public will like them. Not the informed public, when glass is involved.

If you plan to buy a dusty, cloudy or milky piece of glass, consider carefully whether or not it is cleanable. If not, the value at once goes down. If you feel you must buy a piece of sick or dying glass just as a specimen or as one of a kind, then be sure the price is fully discounted.

Some stains can be removed from bottles, decanters and cruets by soaking overnight in a solution of two or three tablespoons of mild detergent and a cup or two of tepid water. Hot or cold water should never be used on valuable glass. Strong detergents, alkaline soaps, and ammonia should be avoided as cleansers.

Any detergents are death to glass decorated in gold or enamels and may eat away the design in minutes. Keep such glass clean by careful dusting, but if you must wash it, use a soap solution of a very mild soap, such as castile. Dry by blotting, not rubbing.

Some inferior glass has only a surface coating of color, for instance, a certain ruby-red Bohemian ware (but not all). This color can be scratched off by silverware, even by fingernails.

Among the most temperamental glass objects are paperweights. Because they are subject to what may seem to be spontaneous cracking, they require coddling. As they sometimes have unknown internal pressures, it's a sound precaution to keep them packed against vibrations, as well as from sharp temperature changes. Let's say that you have the paperweight of your dreams—a Larson or a Barber rose—and decide to take a photograph of it. You turn on hot floodlights while you focus, and suddenly your dream may explode.

Fig. 237 ROSE-COLORED VASE with delicate green foot and spool stem. Attributed to Whitney, at Alfred B. Maclay sale of 1935. South Jersey flips in deep sapphire blue, also attributed to Whitney. *Maclay sale. Photo by Taylor and Dull.*

Glossary

Annealing: gradual cooling of hot glass in an annealing oven or lehr.

Baluster: a stem with a curved silhouette similar to stone or wooden spokes in a balustrade.

Batch: mixture of raw ingredients ready for melting into glass.

Battledore: wooden paddle used in shaping feet of glass vessels.

Block: wooden dipper used to give preliminary shape to the parison of molten glass.

Blown-molded: glass blown into a mold to give pattern or shape.

Blowpipe (blowing iron): hollow iron tube 2 to 7 feet long, into which the glassmaker blows in order to give expansion to the parison or the gather of glass.

Bottle glass: glass which has neither been decolored or chemically treated to add color; also called green-glass, though the untreated color may not be green; a rather coarse, utility glass with an alkaline base of soda or potash.

Chair: wooden bench with sloping arms on which the gaffer rolls his irons while shaping a glass object.

Charge: to load the melting pot with the batch for making glass.

Cowl board: wooden face-mask which furnace tenders and gatherers formerly wore as protection against heat.

Crimp: flower-like form of metal used to shape the rose or lily in Jersey paperweights.

Crimped: a goffered or pie-crust edge often used on the foot or rim of a vessel.

Crucible: melting pot for glass.

Crutch: a wooden shaper such as a block, but cut away on one side and with a short leg that was hand-held.

Crystal: top quality clear glass, colorless and without defects.

Cullet: broken glass, especially that left after a period of glassblowing; a certain proportion of cullet is essential for proper fusion in firing a new batch.

Dip mold: 1-piece mold open at the top, for impressing a pattern.

Fire polishing: final reheating, usually at the glory hole, of finished glassware so as to remove tool- and mold-marks and give brilliance.

Flint glass: lead glass, made with sand, potash and oxide of lead; the latter produces glass of far greater clarity, brilliance and resonance than does metal made with lime.

Flux: an alkali, such as potash and carbonate of soda, or a metal such as oxide of lead, which are added to the glass batch in order to fuse the sand.

Free-blown glass: that which is formed by blowing and shaping with tools, as opposed to molds.

Gaffer: master blower; head of a shop; sometimes also a term meaning a finisher of glassware.

Gather: the blob of molten glass dipped up from the melting pot with the end of a blowpipe.

Gatherer: blower's assistant who secures the gather of glass on the end of the blowing iron.

Gauffered: goffered or fluted to give a pinched or crimped effect.

Gimmal bottle: a pair of bottles or flasks joined as one but with separate compartments.

Glass pots: hard clay pots set into the furnace, in which the glass batch is melted.

Glory hole: small furnace used for the numerous reheatings needed to keep glass from hardening as it is being shaped; also essential for fire polishing.

Green-glass: common glass, not necessarily green in color but with color neither added nor subtracted; principal base is soda or potash.

Guilloche: A chain-like decoration applied to glass from heavy threads of the metal.

Hand-blown glass: usually refers to all glass made with a blowpipe, as opposed to pressed glass or lamp work; more strictly, glass which is not blown in a mold.

Jockey pot: small melting pot that rides atop the main furnace and is used for small batches; also called a monkey pot.

Knop: a bulbous knob, either solid or hollow, in the stem of a glass object.

Lead glass: made with oxide of lead as the flux, which gives the metal the appearance of natural rock crystal; often called flint glass, though flint has rarely been used in the batch.

Leer (lehr, Ger.): annealing oven for gradual cooling of hot glass to prevent cracking.

Lily-pad decoration: applied in almost free-form style which resembles waves rather than lily pads; believed to have been first introduced by Jersey glassblowers from the German Palatine.

Lime glass: that made with soda and lime as a flux, in a formula discovered in 1864 by William Leighton of Hobbs, Brockunier & Company, Wheeling, West Virginia. Lighter in weight than lead glass, nearly as clear, and much cheaper to make, lime glass produced a great expansion of the industry. Sometimes called flint glass, though containing no flint.

Marver: a polished metal or a stone slab *(marbre,* Fr.) on which the gather of molten glass is rolled into a small cylinder before being blown.

Metal: glass either in its hardened or viscous state, more often the latter.

Melting pot: baked clay pots set within the furnace, in which the glass batch is fused at intense heat.

Mold-blown: glass which is blown, but not pressed, into a mold to give shape and usually a pattern, as in historical flasks.

Monkey pot: small crucible set on top of the main furnace; used for test batches or when small amounts of colors are needed.

Off-hand blown: glass which is blown, not mechanically pressed, sometimes into a dip-mold to give shape and pattern, as in swirled flasks.

Opal glass: opaque white glass with opalescent glints; incorrect term for ordinary opaque white metal.

Parison: a slightly inflated, pear-shaped gather of glass before shaping; also called a blow.

Pattern-molded: glass molded for pattern only, and not for shape, in a part-size piece-mold and then inflated.

Piece mold: hinged iron mold made of two or more pieces, either part- or full-sized.

Pontil, punty or *punty rod*— long iron rod similar to blowpipe but usually not hollow. Used to hold base of an object after release from blowpipe and during finishing.

Pontil mark: scar or indentation left on a finished glass vessel where it has been snapped off the pontil rod; scar is sometimes ground smooth.

Plated glass, cased glass: objects in which one or more layers of glass, often of contrasting colors to be cut away in patterns, are applied over an inner core. In cased glass the extra layer is applied inside.

Pressed glass: pressed manually or by machine into molds and not blown during any stage.

Prunt: a blob of glass or a stamped seal applied to a glass object.

Pucellas or *steel jack:* iron or steel spring-tool like a pincers, for shaping glass after it has been blown.

Quilling: applied ribbons of glass pinched into a series of short prongs or teeth.

Rigaree: narrow ribbons of glass tooled horizontally into parallel ribs.

Servitor: the blower who is first assistant to the gaffer.

Shearer: furnace tender.

Shop: a gaffer and his assistants: a gatherer, a servitor or blower, a carrying-in boy, and any others needed at one working part of a furnace.

Siege: platform in the furnace on which melting pots rest.

Snap case: a device developed about 1850 with arms to hold a glass object during the finishing; attached to the pontil rod, the snap case obviated the pontil scar.

Soda glass: that in which the principal flux is soda; the auxiliary flux is usually carbonate of lime.

Threading: fine threads of glass wound round and round glass vessels either at neck or in all-over design.

White glass: transparent colorless glass.

Selected Bibliography

Barber, Edwin Atlee, *American Glassware.* Phila., 1900.

Barber, John W., and Howe, Henry, *Historical Collections of the State of New Jersey.* S. Tuttle, New York, 1844 and 1868.

———, *Historical Collections of the State of Pennsylvania.* G. W. Gorton, Phila., 1843.

Barrett, Clark S., and Scull, Kenneth N., *Tall Pines at Catawba.* Laureate Press, Inc. Egg Harbor, N.J., 1968.

Biographical Review of Leading Citizens of Cumberland County, New Jersey, Boston, Mass., 1896.

Bishop, J. Leander, *A History of American Manufacturers.* Phila., 1861.

Boire, Harold A., Redford, Rare American Glass. *Antiques,* Aug. 1955.

Bole, Robert D., and Walton, Edward H., Jr., *The Glassboro Story, 1779 to 1964.* Maple Press Co., York, Pa., 1964.

Brothers, J. Stanley, Jr., How Glass Paperweights Are Made, *Antiques,* Aug. 1937.

Boyer, Charles S., (with Stephen Van Rensselaer), History of South Jersey Glass Works, *Annals of Camden,* 1926, vol. 5.

Buechner, Thomas S., Origins of American Glass. *Antiques,* Dec. 1955.

Chalmers, Kathryn, *Down The Long-a-Coming.* Moorestown News Chronicle, 1951.

Cloak, Evelyn Campbell, *Glass Paperweights of the Bergstrom Art Center.* Crown Publishers, Inc., New York, 1969.

Crompton, Sidney, *English Glass.* Ward Lock & Co. Ltd., London 1967.

Cummins, George W., *History of Warren County, N.J.* Lewis Historical Publishing Co., New York, 1911.

Cunz, Dieter, *Egg Harbor City: New Germany in New Jersey.* Proc. New Jersey Historical Society, 1955, vol. 73, p. 89.

Cushing, Thomas, and Sheppard, Charles. *History of the Counties of Gloucester, Salem and Cumberland, New Jersey.* Everts & Peck, Phila., 1883.

Daniel, Dorothy, *Cut and Engraved Glass 1771-1905.* M. Barrows & Co., Inc., New York, 1966.

Davids, Richard Wistar, *The Wistar Family.* Phila. 1896.

Davidson, Marshall, *Early American Glass.* Metropolitan Museum of Art, N.Y., 1946.

Davis, Pearce, *The Development of the American Glass Industry.* Harvard University Press, Cambridge, Mass., 1949.

Drinker, Elizabeth. *Extracts from the Journal of Elizabeth Drinker, 1759 to 1807.*, ed. by Henry D. Biddle. J.B. Lippincott Co., Phila., 1889.

Dyott, T.W., M.D., *An Exposition of the System of Moral and Mental Labor established at the Glass Factory of Dyottville in the County of Philadelphia.* Philadelphia, 1833.

Elmer, Lucius Q. C., *History of the Early Settlement and Progress of Cumberland County, New Jersey.* George F. Nixon, Bridgeton, N.J. 1869.

Elville, E. M., *English and Irish Glass 1790-1950,* Country Life, Ltd., London, 1955.

Farber, Samuel, Durand Glass, *The Antiques Journal,* Aug. 1960.

Feld, Stuart P., *Nature in Her Most Seductive Aspects.* Bull. Metropolitan Museum of Art. Nov. 1962.

Fowle, Arthur E., *Flat Glass.* Libbey Owens Sheet Glass Co., Toledo, Ohio, 1924.

Garrison, Winton C. *The Industrial History of New Jersey,* Bureau of Statistics, State of New Jersey, Trenton, 1909.

Gillingham, Harrold E.; *Pottery, China and Glass Making in Philadelphia.* Pennsylvania Mag. of Hist. and Biog. 1930, 54:97.

Gordon, Thomas F., *Gazetteer of New Jersey,* Daniel Fenton, Trenton, N.J., 1834.

Grover, Ray and Lee: *Art Glass Nouveau,* Charles E. Tuttle Co., Inc. Rutland, Vt., 1967.

Harrington, J.C., *Glassmaking at Jamestown.* Dietz Press, Richmond, Va., 1952.

Heston, Alfred M., *Absegami: Annals of Eyren Haven and Atlantic City, 1609 to 1904.* Camden N.J. 1904.

———, ed., *South Jersey: A History, 1664-1924.* Lewis Publishing Co., New York, 1924.

Hone, Philip, The Diary of; edit. Bayard Tuckerman. Dodd, Mead and Company, New York, 1889.

Hunter, Frederick William, *Stiegel Glass.* Dover Publications, New York, 1950.

The Industries of New Jersey, part 2. Historical Publishing Co. Newark, N.J. 1882.

International Commission on Glass, Committee B. *Newsletters,* May 1968 and Aug. 1969; ed. Paul N. Perrot. Corning Museum of Glass.

Johnson, Amandus, *The Journal and Biography of Nicholas Collin: 1746-1831.* New Jersey Society of Pennsylvania, Phila., 1936.

Knittle, Rhea Mansfield, *Early American Glass.* Garden City Publishing Co., Garden City, N.Y., reprint ed. 1948.

Knittle, Walter A. *Early Eighteenth Century Palatine Emigration.* Phila., 1937.

Koch, Robert, *Louis C. Tiffany—Rebel in Glass.* Crown Publishers, Inc., N.Y. 1964.

Kramer, LeRoy, *Johann Baltasar Kramer, Pioneer American Glassblower.* Privately printed 1939.

Lagerberg, T.C. and Viola. *Emil J. Larson and Durand Glass.* New Port Richey, Fla., 1967.

Lee, Francis Bazley, *New Jersey as a Colony and as a State.* 4 vols. Publishing Society of New Jersey, N.Y., 1903.

Lee, Ruth Webb, *Antique Fakes and Reproductions.* Ferris Printing Co., N.Y. 1938.

———, Ralph Barber and the Millville Rose Paperweight. *American Collector,* April 1938. 7:8-9.

———, Counterfeit Bottles. *American Collector,* Sept. 1939, 8:15.

———, The Newest South Jersey Glass. *American Collector,* June 1939, 8:15.

Maxwell, Florence, Wistarberg, Yesterday and Today, *Antiques,* Sept. 1951.

McKearin, George S. and Helen, *American Glass.* Crown Publishers, Inc., New York, 1959 (13th printing).

———, *Two Hundred Years of American Blown Glass.* Crown Publishers, Inc., New York, 1958 (9th printing).

———, Helen, *American Historical Flasks.* Corning Museum of Glass, Corning, N.Y. 1953.

McMahon, William. *The Story of Hammonton.* Laureate Press, Inc. Egg Harbor, N.J. 1966.

Melvin, Jean S., *American Glass Paperweights and Their Makers.* Thomas Nelson & Sons, Camden, N.J., 1967.

Minns, Edward W., Paperweight Making as Done at Millville, *American Collector,* Nov. and Dec. 1938.

Minton, Lee W., *Flame and Heart,* A History of the Glass Bottle Blowers Association. Merkle Press, Inc. 1961.

Myers, Albert Cook, ed., *Sally Wister's Journal,* 1777-1778. Ferris & Leach, Philadelphia, 1902.

Nichols, I.N., *The City of Bridgeton, N.J.* Burk & McFetridge, Phila. 1889.

Odenwelder, Asher J. Jr., *The Collector's Art, A and Z.* vol. 26. Kutztown Publishing Co., Kutztown, Pa., 1948.

Ormsbee, Thomas H., Solomon H. Stanger, Glassboro Bottlemaker, *American Collector,* May 16, 1935.

———, Marked and Lacy Sandwich Salt Dishes, *American Collector,* Aug. 1939.

Parker, Robert Allerton, *A Family of Friends: The Story of the Transatlantic Smiths.* Museum Press, London, 1960. Random House ed. 1959.

Pellatt, Apsley, *Curiosities of Glass Making.* London, 1849.

Perrot, Paul N., *A Decade of Glass Collecting. Selections from the Melvin Billups Collection.* Corning Museum of Glass, Corning, N.Y. 1962.

Pierce, Arthur D., *Smugglers' Woods.* Rutgers University Press, New Brunswick, N.J.

Prowell, George R., *History of Camden County, N.J.*, L.J. Richards & Co., Phila., 1886.

Revi, Albert Christian, *American Art Nouveau Glass,* Thomas Nelson & Sons, Camden, N.J., 1968.

———, *Nineteenth Century Glass,* Thomas Nelson & Sons, Camden, N.J., 1959.

———, Ferroline, *Spinning Wheel,* Nov. 1967.

Rose, James, American Blown Glass in the Seigfred Collection. *Antiques,* June 1967.

Rupp, I. Daniel, *A Collection of Thirty Thousand Names (German, Swiss, Dutch, French and Other Immigrants to Pennsylvania) From 1727 to 1776.* Leary, Stuart & Co., Phila., 1898.

Sandburg, Carl, *In Reckless Ecstasy,* Asgaard Press, Galesburg, Ill. 1904.

Savage, George, *Glass, Pleasures and Treasures.* G. P. Putnam's Sons, N.Y., 1965.

Sinnott, Mary Elizabeth, *Annals of the Sinnott, Rogers, Reeves, Bodine and Allied Families.* J. B. Lippincott Co., Phila. 1905.

Snell, James P., *History of Sussex and Warren Counties, New Jersey.* Everts & Peck, Phila. 1881.

Stewart, Frank H., excerpts from the *Journal of Samuel Huffsey.* 1930 Yearbook, New Jersey Society of Pennsylvania.

———, *Notes on Old Gloucester County, New Jersey.* 3 vols. New Jersey Society of Pennsylvania, Camden, N.J. 1917.

Torgerson, Dorothy, and Tozour, Rachel. *Cape May County Magazine of History and Genealogy,* vol. 5, p. 239, June 1960.

Toulouse, Julian Harrison. *Fruit Jars,* Thomas Nelson & Sons, Camden, N.J., and Everybodys Press, Hanover, Pa., 1969.

Van Rensselaer, Stephen, *Early American Bottles and Flasks,* Peterborough, N.H. Revised ed. 1926.

Wakefield, Hugh, *Nineteenth Century British Glass.* Thomas Yoseloff, N.Y., 1961.

Watson, Richard, *Bitters Bottles,* Thomas Nelson & Sons, N.Y., 1965.

White, Harry Hall, Migrations of Early Glassworkers, *Antiques,* Aug. 1937.

———, New York State Glasshouses, *Antiques,* Sept. and Nov. 1929; July and Sept. 1930.

Wilbur, H. W. and Hand, W. B., *Illustrated History of the Town of Hammonton.* The Mirror Steam Printing House, Hammonton, N.J. 1889.

Wilson, Kenneth M., Gloucester Glass Works, *Journal of Glass Studies,* 1968, p. 191.

———, The Bremen Excavation, *The Glass Club Bulletin,* March 1964.

———, The Glastenbury Glass Factory Company, *Journal of Glass Studies,* 1963, p. 117.

Wistar, Isaac Jones, *Autobiography: 1827-1905.* Harper & Bros. New York, 1914.

Woodward, E.M., and Hageman, John F., *History of Burlington and Mercer Counties, New Jersey.* Everts & Peck, Phila. 1883.

FAIRS AND AWARDS

American Institute of the City of New York. Annual Reports, 1830-1888.

Franklin Institute. Reports of the Committee of Premiums, 1824-1874. Phila.

New York Exhibition of the Industry of All Nations. New York, 1853.

International Exhibition 1876, Official Catalogue. Phila., 1876.

Awards of the United States Centennial Commission at Philadelphia. Phila., 1876.

MANUSCRIPTS

Batsto Glassworks Records and Store Books, New Jersey State Library, Trenton.

Cumberland County Deeds, Cumberland County Courthouse, Bridgeton.

Estellville Papers, privately owned.

Marshallville Ledgers and Store Books, privately owned.

Smith, Hannah Whitall, *Capt. John M. Whitall, the Story of His Life,* Historical Society of Pennsylvania.

Christian L. Stanger's Receipt Book, privately owned.

Frank H. Stewart Papers, Glassboro State College Library.

Wistar Papers, Historical Society of Pennsylvania.

CATALOGS OF EARLY AMERICAN GLASS

Collection of George S. McKearin, Girl Scouts Loan Exhibition, 1929.

Collection of Mrs. William Greig Walker; ex-collection of John Hays Hammond, Jr. The Art Center, New York, 1930.

Collection of George S. McKearin. Anderson Galleries, Inc. Part I, 1931; Part II, 1932.

Collection of Herbert Delevan Mason. Anderson Galleries, Inc., 1932.

Collection of Alfred B. Maclay. Parke-Bernet Galleries, Inc., 1939.

Collection of Mrs. Frederick S. Fish. Parke-Bernet Galleries, Inc., 1940.

Collection of William T. H. Howe, Parke-Bernet Galleries, Inc., 1940.

Collection of William W. Wood, Parke-Bernet Galleries, Inc., 1942.

Fig. 238 Map of glassmaking towns, drawn by Jerry Thorp.

GLASSMAKING TOWNS OF NEW JERSEY

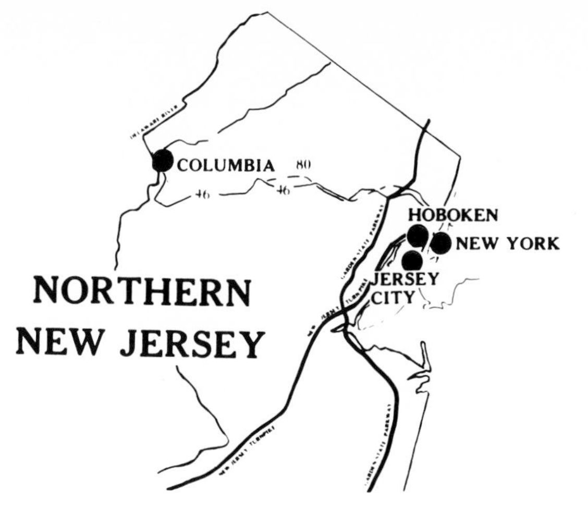

NORTHERN NEW JERSEY
COLUMBIA
80
46
HOBOKEN
NEW YORK
JERSEY CITY

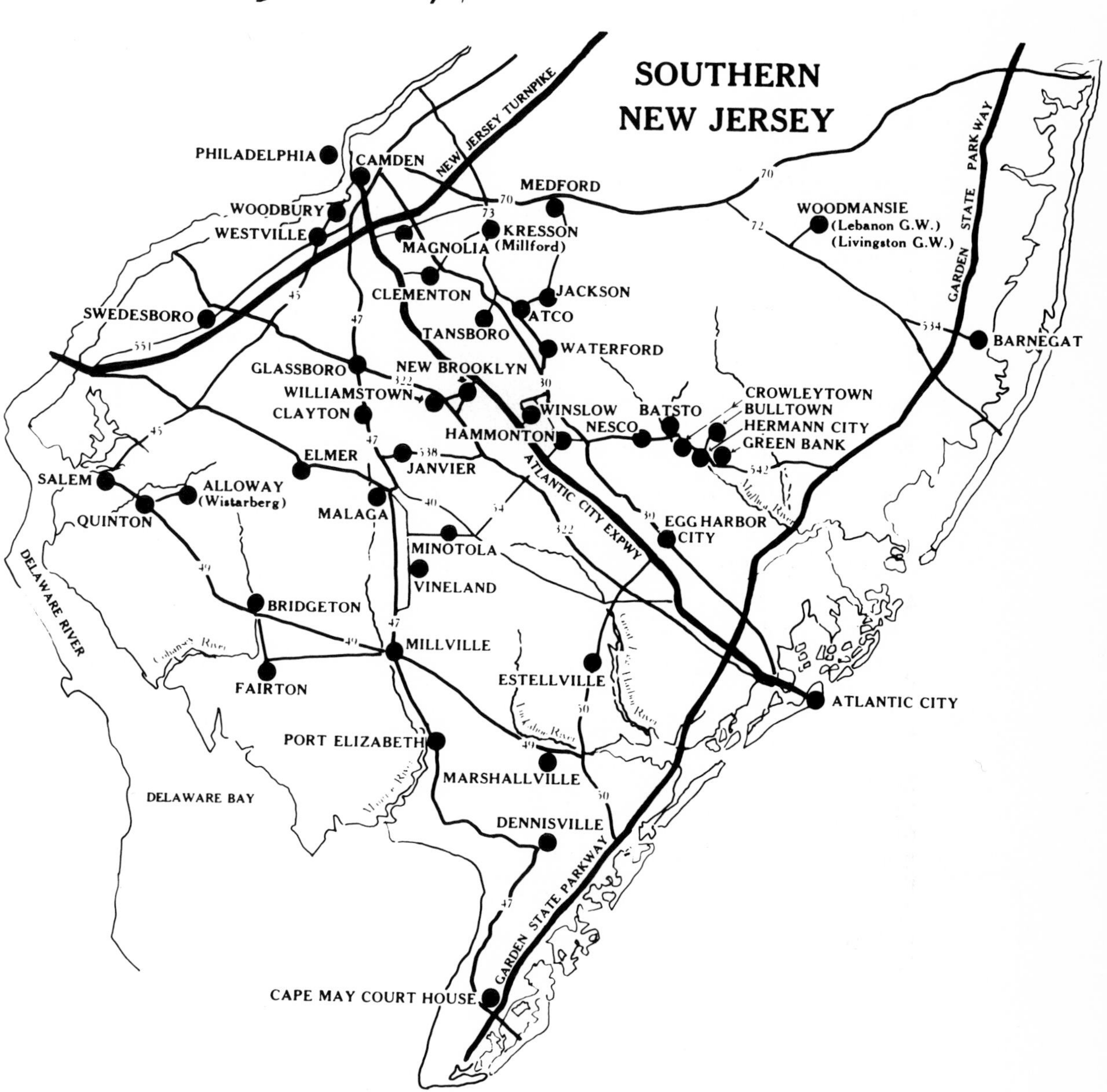

SOUTHERN NEW JERSEY
PHILADELPHIA
CAMDEN
NEW JERSEY TURNPIKE
WOODBURY
WESTVILLE
MEDFORD
70
73
KRESSON (Millford)
MAGNOLIA
WOODMANSIE (Lebanon G.W.) (Livingston G.W.)
72
GARDEN STATE PARKWAY
CLEMENTON
JACKSON
ATCO
SWEDESBORO
TANSBORO
WATERFORD
534
BARNEGAT
551
45
47
GLASSBORO
NEW BROOKLYN
322
WILLIAMSTOWN
CLAYTON
30
WINSLOW
BATSTO
CROWLEYTOWN
BULLTOWN
HERMANN CITY
GREEN BANK
NESCO
HAMMONTON
542
ELMER
538
JANVIER
SALEM
ALLOWAY (Wistarberg)
QUINTON
MALAGA
40
54
ATLANTIC CITY EXPWY
39
EGG HARBOR CITY
MINOTOLA
VINELAND
DELAWARE RIVER
49
BRIDGETON
MILLVILLE
FAIRTON
ESTELLVILLE
ATLANTIC CITY
50
PORT ELIZABETH
MARSHALLVILLE
DELAWARE BAY
DENNISVILLE
CAPE MAY COURT HOUSE

Index

C

D

E

F

G

H

I

J

K

N

O

P

T

U

V

W

Fig. 239 SUNBURST AND DIAMOND pattern-molded pitcher is a 1940s Clevenger copy of 3-mold pitchers made at some New England glassworks of the early 1800s. Pinkish amethyst non-lead glass; rough pontil. (McKearin No. 1 sunburst motif.) H. 7¾ inches.

Fig. 240 EXPERT STILL AT 82, the late Otis Coleman, gaffer who died in 1970, made much of the freeblown and mold-blown glass at Clevenger's from 1930 to mid-1960s.